It is essential that we create a new normal—in our homes, in our nations, and in these United States—and that is what the dedicated and talented women and men whose voices are represented in this book are doing every day. The book is a treasure because it tells their stories.

Gloria Steinem, author, lecturer, editor, and feminist activist

Women and girls keep this world spinning; they are also the key to keeping it from spinning out of control. *Women and Girls Rising* moves smoothly between personal and particular accounts—stirring testimony from Brazil, Iran, Pakistan, China, Uganda, China, and the United States graces this volumes—and analysis, eschewing policy-speak without abandoning policy or politics. The result is humane and instructive, a data-driven but never arid defense of the feminism needed to promote social justice in a world in need. Read this book and see a vibrant and global movement placing women and girls at the center of agendas for health and human rights—and for social and economic progress that doesn't wreck our fragile and beautiful planet.

Paul Farmer, M.D., Harvard University and
Partners In Health

Women and Girls Rising

A growing body of evidence demonstrates that improvements in the status of women and girls—however worthy and important in their own right—also drive the prosperity, stability, and security of families, communities, and nations. Yet despite many indicators of progress, women and girls everywhere—including countries of the developed world—continue to confront barriers to their full and equal participation in social, economic, and political life.

Capturing voices and experiences from around the world, this work documents the modern history of the global women's movement—its many accomplishments and setbacks. Drawing together prominent pioneers and contemporary policymakers, activists, and scholars, the volume interrogates where and why progress has met resistance and been slowed, and examines the still unfinished agenda for change in national and international policy arenas. This history and roadmap are especially critical for younger generations who need a better understanding of this rich feminist legacy and the intense opposition that women's movements have generated.

This book creates a clear and forceful narrative about women's agency and the central relevance of women's rights movements to global and national policy-making. It is essential reading for activists and policymakers, students and scholars alike.

Ellen Chesler, Ph.D., is a senior fellow at the Roosevelt Institute, where she directs the Women and Girls Rising program.

Terry McGovern, J.D. is Professor of Population and Family Health at Columbia University's Mailman School of Public Health.

Global Institutions

Edited by Thomas G. Weiss
The CUNY Graduate Center, New York, USA
and Rorden Wilkinson
University of Sussex, Brighton, UK

About the series

The "Global Institutions Series" provides cutting-edge books about many aspects of what we know as "global governance." It emerges from our shared frustrations with the state of available knowledge—electronic and print-wise, for research and teaching—in the area. The series is designed as a resource for those interested in exploring issues of international organization and global governance. And since the first volumes appeared in 2005, we have taken significant strides toward filling conceptual gaps.

The series consists of three related "streams" distinguished by their blue, red, and green covers. The blue volumes, comprising the majority of the books in the series, provide user-friendly and short (usually no more than 50,000 words) but authoritative guides to major global and regional organizations, as well as key issues in the global governance of security, the environment, human rights, poverty, and humanitarian action among others. The books with red covers are designed to present original research and serve as extended and more specialized treatments of issues pertinent for advancing understanding about global governance. And the volumes with green covers—the most recent departure in the series—are comprehensive and accessible accounts of the major theoretical approaches to global governance and international organization.

The books in each of the streams are written by experts in the field, ranging from the most senior and respected authors to first-rate scholars at the beginning of their careers. In combination, the three components of the series—blue, red, and green—serve as key resources for faculty, students, and practitioners alike. The works in the blue and green streams have value as core and complementary readings in courses on, among other things, international organization, global governance, international law, international relations, and international political economy; the red volumes allow further reflection and investigation in these and related areas.

The books in the series also provide a segue to the foundation volume that offers the most comprehensive textbook treatment available dealing with all the major issues, approaches, institutions, and actors in contemporary global governance—our edited work *International Organization and Global Governance* (2014)—a volume to which many of the authors in the series have contributed essays.

Understanding global governance—past, present, and future—is far from a finished journey. The books in this series nonetheless represent significant steps toward a better way of conceiving contemporary problems and issues as well as, hopefully, doing something to improve world order. We value the feedback from our readers and their role in helping shape the on-going development of the series.

A complete list of titles appears at the end of this book. The most recent titles in the series are:

Women and Girls Rising (2015)
by Ellen Chesler and Terry McGovern

The North Atlantic Treaty Organization (2nd edition, 2015)
by Julian Lindley-French

The African Union (2nd edition, 2015)
by Samuel M. Makinda, F. Wafula Okumu and David Mickler

Governing Climate Change (2nd edition, 2015)
by Harriet Bulkeley and Peter Newell

The Organization of Islamic Cooperation (2015)
by Turan Kayaoglu

Contemporary Human Rights Ideas (2nd edition, 2015)
by Bertrand G. Ramcharan

The Politics of International Organizations (2015)
edited by Patrick Weller and Xu Yi-chong

Women and Girls Rising

Progress and resistance around
the world

Edited by
Ellen Chesler and Terry McGovern

LONDON AND NEW YORK

First published 2016
by Routledge
2 Park Square, Milton Park, Abingdon, Oxon OX14 4RN

and by Routledge
711 Third Avenue, New York, NY 10017

Routledge is an imprint of the Taylor & Francis Group, an informa business

British Library Cataloguing in Publication Data
A catalogue record for this book is available from the British Library

Library of Congress Cataloging in Publication Data
Women and girls rising : progress and resistance around the world /
edited by Ellen Chesler and Theresa McGovern.
    pages cm. – (Global institutions)
Includes bibliographical references and index.
    1. Women–Social conditions–Developing countries. 2. Women–
Economic conditions–Developing countries. 3. Women's rights–
Developing countries. I. Chesler, Ellen, editor. II. McGovern,
Theresa M., editor.
    HQ1870.9.W636 2016
    305.409172'4–dc23
    2015004362

ISBN: 978-1-138-89876-9 (hbk)
ISBN: 978-1-138-89877-6 (pbk)
ISBN: 978-1-315-70837-9 (ebk)

Typeset in Times New Roman
by Taylor & Francis Books

Printed and bound in the United States of America by
Edwards Brothers Malloy on sustainably sourced paper

For: Celia Sloban Chesler,   1918–2000
Belle Wechsler Mallow, 1908–1974
Ann Walsh McGovern, 1932–9.11.2001
in loving memory

Contents

Contributors

Aala Abdelgadir is a research associate for the Civil Society, Markets, and Democracy Initiative at the Council on Foreign Relations (CFR). Prior to joining CFR, she was a Woodbridge Fellow at Yale University. Through this year-long fellowship, she worked on expanding university outreach and efforts in Africa and also established youth development projects in Sudan expanding access to higher education and professional enrichment. She has written for CFR blogs and external publications about political transitions, youth movements, and internet censorship. A Mellon Mays Fellow at Yale, Abdelgadir earned her BA with distinction in political science.

Mahnaz Afkhami is Founder and President of the Women's Learning Partnership, an international organization that empowers women to become leaders in politics, business, and civil society. She helped create the concept and mobilize support for establishing the United Nation's Asian and Pacific Centre for Women and Development and its International Research and Training Institute for the Advancement of Women (INSTRAW). She serves on the boards and steering committees of several organizations, including the Women's Rights Division of Human Rights Watch, the Freer/Sackler Galleries of the Smithsonian Institution and the Foundation for Iranian Studies. Among her publications are *Faith and Freedom: Women's Human Rights in the Muslim World, Women in Exile*, and *Victories Over Violence*. She has also co-authored manuals on leadership and political participation that have been translated into 20 languages. Prior to the Islamic revolution in Iran, Afkhami taught English literature at the National University of Iran, where she founded and directed the Association of University Women. She served as Secretary General of the Women's Organization of Iran (1970–1979) and Iran's Minister for Women's Affairs (1975–1978).

Kalpona Akter is Executive Director of the Bangladesh Center for Worker Solidarity (BCWS), one of Bangladesh's most prominent labor rights advocacy organizations, and is herself a former child garment worker. BCWS is widely regarded as among the most effective grassroots labor organizations in the country. Levi Strauss & Co. calls BCWS "a globally respected labor rights organization, which has played a vital role in documenting and working to remedy labor violations in the apparel industry in Bangladesh." Akter has traveled widely to speak about the deplorable conditions that Bangladeshi garment workers face every day. She has been interviewed extensively by local and international media, particularly following the Tazreen fire and the Rana Plaza building collapse.

María Antonieta Alcalde is Director of Advocacy for the International Planned Parenthood Federation/Western Hemisphere Region (IPPF/WHR) and Director of the IPPF UN Liaison Office. Originally from Mexico, she co-founded several regional organizations, including the Latin American Youth Network for Sexual and Reproductive Rights and the Youth Coalition and was the general coordinator of Balance, Promotion for Development and Youth in Mexico City. Alcalde is a member of the UN's High Level Task Force for ICPD and has served on the boards of the Center for Development and Population Activities (CEDPA), Fundación Mexicana para el Planeamiento de la Familia, and as the North America NGO representative of the Joint United Nations Programme on HIV/AIDS Coordinating Board. Alcalde has participated in several international conferences related to sexual and reproductive health and rights, including the 5-, 10-, and 15-year reviews of the Cairo and Beijing Conferences She holds a degree in accounting from the Universidad Nacional Autónoma de México.

Carol Bellamy was Executive Director of UNICEF from 1995 to 2005. Under her leadership, UNICEF became a champion of global investment in children, arguing that efforts to reduce poverty and build a more secure world can only be successful if they ensure that children have an opportunity to grow to adulthood in health, peace, and dignity. In April 2009, Bellamy was appointed as Chair of the International Baccalaureate Board of Governors. Additionally, she recently completed a three-year term as Chair of the Global Partnership for Education. From 1993 to 1995, Bellamy served as director of the Peace Corps. In 1977, she was elected the first female president of the New York City Council. She holds a BA from Gettysburg College and a JD from the New York University School of Law.

Ellen Bravo directs the Family Values @ Work Consortium, a network of coalitions in 21 states working for policies such as paid sick days and family leave insurance. Previously, she was the director of the organization 9to5. Her most recent book is *Taking on the Big Boys, or Why Feminism is Good for Families, Business and the Nation* (The Feminist Press at CUNY, 2007). Bravo has served on several state and federal commissions, including the bi-partisan Commission on Leave appointed by congress to study the impact of the Family and Medical Leave Act. She has also taught women's studies at the University of Wisconsin-Milwaukee, including masters level classes on family-friendly workplaces. She is on the boards of Working America and the National Domestic Workers Alliance. Among her commendations are the Ford Foundation's Visionary Award, the Francis Perkins Intelligence and Courage Award, and the Families and Work Institute Work Life Legacy Award. Bravo lives in Milwaukee with her husband; they have two adult sons.

Judith Bruce is a senior associate and policy analyst with the Population Council's Poverty, Gender and Youth program. Bruce leads the council's efforts to develop programs that protect health and well-being and expand opportunities for adolescent girls in the poorest communities. She was among the first to illuminate the scope and negative impact of child marriage, insisting on the term "child marriage" rather than "early marriage," as the latter suggests a desirable precocity, concealing the fact that the practice is a serious human rights abuse. Recently Bruce served as co-chair of the UN Expert Group Meeting on the elimination of all forms of discrimination and violence against the girl-child. She has been a member of the Council on Foreign Relations since 1977. In 1993 she received the Association for Women in Development's bi-annual award for outstanding contributions to the field. She is a graduate of Harvard University.

Charlotte Bunch is the Founding Director and Senior Scholar at the Center for Women's Global Leadership and Board of Governor's Distinguished Professor in Women's and Gender Studies, Rutgers University. Previously, she was a fellow at the Institute for Policy Studies in DC and a founder of Washington DC Women's Liberation and of *Quest: A Feminist Quarterly*. Bunch has been an activist, writer, and organizer in the feminist, LGBT, and human rights movements for over four decades. Her contributions have been recognized by many, including the National Women's Hall of Fame, the White House Eleanor Roosevelt Award for Human Rights, a

Nobel Peace Prize nomination as one of "1000 Women Peace Makers" in 2005, and an Honorary Doctor of Laws Degree from the University of Connecticut. Bunch is currently on the board of Association for Women's Rights in Development (AWID) and the Advisory Committee for the Women's Rights Division of Human Rights Watch, and serves on the Global Civil Society Advisory Group to UN Women.

Roxanna Carrillo worked for 20 years at the United Nations and is currently an independent consultant in the areas of gender, human rights, development, and peacebuilding, with a focus on issues related to equality and violence against women. She was the Chief of Policy and Planning in the UN Peacebuilding Support Office. She also served as head of the Conduct and Discipline Unit at the UN Peacekeeping Mission in Burundi. Prior to that she was at UNIFEM, where she started the women's human rights program and led UNIFEM's work at the 1993 World Conference on Human Rights in Vienna. She also set up the UN Trust Fund to End Violence against Women. She co-founded the Center for Women's Global Leadership at Rutgers University and worked for many years prior as an NGO advocate and a journalist in Peru. She holds an MA in political science from Rutgers University and a degree in Spanish literature and linguistics from Universidad Nacional Mayor de San Marcos, Lima.

Hannah Chartoff is a research associate in the Women and Foreign Policy program at the Council on Foreign Relations, where she previously focused on issues of political Islam, radicalization, and terrorism. Prior to her work at the Council, Chartoff was a White House intern in Washington, DC and a Fulbright Scholar in Egypt. She holds a BA from Duke University.

Wendy Chavkin, MD, MPH is Professor of Public Health at the Mailman School and Professor of Obstetrics and Gynecology at the College of Physicians and Surgeons of Columbia University. She is also co-founder of Global Doctors for Choice and previously served as chair of the board of directors of Physicians for Reproductive Choice and Health. In 2004–2005 she was a Fulbright New Century Scholar for her research on fertility decline and the empowerment of women. From 1994 to 2002, she was editor-in-chief of *the Journal of the American Medical Women's Association*, and from 1984 to 1988, the director of the Bureau of Maternity Services and Family Planning in New York City's Department of Health. She has written extensively about women's issues, including the consequences of welfare reform for the health of women and children and conscientious objection to providing reproductive health care. She has received numerous awards from public health organizations for advocacy including the Jean Pakter and Allan Rosenfield awards.

Ellen Chesler, Ph.D., is a senior fellow at the Roosevelt Institute, where she directs the Women and Girls Rising program. She is author of *Woman of Valor: Margaret Sanger and the Birth Control Movement in America* (1992), which remains in print in a new paperback edition released in 2007. She is co-editor with Wendy Chavkin, MD MPH of *Where Human Rights Begin*, a volume of essays that emerged from a fellowship program they directed for the Open Society Foundation. Chesler has also written extensively for academic and public policy anthologies, journals, newspapers, magazines, and blogs. Over a 40-year career, she has held positions in government (chief of staff to New York City Council President Carol Bellamy, 1978–84); philanthropy (Open Society Foundation, 1997–2006, and the Twentieth Century Fund, 1992–1997); and academia (Hunter College of the City University of New York, 2007–10, and Barnard College, 1988–9, 1992–3) and is widely respected for both the intellectual and practical perspectives she brings to her work. She is currently a member of the advisory committee of the Women's Rights Division of Human Rights Watch and of the Council on Foreign Relations. She served for many years on the board of the Planned Parenthood Federation of America and as chair of the board of the International Women's Health Coalition. She has three times been a member of the US delegation to the UN Commission on the Status of Women. She holds a BA from Vassar College and an MA and PhD, with distinction in history, from Columbia University.

Hillary Rodham Clinton After nearly four decades of public service as an advocate for children and families, First Lady, Senator, and US Secretary of State, Hillary Rodham Clinton is currently a candidate for President of the United States. Until recently, she helped lead the Bill, Hillary & Chelsea Clinton Foundation, with a special interest in women and girls and in helping young people get the skills they need to find good jobs and participate in the global economy. She is also the author of the new book, *Hard Choices*, which chronicles her efforts to restore America's leadership after eight years in which it was badly eroded. Thanks in large measure to Hillary's leadership, people were finally able to say: America's back. She championed human rights, internet freedom, religious freedom, and rights and opportunities for women and girls, LGBT people, and young people, and went to bat for American workers and companies around the world, as she has her entire career.

Isobel Coleman was recently confirmed as the US Representative to the United Nations for Management and Reform. She was previously a senior fellow and director of the Civil Society, Markets, and Democracy Initiative at the Council on Foreign Relations (CFR) where she also directed the Women and Foreign Policy Program. Her areas of expertise include democratization, civil society, gender, and economic development. She is the author or co-author of numerous books, including *Pathways to Freedom: Economic and Political Lessons from Democratic Transitions* (CFR, 2013) and *Paradise Beneath Her Feet: How Women are Transforming the Middle East* (Random House, 2010). Coleman's writings have also appeared in *Foreign Affairs, Foreign Policy*, the *New York Times*, the *Washington Post*, and the *Financial Times*. A Marshall scholar, Dr. Coleman holds a BA in public policy and East Asian studies from Princeton University and MPhil and DPhil degrees in international relations from Oxford University. In 2011, *Newsweek* named her one of "150 Women Who Shake the World."

Sonia Correa Since the late 1970s, Sonia Correa has been involved in research and advocacy activities related to gender equality, health, and sexuality. Between 1992 and 2009 she was the research coordinator for sexual and reproductive health and rights at Development Alternatives with Women for a New Era (DAWN). In that capacity, she closely followed United Nations conferences like the International Conference on Population and Development (Cairo, 1994) and the Fourth World Conference on Women (Beijing, 1995) and also the five- and 10-year review processes of those conferences. Since 2002, she has co-chaired Sexuality Policy Watch, a global forum engaged in analyzing global trends in sexuality-related policy and politics. Correa's publications include (with Rebecca Reichmann) *Population and Reproductive Rights: Feminist Perspectives from the South* (Zed Books, 1994), and (with Rosalind Petchesky and Richard Parker) *Sexuality, Health and Human Rights* (Routledge, 2008).

Jan Eliasson currently serves as the UN Deputy Secretary General. His career began in 1982 as Diplomatic Adviser to the Swedish Prime Minister before moving to New York to serve as the Swedish Ambassador to the United Nations. As ambassador from 1988 to 1992, he was part of the UN mediation missions in the war between

Iraq and Iran. He has since served as the first UN Under-Secretary General for Humanitarian Affairs (where he was involved in numerous operations in Somalia, Sudan, Mozambique, and the Balkans), Swedish State Secretary for Foreign Affairs, Swedish Ambassador to Washington, and President of the UN General Assembly. Prior to taking office as Deputy Secretary General, Eliasson was the UN Secretary General's Special Envoy for Darfur from 2007 to 2008.

Annabel Erulkar currently heads the Population Council in Ethiopia and has programmatic, financial, and administrative leadership responsibilities for the country office. She was the principal investigator for the Berhane Hewan program, named best UNFPA "good practice" for adolescents and youth, and is currently principal investigator for a multi-country study testing efforts to delay the age of marriage in multiple hotspots across Africa. Erulkar has authored numerous reports and journal articles related to adolescence in Sub Saharan Africa, including gender-based violence, early marriage, and child domestic work. Before joining the Council in 1995, Erulkar was responsible for research at the Family Planning Association of Kenya, the country's largest non-governmental family planning organization. She holds a BA in anthropology from Bryn Mawr College, an MSc in population sciences from Harvard University and a PhD in social statistics from the University of Southampton, United Kingdom.

Adrienne Germain is President Emerita of the International Women's Health Coalition. She has worked for women's health and human rights for 43 years. Following 14 years with the Ford Foundation, she led IWHC's work on international health and population policy with the UN system, governments, and NGOs. Germain was a pivotal member of US government delegations to the International Conference on Population and Development (ICPD) and the UN Fourth World Conference on Women in Beijing. She has published widely, including edited volumes and many articles in peer-reviewed journals, such as the *WHO Bulletin*. In November 2012, she was a Menschel Senior Fellow in Health Policy at the Harvard University School of Public Health. Germain advises the US State Department and UNFPA, as well as other United Nations, corporate, foundation, and NGO leaders. She holds a BA from Wellesley College and an MA in sociology and demography from the University of California at Berkeley.

Anne Marie Goetz joined New York University's Center for Global Affairs, in January 2014, where she teaches international relations. She worked before this as Chief Advisor on peace, security, and governance to UNIFEM (since 2005) and UN Women (since 2011). Prior to joining UNIFEM she was a Professor of Political Science at the Institute of Development Studies, University of Sussex where she had worked since 1991. She also served the United Nations Development Program in Chad and Guinea in the mid-1980s. While at the UN, Dr. Goetz spearheaded initiatives to promote women's empowerment in the UN's peacebuilding work in fragile states and post-conflict situations. Dr. Goetz specializes in research on public policies in fragile states that promote the interests of marginalized social groups, particularly poor women. Additionally, she is the author of eight books on the subjects of gender, politics, and policy in developing countries, and on accountability reforms.

Devaki Jain graduated in economics from Oxford in 1963 and taught at Delhi University for six years. She is one of the founders of a wide range of institutions including Development Alternatives for Women for a New Era (DAWN), a Third World network of women social scientists who provide an alternative framework for understanding and advancing the cause of poor women of the South. She was a member of the Advisory Committee for the UNDP Human Development Report on Poverty, 1997 and the Eminent Persons group associated with the UN's Graca Machel Committee on the Impact on Children of Armed Conflict. She has also served on the National Preparatory Committee convened by the Government of India to prepare for the UN World Conferences in Nairobi, 1985; Cairo, 1995; and Beijing, 1995. Currently, she is a member of the South Commission headed by Julius Nyerere.

Rob Jenkins is Professor of Political Science at the Roosevelt House Public Policy Institute and Senior Fellow at the Ralph Bunche Institute for International Studies of CUNY. He specializes in international and comparative development politics and post-conflict peacebuilding. He is also an editorial board member of several publications, including the *Journal of Commonwealth and Comparative Politics*. Previously, Jenkins was a Senior Consultant at the United Nations Secretariat's Peacebuilding Support Office and lead author of the 2010 Report of the Secretary General on Women's Participation in Peacebuilding. Prior to that, he was Professor of Political Science at the University of London. Jenkins holds a BA from Harvard University and a DPhil from the University of Sussex.

Naila Kabeer is Professor of Gender and Development at the Gender Institute, London School of Economics and Political Science. Prior to that, she was Professor of Development Studies at the School of Oriental and African Studies at London University and Professorial Fellow at the Institute of Development Studies, Sussex. She has also worked as a Senior Research Fellow at the Department for International Development, UK. Her research interests include gender, poverty, social exclusion, labor markets and livelihoods, social protection, and citizenship. Her publications are numerous, including *Reversed Realities: Gender Hierarchies in Development Thought*. She has carried out extensive training and advisory work with national and international NGOs, as well as for a number of international development agencies. Kabeer is currently on the advisory editorial committee for the journals *Feminist Economics, Development and Change*, and *Gender and Development* and on the board of the Feminist Review Trust.

Bohong Liu is a professor at the China Women's University, former Senior Research Fellow and Deputy Director of the Women's Studies Institute of China and former Coordinator for the Chinese Women's Health Network. She is also the Deputy Secretary General of the Chinese Women's Research Society and a professor at Beijing Foreign Studies University, teaching Gender and Development. Since the 1995 UN conference in Beijing, she has worked with the Chinese government system to teach leaders about the relevance of gender to laws and policies. She has participated in formulating national programs that implement the 1995 UN Platform for Action and CEDAW, and currently, in activities on Beijing+20 in China.

Wanjira Mathai is Project Leader at the Wangari Maathai Institute for Peace & Environmental Studies (WMI) in Kenya. Prior to this she directed international affairs at the Green Belt Movement (GBM), where she managed international outreach and resource mobilization. For six years prior to joining GBM, she worked as a senior program officer at the Carter Presidential Center in Atlanta, Georgia. Since 2002, Mathai has directed International Affairs at GBM, which was founded by her mother, the late Nobel Peace Laureate Wangari Maathai. Today, she directs the new Partnership for Women's Entrepreneurship on Renewables Hub at the Wangari Maathai Institute. She is also a World Future Councilor, Advisory Council Member (Global Alliance for Clean Cookstoves), a member of the Global Restoration Council and a member of the Earth Charter International Council. Mathai is a graduate of Hobart & William Smith Colleges. She earned graduate degrees in public health and business from Emory University's Rollins School of Public Health and the Goizueta School of Business (USA).

Eileen McGivney is a research analyst in the Center for Universal Education at the Brookings Institution. Her work focuses on a variety of issues related to access to and quality of education in developing countries, including challenges facing girls' education, links between education and the labor market, and new school models. Prior to Brookings, Eileen worked as a researcher at Education Reform Initiative in Istanbul, analyzing equity in the Turkish education system. She received a masters' degree in public policy from Sabanci University in Istanbul and a BA from the University of Illinois Urbana-Champaign.

Terry McGovern, J.D. is Professor of Population and Family Health at Columbia University's Mailman School of Public Health, where she directs the Health and Human Rights Certificate and teaches human rights and environmental justice. From 2006 to 2012, Terry was a senior program officer in the Gender Rights and Equality Program at the Ford Foundation. She developed a highly successful health and human rights policy initiative in the US and helped build the strategic policy capacity of groups working globally to advance the health and human rights of women and girls, LGBT individuals, and other marginalized populations. McGovern founded the HIV Law Project in 1989, where she served as Executive Director for 10 years and litigated numerous cases against the federal, state, and local governments, including a successful class action charging that the US government had discriminated against women in its response to the AIDS epidemic. McGovern has published extensively and testified numerous times before the US Congress and other policymaking entities. She is a graduate of the Georgetown School of Law.

Hayat Mirshad is a co-founder of FE-MALE, an editor at the Sawt Al Shaab Lebanese radio station, and a volunteer producer of the first feminist radio program in Lebanon and the Middle East, "Sharika wa Laken." Mirshad also works as a media officer and project coordinator for the *Women's Response to the Arab Spring* project at the Lebanese Democratic Women Gathering. She is active with many civil society and women's organizations and campaigns, such as the Lebanese Women Right to Nationality campaign. Mirshad has also worked at the Collective for Research and Training on Development-Action for four years as a project officer with the active citizenship and gendered social entitlements project. She also works as a freelance reporter for Aljadeed TV.

Lissa Muscatine is co-owner with her husband, Bradley Graham, of Politics & Prose Bookstore in Washington, DC. Before acquiring the store in 2011, she served in the Obama Administration as Director of Speechwriting and Senior Advisor to Secretary of State Hillary Clinton. Previously, she had been a senior advisor on Hillary Clinton's presidential campaign and a collaborator on Clinton's White House memoir, *Living History*. During the Clinton administration, she served as a Presidential Speechwriter, Chief Speechwriter to the First Lady, and later, as Director of Communications to the First Lady and Deputy Assistant to the President. In a prior career in journalism, she worked at the *Delta Democrat-Times* in Greenville, Mississippi, the *Washington Star*, and for 12 years at the *Washington Post*, covering beats from politics to sports. She has contributed commentary pieces to the *New York Times*, the *Washington Post*, the *Huffington Post*, and she blogs for PunditWire.com and the Politics and Prose website. She has served as well on a variety of non-profit boards and is currently chair of the Board of Trustees at the Sidwell Friends School in Washington, D.C. She earned her B.A. from Harvard University and was among 13 American women awarded Rhodes Scholarships in 1977 – the first year women could apply. At Oxford, she studied contemporary European politics.

Noelene Nabulivou works with Diverse Voices and Action for Equality in Fiji. She is also an associate of Development Alternatives with Women for a New Era (DAWN), a network of feminist scholars and activists from the economic South. Nabulivou has been an organizing partner of the Women's Major Group on Sustainable Development, working across the Post Rio+20, SIDS and Post 2015 Development Agenda processes and linking with ICPD Beyond 2014. For the past 30 years, Nabulivou has used south-feminist political economy-based approaches to work on various aspects of gender equality and human rights, social and economic justice, and ecological sustainability.

Jocelyn Olcott is Associate Professor of History, Women's Studies and International & Comparative Studies at Duke University. She is author of *Revolutionary Women in Postrevolutionary Mexico* (Duke University Press, 2005) and is co-editor with Mary Kay Vaughan and Gabriela Cano) of *Sex in Revolution: Gender, Politics, and Power in Modern Mexico* (Duke University Press, 2006, in translation with Fondo de Cultura Económica, 2009). She is completing a book for Oxford University Press on the 1975 International Women's Year Conference in Mexico City, *The Greatest Consciousness-Raising*

Event in History: International Women's Year and the Challenge of Transnational Feminism. She is currently a senior editor of the *Hispanic American Historical Review,* and has published articles in the *Journal of Women's History,* the *Hispanic American Historical Review, Gender & History,* and *International Labor and Working-Class History,* as well as numerous chapters in edited collections. She holds an AB from Princeton University and an MA and PhD from Yale University.

Jacqueline Pitanguy, one of the 1,000 women proposed for the Nobel Peace Prize in 2005, is one of Brazil's best-known feminist activists. She was strong in opposing the military junta in Brazil and resisted dictatorship. When it was overthrown in 1985, she helped to incorporate gender issues into the country's new constitution. She held a cabinet-level position as president of the National Council for Women's Rights (1986–89) and is a recipient of the Medal of Rio Branco, the highest decoration of the Brazilian Ministry of Foreign Affairs. Pitanguy is currently the founder and director of Cidadania, Estudo, Pesquisa, Informação e Ação, a NGO based in Rio de Janeiro, where she coordinates research on gender issues and facilitates advocacy on issues of violence against women and reproductive health. She has been a Professor at the Pontificia Universidade Catolica de Rio de Janeiro and at Rutgers University, where she held the Laurie New Jersey Chair in Women's Studies from 1991 to 1992.

Catherine Powell is a fellow in the Women and Foreign Policy program at the Council on Foreign Relations. She is also a professor at Fordham Law School, where she teaches international law, constitutional law, and comparative law. She took a leave from academia from 2009 to 2012 to serve on Secretary of State Hillary Clinton's Policy Planning Staff and on the Obama administration's National Security Staff as director for human rights. She was founding director of both the Human Rights Institute and the Human Rights Clinic at Columbia Law School, where she was a clinical professor from 1998 to 2002. She is widely published on gender, human rights, and national security matters. She has been a member of the board of Human Rights Watch and a consultant to the Center for American Progress. She is a graduate of Yale College, Yale Law School, and the Woodrow Wilson School of Public and International Affairs at Princeton University.

Renu Adhikari Rajbhandari is a Nepalese physician and women's rights activist. She is founder and chair of the National Alliance of Women Human Rights Defenders (NAWHRD), where she advocates for women's human rights through a variety of campaigns; and founder and chair of the Women's Rehabilitation Center (WOREC), which she established in June, 1991 to fight human trafficking and advocate for women's human rights and served for many years as Executive Director. Previously, she worked at the Central Health Laboratory in Nepal and various hospitals. She holds degrees from the Institute of Medicine, Kathmandu, and Moscow Medical Institute.

Gita Sen has worked for over 35 years on population policies, reproductive and sexual health, gender equality, and women's human rights. She is currently an adjunct professor of global health and population at Harvard University and was, until 2013, a professor of public policy at the Indian Institute of Management in Bangalore, India. She is a founder and member of the Executive Committee of Development Alternatives with Women for a New Era (DAWN). She was lead consultant for drafting UNFPA's India Country Population Assessment document for 2003–2007. She currently serves on the Scientific and Technical Advisory Group of WHO's Department of Reproductive Health and Research. In India she is a member of the governing board of the National Health Systems Resource Centre. She was previously a member of the Millennium Project's Taskforce on Gender Equality, and was the first chairperson of the World Bank's External Gender Consultative Group. Sen holds a PhD in economics from Stanford University.

Farida Shaheed is the UN Special Rapporteur on Cultural Rights, Executive Director of Shirkat Gah – Women's Resource Centre in Pakistan, and a founding member of the national lobby, Women's Action Forum, formed in 1981 to resist the systematic rescinding of women's rights. For more than 25 years, she has promoted women's rights and social justice. Activism informs her scholastic work; conceptual analyses and understanding underpin practical grassroots work, knowledge transfer, and building capabilities. She has published widely on the interface of women, identity, state-citizenship and how this impacts rights. She has led efforts to bring home the commitments made under the Beijing Platform for Action and the CEDAW.

Gloria Steinem is a writer, lecturer, editor, and feminist activist. In 1972, Steinem co-founded *Ms. Magazine* and continues to serve as a consulting editor. She is particularly interested in the shared origins of sex and race caste systems; gender roles and child abuse as roots of violence; non-violent conflict resolution; the cultures of indigenous peoples; and organizing across boundaries for peace and justice. Steinem helped found the Women's Action Alliance, the National Women's Political Caucus, Voters for Choice, Choice USA, the Ms. Foundation for Women, and the national Take Our Daughters to Work Day. She has published several bestselling books and is currently working on *Road to the Heart: America as if Everyone Mattered.* She graduated Phi Beta Kappa from Smith College and has since received many honorary degrees and awards, such as an induction into the National Women's Hall of Fame in Seneca Falls and the Presidential Medal of Freedom awarded in 2013 by President Obama.

Sylvia Tamale is a feminist lawyer and academic based in Kampala, Uganda. She was elected as the first female Dean of Law at Makerere University in 2004. Tamale founded and serves as coordinator of the Law, Gender & Sexuality Research Project and has published widely on a variety of topics, including her latest anthology *African Sexualities: A Reader* (Pambazuka Press, 2011). Tamale has won several awards for her work in defending the rights of marginalized groups, including women, sexual minorities and refugees. She holds a Bachelor's degree in law from Makerere University, a Master's from Harvard Law School, and a PhD in Sociology and Feminist Studies from the University of Minnesota.

Dorothy Q. Thomas is an independent scholar and feminist human rights activist. From September 2013 to May 2014 she served as the interim president and CEO of the Ms. Foundation for Women. Previously, Thomas was a senior strategist at the Sunrise Initiative on Human Rights in the United States and at the US Human Rights Fund, which she co-founded in 2005. From 2009 to 2011, she was a research associate at the University of London and, in 2008, she received a visiting fellowship at the London School of Economics' Centre for the Study of Human Rights. Thomas founded the Women's Rights Division of Human Rights Watch and served as its director from 1990 to 1998. She was awarded a 1998 MacArthur fellowship, a 1995 Bunting Fellowship at the Radcliffe Institute for Advanced Study at Harvard University, and, in 1998, received the Eleanor Roosevelt Human Rights Award from President and Mrs. Clinton. She is a member of the board of the Lambent Foundation for Art and Social Justice. She holds an MA from Georgetown University, which awarded her an honorary doctorate in 1995.

Nisha Varia is associate director of the Women's Rights Division of Human Rights Watch. She focuses on migration, labor rights, forced labor, and trafficking, and has conducted extensive research, published several reports, and carried out advocacy campaigns on migrant domestic workers' rights across Asia and the Middle East, including Indonesia, Malaysia, Sri Lanka, Singapore, Saudi Arabia, and Kuwait. She co-led Human Rights Watch's involvement in the development of the International Labour Organization's 2011 Domestic Workers Convention and 2014 Forced Labor Protocol. Varia is a term member of the Council on Foreign Relations and is a lecturer on human rights research methods at the New School in New York City. Before joining Human Rights Watch, she worked at the International Center for Research on Women and was a Fulbright scholar to India. She holds an MA from Columbia University's School of International and Public Affairs and a BA from Stanford University.

Ravi Verma is regional director for the International Center for Research on Women's (ICRW) Asia Regional Office in New Delhi, India. In this role he leads ICRW's local and regional efforts to conduct research, provide technical support, build capacity, and partake in policy dialogue on an array of issues, including adolescent girls, reproductive health, HIV/AIDS, gender-based violence, and engaging men and boys and economic development. Prior to joining ICRW in 2007, he was a program associate with Population Council/Horizons, where he collaborated with partners to design, implement, and evaluate innovative operations research projects on gender and HIV. For more than 20 years, he was a professor in the department of population policies and programs at the International Institute for Population Sciences in Mumbai, India.

Rebecca Winthrop is a senior fellow and Director of the Center for Universal Education at the Brookings Institution. She is an international expert on global education, particularly in contexts of armed conflict. Prior to joining Brookings in June 2009, Winthrop spent 15 years working in the field of education for displaced and migrant communities, most recently as the head of education for the International Rescue Committee. She has authored chapters for numerous books, including "Learning from Humanitarian Aid" in *Delivering Aid Differently* (Brookings, 2010); "Home-based Schools: A Transitional Education Model in Afghanistan" in *Education, Conflict and Reconciliation: International Perspectives* (Peter Lang, 2007); and "Female Classroom Assistants: Agents of Change in Refugee Classrooms in West Africa?" in *The Structure and Agency of Women's Education* (SUNY Press, 2007). She holds a BA from Swarthmore College, an MA in International and Public Affairs from Columbia University and a PhD from Columbia University's Teachers College.

Cai Yiping is an executive committee member of Development Alternatives for Women for a New Era (DAWN) and a member of the UN Women's Asia-Pacific Regional Civil Society Advisory Group. In 2012, she collaborated with the Ford Foundation on "Women's Organizations in the Asia Region and the post-MDG Process," a project examining the work of Chinese women's organizations. She has also worked as a researcher at the Women's Studies Institute of China, where she authored *International Conventions and Protection of Women's Human Rights in China: A Case Study on CEDAW*. She has also worked as a consultant for UNIFEM, UNFPA, AusAID, ILO, DFID, and the World Bank. She attended the NGO forum of the 1995 Fourth World Conference on Women in Beijing as a journalist and youth participant. She holds a Master's degree in History from Peking University.

Malala Yousafzai is the youngest person to win a Nobel Peace Prize, awarded in 2014 for her advocacy for Pakistani women's rights and girls' education. After the Taliban began attacking girls' schools in her hometown of Swat Valley, she began blogging for the BBC under an alias about the hardship of getting an education under the Taliban's threats. She was awarded Pakistan's National Youth Peace Prize for her activism. In 2012, she was shot by a Taliban gunman on her way home from school. Malala made a full recovery and gave a speech at the United Nations in 2013. She has also written a best-selling autobiography, *I Am Malala: The Girl Who Stood Up for Education and Was Shot by the Taliban* (Orion Publishing Group, 2013).

Hala Youssef is Egyptian Minister of State for Population. Through 2014, she served as rapporteur for the National Population Council of Egypt. She holds a PhD in public health and has over 20 years of experience in the fields of population, sexual and reproductive health, family planning research, and improvement of health services. She is a strong advocate for protecting the rights of Egyptian women and girls.

Foreword

Gloria Steinem

Welcome to an adventure. This anthology documents the progress of the global women's movement and also the resistance it has encountered. It celebrates our many achievements in raising consciousness and changing behaviors, but also identifies the many places where promises to advance women's rights and opportunities have not yet been met. Just a few little things like that.

My hat is off to Ellen Chesler, the principal organizer of this effort, who doesn't think small. The conference at the Ford Foundation in New York in September 2014, from which these chapters are derived, was a harmonic convergence. With so many great minds and good hearts in one place, the entire building seemed to levitate—as Ford deserved to do for supporting and hosting such a historic event, one aptly called *Women and Girls Rising*.

But the truth is that none of us have really thought small since the United Nations World Conferences on Women began in 1975, and especially since the Fourth World Conference on Women in Beijing, where women declared themselves equal human beings with full human rights. We would no longer be used as the means of reproduction, our bodies controlled by religion, state, tribe, caste, or family. We would no longer be the world's largest source of unpaid or underpaid labor, our hard work underwriting the profits of others—individual patriarchs or multi-national corporations. As full human beings we would finally say—and help men to say, too—that the power of the state stops at our skins. We support each other's human rights.

I think about the enormous courage it took to say this, and I realize that we gathered last year, and we raise our voices again in this volume, because of many women who are no longer with us—women we must remember and venerate.

I think first of Bella Abzug, who was always a global thinker from the days of Women's Strike for Peace. Indeed she was often better known in other countries than she was in her own. I remember with great pleasure a young activist who arrived at the UN, and introduced herself by saying, "I am the Bella Abzug of Mongolia." I remember Bella's memorial in the great hall of the General Assembly. Secretary General Kofi Annan said that Bella's global organizing had opened the doors of the United Nations to people, not just nations, and then he memorably pledged to keep them open.

I think too of Geraldine Ferraro, whose savvy political skills were so critical during her service on the United Nations Commission on Human Rights—and later on the US delegation in Beijing.

And I remember so many others as well. Many of us, especially we older ones, must channel lost spirits no longer with us.

And doing so provides me a moment to explain why I cared so much about Beijing that I actually didn't go to the conference in 1995.

If you happen to be a media worker, as I alas have long been, people feel they know you. They tend to ask your opinions instead of seeking out real experts on the subjects they want to understand. I didn't go to Beijing because I realized that people would ask *me* questions, instead of asking them of all the better informed or more representative women attending that historic forum, whom they might not recognize.

This was not false modesty. I also wanted to make a larger point. Though I may be well-known, I also believe that it's obviously wrong to anoint anyone as "the face of feminism." The face of feminism is the face you see in the mirror—and that's true for men as well as women.

Still, I am especially delighted to introduce this book, because I have known from the beginning that feminism is global. I owe this to my oldest friend in the world, Devaki Jain, who is among the many distinguished authors and activists represented here. We discovered each other when I lived in India for two years after college, more than 50 years ago. Each one of us here is a link in the chain that never ends.

And, yes, there's a great deal of bad news to face together. Violence against women has become so great that we are no longer half the passengers on this spaceship, Earth.

And yes, the United Nations is only a partial answer to this problem. Still, it is very, very important that we get our issues into its platform. What the United Nations does is to create the new normal—and that is so crucial. Every day, no matter how long our engagement with feminism, we learn more. For instance, we can now prove that the biggest determinant of whether a country is violent within itself—or will use military violence against another country—is not poverty, access to natural resources, religion, or even degree of democratic practice. It is violence against females that normalizes all other violence and creates the roles of subject, object, dominator, and dominated. It sets a deep pattern for racism, caste, and class. You can't continue those divisions in the long run without controlling reproduction—and that redoubles the need to control female bodies.

So it is essential that as we create a new normal—in our homes, in our nations, and in these United States—and that is what the dedicated and talented women and men whose voices are represented in this book are doing every day. The book is a treasure because it tells their stories.

And their stories compel us to remember, as feminists working to achieve peace and security often remind us, that the human race has two wings.[1] If one is broken, no-one can soar.

Note

1 For these final thoughts I am indebted to Valerie Hudson, Bonnie-Ballif-Spanvill, Mary Caprioli, and Chad Emmet, *Sex and World Peace* (New York: Columbia University Press, 2012).

Acknowledgements

This book and the conference from which it derives would not have been possible without generous support from LaShawn Jefferson and Margaret Hempel of the Ford Foundation, Cynthia Eyakuze at the Open Society Foundation, Kathy Bushkin Calvin of the United Nations Foundation, Felice Gaer of the Jacob Blaustein Institute for the Advancement of Human Rights, and Barbara Dobkin of the Dobkin Family Foundation. We are grateful as well to Darren Walker, Alfred Ironside, and many others at Ford who provided strong personal and technical support. And we warmly acknowledge the esteemed colleagues who graciously served as an advisory board for the project: Hakima Abbas, Carmen Barroso, Kathy Bonk, Charlotte Bunch, Mallika Dutt, Felice Gaer, Leisl Gernholtz, Seema Jalan, LaShawn Jefferson, Anita Nayar, and Joanne Sandler. A full agenda for the conference, which featured many fine speakers in addition to those anthologized in this volume, can be found on the web at www.womenandgirlsrising.com.

We also thank Anna Eleanor Roosevelt and Felicia Wong, chair of the board and president respectively of the Roosevelt Institute, along with Nataya Friedan, project manager for Women and Girls Rising; our associate, Sonia Haerizadeh; our devoted interns, Paula Garcia-Salazar, Lauren Stauffer, and Hannah Zhang; and the outstanding staff members at Roosevelt, too numerous to mention, who also contributed to the success of the undertaking. The Mailman School of Public Health of Columbia University provided valuable support as well. Finally, we acknowledge with gratitude Thomas G. Weiss and Rorden Wilkinson, editors of the Routledge Global Institutions Series, and Devaki Jain, who generously introduced us to them.

Ellen Chesler and Terry McGovern
New York
January, 2015

Abbreviations

ACGEN	Active Citizenship and Gendered Social Entitlements Project
ACLU	American Civil Liberties Union
ACPD	Action Canada for Population and Development
ACWF	All China Women's Federation
AHA	Anti-Homosexuality Act (in Uganda)
AIDS	Acquired immune deficiency syndrome
AIWC	All India Women's Conference
AP	Associated Press
APA	Anti-Pornography Act (in Uganda)
APCWD	United Nations Asian and Pacific Centre for Women and Development
APWLD	Asia Pacific Forum on Women, Law and Development
ARTs	Assisted reproductive technologies
AWID	Association for Women's Rights in Development
BCWS	Bangladesh Center for Worker Solidarity
BPFA	Beijing Platform for Action
BRICS	Brazil, Russia, India, China, South Africa
BSA	Bilateral security agreement
CAPMAS	Central Agency for Statistics (in Egypt)
CCTs	Conditional cash transfers
CEDAW	Convention on the Elimination of Discrimination against Women
CEDPA	Center for Development and Population Activities
CLADEM	Caribbean and Latin American Committee for the Defense of Women's Rights
CNDM	National Council for Women's Rights (in Brazil)
COP	Conference of Parties
CPD	Commission on Population and Development
CPR	Contraceptive prevalence rates

CRC	Convention on the Rights of the Child
CRTDA	Collective for Research and Training on Development Action
CSW	Commission on the Status of Women
CWGL	Center for Women's Global Leadership
DAW	Division for the Advancement of Women
DAWN	Development Alternatives in the New Era
DDR	Disarmament, demobilization and reintegration
DEDAW	Declaration on the Elimination of Discrimination against Women
DFID	Department for International Development
DHS	Demographic and health surveys
DPA	Department of Political Affairs
DPKO	Department of Peacekeeping Operations
DVAW	Declaration against Violence against Women
ECA	Economic Commission of Africa
ECE	Economic Commission of Europe
ECLAC	Economic Commission of Latin America and the Caribbean
ECPAT	End Child Prostitution, Child Pornography and Trafficking of Children for Sexual Purposes
EDHS	Egypt's Demographic and Health Survey
EFA	Education for All
ESCAP	Economic and Social Commission for Asia and the Pacific
ESCWA	Economic and Social Commission of West Africa
EU	European Union
FGM	Female genital mutilation
FWCW	Fourth World Conference on Women
GA	General Assembly
GACC	Global Alliance for Clean Cookstoves
GBM	Green Belt Movement
GCPEA	Global Coalition to Protect Education from Attack
GDP	Gross domestic product
GEC	Girls Education Challenge
GEEJ	Gender, Economic and Ecological Justice Initiative
GEMS	Gender Equity Movement in Schools
GMR	Global Monitoring Report
GPE	Global Partnership for Education
GSP	Generalized system of preferences
HAPCA	HIV and AIDS Prevention and Control Act (in Uganda)

HERA	Health, Empowerment, Rights and Accountability
HIV	Human immunodeficiency virus
HRW	Human Rights Watch
ICERD	International Convention on the Elimination of All Forms of Racial Discrimination
ICPD	International Conference on Population and Development
ICRW	International Center for Research on Women
IDWF	International Domestic Workers' Federation
IDWN	International Domestic Workers Network
ILO	International Labor Organization
IMF	International Monetary Fund
INSTRAW	International Research and Training Institute for the Advancement of Women
IPCC	Intergovernmental Panel on Climate Change
IPPF	International Planned Parenthood Federation
IPSO	International Program on the State of the Ocean
ISIL	Islamic State of Iraq and the Levant
ITUC	International Trade Union Confederation
IUF	International Union of Food, Agricultural, Hotel, Restaurant, Catering, Tobacco and Allied Workers' Associations
IWHC	International Women's Health Coalition
IWTC	International Women's Tribune Center
IWY	International Women's Year
LGBTQI	Lesbian Gay Bisexual Transgender Queer and Intersex
MARP	Most at-risk population
MDGs	Millennium Development Goals
MENA	Middle East and North Africa
MOI	Means of implementation
NAACP	National Association for the Advancement of Colored People
NAP	National action plan
NFIW	National Federation of Indian Women
NGOs	Non-governmental organizations
NPC	National People's Congress (in China)
NPC	National Population Council (in Egypt)
NWCCW	National Working Committee on Children and Women (in China)
OCHA	Office for the Coordination of Humanitarian Affairs
ODA	Overseas development assistance

OECD	Organization for Economic Cooperation and Development
OWG	Open Working Group
PCM	Prevention of Child Marriage (strategy in Egypt)
PEPFAR	President's Emergency Plan for AIDS Relief
PFSC	Pacific Feminist SRHR Coalition
PPGCCSD	Pacific Partnerships to Strengthen Gender Climate Change and Sustainable Development
Prep Com	Preparatory Committee
RedLac	Latin American and Caribbean Youth Network for Sexual and Reproductive Rights
RETRASEX	Latin American Network of Sex Workers
SCR	Security Council Resolution
SDGs	Sustainable Development Goals
SEWA	Self-employed Women's Association
SIDA	Swedish International Development Cooperation Agency
SLACC	Some Latin American and Caribbean Countries
SOEs	State-owned enterprises
SPM	Secretaria de Politicas para as Mulheres
SRB	Sex ratio at birth
SRH	Sexual and reproductive health
SRHR	Sexual and reproductive health rights
TNCs	Transnational Corporations
TOT	Train the Trainer
UDHR	Universal Declaration of Human Rights
UN	United Nations
UNAIDS	Joint UN Programme on HIV and AIDS
UNDP	United Nations Development Program
UNESCO	United Nations Organization for Education, Science and Culture
UNFCCC	United National Framework Convention on Climate Change
UNFPA	United Nations Population Fund
UNGASS	United Nations General Assembly Special Session
UNICEF	United Nations Children's Fund
UNIFEM	United Nations Development Fund for Women
UNOHCHR	United Nations Office of the High Commissioner for Human Rights
UNOHCR	United Nations Office for the High Commissioner for Refugees
USAID	United States Agency for International Development

USHRN	United States Human Rights Network
VAW	Violence against women
VAWA	Violence against Women Act (in the United States)
VCT	Voluntary counseling and testing
VDPA	Vienna Declaration and Program of Action
WAND	Women and Development Unit of the University of the West Indies
WEDO	Women's Environment and Development Organization
WEMC	Women's Empowerment in Muslim Contexts
WHO	World Health Organization
WIDE	World Inequality Database on Education
WIDF	Women's International Democratic Federation
WIEGO	Women in Informal Employment: Globalizing and Organizing
WILDAF	Women in Law and Development in Africa
WILPF	Women's International League for Peace and Freedom
WLP	Women's Learning Partnership
WLUML	Women Living Under Muslim Laws
WMG	Women's Major Group
WOI	Women's Organization of Iran
WOREC	Women's Rehabilitation Centre (in Nepal)
WPA	World Plan of Action
WPF	World Population Fund
WPS	Women peace and security
WTO	World Trade Organization
WWB	Women's World Banking
YC	Youth Coalition
YWCA	Young Women's Christian Association

Introduction

Ellen Chesler and Terry McGovern

Many years ago Eleanor Roosevelt went to the United Nations hoping to shape a post-Second World War order secured morally and legally by human rights instruments and safeguarded by an unprecedented array of new development and humanitarian institutions. She helped expand definitions of rights across civil, political, social, and economic sectors and recognized that such rights are indivisible. Although she originally envisioned a gender-neutral architecture for this enterprise, she listened to women gathered from around the world and included special provisions to address sex discrimination within it.

More than a half century of effort has since confirmed that meaningful improvements in the lives of individuals and in the well-being and security of nations occur only when strategies to allocate resources are delicately balanced with obligations to address fundamental violations in human rights. A double lens of accountability to development and rights is the unique intellectual and moral framework that continues to guide the efforts of the United Nations, the institution that remains Franklin and Eleanor Roosevelt's enduring global legacy. And nowhere has this legacy been more significant than in establishing conditions that are helping to advance rights and opportunities for women and girls.

Historical perspective on women's human rights

Mrs. Roosevelt was one of only 17 female delegates from 11 countries at the UN's founding in London in 1946, but supported by a robust non-governmental community of activists, they immediately issued a statement calling for women to engage in public affairs—to come forward and share in the work of peace and reconstruction, as they had done in the war itself.[1] They created an independent Commission on the Status of Women (CSW) and then prevailed upon the Human Rights

Commission to guarantee explicit rights to "all human beings" in the Universal Declaration of Human Rights (UDHR), not just to men.

The UDHR thus stakes a landmark claim that discrimination against women be viewed as a necessary and appropriate matter of international concern, not as a category privileged and protected by local sovereignty or by local customary or religious practices governing marriage and family relations. It also recognizes that women oppressed in private places cannot realistically claim their legitimate rights as human beings. The state must be obligated to extend rights to women and eliminate everyday forms of discrimination.[2]

Off the radar screen of Cold War warriors skeptical of human rights, the CSW then managed to draft and negotiate the adoption of binding treaties governing women's political rights, nationality rights, consent and minimum age of marriage, property rights, educational opportunities, and labor standards. Path breaking studies were also conducted documenting continued challenges and leading to a new emphasis on the responsibility to provide women not just legal protections, but also greater benefits of development assistance. This work belies the common accusation that this agenda was a Western invention.

In 1967, a formal Declaration on the Elimination of Discrimination against Women was written, and the following year the UN marked the 20th anniversary of the UHDR with a special conference in Tehran, where women's rights provided a rare arena of agreement between Russians, eager to call attention to the educational and employment opportunities their government had granted women, and Americans, for whom these issues were gaining momentum as a result of an emerging second wave of feminism. The conference adopted resolutions encouraging support for a legal rights project to address gender discrimination and development assistance targeted to women, especially in largely agricultural economies based on women's labor. Most significantly, it identified family planning as a basic human right and paved the way for the establishment of a UN fund for population.[3]

Between 1975 and 1995, the UN sponsored four international conferences on women that produced wildly optimistic blueprints for the achievement of concrete gains. They have since been dismissed by some as lacking both focus and practical strategies for implementation, while others insist that however often they may still be unrealized or violated, these programs for action have raised awareness, shaped aspirations, and in countless significant and concrete ways helped change laws and alter behaviors.

In 1979, following two decades of documentation and deliberation, the UN Declaration on Women was codified as the Convention on the

Elimination of All Forms of Discrimination against Women, commonly known as CEDAW. This visionary international women's bill of rights cautiously acknowledges the importance of traditional obligations to the family but also establishes new norms for participation by women in all dimensions of life. It gives precise definition and actionable protection to a broad range of women's rights in marriage and family relations, including property and inheritance and access to health care, with an explicit mention of family planning. It establishes the principle of equal protection for women as citizens in their own right entitled to suffrage, political representation, and other legal benefits; to education, including elementary and secondary education that provides professional and vocational training free of gender stereotypes and segregation; and to formal employment, deserving of equal pay, social security benefits, and protection from sexual harassment and workplace discrimination on the grounds of marriage or maternity.

One-hundred and eighty-eight UN member states have now ratified CEDAW—giving it the active participation of more UN member states than any other treaty—with the stunning exception of the United States, which continues to reside in the unlikely company of Iran, Sudan, Somalia, and a few Pacific Island nations in having failed to ratify. President Jimmy Carter signed the treaty in 1979 and sent it to the Senate, where it has languished ever since because of the high bar of 67 votes necessary for ratification and the fierce opposition of conservatives to international entanglements and women's rights.

In 1992, CEDAW was expanded so that gender-based violence is also formally identified as a fundamental violation of human rights, and governments are encouraged to take action. This breakthrough drew on claims by feminists of evidence of demonstrable abuses of women "including torture, starvation, terrorism, and even murder" that continue to be routinely accepted without legal recourse in many places. "Crimes such as these against any group other than women would be recognized as a civil and political emergency as well as a gross violation of the victim's humanity," Charlotte Bunch of the Center for Women's Global Leadership at Rutgers University, and one of our distinguished contributors, wrote in a path breaking 1990 article in *Human Rights Quarterly*. In 1993, at the Vienna Conference on Human Rights, drawing on a slogan that originated with a grassroots coalition of Philippine women, Bunch first made the claim that "women's rights are human rights," which Hillary Rodham Clinton, another prominent contributor to this volume, then memorably incorporated into her remarks at the UN Fourth World Conference on Women in Beijing in 1995 and made a global mantra.[4]

Recent policy challenges and responses captured in this volume

In recent years, a growing body of evidence has demonstrated even more clearly that improvements in the status of women and girls—however worthy and important in their own right—also drive the prosperity, stability, and security of families, communities, and nations. Yet despite many indicators of progress, women and girls everywhere—including the United States and elsewhere in well-developed, not just developing, societies—continue to confront barriers to their full and equal rights and participation. Meeting the challenges they face will require significantly increased financial capital and political will.

As we work toward this goal, we can only benefit from having women who work on the ground around the world share the strategies they have developed, the lessons they have learned and the resistances they have faced. To this end, on 11–12 September 2014, the Roosevelt Institute convened a two-day conference at the Ford Foundation in New York City. The intent was to create a clear and forceful narrative about the modern movement for women's rights, its central relevance to global and national policymaking, and its agenda for the future.

The convening brought together a diverse group of 67 prominent policymakers, activists, and scholars from 30 countries—gathered from across geographies and generations, ethnic and religious divides, policy specializations, and academic disciplines. Several hundred more distinguished guests comprised the live audience, while several thousand more in the United States and around the world participated virtually through digital streaming of the proceedings.

From the highlights of the conference and the background papers prepared for it, we are pleased to present this edited volume. The core of the book features chapters across a range of issues, each empirically grounded and well-sourced, but also provocatively argued, clearly written, and thus intended to be accessible to a broad audience of policymakers, journalists, public intellectuals, academics, and students.

Prominent pioneers in the global women's movement provide lessons from the past to learn from and build on. Contemporary policymakers, activists, and scholars present their best assessment of today's policy and programmatic innovation, often challenging conventional assumptions. And interspersed throughout are also a number of shorter, more personal reflections, which address the conditions that inspire recent work and shape hopes and concerns for the future.

Capturing an array of voices and experiences, our contributors interrogate gains secured, controversies inspired, and oppositions unleashed. While the anthology, of course, does not aspire to be definitive, the chapters individually and collectively do present an inspiring story of major accomplishments in the advancement of the normative and legal frameworks that today help shape the aspirations of women and girls. By examining continuing struggles, however, they also illuminate the difficulty of realizing rights and opportunities, especially in light of sustained controversies around gender, but also because of circumstances wrought by economic crises, global and regional political conflicts, and epidemic health challenges, including HIV-AIDS, largely unforeseen when commitments and goals to achieving gains for women were first established.

Intended to help inform future agendas in national and international arenas, many of the chapters also provide rich content that identifies and analyzes urgent issues of strategy, policy, and program, as well as resource allocation. This history and roadmap are especially critical for younger generations who need a better understanding of this rich feminist legacy. On the whole, our contributors present a powerful narrative of women's agency, not one of victimization. Yet they also avoid an all too common tendency to oversimplify and overpromise what women can accomplish, and to isolate gender as a category of concern and analysis from the larger economic, social, and political circumstances, including class and racial hierarchies, in which it must be located and understood.

The urgency of this effort is great. We approach the 20th anniversary of the Beijing summit with growing interest of policymakers in the issues raised there, but with public support compromised by increasing politicization—too often verging on demonization—of the women and girls' agenda. The UN—where women have long gathered with big dreams and secured historic legal and institutional changes to achieve them—has itself come under renewed and relentless attack as it seeks to build on the accomplishments and address the failures of its much heralded Millennium Development Goals (MDGs) with a new and refined set of aspirations for sustainable development post 2015. Criticism comes not only from conservatives opposed to multi-lateral alliances and to the universal standards for human rights and social justice the UN has long promoted, but also from many progressives understandably troubled by the institution's structural weaknesses, inefficiencies, and frequent failure to deliver on the promises it makes. Still, our contributors—many of whom have spent decades working within or lobbying around the UN—remain committed to holding the institution accountable, along with its member states.

Organizational overview

Our book is organized in five sections. The first examines critical developments in the space that the UN, working in partnership with diverse women's movements, has created for the formulation and advancement of global gender norms. The second looks bottom-up at the realization of rights in national and local contexts. The third offers several broad overviews and a number of regional or country case studies of efforts to achieve full economic justice for women and girls. The fourth dissects cultural, structural, and resource barriers to educating girls and eliminating the burdens on individuals and societies of child or early marriage. Two brief final chapters reflect on the specific gender challenges presented by climate change and urgent new threats to our natural environment. And a final word goes to Hillary Clinton, former US First Lady, Senator, and Secretary of State—now again a candidate for president—in an intimate, reflective conversation with Lissa Muscatine, one of the principal aides who accompanied her to Beijing.

Our many contributors deliberately present a variety of perspectives and are not meant to achieve a consistent point of view. Growing recognition of gender as a category of concern across sectors has not necessarily strengthened agreement on important ideological and instrumental questions about how best to advance the status of women and girls. In fact, the opposite may be true—with disputes intensifying as the stakes grow higher and obstacles to progress become more difficult to comprehend and to untangle from larger geopolitical circumstances and complexities.

Common themes

Still, from this diverse set of analyses and reflections, a number of common themes do emerge.

Misguided macroeconomic policies devastate poor women and families

First, many of our contributors comment on the profound and troubling lack of coherence between macroeconomic policies of recent decades and bold commitments to advance gender equality. The resources to help realize rights have simply not materialized, betraying Eleanor Roosevelt's original injunction about keeping the two in balance. The UN and its affiliated institutions are simply running out of money. They increasingly find themselves having to justify the high costs and sustainability of their huge bureaucracies and needing to raise funds from the private sector without adequate mechanisms for accountability or transparency.

Meanwhile, countries starved for funding, especially in light of the global recession of 2008, have embraced austerity and shrunk their budgets, making it impossible to translate good intentions into realities.[5] Misguided policies together with questions of accountability are critical here. Through the 1980s and 1990s, at the urging of international financial institutions, most developing countries—many of which had earlier experimented with state socialism outright or with mixed economies that heavily emphasized public investment—were made to reverse course and privatize many services, with governments becoming regulators, rather than providers, of such core elements of the social and economic rights agenda as education, employment, and health care. This restructuring, with its adverse consequences for tax revenue, social insurance, and the imposition of user fees—and for the flow of external aid on which many poor countries still rely—has had devastating impacts.[6] In more than 60 percent of them, for example, out of pocket spending rose to an estimated 40 percent of total spending on health care alone. And even in countries like China and India, experiencing overall economic growth, worsening inequalities have slowed or reversed gains for women and girls, as clear-sighted assessments by Liu Bohong and Yaiping Cai and by Devaki Jain attest.

UN Deputy Secretary General Jan Eliasson offers a powerful statement that equity and advancement for women and girls is the missing ingredient without which the institution's larger aspirations to advance rights, development, and security cannot succeed. Secretary Clinton makes the same forceful argument she has long advanced that investing in women and girls is the right and the smart thing to do. But gender-sensitive policies, however well meaning, will not succeed absent larger strategies to promote economic growth and address the persistent divide between rich and poor.

Inclusive growth requires special attention to "structures of constraint"

Naila Kabeer also reminds us that while the formal participation of women in economies most always boosts economic growth, the reverse proposition—that economic growth reduces gender inequalities—is not always true. Economic growth only benefits women when special attention is given to the structural constraints of workplaces that still typically segregate women in low-paying jobs, pay them less than men for the same work, and assume their primary responsibility for child-rearing and other household obligations. Wendy Chavkin points out that outside of several advanced Scandinavian countries that offer generous benefits to both mothers and fathers, women typically respond by having fewer children, a situation that results in overall fertility declines, which, in turn, after providing a temporary demographic dividend from women's economic participation, may wind up further depleting public coffers needed to sustain robust programs for social security. From a different vantage point, Isobel Coleman and Aala Abdelgadir demonstrate how cultural constraints continue to limit women's advancement and overall progress in countries of the MENA region with strong conservative values, where women typically leave the workforce when they marry. And, finally, Ellen Bravo describes how Washington's failure to provide adequate support for work-family balance in the United States has inspired several progressive states and municipalities to meet the challenge and provide replicable models for a national policy reassessment.

Resource-strained governments in many developed countries are responding by tolerating the transnational migration of women to provide domestic services and other caregiving. This, in turn, as Nisha Varia recounts, has required determined efforts to protect the rights of domestic workers through labor unions, where strategies are being modeled on previously successful efforts in the formal sector, such as those Kalpona Akter describes in moving reflections on her work in the garment factories of Bangladesh.

Arguments for cultural pluralism fuel a backlash

Success in advancing universal norms has unleashed a perhaps predictable response, with criticisms of the human rights doctrine for denying cultural self-determination now uniting elements of the extreme right and left. Feminists Farida Shaheed, Charlotte Bunch, and Roxanna Carrillo respond eloquently that if the rights of half of humanity can be conditioned in the name of culture, religion, or nationality, then the concept has no meaning. Still, the UN remains an often unwieldy institution whose governance requires near unanimity to move forward on matters of rights and development under the jurisdiction of the General Assembly. With the rise of conservative social forces in many G77 countries, in the Middle East, Eastern Europe, and elsewhere—many of them also amply resourced by Catholic and Evangelical churches exporting an ideological agenda—consensus is becoming more and more difficult to achieve, as Adrienne Germain, Gita Sen, and Sonia Correa, 40-year veterans of pitched battles over the sexual and reproductive health and rights of women and girls, also remind us. What is more, as Sylvia Tamale's chapter on Uganda demonstrates, we still have a long way to go to fully realize individual rights of sexual expression, orientation, and identity everywhere. The powerful force that traditional values exert on cultures, and the many ways in which they are reconstructed to serve prevailing political interests and to foster regional and global conflict, are concerns that inform the fine chapters that also comprise the section of this volume devoted to policy on advancing girls' education and eliminating child marriage. Carol Bellamy, for example, offers poignant evidence of how conflict in Syria is reversing hard-won gains and again raising rates of child marriage. Especially valuable, therefore, are the strategies offered from India, Egypt, and Ethiopia on ways to involve men and boys more meaningfully to overcome gender stereotypes and end violations against women and girls.

Data limitations narrow our sights and our impact

US historian Jocelyn Olcott leads off this volume by examining the first International Women's Year Conference in Mexico City in 1975 as a foundation for subsequent progress because, among other legacies, it is credited with having created INSTRAW, the UN agency that collects essential data to monitor women across a host of social and economic indicators. Secretary Clinton, however, closes the book by decrying the continued limitations of available metrics and calling for better ones. In between, several contributors address the hazards of tethering policy to national data sets that conceal or distort important sub-national variations. They also point to a paucity of usable data on adolescents, which limits the ability of policymakers to design useful interventions in education or sexual and reproductive health care, for example. Without gender disaggregation of data, moreover, specific impacts on women and girls in such crises as the HIV-AIDS epidemic tend to be overlooked for too long.

Continuing efforts require a commitment by governments to assemble metrics that disaggregate expenditures by gender and involve a range of actors—finance and sector ministries, national machineries for the advancement of women, statistical and planning bureaus, parliamentarians, international organizations and donors, local civil society, and media. The relative powerlessness of health and gender ministries compared with finance ministries that actually negotiate loans and allocate national budgets may have also slowed women's advancement, as several of our chapters attest.[7]

At the same time, we are cautioned to be wary of placing too much emphasis on gender analysis as an end in itself—in other words, not to conflate greater awareness of women and girls with automatic progress on their behalf. Since introduction of the concept in the Beijing Platform for Action, gender mainstreaming has actually proven to be a technically confusing tool. Policies addressing gender equality often "evaporate" in budget processes and implementation stages or in their translation from legal and policy commitments to actual realities.[8] A recent Organisation for Economic Co-operation and Development (OECD) study found that "donors tended to lack well-defined priorities and objectives and rarely had specific, dedicated and well-resourced budgets in place," and that 74 percent of aid marked with gender equality as a principal or significant objective was not held accountable for the translation of budget and policy revisions into actual programs.[9]

Above all, we need more investments in women's movements on the ground

Investing in women and girls has become a development trend that is not, alas, matched by a commitment to investing in women's rights organizing or advocacy work.[10] An Association for Women's Rights in Development (AWID) 2011 survey of over 1,000 women's organizations found that only 7 percent had 2010 budgets of over USD $500,000; 48 percent had not received core funding; and 52 percent did not receive multi-year funding.[11] Yet, research across 70 countries shows that the "autonomous mobilization of feminists in domestic and transnational contexts—not leftist parties, women in government or national wealth—is the critical factor for achieving policy change."[12]

This volume amply confirms this finding with rich personal stories and qualitative analysis. Over and over again our contributors demonstrate the significant role women's movements have played in working with actors inside governments and global institutions to achieve change. This was especially true at the UN global forums in Cairo, Vienna, and Beijing during the 1990s, which are intimately remembered here. Most compelling, as well, are the recollections of former Women's Minister of Iran, Mahnaz Afkhami, about how women's organizing in pre-revolutionary Iran informed the agenda of the 1975 first UN conference on women in Mexico City, and how, in turn, its platform for action further influenced Iran and left a legacy of institutions and progress for women that the forces of reaction, however determined, have not been able to unravel completely.

Our section on realizing rights further confirms the importance of autonomous feminist organizing, beginning with a chapter from the distinguished advocate and scholar, Jacqueline Pitanguy on the parallel evolution of women's rights and democratic institutions in Brazil. Farida Shaheed of Pakistan, who is currently serving as UN Special Rapporteur on the Right to Culture, also reflects on the importance of building the women's rights movement and leveraging lessons from global conferences to inform local realities, a theme then explored in chapters from Lebanon, Nepal, and elsewhere.

Finally, several of our contributors reflect on prospects for building new relationships between women's organization and private sector actors, who may well be the most influential new players in development. As major players like the World Bank explicitly call for the "gendering" of development, public-private partnerships are expanding to include development agency foundations, corporations, and NGOs. This trend is also shifting development discourse "from aid to investment" and encouraging corporate management models with an emphasis on results-based monitoring and evaluation systems, and an increased focus on narrow solutions.

Women's rights organizations are struggling to maintain context-specific innovations targeting underlying rights issues, as donors emphasize results-oriented, short-term programs.[13] Specific, tangible aid objectives aligned with larger demands for accountability, a model increasingly more influential in setting the aid agenda, also drives donors, to experiment and to jump from one issue to another.[14] This may undermine efforts to transform deep-rooted historical inequities that by their very nature take time. We need greater scrutiny of recent trends in development practice along with accountability measures—most especially to monitor adherence of businesses and corporations to human right agreements. The emergence of right-leaning governments in a number of OECD countries reinforces the importance of these arguments. A less transformative approach to development may appeal to governments that are eager to limit their own public aid expenditures and reluctant to use aid money for advocacy.[15]

Success is a good thing by and large. We are pleased to see more and more projects that advance the legal and social empowerment of women,[16] along with a growing perception of a gender-progressive public sector. This volume reminds us, however, that we still need independent women's rights organizations to tackle inextricable, cultural and legal discrimination, and deeply embedded structural inequalities. Long-term success in shifting practices that harm women and girls will require continued support for instrumental, ground-based strategies at work alongside strong, sustainable advocacy movements. This is what policymakers often refer to as an "enabling environment."[17] Happily, there are visionary funders willing to take on this "riskier," less obviously measurable work. We just need more of them.

There is no better way to make this argument than by pointing to recent efforts of feminists in the movement for environmental justice, which claims our attention as climate change threatens the planet and governments, often hostage to private interests, are slow to respond. Taking a page from Eleanor Roosevelt and Hansa Mehta of India (who first encouraged Mrs. Roosevelt's special attention to women), Fiji activist Noelene Nabulivou examines the gendered impacts of climate change and calls on the UN to provide greater opportunity for participation and more accountability to women in its ongoing formulation of environmental policy. Wanjira Mathai of Kenya then describes a practical program of environmental stewardship, which engages women entrepreneurs to provide efficient cookstoves that do not depend for fuel on wood that is felled from precious forests and releases harmful pollutants when burned.

Their reflections provide evidence—amplified elsewhere in this volume—that women and girls are, indeed, continuing to rise in courageous, innovative, and effective ways. We honor that history and hope our book inspires its future.

Notes

1 Ellen Chesler, "The shoulders we stand on: Eleanor Roosevelt and roots of the Women's Rights Revolution," in *The Unfinished Revolution: Voices from the Global Struggle for Women's Human Rights*, ed. Minky Worden (New York: Seven Stories Press, 2012), 20–25, informs this first section.
2 Eleanor Roosevelt, "Making Human Rights come alive," Speech to the Second National Conference on UNESCO, 1949, www.udhr.org/history/114.htm; Felice D. Gaer, "And never the twain shall meet? The struggle to establish Women's Rights as International Human Rights," in *The International Human Rights of Women: Instruments of Change*, ed. Carol Elizabeth Lockwood (Washington, DC: American Bar Association, 1998), 8.
3 Arvonne S. Fraser, "Becoming human: The origins and development of Women's Human Rights," *Human Rights Quarterly* 21, no. 4 (1999): 891.
4 "Convention on the elimination of all forms of discrimination against women (CEDAW), 18 December 1979, in *The International Human Rights of Women: Instruments of Change*, ed. Lockwood, 269–280; Charlotte Bunch, "Women's Rights as Human Rights: Towards a re-vision of Human Rights," *Human Rights Quarterly* 12, no. 4 (1990): 486.
5 Maitrayee Mukhopadhyay and Rosalind Eyben, "Rights and resources: the effects of external financing on organising for Women's Rights," Royal Tropical Institute and Pathways of Women's Empowerment, March 2011,

http://www.pathwaysofempowerment.org/Rights_and_Resources.pdf; and Caroline Moser and Annalise Moser, "Gender mainstreaming since Beijing: A review of success and limitations in International Institutions," *Gender and Development* 13, no. 2 (2005): 11–22.

6 Marge Berer, "Health sector reforms: Implications for sexual and reproductive health services," *Reproductive Health Matters* 10, no. 20 (2002): 6–15; and Tania Dmytraczenko, Vijay Rao, and Lori Ashford, "Health sector reform: How it affects reproductive health," Population Reference Bureau, 2003.

7 United Nations, Division for the Advancement of Women and Department of Economic and Social Affairs, *Report of the expert group meeting: Financing for Gender Equality and the Empowerment of Women*, (EGM/FFGE/2007/REPORT), 4–7 September 2007.

8 Letty Chiwara and Maria Karadenizli, "Mapping aid effectiveness and gender equality: Global findings," United Nations Development Fund for Women (UNDP), 2008.

9 OECD/DAC, "Aid in support of gender equality and women's empowerment: Statistical overview," October 2012.

10 Terry McGovern, "No Risk, No Gain: Invest In Women and Girls By Funding Advocacy, Organizing, Litigation and Work to Shift Culture," 86–102.

11 Cindy Clark and Ellen Sprenger, "Where is the money for Women's Rights? Assessing resources and the role of donors in the promotion of Women's Rights and the support of Women's Organizations," AWID, February 2006.

12 Angelika Arutyunova, "Watering the leaves and starving the roots: The status of financing for women's rights organizing gender equality," AWID, 2013.

13 Maitrayee Mukhopadhyay and Rosalind Eyben, "Rights and resources: the effects of external financing on organising for Women's Rights."

14 Fernanda Hopenhaym, "Fund*Her* Brief 2008: Money watch for Women's Rights movements and organizations," AWID, 2008, 47.

15 Rosalind Eyben, "Issue 4: What is happening to donor support for women's rights?," *Contestations: Dialogues on women's empowerment*, www.contestations.net/issues/issue-4/what-is-happening-to-donor-support-for-women%E2%80%99s-rights/.

16 Asia Development Bank, "Legal Empowerment for women and disadvantaged groups," 2009, 123; and Deutsche Gesellschaft Fur Internationale Zusammenarbeit (GIZ) GmbH, *Promotion of legal and social empowerment of women*, www.giz.de/themen/en/20298.htm.

17 United Nations, "Joint program on fostering an enabling environment for gender equality in Turkey: Inception report," October 2011, 37; Canadian International Development Agency, "Gender Equality: Policy and tools—CIDA's Framework for assessing Gender Equality results," 2010, 28.

Part I
Establishing new norms at the United Nations

1 The century of women

A reflection

The Honorable Jan Eliasson

UNITED NATIONS DEPUTY SECRETARY GENERAL

I see the glorious Four Freedoms Park on Roosevelt Island every morning from my 38th floor office in the United Nations. It is a daily reminder of Franklin Roosevelt's commitment to securing freedom of expression, freedom of religion, freedom from fear and freedom from want—everywhere in the world.

I also have a booklet on my desk that was given to me by a woman who, back in 1950, had attended a seminar with Eleanor Roosevelt about the Universal Declaration of Human Rights. This was shortly after this landmark document was crafted by the UN Human Rights Commission under Mrs. Roosevelt's gifted leadership.

"She was so impressive," the woman told me, "that I asked for her autograph." "I paid just 25 cents, but I've kept this in my library all these years, and now I want you to have it."

I opened up the nice brochure, and on the first page it says "With good wishes, Eleanor Roosevelt."

I keep this in a very special place.

Today, in a time of renewed turmoil and uncertainty across the world, people are again looking for hope. This is why I'm so glad to join you today for what is a powerful statement of optimism: namely, *Women and Girls Rising*.

Nothing can rival the hopeful message of the empowerment, engagement, and elevation of women and girls in today's world. I firmly believe, and I say it often, that this will be the century of women—one in which women and girls enjoy their rights and realize their potential as never before—a time when they finally live free from discrimination and violence—from ignorance and want.

We are not there yet, as we all know. And the journey to that necessary destination has been far too long and far too arduous. In 1995, however, we reached a milestone in this struggle when 189 governments set out a visionary agenda for achieving women's empowerment, women's rights, and gender equality at the UN's Fourth World Conference on Women in Beijing, China.

As we approach the 20th anniversary of this landmark achievement, it is critical to take stock of our progress. Over the past 20 years much has been achieved by, and within, the UN system. Secretary General Ban Ki Moon has made gender equality a priority. He has appointed more women to senior leadership positions than all of his predecessors combined. And UN bodies have made gender equality an integral part of their mandates.

And, of course, a key development has been the establishment of UN Women in 2010, which now plays a critical role in advancing global standards and knowledge on gender equality for the UN itself and in supporting member states and civil society to live up to those standards on the ground. Important gains have also been made on women's access to decent work and social protection and on women's sexual and reproductive health and rights.

And we are holding ourselves accountable. A catalyst for our efforts was the adoption of the UN system-wide action plan on gender two years ago. This is the first framework to systematically measure progress on gender equality and women's empowerment across the UN system, and it gives us a clearer picture of where there is progress in mainstreaming gender into its own policies and programs—of strengths and also of weaknesses.

For example, we have worked to strengthen the role of women in peace and security. Today women are more involved in peacekeeping than ever before. Five of 16 operations are now led by women special representatives. Our operation in Cyprus is particularly interesting, following the appointment of the first woman as commander of forces, a general from Norway. Women are also serving in UN police contingents in greater numbers than ever, but still the negotiation table remains a men's club.

I have mediated six conflicts in my time, and I've always had women in my delegations, but never one in front of me. A recent UN survey of 31 peace processes from 1992 to 2011 showed that women comprised only 4 percent of signatories, 2.4 percent of chief mediators, 3.7 percent of witnesses, and 9 percent of the negotiators. This underrepresentation in peace processes is much more marked than in other decision-making forums.

The main institutional actors, including the UN Security Council, now recognize the importance of opening doors and opportunities to women in conflict prevention and peacemaking. With the well-known prescription of Resolution 1325, these institutions are now committed to positive change, and we must hold them to this promise.

We must also work harder to address formidable inequalities that remain on the ground. Although equality in primary school enrollment has clearly improved, large gender gaps in education persist at and above secondary levels. Girls and young women continue to endure various forms of discrimination and abuse in their quests for education. Far too many women are also still denied their sexual reproductive health and rights, and here we should note that our special working group on Sustainable Development Goals sent a strong message in this field. We hope the negotiations next year will heed that and confirm the working group's findings. This is very important.

New rules and policies on domestic violence are also helping strengthen state accountability, even as violence against women worldwide continues at unacceptable levels. It is crucially important to engage men and boys in this work. UN Women has launched a solidarity platform *#heforshe*, which aims to amplify the voices of men and boys speaking out for gender equality. We should all try to help promote that work in this age of social media.

Sexual violence, indeed all violence against women and girls, is fueled by unequal power relationships between men and women. Notions of masculinity are deeply rooted in dominance, female objectification, and sexual aggression. Changing these social norms and gender stereotypes is essential to tackling all forms of violence. By adopting a positive, more mature perception of masculinity, men and boys can become partners in preventing violence.

I remember working with my prime minister in Sweden in the 1980s on a speech he was to deliver, whose working title was "The Importance of the Emancipation of Women." He looked at us, and said: "You don't understand. 'It's not the emancipation of women. It's the emancipation of man!'" This was 30 years ago!

Promoting women's leadership is critical to addressing these problems, but as you know, the number of women in power remains low. Only one in five parliamentarians worldwide is a woman, with Rwanda and Sweden at parity and leading all nations. This is a considerable improvement from 1995, when only one in ten was a woman, but it is still slow progress. Further gains must be achieved by surmounting the barriers women face in electoral politics because gender bias in most cultures makes winning the support of political parties, raising funds, and securing fair representation by the media much more difficult for women.

A range of measures can be adopted to address the unequal participation of women in political life—from ensuring that women get selected as candidates in the first place, to voluntary or legislative focus. Our political systems must be fully representative of all the people they serve, women as well as men. It benefits us all.

The global political and economic landscape continues to change rapidly and dramatically. Conflicts, financial economic crisis, food insecurity, and climate change, as well as pandemics like Ebola, have intensified vulnerability with specific impacts on women and girls.

Responding to this new landscape—creating a safe and equitable world for generations to come—is the most urgent challenge of this century. The Beijing anniversary and the elaboration of the post-2015 development agenda provide an historic opportunity to place gender equality at the center of the global agenda. This is important in itself and also as a means to achieve sustainable development and lasting peace.

The future we want demands a bold and transformative approach to addressing structural barriers in gender equality. Without this focus our work for human rights—our work for sustainable development— our work for lasting peace is futile and incomplete. We must seize every opportunity at all levels to realize the human rights of women and girls and their full and equal participation in society.

We must make this the century of women. In a time of great uncertainty, that is a truly inspiring challenge and promise for the future.

2 From the time of creation

Legacies and unfinished business from the first International Women's Year Conference

Jocelyn Olcott

Four decades have passed since thousands of people descended on Mexico City for the very first UN International Women's Year (IWY) Conference in the summer of 1975. In addition to delegates from UN member states and invited liberation movements and non-governmental organizations (NGOs), the event drew roughly 2,000 journalists and 6,000 participants in the parallel NGO tribune. Indeed, the IWY Conference was among the very first UN conferences to include a full-scale NGO meeting, it started out as a small preconference of consultative-status NGOs, then expanded to a tribune to run the length of the conference and include anyone who registered in advance, and finally—during the program itself—opened up to anyone who showed up. Not the least because of this dramatic opening of the NGO tribune, IWY metamorphosed from a more conventional UN conference into a "happening"—what journalists and promoters alike dubbed the "greatest consciousness-raising event in history".[1]

This chapter draws on research for the first book-length study of the Mexico City conference. There are quite a few shorter, first-hand accounts, including those by journalists and participants. But journalists attended mostly to the spectacular—confrontations at the NGO tribune; delegates walking out on Israeli First Lady Leah Rabin's speech at the government conference; embodied performances conveyed through hair, clothing, voice, and posture—and, with a few exceptions, paid little attention to the day-to-day efforts by thousands of participants. The Associated Press (AP) reporter Peggy Simpson has recounted that her editors pushed for such coverage. They even ran under her byline a story about the "sex appeal of the Soviet cosmonaut" Valentina Tereshkova, who led the Soviet delegation, and sent out a photo from the NGO tribune that erroneously portrayed it as a "global catfight."[2] The participants' accounts are necessarily partial, reflecting their own backgrounds, the moments they witnessed, and the points at which they entered and exited this story.[3] What has ended up in the secondary literature results from what amounts to a game of telephone—stories that have been altered on each retelling to reflect more about expectations than events. As a result, much of what we think we know about this conference is surprisingly apocryphal. Almost every account in the academic literature—all of which are quite brief—centers on an imagined smackdown between the white, liberal, US feminist Betty Friedan on one side and the indigenous, Marxist, Bolivian labor-union militant Domitila Barrios de Chungara on the other.[4] A well-regarded political scientist substitutes Gloria Steinem in for Betty Friedan in her description of the NGO tribune dynamics and relates an entirely fictional account of audience members throwing tomatoes at United States Agency for International Development (USAID) Director Daniel Parker.[5]

It is possible to trace how most of these stories came into being, but if we want to learn from that first IWY conference, we need to understand what actually happened to interpret the stories we have come to tell ourselves. My research for this project starts with the Communist-oriented Women's International Democratic Federation (WIDF) first proposing International Women's Year in 1972 and extends through the aftermath of the Mexico City conference; it includes research in archives all over the world, including Mexico City, Paris, Canberra, and New York, as well as important documentation at the Sophia Smith Collection at Smith College and the Schlesinger Library at the Radcliffe Institute.

A *sui generis* conference

It is important to remember that the Mexico City conference and tribune were *sui generis*. Unlike later conferences there was no script to work from, and for many participants—even at the government conference but particularly at the tribune—this was their first experience with a UN conference. Tribune participants often had not realized that they would not have an opportunity to participate in deliberations at the government conference, which at any rate took place five kilometers away in traffic-congested Mexico City. Even those few activists who managed to make contact with those participating in the government conference often found themselves stymied by the limited influence they could have on instructed delegations. Although there had been noises about the idea of a follow-up conference, given the difficulty of making the IWY conference happen, many feared it would end up being their only chance to get their message out and to make things right. It turned out that the IWY conference was a historic, game-changing event both for the UN and for transnational women's organizing, but at the time, it felt more like a seat-of-the-pants operation, which a committed group of women had managed to pull off against some very long odds. The conference had been planned at a break-neck pace and with no budget allocated by the UN—organizers would have to rely on contributions to a voluntary fund that remained paltry until Iran's Princess Ashraf Pahlavi donated a million dollars.[6]

Legacies of Mexico City

Enduring structures and initiatives emerge

Despite all of these challenges, the Mexico City conference and, perhaps as importantly, the buzz surrounding it, left important legacies for the burgeoning transnational women's movement. Most immediately, IWY—both the year and the conference—fostered enduring structures. Princess Ashraf donated another million dollars to create a research and training institute in Tehran, which, after the 1979 Iranian revolution, became the United Nations International Research and Training Institute for the Advancement of Women (INSTRAW), now head-quartered in Santo Domingo, Dominican Republic. Preparations for the IWY conference clearly demonstrated the need for an institution such as INSTRAW for two principal reasons. First, the United Nations and even its member states had very weak data about many questions relating to women's status—ranging from political and property rights to literacy levels and health concerns. Compliance with the reporting requirements of the 1967 Declaration on the Elimination of Discrimination against Women (DEDAW) was weak, even among those states who had signed it, and a UN-based research institute would provide the means and the structure for collecting and analyzing the vast amounts of missing data about women.

The IWY conference also generated two critical financial institutions. The IWY Voluntary Fund became the UN Development Fund for Women (UNIFEM), which has provided indispensable financial and technical assistance to women's programs and has pressed member states to develop gender-sensitive budgeting procedures. Originally directed by Margaret Snyder, who had directed women's programs for the UN's Economic Commission on Africa, UNIFEM now operates under the umbrella of UN Women.[7] The second institution was Women's World Banking, which emerged from discussions at the Women in Development seminar—organized by Irene Tinker and sponsored by the American Association for the Advancement of Science—that took place in Mexico City during the three days preceding the conference.[8] The women who participated in those discussions—including Ghanaian businesswoman Esther Ocloo; the founder of India's Self-Employed Women's Association, Ela Bhatt; and Michaela Walsh, who had left Merrill Lynch to work for the Rockefeller Brothers Fund—recognized the difficulties women experienced in gaining access to credit and established a 15-member planning committee the following year, and Women's World Banking (WWB) in 1979.[9]

Arguably even more important than centralized institutions such as INSTRAW, UNIFEM, and WWB, were the countless local initiatives that IWY galvanized, ranging from constitutional amendments to the founding of grassroots organizations. In December 1974, having just agreed to host the IWY conference, Mexico amended its constitution to state, "man and woman are equals before the law." On International Women's Day (8 March) 1975, Cuba passed its Family Code, which mandates that men and women share equally in family and domestic labor obligations. (To this day, every wedding in Cuba requires a notary to read the four articles of the marital code mandating that husbands and wives share equally in household and family duties and offer "reciprocal cooperation" for each to pursue studies, skills or professions.) Australia created a new position of the Advisor to the Prime Minister on Women's Affairs and filled it with the young and brilliant feminist Elizabeth Reid.[10] Even in countries whose national governments were less inclined to take women's concerns seriously, grassroots activists took advantage of the UN's imprimatur to gain access to resources—funding, spaces, books, technology, personal contacts, half-working jalopies—that helped them go out into communities and establish women's organizations.[11] The 1970s had brought an explosion of NGOs of all kinds, mushrooming from the small number of consultative-status NGOs to proliferating upstart organizations.[12] These newer NGOs often relied on more established foundations and political parties for support, but they nonetheless became a dynamic—if ambiguous—part of the growing transnational women's movement.

When the Nobel Laureate Wangari Maathai explained to a US radio interviewer how she ended up starting Kenya's Green Belt Movement, she recounted:

[I]t was around the mid-1970s, and many women will remember that was the year when women of the world met in Mexico during the very first United Nations conference on women. It was that conference, by the way, that declared the first women's decade, and we were preparing in Kenya for us to go and participate at that meeting. And it was during that preparation that I listened to the women from the rural areas, and as they articulated their issues, their agendas, their concerns, I noticed that they were talking about the need for firewood, the need for energy, the need for clean drinking water, the need for food and the need for income, and all of these connected very closely to the environment.[13]

Versions of Maathai's experience occurred all over the world around a panoply of issues.

Recognition of the importance of diverse participation

Another significant legacy of the Mexico City conference and, more emphatically, the NGO tribune, was the greater recognition given to the importance of diverse perspectives. This recognition stemmed partly from the particular moment in UN history: as the wave of decolonization movements crested, the Group of 77—effectively the UN's iteration of the Non-Aligned Movement—had taken over the General Assembly and made recognition of racism and racial discrimination a central demand.[14] In its 1974 session the UN General Assembly (GA) had suspended South Africa's credentials because of its *apartheid* policies and had passed the Charter on the Economic Rights and Duties of States, which calls for economic sovereignty of all nations and a more equitable distribution of wealth. In response to objections against Western domination of communications media and broadcast satellite technology, the UN's Center for Economic and Social Information had organized a "journalists encounter" for the three days prior to the conference—running parallel to the women in development seminar—and also sponsored 50 media fellows from Third World countries to participate, allowing them both to cover the IWY proceedings first-hand and to educate journalists from other regions about their home countries.[15]

In part because of these geopolitical factors, and in part because some of the key figures planning the tribune had been powerfully shaped by the US civil rights movement, the tribune organizers worked tirelessly to promote diverse participation. The government conference was, of course, inevitably diverse—it included one delegation from each member state, liberation movement, or consultative-status NGO in attendance. The tribune, however, ran the risk, as the organizers saw it, of being "overrun" by US feminists. Mildred Persinger, the chair of the tribune organizing committee, and Marcia-Ximena Bravo, its executive director, worked tirelessly to raise funds to sponsor Third World participants. Nearly every piece of correspondence from the months leading up to the conference includes a plea for names and contacts. They offended several prominent US feminists by discouraging them from attending, although most disregarded their pleas. But funding organizations—the Ford Foundation in particular—saw Third World participants playing a didactic role: they would teach US feminists and "Women's Libbers" as well as a broader public who might learn about the conference through press coverage about the "breadth and depth of the issues beyond narrow feminist concerns."[16]

As a result of this commitment to diversity, the tribune's formal program—to say nothing of the informal meetings, coffee klatches, and rap sessions organized on the fly—included a strikingly diverse array of speakers. The organizers had left the last three days of the NGO tribune program unscheduled to allow for sessions that would address issues arising during the tribune itself. Of the 109 scheduled speakers, 26 were from Latin America and the Caribbean, 21 from Africa, 15 from Asia (including South and Southeast Asia), four from the Middle East (Lebanon and Iran) and three from Oceania (Fiji and Australia). Of the remaining speakers, 18 were from Western Europe, six from Eastern Europe, and 16 from the United States (of whom four were from the underrepresented category of men and five were confined to the role of session chair).[17]

Unfinished business

All this is not to say the tribune achieved some ideal of diversity, whatever that ideal might be. Indeed, one of the items of unfinished business from 1975 is the need to think more intentionally about what we want this diversity to achieve. Because of Cold War ideologies, the New York-based organizing committee had kept the WIDF at arm's length, losing out on the NGO's extensive connections in the postcolonial world. And most of the Third World participants in the tribune could be described as Third World cosmopolitans. They often had received advanced degrees in places like London or Paris and had lived abroad for much of their lives before returning to places like Lagos or Delhi. Without question, they offered more diverse perspectives than any previous women's conferences, or than might have been the case had the organizing committee simply taken the path of least resistance and put together a program of the many women clamoring for a speaking part at the tribune. Nonetheless, they fell along what cultural geographer Cindi Katz would call the same contour lines as the New York organizers—those lines that disregard geopolitical boundaries but follow the same elevation.[18] As the economist Devaki Jain told an interviewer during the tribune:

In many of our countries—and I think this is true even in advanced countries, but particularly in those that you call under-developed or developing—we have an elite class that has had the benefits of education and also income improvement, and very often we take their decisions for the rest, and we also influence world opinion on what is necessary in our countries. I feel now that this must be changed because our concerns are very different from those who are, say, the fifty percent of India's population who are in rural areas living very traditional lives, where labor is not male/female but family labor.[19]

As the feminist theorist Gayatri Spivak has noted, this dynamic of elite women representing poor countries persisted through the 1995 Beijing conference:

People going to these conferences may be struck by the global radical aura, but if you hang out at the other end, participating day-to-day in the (largely imposed) politics of how delegations and NGO groups are put together … you would attest that what is left out is the poorest women of the South as self-conscious critical agents, who might be able to speak through those very non-governmental organizations of the South that are not favored by these object-constitution policies.[20]

So gains in diversity fall in both categories under consideration here—both legacy and unfinished business. The appearance of diversity at the UN Women's conferences certainly grew between Mexico City and Beijing, not least because participation in general grew and because the Mexico City conference had established that these gatherings were consequential, but research remains to be done to establish whether discussions have really opened up considerably from what took place in 1975.

Devaki Jain's comment points to the second item of unfinished business: the thorny problem of women's household labor obligations. In Mexico City, government delegates, development specialists, and grassroots activists all agreed that the single most significant obstacle to improving women's status was the crushing burden of reproductive labor—not only the caring and cleaning for family members, but also hauling water and fuel, subsistence agricultural production, and informal marketing and bartering, which all are critical to a family's survival.[21] All the proposed literacy programs, health clinics, and vocational schools would be for naught if women never have the time or energy to avail themselves of them. Many participants in Mexico City had been deeply influenced by Ester Boserup's landmark book showing that most development schemes actually increase women's labor burdens and further marginalize them socially and economically.[22] Others protested energetically that policymakers' fetishization of GDP—a metric that only includes commodified labor—excludes the vast amounts of economic activity that women perform.

Three recommendations circulated in Mexico City. Those from countries with stronger welfare states—particularly socialist countries but also social democratic countries—advocated the socialization of many of these labors by creating public childcare facilities, communal kitchens and the like, collectivization schemes which generally still depended on undervalued women's labor, however. A smaller contingent favored recognizing women's labor through some version of wages for housework, by which states would provide compensation and pension benefits to those who perform household labor. A few countries like Sweden, Norway, and Cuba placed particular emphasis on resocializing men and women alike so that both sexes would take responsibility for household labor obligations. US-based development experts concentrated on getting women into the "productive" economy—meaning commodified labor—and had faith that technological improvements would reduce the labor needs. The model of more women entering the labor market in practice often depends on paying someone else to perform the necessary household labors, which across cultures remains sexed, racialized, and underpaid.

Conclusion

While the Mexico City conference and tribune did not resolve these problems, it put them squarely on the table. Neither women's activism nor the UN would ever look the same afterwards. The UN could no longer sideline women's concerns or address them only in an instrumental fashion as they coincided with concerns about population or economic development, for example. The UN itself would have to change, including more women in its professional ranks and pressing member states to send more women with their delegations. The 1975 IWY conference fostered connections and networks that endured and flourished over the coming decades, many facilitated by the International Women's Tribune Centre that emerged out of IWY. The activities in Mexico City—of having a full-scale NGO tribune with a daily newspaper, of creating avenues by which activists and policy-makers could exchange views, of carving out space for deep policy discussions across ideological and cultural divides—set a high bar for the subsequent conferences in Copenhagen, Nairobi, and Beijing.

Notes

1 See, for example, UN Secretariat member Margaret Bruce's remarks to the AAUW-organized seminar at UN headquarters in November 1974; Mexican IWY planner Gloria Brasdefer's comments to the press (*Excélsior*, 18 June 1975, 1-B); as well as *New York Times*, 4 June 1975 (45), 19 June 1975 (41), and 3 July 1975 (1); *The Nation*, 19 July 1975, 36; *The Economist*, 5 July 1975, 72; *Newsweek*, 7 July 1975, 28; video "Report from Mexico City" (Sacramento, Calif.: KVIE).

2 Peggy A. Simpson, "The Washington Press Club Foundation's Oral History Project: Getting Women Journalists to Speak of Themselves, for Themselves, for Herstory's Sake," in *Women Transforming Communications: Global Intersections*, ed. Donna Allen, Ramona R. Rush, and Susan J. Kaufman, (London: SAGE Publications, 1996); Peggy A. Simpson, "Covering the Women's Movement," *Nieman Reports*, Winter 1999/2000.

3 See for example, Virginia R. Allan, Margaret E. Galey, and Mildred E. Persinger, "World Conference of International Women's Year," in *Women, Politics, and the United Nations*, ed. Anne Winslow (Westport, Conn., and London: Greenwood Press, 1995); Domitila Barrios de Chungara and Moema Viezzer, *Let Me Speak!: Testimony of Domitila, a Woman of the Bolivian Mines*, trans. Victoria Ortiz, (New York: Monthly Review Press, 1978); Betty Friedan, "Scary Doings in Mexico City," in *"It Changed My Life": Writings on the Women's Movement* (Cambridge, Mass.: Harvard University Press, 1998); Devaki Jain, *Women, Development, and the UN: A Sixty-Year Quest for Equality and Justice* (Bloomington and Indianapolis: Indiana University Press, 2005); Anne Winslow, *Women, Politics, and the United Nations* (Westport, Conn.: Greenwood Press, 1995); Joan McKenna, *Women in Action* (Al-Ber Costa Chapter of the United Nations Association, 1976).

4 See for example, Bina Agarwal, "From Mexico 1975 to Beijing 1995," *Indian Journal of Gender Studies* 3, no. 1 (1996): 88; Francesca Miller, *Latin American Women and the Search for Social Justice* (Hanover and London: University Press of New England, 1991), 200; Göran Therborn, *Between Sex and Power: Family in the World, 1900–2000* (London and New York: Routledge, 2004), 103.

5 Mary E Hawkesworth, *Globalization and Feminist Activism* (New York: Rowman & Littlefield Publishers, 2006), 121.

6 The UN's Economic and Social Council (ECOSOC) approved funding of the conference by the creation of a voluntary fund on 16 May 1974 (E/RES/1851).

7   Margaret Snyder, "The Politics of Women and Development," in *Women, Politics, and the United Nations*, ed. Anne Winslow, (Westport, Conn.: Greenwood Press, 1995); Margaret Snyder, "Walking My Own Road: How a Sabbatical Year Led to a United Nations Career," in *Developing Power: How Women Transformed International Development*, ed. Arvonne S. Fraser and Irene Tinker, (New York: Feminist Press at the City University of New York, 2004).

8   Margaret Snyder, "The Politics of Women and Development"; Michaela Walsh, *Founding a Movement: Women's World Banking, 1975–1990* (New York: Cosimo Books, 2012).

9   Ibid.

10 Hester Eisenstein, *Inside Agitators: Australian Femocrats and the State* (Philadelphia, Penn.: Temple University Press, 1996).

11 The citations are too numerous to list here, but scholars of places all over to the world mention 1975 as a turning point in women's activism, often explicitly linking this periodization to the attention brought by IWY. For a small sampling, see, Zarina Bhatty, "A Daughter of Awadh," *A Space of Her Own: Personal Narratives of Twelve Women* (New Delhi: SAGE Publications, 2005); Yoshie Kobayashi, *A Path Toward Gender Equality: State Feminism in Japan* (New York: Routledge, 2004); Saba Mahmood, *Politics of Piety: The Islamic Revival and the Feminist Subject* (Princeton, N.J.: Princeton University Press, 2004); Millie Thayer, "Transnational Feminism: Reading Joan Scott in the Brazilian *sertão*," *Ethnography* 2, no. 2 (2001).

12 Akira Iriye, *Global Community: The Role of International Organizations in the Making of the Contemporary World* (Berkeley: University of California Press, 2002).

13 "Wangari Maathai," in *Connection*, ed. Dick Gordon (Boston, Mass.: WBUR, 2005).

14 Paul M. Kennedy, *The Parliament of Man: The Past, Present, and Future of the United Nations*, 1st edn (New York: Random House, 2006); Mark Mazower, *Governing the World: The History of an Idea* (New York: Penguin, 2012); Stanley Meisler, *United Nations: A History* (New York: Grove Press, 2011).

15 For a more extended discussion of the journalists' encounter and the media's role in IWY, see Jocelyn Olcott, "Empires of Information: Media Strategies for the 1975 International Women's Year," *Journal of Women's History* 24, no. 4 (2012).

16 Adrienne Germain (Ford Foundation) to R.G. Livingston (German Marshall Fund), 19 March 1975, Ford Foundation archive, grant no. 75–224.

17 "Report: International Women's Year Tribune—1975," November 1975, Sophia Smith Collection (Smith College), International Women's Tribune Center papers, Box 3.

18 Cindi Katz, "Vagabond Capitalism and the Necessity of Social Reproduction," *Antipode* 33, no. 1 (2001).

19 "Report from Mexico City" (Sacramento, Calif.: KVIE).

20 Gayatri Chakravorty Spivak, "'Woman' as Theatre: United Nations Conference on Women, Beijing 1995," *Radical Philosophy* (1996).

21 On IWY deliberations over women's subsistence labors, see Jocelyn Olcott, "The Battle within the Home: Development Strategies, Second-Wave

Feminism, and the Commodification of Caring Labors at the 1975 International Women's Year Conference," in *Workers across the Americas: The Transnational Turn in Labor History*, ed. Leon Fink (New York: Oxford University Press, 2011).

22 Ester Boserup, *Women in Economic Development* (London: Earthscan, 1970).

3 Women's rights are human rights
A concept in the making

Charlotte Bunch and Roxanna Carrillo

"Women's rights are human rights" is a powerful concept that resonates globally today. Awareness of the routine violation of women's rights has grown exponentially in recent years, particularly with regard to domestic and state-sanctioned violence. We know more about the range of this violence, its multiple manifestations, the extent and diversity of its geography, and the universality of its reach. The media now reports regularly on the matter and many organizations in different sectors carefully document its incidence.

Multiple UN agencies study the problem and fund programs to end it. UN Women, the UN Population Fund (UNFPA), and the office of the UN High Commissioner for Human Rights (OHCHR) all have violence against women (VAW) as a major pillar of their work. The World Health Organization (WHO) produces multi-country reports on intimate partner violence. The International Labor Organization (ILO) studies sexual harassment in the workplace. The Office of the UN High Commissioner for Refugees (UNHCR) addresses the protection of internally displaced women and refugees. UNICEF deals with child marriage and violations of the girl child. In 2006, in response to a mandate by the General Assembly, the UN Secretary General issued a "Study on Ending Violence against Women: From Words to Action."[1]

There have been numerous changes in national law and policy as well. According to the UN Special Rapporteur on Violence against women, only a handful of countries had addressed the issue of domestic violence in any form in 1994, but nine years later every UN member state, except Bhutan, had passed legislation or formulated national programs to deal with it.[2]

However widely embraced today, the concept of VAW as a breach of fundamental human rights first came to light through the work of women's groups from around the world working collaboratively. The idea took root at the UN World Conference on Human Rights in

Vienna in 1993, which first mainstreamed gender into human rights discourse and recognized VAW as worthy of universal response and condemnation.

Women organized for Vienna as part of an emerging global feminist movement that transcended geographies of North and South and looked to the UN as an important arena for advancing policies and programs. Global feminism in these years moved beyond traditional silos of "women's issues" and brought a gendered analysis to bear on concerns about peace and security, rights, development, health, and the environment. The UN World Conferences of the 1990s—Rio's Earth Summit, Vienna's on human rights, Cairo's on population and development, Copenhagen's Social Development Summit—provided key arenas for this work. They also prepared the way for a far more expansive treatment of women's issues than ever before at the UN Fourth World Conference on Women in Beijing. This paper briefly tells this story.

Global feminism and human rights pre-Vienna

Framing women's rights as fundamental human rights was an idea whose time had come. It surfaced through feminist organizing around the UN world conferences on women. Peggy Antrobus sums up the impact of the UN Decade for Women which encompassed three World Conferences on Women—Mexico City in 1975, Copenhagen in 1980, and Nairobi in 1985:

> It was within this context that women from around the world first encountered each other in a sustained and ever-deepening process focused on their position and condition. The Decade was to nurture and expand this movement in a way that not even its strongest protagonists could have imagined.[3]

Occurring before the Internet transformed mass communications, these conferences were rare and precious opportunities that shaped a generation of civil society activists.[4] At each of them women eager to work across cultures teamed up to advocate around specific issues and debated strategies for feminist theory and activism. This contact broadened understandings of the diverse conditions women face, as well as the common struggles. It also laid the foundation of personal trust and political awareness necessary to engage in collective activism across cultures.

Deconstructing this history uncovers valuable lessons. At the NGO Forum held parallel to the Second UN World Conference on Women in Copenhagen, for example, Bunch and Antrobus, of the Women and Development Unit (WAND) of the University of the West Indies collaborated on a video called "World Feminists," shown daily.[5] It generated considerable dialogue on linking feminism and other social movements and their critiques of power. In a section of the Forum on "International Feminist Networking," sponsored by the International Women's Tribune Center (IWTC) and ISIS International, informative cross-cultural discussions of VAW emerged.[6] The Copenhagen conference has been remembered for its heated exchanges between North and South, but these sessions, by contrast, revealed commonalities, with an eager exchange of stories, laughter, and tears across what elsewhere seemed insurmountable cultural divides. VAW existed everywhere—no country was really "developed" on this, and no government had a solution. The convergence of prevailing social attitudes and of feminist strategies in response was striking—even as specific manifestations of violence varied by culture, race, class, religion, and other context-specific factors.

The process worked in two directions with local and regional activism also leading upstream to new global understandings. For example, in 1981, the Latin American women's movement's first regional "Feminist Encuentro"[7] declared 25 November a day to call attention to VAW in commemoration of the Trujillo regime's assassination of the Mirabal sisters in the Dominican Republic. The day quickly became a "classic" of the feminist calendar—an opportunity to raise consciousness and mobilize for action. Eighteen years later, the UN officially recognized 25 November as the International Day for the Elimination of Violence against Women.[8]

In Latin America, a region known for its struggles against military dictatorships, the predisposition to understand feminism as central to human rights and democratic practice was especially strong. Key conceptual breakthroughs on state responsibility for VAW, in particular, the decision by the Inter-American Court of Human Rights in *Velasquez-Rodriguez v. Honduras*,[9] come from this region's struggle to identify those responsible for the disappeared during the "dirty wars" of the 1970s and 1980s. This decision broke new ground in identifying states' duty to prevent, prosecute, and punish violent acts of private perpetrators.

The Third UN World Conference on Women in Nairobi provided a venue for even more robust cross-cultural strategizing. At both the NGO Forum and the official intergovernmental conference, issues of gender-based persecution and violence were more visible than they had been five years earlier. In a number of countries, women were working against rape, domestic violence, sex tourism, forced prostitution, and female genital mutilation, and these issues were avidly discussed, although still not conceptualized formally as matters of human rights.

In Nairobi, feminists from the Global South became more visible, as did the expansion of women's movements everywhere. Regional women's events multiplied, and global initiatives emerged in many fields—women's studies, feminist publishing, lesbian rights, women's health and reproductive rights, etc. For example, Development Alternatives with Women for a New Era (DAWN), a network of Southern-based researchers and activists, was launched to promote Third-World feminist perspectives at Nairobi. Women in Law and Development sessions at Nairobi led to regional networks on this theme—Asia Pacific Forum of Women, Law and Development (APWLD) in Asia, Caribbean and Latin American Committee for the Defense of Women's Rights (CLADEM) in Latin America, and Women in Law and Development in Africa (WILDAF) in Africa.[10] In 1987, the Network of Women Living under Muslim Laws (WLUML) was founded to create solidarity among activists.[11]

Interest in the human rights framework grew among feminists looking for ways to hold governments responsible for the plight of women, demanding more effective mechanisms to lift gender-based violations out of the shadows. Why were women trafficked for sex tourism treated as criminals and not given refugee status in the countries in which they landed? Why were women raped in war not offered asylum elsewhere? Why had the sexual torture of female political prisoners in the "dirty wars" of Latin America, or the organized rape of "comfort" women by Japan in the Second World War, been excluded from international justice proceedings? Feminists everywhere were examining the gendered exclusion of women's experiences from mainstream human rights considerations.

The Gabriela Women's Coalition in the Philippines launched a campaign in 1988 under the banner "women's rights are human rights." The Latin American Feminist Encuentro in Argentina in 1990 buzzed with discussion of this evolving paradigm. In 1992, Rebecca Cook organized a landmark consultation of lawyers at the University of Toronto to bring "legal theory and practice to bear on the relationship between international human rights and women's rights."[12] Immediately after, the North-South Institute brought together activists with these lawyers for an international conference: "Linking Hands for Changing Laws: Women's Rights as Human Rights around the

World."[13] Both events became mobilizing forces for subsequent advocacy at Vienna. The International Interdisciplinary Congress on Women in Costa Rica in early 1993 provided another global opportunity to expand on this perspective. Leading up to Vienna, feminists repeatedly discussed the idea that women's rights and human rights are indivisible.

Women's caucuses also formed within mainstream human rights organizations such as Amnesty International. Human Rights Watch established a Women's Rights Division to research and document global abuses in the context of international law.[14] The expertise of human rights specialists who brought a sophisticated understanding of human rights mechanisms was crucial to advancing methodology, documenting abuses, and demanding government accountability for violations of women.

Our own personal journeys converged at this time, and we co-organized workshops on global feminism in Latin America, South Asia, and at the Nairobi Conference. In 1987, we both went to Rutgers University in New Jersey, where Charlotte was a visiting scholar and Roxanna a graduate student. In Charlotte's seminar on "Global Feminism and Human Rights," we further developed our ideas and made contact with activists and scholars from around the world working on this topic.[15] Two years later we founded the Center for Women's Global Leadership (CWGL) to develop and advocate for women's rights as human rights, using VAW as a prism. At the first CWGL Women's Global Leadership Institute in June 1991, two key strategies emerged. We would organize for this concept at the upcoming 1993 UN World Conference on Human Rights and we would develop a "16 Days of Activism against Gender Violence" campaign. The 16 Days explicitly linked human rights and VAW during the period between 25 November, International Day for the Elimination of Violence against Women, and 10 December, International Human Rights Day.[16]

CWGL convened a working group on women's human rights in the New York area, which brought together local activists, lawyers, and academics who regularly exchanged perspectives and strategies. We also organized similar conversations cross-culturally, and in February 1993 held an international strategy meeting to coordinate plans for Vienna.[17]

Meanwhile at the UN itself, norm-setting initiatives on VAW were put in play by the Commission on the Status of Women (CSW) and the Division for the Advancement of Women (DAW), which produced an early UN study of domestic violence in 1989.[18] The CEDAW

Committee (the treaty body monitoring government compliance with the Convention on the Elimination of all Forms of Discrimination against Women) sought to remedy its earlier omission of VAW from the women's convention by developing General Recommendation 19,[19] which interprets VAW as a form of discrimination as defined in Article II of CEDAW. The potential of a specific Convention on Violence against Women was explored, but political consensus and resources to do that did not materialize internationally, and instead an optional protocol for CEDAW was authorized.

On the operational side, the UN Development Fund for Women (UNIFEM), which had been created to support initiatives in the developing world, found its hands tied on this still volatile subject. Few development specialists and few national governments at the time saw VAW as part of "development," even as income-generating projects fell short of anticipated outcomes, and entrenched traditions of sex discrimination and domestic violence were recognized as obstacles.

UNIFEM therefore asked Roxanna to write a formal policy brief on the subject of VAW as an obstacle to development.[20] Some Southern governments were initially opposed, fearing that the stigma of the issue would unfairly attach only to them. Underscoring the universality of the problem, however, UNIFEM Executive Director, Sharon Capeling-Alakija, and her Deputy, Thelma Awori, won the day. UNIFEM directed funds to support groups working on it, and in 1991 Roxanna became the staff person with responsibility for this portfolio. With preparations for Vienna under way, she also became UNIFEM's liaison in interagency UN meetings with direct access to the official planning process.

A movement for women's rights as human rights

The Vienna Conference, the UN's first global human rights convening since 1968, took place soon after the demise of the Soviet Union, when new thinking on the subject became possible. As the Cold War waned, dictatorships fell, and democratic movements gained momentum in Eastern Europe, Latin America, and Asia, human rights gained greater influence as the world's shared ethical frame. At the same time, global media attention was exposing the brutality of rape as a weapon of war in Bosnia—in the heart of Europe.

The Global Campaign for Women's Human Rights kicked off in 1991 with a petition asserting simply that "violence against women violates human rights." It called on the forthcoming UN conference "to comprehensively address women's human rights at every level of its proceedings." Initially circulated by CWGL, the International Women's Tribune Center (IWTC) and the World Young Women's Christian Association (YWCA), the petition became the first action of the 16 Days of Activism against Gender Violence campaign. Seeking individual signatures as endorsements from around the world, it served as a vehicle for drawing women into the preparatory processes for the Vienna conference. Touching a nerve, it was translated at the grassroots level into over 25 languages and circulated in 124 countries. In this pre-Internet age, boxes of signed paper petitions were soon mailed back to CWGL from faraway places, some signed with thumbprints by illiterate women. The process awakened widespread debate over women's rights in human rights discourse.

At local hearings women testified on how violence constitutes a human rights violation under covenants prohibiting torture or terrorism, and therefore demands state accountability. Women lobbied national governments and mainstream human rights groups, becoming a forceful presence at UN preparatory meetings for Vienna in Tunis, San Jose, Bangkok, and Geneva. Latin American feminists held a parallel event—"La Nuestra,"[21] which developed demands and an advocacy strategy presented at plenary sessions of the governmental meeting. WILDAF held sub-regional meetings where participants contributed ideas and demands to a paper for Tunis. Through these experiences in caucusing, lobbying, and drafting text for inclusion in official documents, women learned critical skills, including how to present their demands persuasively in human rights terms.

UNIFEM made the collaboration of civil society and governments a central goal. It brought a dozen women from the Global South to Geneva where they formed a women's caucus and came to know the negotiators of the outcome document who would become key players in Vienna. UNIFEM also convened a meeting on "International Strategies to End Violence against Women," cosponsored by the government of the Netherlands and the North-South Institute of Canada.[22] The Dutch underwrote the event, which brought some 80 women's rights activists, many from the South, to The Hague, most of whom then travelled on to Vienna.

The Vienna conference and the VDPA

In Vienna, women worked across geographies and across sectors (UN staff, government delegations, and NGOs) to influence conference outcomes, and to gain media attention. The Global Campaign's initial background paper, and its work as rapporteur on women's issues in the

NGO pre-event, guided a working group of over 200 who eventually agreed on demands endorsed by the NGO Forum as the basis for lobbying the official conference.

As a result of efforts by UNIFEM and the NGO Women's Caucus at Geneva, roughly half of all participants in the NGO space at Vienna were female. Many sessions were held on women's rights and a designated "Women's Rights Place" provided a hub for orientation, information-sharing, and networking. Global Campaign organizers also worked with a media team from the Communications Consortium Media Center in Washington, DC, led by Kathy Bonk, who trained a group of savvy spokespersons.

The campaign's key event was a day long "Global Tribunal."[23] Feminist networks from around the world selected key cases, and 33 women gave testimony covering a wide range of issues including domestic violence, rape in war, trafficking, compromise of bodily integrity, abuse of migrant women, and the political persecution of lesbians. This riveting event demonstrated in graphic terms that the simple fact of being female can be life-threatening—that the inhuman and degrading treatment women too often experience conforms to conventional definitions of torture, terrorism, or slavery prohibited under human rights accords. Four prominent judges from different regions—two male and two female, working with a diverse team of women lawyers—issued powerful conclusions on why women's rights should be a priority. This judgment, along with over 250,000 petition signatures, was presented at the official conference. The campaign did not present women only as victims, but also as activists with agency, claiming our place as a constituency that would strengthen and revitalize the overall movement for human rights.

Official conference negotiations leading up to Vienna often foundered and broke down completely between North and South over approaches to definitions of social and economic rights as human rights. An agreed draft document did not emerge until after the last preparatory committee meeting in Geneva in April, where concern grew that overall consensus could not be reached in Vienna. In this context, women's rights emerged as a rare area of agreement coming from all regions, with draft text that arrived in Vienna almost free of brackets, to the surprise of mainstream human rights organizations, which still viewed women's issues as marginal.

The final Vienna Declaration and Programme of Action (VDPA)[24] affirms that "the human rights of women and of the girl child are an inalienable, integral and indivisible part of universal human rights" not to be subject to limitations. It recognizes VAW as an abuse to be eliminated and recommends the appointment of a special rapporteur to report on it. The far-reaching implications of these changes were only barely understood by the governments who adopted them and even by many of us who advocated for them.

Beyond this landmark recognition of women's rights as human rights, the VDPA has also been critical in other respects.[25] Its affirmation that the "promotion and protection of all human rights is a legitimate concern of the international community" is crucial to global activism on behalf of women's human rights everywhere. Its defense of the universality of rights has also been central to women's rights defenders, who, in turn, have advanced the principle. If violating the rights of half of humanity can be conditioned in the name of culture, religion, or nationality, then the concept has little meaning.

The VDPA also reaffirms the indivisibility of human rights—civil, political, social, and economic—and underscores their interdependence. Again, women have advanced this concept, because the multiple violations of our rights are so often hard to distinguish and categorize. Feminists helped strengthen an intersectional approach to rights—understanding that discrimination in one area usually affects another—that violations on the basis of gender, race, class, and other factors intersect in the abuse most women experience.

Vienna opened the door to greater participation of NGOs in UN human rights deliberations, and particularly to those marginalized previously at the UN, including indigenous peoples, women, and groups from the Global South. This process continued with the creation of OHCHR, another outcome of Vienna, and as representatives of social movements gained greater access to the Human Rights Commission (now the Human Rights Council) and other human rights bodies and special mechanisms.

Vienna to Beijing

With feminists regularly lobbying in Geneva, New York, and locally, the UN advanced more systematic standard-setting on women's human rights, especially around gender-based violence. The UN General Assembly adopted the Declaration on the Elimination of Violence Against Women (DVAW) in December of 1993, and the Human Rights Commission at its first session after Vienna appointed a "Special Rapporteur on Violence against Women, its Causes and Consequences." These appointees have produced a rich body of work codifying human rights standards on gender violence. In 1994, the UN Commission on Human Rights also adopted its first resolution on gender integration, which has since evolved into annual sessions on the topic at the Human Rights Council, as well as a range of efforts to integrate women's perspectives more fully in all areas of human rights.

The success of the "women's rights are human rights" claim in Vienna also became a guiding framework in arenas beyond the formal human rights system. It has influenced the health, population and development, and peace and security dimensions of UN operations. Language negotiated in Vienna framed the conceptualizing of women's health, reproduction, and sexuality as rights matters at the 1994 International Conference on Population and Development in Cairo. In 1995, the Global Campaign reinforced specific gendered concerns as socio-economic human rights at the UN World Summit on Social Development in Copenhagen. In these settings, and then again at Beijing, a powerful backlash against feminist interpretations of human rights emerged, with conservatives strongly resisting the application of human rights principles to reproduction and sexuality.

The 1995 Beijing Declaration and Platform for Action (BPFA)[26] reaffirms Vienna language on the universality of women's human rights and includes specific chapters on human rights and on VAW. Its 12 critical areas of concern broadly define women's rights to encompass health, education, and development, and specifically addresses rights of girls, such as consent in marriage. Its section on women and armed conflict incorporates a human rights approach to VAW in war and other aspects of a "women, peace and security" agenda that have since taken center stage. Then-First Lady, Hillary Rodham Clinton's famous speech in Beijing advocating "women's rights are human rights" brought added legitimacy and global media attention to the paradigm, helping it become the new norm.

An explosion of activity followed Beijing as women's groups and human rights organizations escalated their documentation of abuses and demands for change. Addressing issues from honor killings in Pakistan to reproductive rights in Peru, welfare and housing rights in the United States, or global questions of environmental justice, feminists have used human rights laws and instruments to try and hold governments accountable. At the same time, bilateral foreign aid, along with funding from multi-lateral institutions and agencies and some private foundations, now pay more attention to women's concerns.

The Vienna, Cairo, and Beijing conferences renewed interest in the Convention on the Elimination of All Forms of Discrimination Against Women (CEDAW) and gave impetus to the creation of an optional protocol, providing redress of individual grievances, which dramatically strengthens the document as a vehicle for implementation of women's rights. Increasing numbers of women's organizations now regularly engage the CEDAW committee and write shadow reports when their governments come up for periodic review. Improved national legislation and policies to help women exercise their rights have become benchmarks of government compliance with these treaties. And CEDAW now regularly informs national laws on issues of sex discrimination in civil status, political representation, employment, education, criminal justice procedures, and the like.

Collaboration among multiple constituencies of women from around the world has, of course, been fraught at times and not always easy. Success in working together—especially in the face of mounting backlash—was exhilarating at these conferences that resulted in strong outcome documents. Many challenges remain, and new obstacles have developed as a result of growing financial challenges, economic inequalities, health epidemics, and political unrest in many regions. Nevertheless, women have achieved a palpable sense of power and impact since Beijing. International organizations, donor resources and new information technologies have advanced this work, but its roots remain in women's movements on the ground. It is those movements that must rise up once again to address a still unfinished agenda.

Achievements

> Hidden from view away from the drama of the use of force and international peace and security, there has been a quiet, creeping revolution in the area of women's and children's rights at the international level which may have far reaching consequences about how we think about international law and its place in the modern world.
> Radhika Coomaraswamy, "Women and Children: The Cutting Edge of International Law," The Grotius Lecture, 2014

The legal advances and human rights mechanisms women achieved after Vienna and Beijing do indeed have revolutionary potential, if implemented. The Beijing call for an Optional Protocol to strengthen CEDAW implementation was adopted in 2000. The number of countries ratifying the convention jumped from 119 in 1994 to 188 in 2014, and significant numbers removed some of their reservations to CEDAW, including a few in the controversial area of family law.

The women, peace, and security agenda has been the focus of considerable high-level attention since the UN Security Council (2000) adopted its first resolution on women. Security Council Resolution (SCR) 1325 reaffirms the importance of participation in the prevention and resolution of armed conflict, and highlights the role of women in peacekeeping and peacemaking. It also addresses VAW in conflict, calling all actors to take special measures for the protection of women and girls. Under pressure from NGOs, national plans of action on SCR 1325 have been drawn up, but implementation is minimal. SCR 1325 has several implementing resolutions (SCRs 1820, 1888, 1889, 1960, and 2106), including one (SCR 1820) that led to the creation of a Special Representative of the Secretary General on Sexual Violence during Armed Conflict, who monitors and reports on this issue to the Security Council. These, unfortunately, only address sexual violence in conflict, leaving aside other aspects of the groundbreaking SCR 1325 and other issues women confront in times of war.

Although these developments have brought greater focus to issues of gender and violence in war and conflict, they have not yet made much difference on the ground where militarism and armed conflicts are still rampant. Significantly, however, the Rome Statute that created the International Criminal Court (1998) includes gender-based persecution and sexual violence as crimes against humanity, and provides for the application of criminal as well as moral sanctions against them. Its rigorous application could have an impact.

Regionally, human rights mechanisms have been created to hasten realization of women's rights. In Latin America, the first ever Convention on the Prevention, Punishment and Eradication of Violence Against Women (Convention of Belem do Para)[27] was adopted in 1994, and has since been a major trigger for significant legislative reform in every participating country. Comparable regional advances include the Optional Protocol on Women's Human Rights to the African Charter on Peoples and Human Rights (2000), and in Europe, the Istanbul Convention on Preventing and Combating Violence against Women and Domestic Violence (2011).

Another promising area is the growth in diversity of women's constituencies claiming rights. Indigenous, Afro-descendant, immigrant, Dalit, disabled, lesbian, younger, and older women, as well as racial, ethnic, and cultural minorities, among others, have come forward with their particularized stories of discrimination and violence. Such diversification has complicated definitions of "women," but also enriched and amplified the conceptual clarity necessary to deal with the intersection of gender and other factors, and thus make possible greater realization of rights for all. Women are also considerably more visible as leaders—often with a feminist perspective—in a range of social movements such as disability and land rights groups.

Given the more visible advocacy role of women on gender and other human rights concerns, the need for their protection and security as human rights defenders has become clear.[28] Feminists and human rights activists have collaborated over the past decade to address the increasingly precarious situation of all human rights defenders, and to understand the particular needs of those working on women's and sexual rights.[29]

Feminist and human rights movements have profoundly affected each other in this and other areas of theory and practice. Feminist thinking created a critique of the socially constructed separation of the public and private spheres, demonstrating how violations readily denounced in "public" spaces, such as battlefields or prisons, are often tolerated or excused in the private space of the family. This added to an expanding understanding of collusion by the state with ostensibly "private actors," such as corporations, private militias, churches, or families.

Feminists have, in turn, adopted key human rights concepts like "due diligence." All three UN Special Rapporteurs on Violence against Women (Radhika Coomaraswamy, Yakin Ertürk and Rashida Manjoo) have delineated state responsibility for working to prevent and respond to acts of VAW committed by private actors, and due diligence is now an accepted international obligation of governments.[30] The NGO Due Diligence Project has spelled out state obligations as the "Five P's—prevention, protection, prosecution, punishment and provision of redress." This framework is aimed at bringing practice in line with norms and standards.[31]

A major contribution of feminist analysis has been to recognize the body as a key site of rights violations. The conceptualization of sexual rights links reproductive rights to rights of sexual expression and pleasure, including sexual orientation and gender identity. It recognizes that many violations are centered on the control of women's sexuality—from criminalization of contraception and abortion, to the practice of female genital mutilation, stoning and "honor killings," or the "corrective rapes" and forced marriages imposed on women who transgress gender norms. Gender constructions are now also understood as a dimension of abuse of gay men and transgender people and as a factor in shaping how all men experience torture, rape, and abuses intended to humiliate them by treating them like women.

Another area of considerable, but insufficient, progress is the growth in resources for women's rights work. In 1996, the UN established a Trust Fund to End Violence against Women, which has since funded cutting-edge initiatives, many of them later replicated by national governments and NGOs. Women's funds have been created in a variety of countries bringing new resources, but total revenues still remain small. The establishment of UN Women in 2010 was meant to create a more powerful and coordinated voice for women's rights and to galvanize more resources. However, the precarious global economic climate leaves UN Women's budget substantially below expectations and far smaller than other operating agencies like UNICEF.

Some global foundations and corporations have increased their interest in women, but not necessarily in funding advocacy around rights or to shift cultural norms. The Association For Women's Rights in Development (AWID) in two recent reports uncovers the disturbing finding that only 18 percent of new resources "for women" fund women's movement organizations and advocacy,[32] but rather fund charities, education, and services. This is disturbing given that supporting women's groups has been shown to be the most effective and efficient way to use such resources, especially in combating VAW.[33]

Backlash and challenges

Norms and laws have changed dramatically in the 40 years since Mexico City and the 22 years since Vienna. Women have claimed their human rights and now play a greater role in the public realms of most countries. However, as we all know too well, the existence of laws and mechanisms, although important, does not mean our work is finished. Closing the gap between the setting of standards and their implementation remains our collective challenge. As the Geneva Academy of International Humanitarian Law and Human Rights concluded in its review of women's rights, "[A] global snapshot of women's enjoyment of their basic human rights in 2014 appears bleak."[34]

Tragically, despite dramatic changes in awareness and even in laws, VAW has shown no discernible decrease in actual prevalence. The UN now estimates that gender-based violence is experienced—often repeatedly—by one of every three women in the world.[35] Rashida Manjoo, the current UN Special Rapporteur on Violence against Women, summed up the problem in a 2013 report on state responsibility:

> Despite numerous developments, violence against women remains endemic, and the lack of accountability for violations experienced by women is the rule rather than the exception in many countries. Some challenges as regards state responsibility include: lack of acceptance of violence against women as a human rights issue;

inadequate state responses; minimum time, effort and resources are devoted to the problem ... also lack of response to addressing both individual and structural aspects of inequality and multiple and intersecting forms of discrimination, which are a cause and a consequence of violence against women.[36]

The forces of backlash against fundamental social change have also grown stronger, especially in intergovernmental negotiations at the UN. Fundamentalist backlash against women's claims to equality, and especially to sexual and reproductive rights, has seized on claims of national, cultural, and religious sovereignty as excuses for perpetuating socially constructed patriarchal practices. Ironically, many who agree on little else will claim that women's rights threaten their "unique culture," and that some aspect of control over women's bodies is intrinsic to their national or cultural identity and/or faith, including, for example, Southern Baptists in the United States, Iranian mullahs, Zulus in South Africa, Russian Orthodox priests, and the Vatican. As Pregs Govender of South Africa has put it, "[p]atriarchy, as a globally shared culture, expresses itself differently in local contexts."[37]

VAW is not some marginalized, exotic practice in remote places, but a critical factor in maintaining the domination of small groups of men in virtually all societies. So strong is the backlash against gains, that previous UN consensus over VAW is now faltering. For example, at the 2003 UN CSW review of the VAW section of the BPFA, no agreed conclusions on it were adopted—the first time the CSW failed to reach consensus in its Beijing reviews. Again at the 2013 session of the CSW on the same topic, agreement was barely reached after endless negotiations watered down the link between VAW, culture, and control over women's bodies.

Conflicts around women and sexual rights are now also threatening past agreement over the principle of universality in human rights. Universality does not mean that all women's lives are the same, or that their choices will be identical. It simply means that every woman is entitled to claim rights and live a life free of discrimination and violence justified in the name of culture or religion.

Cultures are not static or apolitical or unaffected by outside forces. Nor are they detached from prevailing material conditions. Claims called "cultural" or "religious" are also political—reflecting fear of and resistance to prevailing secular and globalized tendencies. Challenging the appropriation of culture by conservative forces and reclaiming women's right to participate in how cultures evolve is an important feminist strategy, long advanced by groups like WLUML, whose global campaign proclaims: "Violence is not our Culture."[38] Backlash is also personal, as witnessed in the increasing number of defenders of women's human rights attacked and recently jailed in places like Azerbaijan, Colombia, and Egypt, or even worse, assassinated in Libya, Somalia, Honduras, and other sites of conflict. The defense of such women by the international community is crucial to women's advancement.

Progress in realizing women's human rights is also threatened by economic challenges in much of the world, resulting in austerity policies bringing reduced public programming and spending to redress inequalities. Conditions of extreme poverty foster deeply entrenched traditions denying women equal rights to education, formal employment, and property ownership, as well as making them vulnerable to abuses such as child marriage, domestic violence, and trafficking. Women's personal and social status will not continue to advance unless the growing gap between extreme rich and poor can be closed.

Finally, we must reassess the role of the UN in advancing human rights and justice. Recent UN meetings and forums have primarily been about preserving past achievements, not advancing new gains or raising questions about the use of valuable resources for minimal results. Further, privatization of many governmental services requires new thinking about non-state actor accountability to human rights norms. These challenges are currently playing out in UN talks over the Post-2015 Sustainable Development Goals.

Conclusion

The world conferences of the 1990s still stand as beacons of hope that concerted collective action can advance respect and the realization of women's rights. Networking across boundaries and dividing lines was key to those achievements, and the challenge today is to find new forms for such collaborations. New generations of women around the world must now carry this message forward. Fortunately, they are rising up everywhere, often in surprisingly brave ways, and frequently with support from young men. The challenge is to build on past gains with new energies and insights.

Notes

1 United Nations, *Ending Violence against Women, From Words to Action: Study of the Secretary General* (New York: United Nations, 2006).

2 Radhika Comaraswamy "Women and Children: The Cutting Edge of International Law" (The Grotius Lecture 2014, Annual General Meeting of the American Society for International Law, Washington, DC, 9 April).

3 Peggy Antrobus, *The Global Women's Movement: Origins, Issues and Strategies* (London: Zed Press, 2004), 37.

4 See "UN Activist Forum" section of the *Journal of Women's History* 24, no. 4 (2012) for a series of reflections by women involved in these conferences. Note also *The Proceedings of the International Tribunal on Crimes against Women,* compiled and edited by Diana E.H. Russell and Nicole Van de Ven (Palo Alto, Calif.: Frog in the Well Press, 1984) for testimony from women around the world involved in the 1977 NGO tribunal held in response to the UN International Women's Year.

5 The *World Feminists* video directed by Martha Stuart as part of her series called "Are You Listening?" was the product of an international workshop sponsored by the Women and Development Unit of the University of the West Indies (WAND), and the United Nations Asian and Pacific Centre for Women and Development (APCWD), held in Stony Point NY in 1980. See Charlotte Bunch, *Passionate Politics* (New York: St. Martin's Press, 1987), 285–292.

6 Charlotte organized this part of the Forum with two key global women's groups: IWTC based in New York (founded out of the Mexico City conference in 1975) and ISIS International (founded in 1976) based in both Geneva and Rome.

7 Latin American feminists have been meeting in an *Encuentro Feminista Latino Americano y del Caribe* (EFLAC) every two to three years to exchange information and strategies, and to affirm regional solidarity. The first meeting took place in Bogota, Colombia in 1982.

8 In December 1999 the UN General Assembly passed resolution 54/134 declaring 25 November as International Day for the Elimination of Violence against Women.

9 The Honduras government argued that it did not have any responsibility for the crimes of the paramilitaries that caused the death of Velásquez Rodríguez, because the perpetrators were "non-State" actors. The Inter-American Court of Human Rights decided against the Honduras government in the judgment of July 29 1988.

10 The acronyms stand for Asia Pacific Women Law and Development, Comité Latinoamericano por la Defensa de los Derechos de la Mujer, and Women in Law and Development in Africa.

11 Charlotte Bunch, Peggy Antrobus, Samantha Frost, and Niamh Reilly, "International Networking for Women's Human Rights," in *Global Citizen Action,* ed. M. Edwards and J. Gaventa (Boulder, Colo.: Lynne Reiner Publishers, 2001).

12 Rebecca Cook, ed., *Human Rights of Women: National and International Perspectives* (Philadelphia: University of Pennsylvania Press, 1994), 3.

13 Joanna Kerr, ed., *Ours By Right: Women's Rights as Human Rights* (London and Ottawa: Zed Press in association with the North-South Institute, 2003).

14 Human Rights Watch, Worden, M. ed., *The Unfinished Revolution: Voices from the Global Fight for Women's Human Rights* (New York: Seven Stories Press, 2012).

15 Some of the earliest writings on women's rights as human rights include: Georgina Ashworth, "Of Violence and Violation: Women and Human Rights," in *Change Thinkbook II* (London, 1986); Alda Facio at *Mujer FemPress* (ILET) Santiago, No. 97, especial "Contraviolencia", December, 1988; Lori Heise, "Crimes of Gender" in *WorldWatch* (March–April 1989): 12–21; Gail Omvedt, *Violence Against Women: New Movements and New Theories in India* (New Delhi: Kali for Women, 1990); Roxana Vasquez and Giulia Tamayo, *Violencia y Legalidad* (Lima: Concytec, 1989).

16 Rutgers Center for Women's Global Leadership, *The Activist Origins of the 16 Days Campaign*, http://16dayscwgl.rutgers.edu/about/activist-origins-of-the-campaign.

17 Center for Women's Global Leadership, *International Campaign for Women's Human Rights, 1992–93 Report* (New Brunswick, N.J.: Center for Women's Global Leadership, 1993).

18 United Nations Centre for Social Development and Humanitarian Affairs. Division for the Advancement of Women, *Violence against Women in the Family*. Prepared by Jane F. Connors (New York: United Nations, 1989).

19 See all General Recommendations to CEDAW and more specifically General Recommendation 19 www.un.org/womenwatch/daw/cedaw/recommendations/recomm.htm.

20 Roxanna Carrillo, *Battered Dreams: Violence against Women as an Obstacle to Development* (New York: UNIFEM, 1992).

21 "La Nuestra" as the feminist regional meeting was called, took place 3–5 December 1992 in San Jose, Costa Rica.

22 *Report of the International Conference on Strategies for the Elimination of Violence against Women*, June 1993 in The Hague. The Netherlands Ministry for International Development and Cooperation, in collaboration with UNIFEM and The North-South Institute; Vienna Declaration and Programme of Action (VDPA), Adopted by the World Conference on Human Rights in Vienna on 25 June 1993.

23 Charlotte Bunch and Niamh Reilly, *Demanding Accountability: The Global Campaign and Vienna Tribunal for Women's Human Rights.* (New Brunswick, N.J.: CWGL; and New York: UNIFEM, 1994). This event is captured in the film *The Vienna Tribunal*, directed by Gerry Rogers, the National Film Board of Canada.

24 *VDPA*, op. cit, 33.

25 Ibid., 34.

26 *Report of the Fourth World Conference on Women* (E.96.IV.13), 4–15 September 1995.

27 Inter-American Convention on the Prevention, Punishment and Eradication of Violence against Women.

28 See the 27 February 2002 groundbreaking report on women human rights defenders prepared by Hina Jilani, Special Representative of the Secretary General on the situation of Human Rights Defenders to the 58th Session of the Commission on Human Rights (E/CN.4/2002/106).

29 Women Human Rights Defenders International Coalition, *Global Report on the Situation of Women Human Rights Defenders* (January 2012); Association for Women's Rights in Development (AWID), "Our Right to Safety: Women Human Rights Defenders' Holistic Approach to

50   Charlotte Bunch and Roxanna Carrillo

Protection" (Toronto, Ontario: Association for Women's Rights in Development, 2014).

30 Radhika Coomaraswamy, *Violence Against Women in the Family* (E/CN.4/1999/68), 19 March 1999; Yakin Ertürk, *The Due Diligence Standard as a Tool for the Elimination of Violence Against Women* (E/CN.4/2006/61), 20 January 2006; and Rashida Manjoo, *State Responsibility for Eliminating Violence Against Women* (A/HRC/23/49), 14 May 2013.

31 Zarizana Abdul Aziz and Janine Moussa, *Due Diligence Framework: State Accountability Framework for Eliminating Violence against Women* (Malaysia: International Human Rights Initiative, 2014).

32 AWID, "New Actors, New Money, New Conversations: A Mapping of Recent Initiatives for Women and Girls" (Toronto, Mexico DF and Cape Town: AWID, 2013).

33 Mala Htun and S. Laurel Weldon, "The Civic Origins of Progressive Policy Change: Combating Violence against Women in Global Perspective, 1975–2005," *American Political Science Review* 106, no. 3 (2012): 548–569.

34 Alice Priddy, *Academy in Brief No. 4.: The Situation of Women's Rights 20 Years After the Vienna World Conference on Human Rights* (Geneva, Switzerland: Geneva Academy of International Humanitarian Law and Human Rights, 2014), 11.

35 WHO, *Global and Regional Estimates of Violence Against Women* (Geneva, Switzerland: World Health Organization, 2013).

36 Rashida Manjoo, *State Responsibility for Eliminating Violence Against Women*.

37 Pregs Govender, "When 'Traditional Values' are a Stick to Beat Women," *Times Live*, 28 February 2010.

38 WLUML campaign "Violence is not our Culture," www.violenceisnotourculture.org.

4 Feminist mobilizing for global commitments to the sexual and reproductive health and rights of women and girls

Sonia Correa, Adrienne Germain and Gita Sen

This chapter analyzes the emergence of sexual and reproductive health and rights (SRHR) as a cornerstone of global women's rights activism and as a central factor in policy conversations addressing poverty eradication, sustainable development, and the realization of human rights. The analysis reflects our experiences in the "eye of the storm," beginning in the 1970s. We review how we helped build an international feminist consensus for the 1994 International Conference on Population and Development (ICPD) in Cairo and the 1995 Fourth World Conference on Women (FWCW) in Beijing. We reflect on the complex SRHR trajectories that emerged and, in particular, on two challenges that even today beset ongoing work to secure a central position for these issues in the United Nation's (UN) post-2015 global agenda. The first challenge is fault-lines—particularly the South–North divide—that pre-dated Cairo. The second is the intersections, convergences, and disjunctions between the feminist agenda for Cairo and the sexual rights agenda, particularly lesbian, gay, bisexual, transgender, queer, and intersex (LGBTQI) rights. We conclude with a summary of, and reflections on, lessons from our continuing experiences that are relevant for the post-2015 agenda process.

Who we are: an important factor in success

We have each worked for the advancement of women's health and human rights for over 40 years. Together and separately, we were, and are, connected as activists to global and regional women's human rights organizations that remain influential actors today, as well as to national and local groups whose work provided the original motivation for conceptualizing and promoting the SRHR agenda. When the UN initiated the global conferences of the 1990s, each of us, and a critical mass of others advocating for women's equality, also had considerable experience working in and with "mainstream" institutions, including our own and other governments, international agencies, especially in the UN system, and public and private philanthropy.

This combination of activism with mainstream experience and contacts fundamentally shaped our strategies, credibility, and impacts. We learned skills for intergovernmental negotiation and compromise along the road—never losing sight of our final destination and never compromising our values. Persistent determination and more than full-time engagement, not for weeks, months, or years, but for decades, were and remain vital.

The 1970s and 1980s: problem definition and building the base for political action

The eruption of interest in reproductive rights among South and North feminists in the 1980s, followed by sexual rights in the 1990s, reflected understandings of struggles for sexual and reproductive freedom from the eighteenth century onward.[1] In the early twentieth century, feminists and other activists, such as Margaret Sanger, promoted access to contraception in the North, followed later by demands for access to safe abortion, ethical standards in contraceptive research, and prohibition of forced sterilization.[2] Since the 1960s, as population control policies, contraceptive research, and family planning services expanded in the South with substantial Northern funding, feminists from both regions pursued the health and human rights of women within a broader frame of opposition to policies and programs aimed at outright population control. Although both these streams of feminist mobilizing are relevant for assessing the contributions of the women's movement to the processes and outcomes of the ICPD and FWCW, this chapter focuses on mobilizing for global policies that primarily affect women in the South.

Feminist pursuit of South-focused SRHR (the content not the term) began as a response to shortcomings in the conceptualization, as well as the implementation, of "population control and family planning" policies and programs by the UN system, international donors, and nation states.[3] At the global level and especially in the large countries of South and East Asia with authoritarian governments, population policies and programs reflected a conviction that rapid growth jeopardizes development and environmental sustainability, and that "family planning," achieved through greatly increased use of modern contraception, is the solution—the so-called magic bullet.

This vertical approach to family planning targeted vast populations of women, delivered large quantities of contraceptive commodities, and focused on "motivating" them to "accept" contraception, especially long-acting methods such as intrauterine devices and sterilization. Many such policies and programs were deliberately designed and managed separately from larger health systems. Safe abortion services were usually excluded, even where contraceptive failure and drop-out rates undermined the desired progress toward reduced fertility, where levels of unsafe abortion remained very high and/or where national abortion laws were fairly liberal, as in India. Essential factors that shape fertility outcomes and contraceptive use were ignored, especially the centrality of sexuality to human life and a consequent need for accurate information and education on sexuality, health, and childbearing from a very young age, the overall quality of family planning services, and the larger cultural norms and social conditions that affect marriage, union, and women's childbearing decisions.

International and national feminist groups criticized these top-down policies and vertical services, including abuses of fundamental human rights, such as avoidable illness and death resulting from poorly delivered or forced contraception. We also faulted the lack of attention to harmful contraceptive side effects and the failure to provide a wide choice of family planning methods. We highlighted the impacts of absence of attention to sexually transmitted infections; to the poor quality of maternal health care overall, including prenatal, obstetric, and postpartum care; to the then-undocumented problem of violence against women, usually perpetrated by intimate partners; and to the effects of such harmful practices related to SRHR as female genital mutilation and child marriage.[4]

During this period, each of us, from different positions, helped raise funds for and build activist women's health and rights organizations across Africa, Asia, Latin America, and the Caribbean.[5] Much of the evidence used in the Cairo and Beijing debates came from these initiatives, as well as from international women's organizations that monitored the effects of global population control and contraceptive research policies, practices, and funding.

The 1980s and 1990s: creating intellectual capital, concepts, and evidence

In the 1970s and 1980s, feminist advocates working for women's health and human rights were widely ignored by prevailing power brokers, as were actors inside mainstream institutions who pressed for improved quality in family planning services, argued against coercion, and promoted access to safe abortion.[6] Throughout this period, as part of our strategy to gain seats at policy tables, those of us with shared concerns collaborated to create and widely disseminate the conceptual policy analysis and empirical findings required as evidence to support and effectively promote our points of view. These efforts are illustrated by our own personal, political, and professional trajectories.

Sonia Corrêa first engaged with reproductive freedom while living in France during the fight for legalization of abortion there. On returning to Brazil she was immersed in the country's struggle for democratization, which included unexpected calls from feminists for abortion rights, homosexual liberation, rights of prostitutes, and, from the mid-1980s on, for the fight against discrimination related to HIV and AIDS. Brazilian feminist collectives advocated for reproductive freedom and often came into conflict with others working for democracy, particularly the Roman Catholic Church.

SOS Corpo, the feminist NGO in Recife which Sonia helped found, promoted the concept of reproductive rights across Brazil immediately after it was legitimized in a conference organized by the Women's Global Network for Reproductive Rights (the Global Network) in Amsterdam in 1984. In the 1990s, two other institutions were created in Brazil, which moved these agendas forward—the Commission for Citizenship and Reproduction and the National Feminist Network on Sexual and Reproductive Health and Rights. As democracy took root and became more stable, these various organizations engaged critically with SRHR policy-formation and monitoring.

Development Alternatives with Women for a New Era (DAWN), which Gita Sen of India co-founded, grew out of a process of dialogue among women who were largely from the Global South, where they were also critics of mainstream development theories, policies, and practices in their countries. Sonia, for example, brought to DAWN the perspectives and experiences of Brazilian feminists, including the lessons learned in their work for SRHR. An important element of DAWN's critique was its challenge to population control policies and programs premised on neo-Malthusian theories of a "population bomb." DAWN's book, *Development, Crises, and Alternative Visions: Third World Women's Perspectives*, produced for the third UN World Conference on Women in Nairobi in 1985, caught the imagination of many researchers and activists with its trenchant critique and search for alternatives.[7]

The UN Conference on Environment and Development, held in Rio in 1992, provided fertile ground for extending this search, this time through in-depth interactions between Southern feminists and Northern environmentalists, many of whom were advocates of population control. Feminist South activists, with support from like-minded women inside Northern environmental groups, persuaded many of these influential organizations to endorse a human rights-based approach to population, using research on population and the environment spearheaded by DAWN.[8] Meanwhile, in preparation for Cairo, then two years away, DAWN also worked to mobilize Southern feminists around a common SRHR platform.

During this time the International Women's Health Coalition (IWHC) in New York City, headed by Joan Dunlop and Adrienne Germain, gathered feminist professionals and activists, including Gita and Sonia, along with top researchers and policymakers from many countries of North and South, to contribute to dozens of publications and policy debates on neglected core elements of SRHR.[9] These included safe abortion, contraceptive choices, safety and quality of family planning services, sexually transmitted infections, and HIV.[10] IWHC also promoted "microbicides," first conceptualized by feminist health advocates, then later adopted, and now under development, by mainstream global health institutions as a tool that women could use and control for prevention of sexually transmitted infections and HIV.[11] Feminists also first directed attention to adolescents in need of services, including appropriate content and approaches to comprehensive sexuality education,[12] which were later adopted as global standards by the Population Council, the United Nations Organization for Education, Science and Culture (UNESCO), and the United Nations Population Fund (UNFPA). The aim of all this substantive work was to integrate women's and human rights perspectives into mainstream population and family planning research and programs, and to engage the interest of the field's leaders in promoting our agenda through collaborative and cross-disciplinary work.

Meanwhile, and just as significantly, in 1985, IWHC also began to invest in grants and professional partnerships with nascent, local women's health and rights groups in Africa, Asia, and Latin America. At the UN conference in Nairobi that year, we also all witnessed the first organized, international action against abortion, contraception, and women's equality mobilized under the "right to life" banner. This opened our eyes to another ominous ideology we would have to confront beyond population control.

In the 1990s, substantive investments by feminists in the conceptualization of SRHR, in global, regional, and national research—and in political action—gained the respect of increasing numbers of mainstream actors in family planning and health, and even in demography. Feminist demographers in Latin America, particularly in Mexico and Brazil, began to critique instrumental family planning policies and undertook research on women's health, contraceptive prevalence, and abortion, which demonstrated the efficacy of new approaches. At the same time, with the support of key professionals inside the World Health Organization (WHO), the Ford Foundation, and UNFPA who were sympathetic to our perspectives, such as Mahmoud Fathalla, Jose Barzelatto, and Anibal Faundes, we began to influence the policies, programs, and research agendas of central global institutions. These diverse activities all helped pave the road to the ICPD and the FWCW.

United Nations conferences in the 1990s

The population control and family planning establishment at first reacted strongly against us. Hoping to use the 1994 Cairo conference to regain support for traditional approaches to population control and family planning (which some believed had already been weakened ten years earlier at the UN World Population Conference in Bucharest), many population professionals attempted to discredit all criticism with such canards as: "Women are in bed with the Vatican and against family planning." The Holy See, opposed to family planning policies of any kind, also sought to silence feminist voices. During negotiations at Rio in 1992, the Vatican introduced a political and negotiating strategy, which not only opposed language that supported contraception and reproductive rights, but also emphasized eradication of poverty and re-balancing of South–North inequalities. This approach captured the hearts and minds of Southern governments and many activists, including some feminists.

Advocates of women's health and rights had to counter both perspectives. We contested the accusations made by the population establishment and, at the same time, revealed the regressive positions on women's rights and autonomy that lurked beneath the Vatican's often compelling rhetoric on poverty and inequality. We also mobilized widely to create a constructive alternative, a "feminist population policy," which Marge Berer, who became editor of the journal, *Reproductive Health Matters*, had called for at the 1990 Women's Health conference organized by the Global Network in Manila.

After Rio, a small international group of women met in London to frame such a policy. We agreed on a core mission to promote and protect the health, sexuality, and reproductive rights of women and girls. To that end we conceptualized a minimum package of voluntary, quality contraceptive services; safe abortion; prenatal, obstetric and postpartum care; STI and HIV prevention and treatment; and comprehensive sexuality education. Further, we called for actionable commitments to change the ways that family planning and population funds were spent. Last but not least, we committed ourselves to forging political consensus among diverse feminist communities worldwide on a single platform, and to sustain and widen consensus in each new stage of the road to Cairo. Forging consensus on substance across our diversity, "following the money," and sustaining our intent for a long and difficult struggle became signature principles of our strategy and also major factors in our success.

Influencing the Cairo conference

With almost no funds, no Internet or even reliable mail and phone links, we circulated our brief, draft "Declaration" for comment to as many women as we could reach worldwide. We established an organizing committee, reflecting wide political, geographic, and disciplinary diversity, to select 220 women from about 700 worldwide applicants for a meeting in Rio in January 1994 to elaborate a more fulsome feminist statement.[13] As a result of extraordinary focus and efforts to build consensus over five days, the Rio meeting yielded the "Women's Platform for ICPD," which IWHC published and widely disseminated on behalf of the participants.[14]

Simultaneously, to engage the respect and attention of mainstream actors at the UN, in foundations and among academics, we also produced a scholarly volume of essays outlining an alternative approach to population policy. With political and financial support from the Swedish International Development Cooperation Agency (SIDA), IWHC and Harvard University jointly published *Population Policies Reconsidered: Health, Empowerment and Rights*, and together launched the book in Zimbabwe in early 1994.[15] The volume's 17 essays by leading economists, health professionals, SRHR advocates, and an ethicist converged in many ways with the "Women's Platform."

With platform and book in hand, we and other colleagues from around the world, turned our attention to the official UN process for Cairo.[16] We participated in the UN's three "Preparatory Committee" (Prep Com) meetings, convened in New York City to negotiate a draft outcome document. We interacted extensively and intensively with governmental delegates and with UNFPA, the conference secretariat; lobbied national capitals and launched press initiatives. Few of us had much direct experience in UN negotiations, and we benefitted greatly from prior work on access to UN processes by Bella Abzug and the international organization she founded, Women's Environment and Development Organization (WEDO).

Although our learning curve was extremely steep, we were fiercely determined and exercised sound common sense about strategy. Two of the most important early decisions we made were first, to focus relentlessly on negotiations over the draft outcome document, and, second, to build and continuously refine an "inside-outside" strategy through which a critical mass of allies secured positions on national delegations to Cairo, while others constituted a disciplined advocacy force of women from countries likely to be key to negotiations leading up to and at the conference itself. We secured vital access to the chairpersons of the Prep Coms and in Cairo, as well as to delegates assigned to chair the working groups tasked to resolve language disputes on such contentious issues as human rights, SRHR, abortion, and adolescents. From the start, we sought official UNFPA support for our platform, but the agency's informal support only came late in the process, when Nafis Sadik, the head of UNFPA, recognized feminist advocates as necessary allies to counter both the moral high ground claimed by the Holy See and also the Vatican's (failed) effort to co-opt the conservative Islamic states.

The web of strategic relationships we and our feminist colleagues built with key actors, our presence in every stage of negotiations and our laser-like attention to the wording of agreements (with astute judgment about whether and when to compromise or not) resulted in a final Programme of Action out of Cairo, which has since been widely described as a "paradigm shift" in population policy because of its overarching human rights frame and emphasis on the interconnections of sexual and reproductive health, gender equality, women's empowerment, and poverty reduction. A path-breaking document, the Programme defines and makes commitments on SRHR, including prohibitions on many abuses still widespread in 1994, including incentive schemes, numerical targets, and forced sterilization. And it recognizes the need for access to safe abortion and for access by adolescents to SRH services and sex education, among other breakthroughs.

Although Cairo secured most of the elements of the Women's Platform, some did not survive. For example, language on "sexual rights" from the original UN negotiating draft was bartered for 42 paragraphs on adolescents' health and rights, representing a vital new element in a global intergovernmental agreement. Despite losing the term "sexual rights," we and other feminists fought for and secured language on the core content of sexual rights in paragraphs that define what constitutes "sexual and reproductive health and reproductive rights."[17]

We also pledged to fight for explicit use of the term, "sexual rights," as well as its content, and other excluded issues at the UN conference on women scheduled for 1995 in Beijing. A core group of ICPD advocates worked together as Health, Empowerment, Rights and Accountability (HERA) to ensure that the Cairo Programme of Action was reaffirmed in Beijing and also to strengthen and augment its commitments. We employed the same strategies and some new tactics based on lessons learned in Cairo.

Among other accomplishments, the Beijing Platform for Action reaffirms the Cairo Programme, and strengthens its language on safe abortion by recommending that countries review and revise punitive abortion laws. Perhaps most notably, the Beijing Platform also provides the first major intergovernmental statement of agreement on sexual rights:

> The human rights of women include their right to have control over and decide freely and responsibly on matters related to their sexuality, including sexual and reproductive health, free of coercion, discrimination and violence. Equal relationships between women and men in matters of sexual relations and reproduction, including full respect for the integrity of the person, require mutual respect, consent and shared responsibility for sexual behavior and its consequences.[18]

This language was negotiated painfully over the course of the conference in a working group led by Monique Essed Fernandes, the exceptional delegate from Surinam who was also a member of HERA, and by Ambassador Merwat Telawi of Egypt who chaired the decisive plenary session on this issue.

While these efforts have provided a solid foundation for all UN negotiations on sexuality and reproduction in the two decades since, Cairo and Beijing hardly provided the last word. Since 1995, determined conservative opponents have consistently opposed efforts to realize sexual rights, provide access to safe abortion, extend services to adolescents, and many other core commitments made two decades ago. And, regrettably, the population and family planning establishment has all too often been willing to compromise on the most "controversial issues" to "protect" family planning,[19] while health officials have ignored such essential elements as access to safe abortion.[20]

Because these battles have been and will continue to be fought at the UN in New York, as well as in other UN forums, regional bodies, and at the country level, SRHR activists from South and North have continued to invest in and train new generations of activists, educate new government delegates, select and participate in key negotiating arenas, and build the political will required for full implementation.[21]

The South–North fault line

At the heart of the very intense debates among feminists in the North and South that preceded Cairo was a suspicion and mistrust bred by a long history of colonial encounters and ongoing neo-colonial domination. Some feminists argued, for example, that the term, "reproductive rights," is just a disguise for old-fashioned Malthusian population control of non-white peoples. Others believed that sexual and reproductive matters are secondary to the "more important" constraints of class structures and of North–South inequalities. It took considerable effort to convince many key leaders and women's groups that SRHR is a core demand, central to redressing other legitimate grievances.

Even as the SRHR agenda has been more widely embraced, however, the South–North fault line among UN member states on population issues continues. A core South position was first articulated at the 1974 UN World Population Conference with the anti-Malthusian assertion: "Development is the best contraceptive." Since then, the right to development, including its financing, has dominated South–North tensions at the UN, with increasing complexity as the global economy and global politics have been buffeted by rapid financialization, neo-liberal economic policies, and rising inequality between and within countries. Today, every global issue addressed by the UN—trade, investment, finance, conflict and security, climate change, human rights—is seen through a South–North lens. This situation sometimes causes acute astigmatism as new economic powers and poles of capital accumulation, for instance Brazil, Russia, India, China, and South Africa (BRICS), have gained prominence. Further, the Group of 77, long the South voice in UN negotiations, remains a powerful force despite the enormous diversity among its constituent countries.

SRHR negotiations are increasingly held hostage to the resolution of these larger debates. In the five, 10, and 20-year reviews of Cairo and Beijing, for example, the Group of 77 challenged the ICPD agreements, yielding to the demands of member states with conservative positions on women's rights, gender equality, and SRHR. An eminently sensible solution was proposed during the 1999 ICPD review by a group of South countries that called themselves Some Latin American and Caribbean Countries (SLACC). SLACC argued, successfully in that case, that the Group of 77's *raison d'être* was and should remain the articulation of a Southern position on economic issues. But, on matters of SRHR, gender equality, and human rights, the member states of the Group of 77 should be free to articulate their own national positions.

While Group of 77 members took independent positions on SRHR in 1999, continuing South–North tensions make this less possible today. As global inequality has increased, Northern intransigence on issues such as development finance (including overseas development assistance (ODA) funds) is a permanent trigger for Group of 77 solidarity. Nowhere has this been more evident than in the ongoing battles over the post-2015 development agenda. The South–North economic divide provides ample grist to the mill of those aiming to drive the Group of 77 position on SRHR to its lowest common denominator.

At the same time, the North has also faced diverse perspectives as governments and alliances among countries change. For instance, in the European Union a small group of countries (Ireland, Poland, and Malta) have exerted a backward force on SRHR issues such as access to safe abortion. In other parts of the North and the South, countries where evangelical Christian Churches are strong have formed alliances with countries influenced by the Roman Catholic Church hierarchy and with conservative Muslim states to oppose SRHR.

All of this adds up to an extremely complex environment for advocacy today. Feminist activists have had to become increasingly adept at influencing both their own governments and the broader UN process just to protect the agreements we have.

The conceptual and political challenges of sexuality

Sexuality entered the ICPD debates through two distinctive pathways. In the late 1980s, in the context of the emerging HIV and AIDS epidemic, staff of the WHO defined sexual health by drawing on the definition of health in the WHO constitution. This language was included, along with "sexual rights," in the draft negotiating text at the start of the Cairo conference, and was strongly supported by many Northern countries and feminist advocates, among others. While feminist advocates promoted attention to sexual violence and STIs, not a few proponents of sexual rights were concerned at least as much with sexual freedom and pleasure.[22] Thus, Cairo opened a window towards the large vista of sexuality, even though the term "sexual rights" did not survive the real politics of negotiation.[23]

Although the Beijing battles on sexual orientation and sexual rights were even fiercer than those in Cairo, and the terms "sexual rights" and "sexual orientation" were excluded in the end, the BPFA, as mentioned above, included the content of women's sexual rights for the first time, and in subsequent UN forums the first sentence of that paragraph has been extended to men and adolescents.[24] The heteronormative nature of the paragraph was, however, criticized by gay activists and also lesbians, who, in Gloria Careaga's analysis, pursued human rights and sexual orientation in Beijing in a well-planned assault on the disciplinary edifice of population, heterosexuality, and procreation that continues today.[25]

In 2003, with support from many activists including feminists, Brazil tabled a resolution on sexual orientation and human rights at the UN Commission on Human Rights. It was not voted on, however, because Brazil retreated under the pressure of its Islamic trade partners.[26] Activists and some governments have, nonetheless, refused to let the issue die. In December 2006, at the UN Human Rights Council (the Council), which replaced the UN Commission on Human Rights, Norway presented a declaration on human rights, sexual orientation, and gender. In March 2007, the "Yogyakarta Principles for the Application of International Human Rights Law in relation to Sexual Orientation and Gender Identity" were also launched at the Council. In 2011 and 2014, two groundbreaking resolutions on sexual orientation and gender identity were also voted on and approved there.[27]

Further, since Cairo the concept of sexual rights has been taken up by many communities: lesbians, gays, trans-people, the HIV and AIDS movement, including UNAIDS, and even sex workers. For instance, in 2006 the Latin American Network of Sex Workers, RETRASEX, adopted sexual rights as one of its guiding principles and their representatives participated in the First Latin American Conference on Population and Development, an intergovernmental meeting to mark the 20th anniversary of Cairo. Despite these expanding constituencies, work to secure comprehensive recognition of sexual rights, including sexual orientation and gender identity, still faces conceptual and political challenges. Conceptually, the developments described above destabilize the heterosexual gender binary that has informed, and still informs, many feminists' views on sexuality. Politically, the construction of coalitions around sexual rights requires that identity politics, and related competition for resources and "victimization," be named and overcome, and that sharp differences of views, on sex work, for example, be faced and processed. This is more easily said than done and is, by no means, yet done.

Politically, global arenas are fraught with unresolved conflicts and fault lines on sexuality. For example, in most global debates, states and sometimes activists define sexual rights as addressing only LGBT rights or sexual orientation and gender identity, ignoring key dimensions of sexual rights, such as gender-based sexual violence, harmful practices that compromise the sexual lives of girls, women, and intersex children, or even human rights violations experienced by HIV-positive persons and sex workers. Recently, some North and South states have supported LGBT rights to project an image of liberalism and "modernity," but have done so to the detriment of their previous commitments to abortion rights and progressive views on sex work. This worrying tendency is not always understood and contested by LGBT groups, and many feminists still resist a fulsome definition of sexual rights beyond heterosexuality and sexual behaviors they see as socially and politically acceptable. This hydraulic politics of global sexual rights debates weakens our ability to sustain a comprehensive definition and application of sexual rights against fierce attacks by conservative forces and dogmatic religious actors, among others.

Conclusion

Intense and sustained follow-up has been and is still required to ensure that global actors and national governments protect, advance, and implement the commitments they made in Cairo and Beijing. Since the late 1990s, most of the global intergovernmental negotiations on these issues have been held at the UN in New York, notably in the Commission on Population and Development and the Commission on the Status of Women, and in Geneva at the Human Rights Council. This means that most delegation positions are driven by UN politics and generalist diplomats rather than by health, gender, and rights professionals. Thanks importantly to feminist advocates and our government allies, we have experienced no major SRHR losses since 1994, but opportunities to advance commitments and implementation have been thwarted by UN politics and conservatism, among other factors, and increasingly, even reaffirmation of existing commitments has been threatened.[28]

Feminist advocacy must increasingly cope with shifting sexual and reproductive rights politics, both south and north of the Equator, which is affected by the growth of conservatism, in particular religious dogmatism; by persistent inequalities; and, almost everywhere, by assaults on, and failure to fulfill, human rights standards broadly speaking. Among

NGOs many important would-be friends of SRHR in the population and family planning communities remain committed to vertical contraception programs, to old indicators and to renewed emphasis on commodities, neglecting desperately needed improvements in the quality of services—even vertical contraceptive services—to meet human rights standards and the needs of users, especially adolescents.[29]

As indicated above, opponents of SRHR have gained political weight. The alliance between the Holy See and the Arab group has recently co-opted Sub Saharan Africa. Latin American countries, strongly supportive of the Cairo agenda in regional negotiations, nonetheless have compromised SRHR in their global negotiating positions.[30] Asian countries have no common SRHR position except, when necessary, the lowest common denominator driven by a few very conservative countries and the wider Group of 77 agenda. The Europe group is also, as noted, hamstrung on key SRHR issues, and the US position, influential in most negotiations, varies widely according to who occupies the White House. Further, SRHR politics, still affected by old North-South tensions, are now also affected by the BRICS as they become global players.[31] Given this complex environment, some governments that have supported SRHR are beginning to suggest avoiding SRHR issues, unless heavily pressed by feminists both at the UN and in their capitals.

Dealing with these politics and covering the multiple UN forums stretches the feminist SRHR movement to its human and financial limits, and has also required modified strategies, particularly in the last decade. The international feminist SRHR movement has grown in numbers and skill in virtually all countries, thanks in part to professional partnerships and advocacy for their funding by transnational feminist networks and organization. Using the Internet for consultations with these and other feminists worldwide, democratically constituted international feminist groups, and now youth activists as well, prepare SRHR negotiating positions for each UN negotiation. With this substantive foundation, relatively small numbers of well-trained and coordinated activists, physically present in each UN forum, have influenced SRHR negotiations using the proven tactics of educating, lobbying, and providing language and strategic support to government delegations.

In addition, SRHR activists work increasingly through new and broader alliances. For example, the "women's major group," which encompasses feminist activists from all sectors, has strongly supported SRHR in the post-2015 agenda process. The group does preparatory work through the Internet, effectively divides labor among advocacy groups for the actual negotiations, and keeps everyone informed worldwide at the level needed for continuous advocacy in New York and in capitals. Sustaining this feminist advocacy is undoubtedly essential to secure a central role for SRHR in the post-2015 agenda so that the gaps in the content and implementation of Cairo's and subsequent SRHR agreements can be closed.

Despite the challenges, we dare to say that the most important legacy of Cairo and Beijing is the political imagination that created and helped win the outcome agreements. That imagination continues to inspire new generations of feminist SRHR advocates to use their own creativity and energy to resist, to keep fighting and to establish and sustain old and new virtuous connections within and outside institutions and across movements. These advocates at national, regional, and global levels, will be instrumental in work to secure a post-2015 agenda that protects and fulfills human rights standards, specifies actions to implement SRHR agreements, requires accountability of all actors at all levels for implementation, and widens the agreed agenda to include sexual rights, among other issues. And, if the post-2015 agenda falls short, they will hold the world accountable, while identifying ways to move forward, as earlier generations have done.

Notes

1 Rosalind Petchesky and Sonia Corrêa, "Sexual and Reproductive Rights from the Feminist Perspective," in *Routledge Handbook of Sexuality, Health and Rights*, ed. Peter Aggleton and Richard Parker (New York: Routledge, 2010).

2 Ellen Chesler, *Woman of Valor: Margaret Sanger and the Birth Control Movement in America* (New York: Simon and Schuster, 1992).

3 Adrienne Germain and Jane Ordway, "Population Policy and Women's Health: Balancing the Scales," in *Beyond the Numbers: A Reader on the Population, Consumption, and the Environment*, ed. L.A. Mazur (New York: Island Press, 1994). (Shortened version of longer article originally commissioned by and published with sponsorship of the Overseas Development Council, New York: International Women's Health Coalition, 1989.)

4 Adrienne Germain and Ruth Dixon-Mueller, *Four Essays on Birth Control Needs and Risks* (New York: International Women's Health Coalition, 1993).

5 Adrienne Germain and Ruth Dixon-Mueller "Population Policy and Women's Political Action in Three Developing Countries," in *Population Policy and Women's Rights: Transforming Reproductive Choice*, ed. Ruth Dixon-Mueller (Westport, Conn.: Praeger, 1993). (Also published in shorter form in *Population and Development Review*, Supplement to Vol. 20, 1994.)

6 Judith Bruce, "Fundamental Elements of the Quality of Care: A Simple Framework," *Studies in Family Planning* 21 (1990): 61–91.

7 Gita Sen and Caren Grown, *Development, Crises, and Alternative Visions: Third World Women's Perspectives* (New York: Monthly Review Press, 1987).

8 Lourdes Arizpe, M. Priscilla Stone and David C. Major, eds., *Population and Environment: Rethinking the Debate* (Boulder, Colo.: Westview Press, 1994). See also, Gita Sen "Creating Common Ground Between Environmentalists and Women: Thinking Locally, Acting Globally?," *Ambio: a Journal of the Human Environment* XXIV (1995): 1.

9 WHO Special Program of Research, Development and Research Training in Human Reproduction and International Women's Health Coalition, *Creating Common Ground: Report of a Meeting Between Women's Health Advocates and Scientists on Women's Perspectives on the Introduction of Fertility Regulation Technologies* (Geneva, Switzerland: World Health Organization, 1991).

10 Adrienne Germain, King K. Holmes, Peter Piot, and Judith N. Wasserheit, ed., *Reproductive Tract Infections: Global Impact and Priorities for Women's Reproductive Health* (New York: Plenum Press, 1992).

11 Peggy Antrobus, Adrienne Germain and Sia Nowrojee, "Challenging the Culture of Silence: Building Alliances to End Reproductive Tract Infections," Report of the meeting co-sponsored with the Women and Development Unit, University of the West Indies (New York: International Women's Health Coalition, 1994).

12 Andrea Irvin, "Positively Informed: Lesson Plans and Guidance for Sexuality Educators and Advocates" (New York: International Women's Health Coalition, 2004).

13 The organizing committee consisted of: Peggy Antrobus, University of the West Indies, Caribbean; Amparo Claro, Latin American and Caribbean Women's Health Network and Isis International; Sonia Correa, National Feminist Health and Reproductive Rights Network, Brazil; Adrienne Germain, International Women's Health Coalition; Marie Aimee Helie-Lucas, Women Living under Muslim Laws; Bene Madunagu, Women in Nigeria; Florence Manguyu, Medical Women's International Association; Alexandria Marcelo, WomanHealth, the Philippines; Rosalind Petchesky, International Reproductive Rights Research Action Group; Jacqueline Pitanguy, Citizenship, Studies, Information, Action, Brazil; Julia Scott, National Black Women's Health Project, USA; Gita Sen, Development Alternatives with Women for a New Era (DAWN); Loes Keysers, Women's Global Network for Reproductive Rights; and Mona Zulficar, Women's Health Improvement Association, Egypt.

14 Claudia Garcia-Moreno, ed., "Reproductive Health and Justice: International Women's Conference for Cairo '94" (New York: International Women's Health Coalition and Citizenship, Studies, Information and Action, 1994).

15 Gita Sen, Adrienne Germain and Lincoln Chen, eds, *Population Policies Reconsidered: Health, Empowerment and Rights* (Cambridge, Mass.: Harvard University Press, 1994).

16 See endnote 13, which lists many of those engaged. Others included Marge Berer, Rhonda Copelon, Joan Dunlop, and Francis Kissling.

17 *Programme of Action adopted at the International Conference on Population and Development* (New York: United Nations Population Fund, 2004), paras 7.2, 7.3.

18 *The Beijing Declaration and Platform for Action* (UN Department of Public Information, 1996), para. 96.

19 Ruth Dixon-Mueller and Adrienne Germain, "Reproductive Health and the Demographic Imagination," in *Women's Empowerment and Demographic Processes: Moving Beyond Cairo*, ed. Harriet B. Presser and Gita Sen (Oxford: Oxford University Press, 2000).

20 Adrienne Germain and Theresa Kim, *Expanding Access to Safe Abortion* (New York: International Women's Health Coalition, 1998).

21 Rounaq Jahan and Adrienne Germain, "Mobilizing Support to Sustain Political Will is the Key to Progress in Reproductive Health," *The Lancet* 364, no. 9436 (2004): 742–744.

22 Rosalind Petchesky, "Sexual Rights: Inventing a Concept, Mapping an International Practice," in *Framing the sexual subject: The politics of gender, sexuality, and power*, ed. Richard Parker, Regina Barbosa and Peter Aggleton (London: Routledge, 2000): 81–103.

23 Sonia Corrêa, Rosalind Petchesky and Richard Parker, *Sexuality, Health and Human Rights* (New York: Routledge, 2008).

24 Susana T. Fried and Ilana Landsberg-Lewis, "Sexual Rights: From Concept to Strategy," in *Women's Human Rights Reference Guide*, ed. Kelly D. Askin and Dorean M. Koenig (New York: Transnational Press, 2001). See also, Paul Hunt, *Economic, Social and Cultural Rights: The Right of Everyone to the Enjoyment of the Highest Attainable Standard of Physical and Mental Health*, Report of the Special Rapporteur on the right of everyone to the enjoyment of the highest attainable standard of physical and mental health, UN Commission on Human Rights, 2004, 60th session.

25 Francoise Girard, "Negotiating Sexual Rights and Sexual Orientation at the UN" in *SexPolitics: Reports from the Front Lines*, ed. Richard Parker, Rosalind Petchesky and Robert Sember (New York: Sexuality Policy Watch, 2007).

26 Magaly Pazello, "Sexual Rights and Trade," *Peace Review: A Journal of Social Justice* 17, 2–3 (2005): 155–162.

27 ARC International 2014, *SOGI Victory at the Human Rights Council*, http://arc-international.net/press-2014sogires. See also, Association for Women's Rights in Development 2014, *The Right To Autonomy Over Our Bodies And Loves: The Resolution On Human Rights, Sexual Orientation And Gender Identity Furthers Dialogue*, www.awid.org/News-Analysis/Friday-Files/The-Right-To-Autonomy-Over-Our-Bodies-And-Loves-The-Resolution-On-Human-Righ ts-Sexual-Orientation-And-Gender-Identity-Furthers-Dialogue.

28 Sonia Correa, Adrienne Germain, and Rosalind Petcheskey, "Thinking Beyond ICPD + 10: Where Should Our Movement be Going?," *Reproductive Health Matters* 13, 25 (2005): 109–19. See also, Gita Sen, "Neolibs, Neocons and Gender Justice: Lessons from Global Negotiations," Occasional Paper No. 9 (Geneva, Switzerland: UN Research Institute for Social Development, 2005).

29 Jane Cottingham, Adrienne Germain, and Paul Hunt, "Using Human Rights to Meet the Unmet Need for Family Planning," *The Lancet* 30, no. 9837 (2012): 172–80. See information on the Family Planning 2020 (FP2020) partnership at www.familyplanning2020.org. See also, Gita Sen, "Integrating Family Planning with Sexual and Reproductive Rights: the Past as Prologue?," *Studies in Family Planning* 41, no. 2 (2010): 143–46.

68 Sonia Correa, Adrienne Germain, and Gita Sen

30 Lilian Abracinskas, Sonia Corrêa, Beatriz Galli, and Alexandra Garita, "The 'unexpected' Montevideo Consensus," *Global Public Health* 9, no. 6 (2014): 631–8.
31 Sonia Corrêa, "Emerging Powers: Can it be that Sexuality and Human Rights is a Lateral Issue?" *SUR International Journal on Human Rights* 11, no. 20 (2014).

5 Taking stock: protection without empowerment?

Evolution of the women, peace, and security agenda since the Beijing Platform for Action

Anne Marie Goetz and Rob Jenkins

This chapter reviews the evolution of what the international community has come to call the "women, peace, and security agenda"—or the challenge of bringing a gender equality perspective to the institutions and practices of international conflict-prevention and peacebuilding. The key components of this worldwide effort are detailed in Section E ("Conflict") of the 1995 Platform for Action of the UN Fourth World Conference on Women in Beijing. At the heart of these assertions of state obligations to protect women in conflict is a conviction that women's leadership and participation in male-dominated security, justice and foreign policy institutions, tied to a commitment to disarmament and demilitarization, will promote more peaceful societies and a safer world. This agenda is grounded in a century of women's peace activism—set out by the Women's Peace Congress in the Hague in April 1915 and carried forward by the world's longest-lasting international women's organization: the Women's International League for Peace and Freedom.[1]

In the 20 years since Beijing, the women, peace, and security (WPS) agenda has become more firmly internalized, or "mainstreamed," within the operation of security institutions than initially expected. In this chapter we will discuss the consequences of this mainstreaming from the perspective of the core commitment to promote women's peace leadership. The normative foundations of the WPS agenda are solid—in addition to important regional commitments there are seven UN Security Council resolutions (SCR) (starting with SCR 1325 in 2000) asserting clearly that women's participation in conflict prevention and recovery is an international peace and security matter, as is the responsibility to stop all forms of violence against women during and after conflict. Since the late 1990s international transitional justice processes have been addressing the crimes to which women are subject in wartime. There is a stronger awareness of the need to engage women in post-conflict economic recovery. CEDAW reporting processes have been amended to include women and conflict issues.[2] The 2013 General Recommendation 30 requires all participating states to report on women's engagement in conflict prevention and recovery processes. At a national level, women are more visible than ever in foreign policy and defense establishments, and almost 50 countries have developed National Action Plans to advance women peace and security goals. Women's participation is particularly marked where local women's groups have found the political space, resources and alliances to demand accountability from national and international actors for adherence to global norms. This has taken place in settings as diverse as Nepal, Colombia, the Philippines, Timor Leste, Aceh, Guatemala, Liberia, and Uganda.

But there is still a long way to go. Mainstreaming has dulled the stress in the Beijing Platform for Action (BPFA) "Section E" on women's leadership and participation. At the international level, there is a growing divergence between the "protection" component of the WPS agenda and the "participation" component that connects women's empowerment to long-term conflict prevention and peace building. International security institutions have responded with greater intensity to the issue of sexual violence in conflict than to the challenge of ensuring women's full and equal access to representation within decision-making bodies, including truth and reconciliation commissions, post-conflict planning bodies and national parliaments. The "mainstreaming" of the WPS agenda in institutions responsible for maintaining security, negotiating peace, and ensuring the rule of law is often reduced to devising inconsequential bureaucratic checklists. All too often the process of creating National Action Plans (NAPs) for the implementation of SCR 1325 has involved specifying lists of organizational-change measures with little practical chance of altering the operation of state institutions, civilian or military. The process of formulating a NAP provides the illusion of action; governments often refer to their NAP as if the creation of a plan were a sufficient substitute for the kinds of actions that might lead to the changes envisioned under SCR 1325. They provide a convenient façade, rather than a substantial framework, for state accountability.

This chapter traces the normative evolution of the WPS agenda. Two sections assess the growing centrality of conflict-related sexual violence in the overall WPS agenda and the challenges of main-streaming its empowerment component through NAPs. A brief con-clusion considers the implications of our findings, including the potential consequences of the twenty-first century global security environment for the pacifist and disarmament-focused voices repre-sented in Beijing, when a more upbeat political atmosphere prevailed, inspired by the end of the Cold War.

The women, peace, and security agenda: normative advances between 2000 and 2014

In 1995, at the time of the Beijing Conference, there had still never been a conviction in an international criminal tribunal for war rape. There had never been a UN-appointed female peace mediator. The first conviction came in 1998,[3] but no woman was designated a UN senior mediator until Mary Robinson was appointed in 2013 as the Secretary-General's Special Envoy for the Great Lakes Region. This ordering of priorities—focusing on protection before promoting lea-dership and participation—is mirrored in patterns of mainstreaming women, peace, and security at the UN.

The complete absence of women's participation in the 1995 Dayton Agreement to end the Bosnian conflict and the UN's introspection about its responsibility to protect civilians after the 1994 Rwandan genocide were among the drivers prompting women's peace organizations to lobby for a firm Security Council commitment to women's participation in conflict prevention. "Women and Peace and Security," as the Security Council titles it, became a regular item on the Security Council's work plan with the passage of SCR 1325 in October 2000. This was at the turn of the millennium, five years after the Beijing Conference, and in the afterglow of the Millennium Declaration,[4] a moment that in retro-spect marked a high point of liberal internationalism and an openness to collaboration to prevent human rights abuses. The Security Council has since become much more hostile to what are seen by some mem-bers as costly "thematic" concerns (others concern children and armed conflict, environmental issues, protection of civilians, etc.).

For eight years, SCR 1325 served primarily as a symbol of the Security Council's good intentions—acknowledged via an annual "Open Debate" in October but lacking any kind of monitoring let alone accountability mechanisms. But starting in 2008, a series of Security Council resolutions set out increasingly detailed obligations for Council, UN, and member state actions. Four resolutions[5] rede-fined sexual violence in conflict not as inevitable wartime "collateral damage," but as (when widespread and systematic) a conscious military strategy for which there is command responsibility that is subject to judicial and political censure and military counter-tactics. These resolutions require peacekeepers to prevent sexual violence, mediators and negotiators to address it in peace talks, judicial authorities to ensure effective prosecutions and redress, and so forth.

A separate resolution, number 1889 (2009), focuses on the central role that women can and should play in preventing conflict recurrence. Resolution 1889 acknowledged that women's access to civil service jobs, elected office, party leadership, business associations, and other positions of decision-making authority is crucial to the state-building/ rebuilding process. The most recent SCR, 2122 (2013), concedes that the Security Council had not done enough to advance this "participation" component of the WPS agenda. SCR 2122 calls for concrete measures to support women's organizations so that they can represent women's views in conflict-resolution efforts, and obligates UN-appointed mediators to meet early and regularly with women's groups.

SCR 2122 also recognizes that gender-based inequality in citizenship rights exacerbates women's vulnerability in situations of displacement. It alludes to the right of women to terminate pregnancies resulting from conflict-related rape. It invokes the principle of provision of humanitarian aid without discrimination to note that sexual and reproductive health services of particular kinds are needed by women who are pregnant because of rape. And it calls on all UN member states to improve implementation of WPS commitments in the run up to the 15th anniversary of SCR 1325 in 2015. It notes *"with concern*, that without a significant implementation shift, women and women's perspectives will continue to be underrepresented in conflict prevention, resolution, protection and peace-building for the foreseeable future."

The period of normative development between 2000 and 2014 was not matched by changes in women's engagement in conflict resolution. This is recognized by SCR 2122, but what precisely the "significant implementation shift" could involve is frustratingly unclear. Diplomats and UN officials often argue that there is extremely little room for taking on new issues and agendas in the delicate art of conflict resolution and recovery. They point out that because post-conflict spending prioritizes the buying off and/or punishing of potential "spoilers," including through expensive (and often ineffectual) Disarmament, Demobilization and Reintegration (DDR) programs, the funds available for initiatives dedicated to women are limited. Other excuses include that too few women have the necessary mediation experience and that negotiating delegations threaten to leave talks if any requirements are imposed regarding the composition of their teams. Under such circumstances, it is often said that the burden of encouraging women's participation could actually undercut peace talks or delay agreement. This was the impression given by UN Special Envoy Lakhdar Brahimi in his foot-dragging over holding meetings with Syrian women's organizations in 2013 and 2014. When Brahimi did eventually attend the introductory and concluding sessions of a conference of Syrian women's organizations in January 2013, he made no commitment to use his influence to press for opportunities for the women to provide even occasional briefings to the negotiators.[6] No consultations with women took place when the Syria negotiations began several weeks later.

National and international peacebuilding continues to be a male-dominated activity. There are exceptions, to be sure. Over the past two decades, Africa has seen post-conflict legislative and constitutional reforms in which women have been able to seize opportunities for change in the "gender regime."[7] Aili Mari Tripp's analysis of these cases in Africa[8] suggests that they show a convergence of factors including large and well-networked women's peace movements, long-duration, high-casualty civil wars resolved via comprehensive agreements that opened space for substantial institutional reform. The influence of international actors also played a role.

In contrast with the environment of liberal internationalism ushered in by the Millennium Declaration in 2000, today there is a backlash against international efforts to promote human rights and protect civilians, in part because of the massive and rising cost of peacekeeping, and in part because past actions to protect civilians, such as in the Security Council-sanctioned air strikes in Libya in 2011, have come to be seen as roundabout methods for leading Western powers to effect regime change. The long-standing tension in international institutions between the promotion of human rights and the defense of state sovereignty (and sovereign immunity) has grown in intensity, as seen in African states' 2013 backlash against the International Criminal Court, which is perceived to be targeting African war criminals exclusively. In this context, the suggestion that women's participation and the promotion of their rights is a national and international responsibility is resented by "sovereignty hawks" as an assault on national sensibilities. The period of normative development in the WPS agenda between 2000 and 2013 may in the years ahead be regarded as an anomaly.

Protection without empowerment? Sexual violence in conflict

One specific aspect of the WPS agenda has enjoyed an easy, if astonishingly delayed, fit with the Council's mandate to uphold international humanitarian law: the responsibility to prevent sexual violence during conflict. Widespread and systematic sexual violence became established in the late 1990s as a key element of international humanitarian law jurisprudence, but it was not a topic directly addressed by the Security Council until the early years of the present century. Conflict-related sexual violence was identified in SCR 1325 itself. Nevertheless, the Council did not make this a major focus of its mandates for peacekeeping missions or for conflict-resolution processes.

In 2008, feminist bureaucrats in OCHA, UNIFEM, UNFPA, UNDP, and the Department for Peacekeeping Operations (DPKO),[9] along with the UK and the US missions, collaboratively developed the first new WPS resolution at the Council since 2000. What would become SCR 1820 affirmed that some acts of sexual violence in conflict can be considered tactics of warfare, requiring application of the security and political responses that the Council brings to other violations of international humanitarian law, including the refusal to recognize amnesties for perpetrators. SCR 1820 took a 1325-informed approach to protection, situating the proposed responses to sexual violence within the established language of women's empowerment. Operational Paragraph 3 of SCR 1820 calls on the Secretary General to "encourage dialogue to address this issue in the context of broader discussions of conflict resolution ... taking into account, inter alia, *the views expressed by women of affected local communities.*" This phrase indicates the need to ensure women's participation in protection initiatives.

SCR 1820 was followed by three subsequent sexual violence resolutions that, in turn, created a dedicated Special Representative of the Secretary General (1888); called for a reporting mechanism that would name perpetrators (1960); established a corps of trained "Women Protection Advisers" to sharpen the UN's response in the field (1960); and included this issue in the designation criteria of sanctions committees (2106).

Through the passage of these resolutions, the Security Council has, to a significant degree, carved the protection-from-sexual-violence element of the 1325 agenda away from those measures aimed primarily at women's empowerment, including their equal representation within rule-formulating and decision-making bodies. In the recent past

Council observers have remarked on the highly detailed language on preventing sexual violence found in UN peacekeeping mission mandates. This is in contrast with the lack of concrete instructions to mission leadership to support women's engagement in reconciliation processes, governance institutions, or the reform of the justice and security sectors.[10]

While implementation of protection and reporting measures has improved, the UN system has been slow to address sexual violence issues meaningfully in its *political* work. It was not until 2012 that the Department of Political Affairs (DPA) issued guidance notes designed to encourage mediators to press for the inclusion of sexual violence issues during UN mediation processes. There is no credible evidence that these guidelines inluenced the practices used by Special Envoys. The one exception, the Special Envoy to the Great Lakes region, Mary Robinson, produced such impressive results that it is difficult to believe that other envoys could not deliver at least something for women who have suffered high levels of sexual violence. She brokered a set of gender-responsive provisions in the 2013 Peace, Security and Cooperation Framework for the Great Lakes Region. Arguably, Robinson's ability to advance the substantive issues involved stemmed from her decision to reinvent the procedures used to generate consensus. Most importantly, she initiated regular consultations with a pre-existing (not donor-created) network of women leaders from the region.

Sexual violence in conflict is an international crime and fits easily in the mandates of the Security Council and other international institutions. The obligation to promote women's participation lacks this type of legal imperative: it is not a crime not to include women in peace talks, for instance. For all the measurement challenges, conflict-related sexual violence is more amenable to tracking than is the notoriously slippery and context-specific concept of women's empowerment. Conflict-related sexual violence also fits securely within traditional gender-role expectations, particularly with respect to gendered descriptions of conflict.[11] The nature of the crime is gendered, regardless of the sex of the victim.

As the primary targets, however, women are framed as more or less passive prey. This reinforces gender stereotypes of women as sexually subordinated. The current focus on sexual violence—particularly efforts to prevent violations from happening—offers (mainly) male security officials the kind of role with which they are comfortable: protectors of women's virtue. Perhaps most importantly, because of the legal need to specify sexual violence as a purely tactical or criminal issue, the international actors who have worked so hard to advance action on this issue may unwittingly have directed attention away from seeing sexual violence as rooted in social relations.

The campaign to prevent conflict-related violence has become perhaps the highest profile international effort to address VAW, moving from a "women's issues" backwater to a major foreign policy concern. This was signaled clearly in the June 2014 Global Summit on Ending Sexual Violence in Conflict, convened by UK Foreign Secretary William Hague. The Summit was the culmination of a two-year strategy by Hague to take advantage of the UK's 2013 presidency of the G8 to place this issue on the agenda of the world's most exclusive club of nations. Representatives from 120 countries, including more than 70 foreign ministers, attended this meeting—an unprecedented demonstration of commitment.

National implementation: substituting planning for action

This section charts the evolution and identifies the limitations of NAPs to advance the WPS agenda in operational terms. Opponents of the 1325 agenda on the Security Council reiterate frequently that implementation is primarily a national responsibility. Since 2004 the Security Council has reiterated a request to UN member states to develop NAPs for the implementation of women, peace, and security objectives. Forty-six had done so as of July 2014; some had also "localized" them to sub-national or local government levels.[12]

No systematic global assessment of the effectiveness of these plans has been conducted. A 2013 Global Review Meeting convened by UN Women on NAPs, examined variations in the design and content of these plans but did not have systematic comparable data on their impact.[13] A technical paper prepared by Natalie Hudson for this meeting demonstrated that these plans vary widely in the extent to which they represent genuine national commitments to gender-related reform to national security, justice, and foreign policy establishments.[14] Inter-departmental operational instructions such as were developed in 2006 for the UK's Foreign and Commonwealth Office, Department of Defense and Department for International Development, have been effective in building coherence in addressing gender issues across conflict-prevention and human security promotion initiatives.

The Hudson overview paper identifies a number of issues of concern: donor country NAPs tend to address WPS issues primarily as a matter of foreign aid, influence in international institutions, and domestic efforts to accelerate the recruitment of women to national armed forces and police. They do not address WPS issues in relation to domestic social tensions—for instance, the US NAP was criticized by US women's organizations for failing to address conflict between communities in the United States or in its immigration policies, notably in relation to Central America. NAPs in conflict-affected countries are distorted by the specific preoccupations of the international institutions supporting NAP development. Uganda's NAP, for instance, focuses very strongly on reproductive health issues—which reflects the influence of its main financial supporter, UNFPA. Many are exceptionally ambitious but lack dedicated financing or inter-departmental agreements to make them feasible. Where NAPs are developed and coordinated primarily by a ministry of women's or gender issues—as in Liberia or Uganda—NAPs suffer from the marginality and ineffectiveness that plague these "National Women's Machineries."

Donor country NAPs do not appear to have resulted in the international supporters of peace processes insisting upon women's inclusion in conflict-resolution. Quite a number of the countries supporting the 2013–2014 talks for Syria had adopted NAPs, yet few made a specific effort to urge the mediator or the negotiating parties to include women in the talks. Nor has the existence of a NAP provided any kind of protection to women upon the outbreak of conflict—Cote d'Ivoire's early 2007 NAP praised for its realistic monitoring framework proved useless in the extreme violence election-related of 2010 and 2011.

There have been some exceptions to this generally disappointing trend. For instance, in the Philippines, the relatively large role played by women and the women's movement in the country's NAP (in 2010) may have had something to do with the unusually large part women played in resolving the conflict and participating in post-conflict institutions. Where coordinating committees are established linking relevant government departments with women's peace organizations in civil society, such as the Women Peace and Security Coordinating Committee in Fiji, established in 2003, and a similar arrangement established in Nepal in 2009, there is stronger government responsiveness to early conflict-alerts from women's groups.[15]

Regrettably, like so many gender mainstreaming initiatives, NAPs are too easily reduced to box-ticking exercises that serve mainly to generate the impression that national authorities are taking WPS seriously. The process of formulating a NAP can signal membership in a community of like-minded states—a means of gaining international legitimacy. Canada's rush to finalize its NAP in 2010 was part of a broader image-enhancement campaign related to Canada's bid for (elected, temporary) Security Council membership, which it lost to Germany. Japan rushed to draw up a NAP in 2013 when it became known that the G8, under the UK presidency that year, would be focusing on conflict-related sexual violence. Japan did not want to be the only other G8 country besides Russia, a more or less open opponent of the WPS agenda, to lack a NAP.

Ironically, the UK government, which would go on to make conflict-related sexual violence a signature issue in 2013, had promised to use an earlier G8 presidency, in 2005, to press for more concerted action by G8 members and the countries with which they partnered, to develop NAPs on SCR 1325. The UK had even made this commitment in its 2004 statement to the Council at the Open Debate on 1325. Needless to say, the initiative on NAPs did not generate anything like the same fanfare as William Hague's 2013 partnership with Angelina Jolie for action on conflict-related sexual violence—once again showing a stronger response to protection than leadership issues.

Conclusion: emerging security challenges and the future of WPS activism

Section E of the BPFA reflected the central preoccupations of the global women's peace movement—an insistence on disarmament, particularly the elimination of weapons of mass destruction, and a focus on promoting peace education and social justice in the interests of long-term conflict prevention. Section E, SCR 1325, and CEDAW's General Recommendation 30 are animated by the conviction that gender-based inequality is one of the drivers of the militarization, extremism, and violent masculinities that destabilize societies.

Twenty years on, key components of the original WPS agenda have been sidelined. The drive to engage the Security Council has in particular required that WPS be framed as a matter of international humanitarian and human rights law. Within this framework, the Council has been able to acknowledge—albeit incompletely—its responsibility to prevent and respond robustly to sexual violence in conflict, but has shown much less interest in realizing its responsibilities to ensure women's participation in conflict resolution and recovery. Evidence of this divergent commitment is clear from the proliferation of Security Council resolutions on sexual violence in conflict, and from the Council's relative consistency in ensuring that its mandates for UN missions address sexual violence. In contrast, the numbers of women participating in peace processes remain low, women's movements' engagement in formal conflict resolution and recovery processes remains limited, and the Security Council remains vague in the instructions it provides UN missions on the promotion of women's participation and is at best inconsistent in tracking field-mission compliance with these instructions.

This ambivalence may mean that WPS concerns will be further sidelined in the context of responses to the new security threats that have emerged since 1995. At the top of the list is the challenge of globally networked extremist insurgencies that appeal to atavistic and highly contested interpretations of Islam. Many such movements have made the imposition of social, political, and economic constraints on women a fundamental part of their ideologies. Their violent repression of women who dare to play non-traditional roles or who defend women's rights has seriously raised the costs of women's activism and has, in many country contexts, completely closed whatever political space for gender-equality advocacy might have existed.

This paper has argued that although there is much to be celebrated in the institutionalization of the WPS agenda, it has come with a cost. The transformative focus on women's empowerment has never been fully welcome in peace and security institutions. Section E of the BPFA, the UN Security Council resolutions on WPS, and CEDAW's 2013 General Recommendation 30 on conflict represent a substantial framework of international law connecting women's rights and empowerment to the security field, explicitly linking women's capacity to engage in peace work with the levels of security that women (and the societies to which they belong) experience. While the framework is legally formidable, the institutions for ensuring its implementation remain politically feeble. The UN has failed to develop, let alone deliver on, initiatives to rapidly increase women's rate of market or political engagement in post-conflict situations. At national levels, it seems that only where women's groups are strong and well networked domestically and regionally are they able to seize opportunities to influence peace processes and recovery. In the context of rising inequality and instability, women's groups face increasing difficulties surviving, let alone engaging in conflict resolution. International accountability for promoting women's peace leadership is needed more than ever. It is the key to effective protection.

Notes

1 In April 2015 WILPF held its Centennial Congress and International Conference on Peacebuilding. See *Women's Power to Stop War: A Global Movement of WILPF,* www.womenstopwar.org/.

2 Office of the High Commissioner for Human Rights, *General Recommendation No. 30 on Women in Conflict Prevention and Post-conflict Situations* (Geneva, Switzerland: United Nations, 2013).

3 In September 1998, the International Criminal Tribunal for Rwanda issued the first verdict by an international tribunal on sexual violence in a civil war, finding it to be an act of genocide when committed with the intent of destroying a particular group.

4 United Nations, *Millennium Summit of the United Nations,* www.un.org/en/development/devagenda/millennium.shtml.

5 Security Council Resolution 1820 (2008); Security Council Resolution 1888 (2009); Security Council Resolution 1960 (2010); Security Council Resolution 2106 (2013).

6 Madeleine Rees, "Syrian Women Demand to Take Part in the Peace Talks in Geneva," *Open Democracy,* 12 January 2013, www.opendemocracy.net/5050/madeleine-rees/syrian-women-demand-to-take-part-in-peace-talks-in-geneva.

7 Raewyn Connell, *Gender* (Cambridge: Cambridge University Press, 2003).

8 Aili Mari Tripp, "Gender and Peace Negotiations in Africa," in *Gendered Insecurities,* ed. Howard Stein and Amal Fadlalla (New York: Routledge, 2012).

9 Office for the Coordination of Humanitarian Affairs, UN Development Fund for Women, UN Population Programme, UN Development Fund, Department of Peacekeeping Operations.

10 Security Council Report, *2014 Cross-Cutting Report on Women, Peace and Security,* www.securitycouncilreport.org/cross-cutting-report/women-peace-and-security.php.

11 Diane Otto, "The Exile of Inclusion," *Melbourne Journal of International Law* 10, no.1 (2009): 11–26; Laura Shepherd, "Sex, Security and Superhero (in)es: From 1325 to 1820 and Beyond," *International Feminist Journal of Politics* 13, no. 4 (2011): 504–133.

12 The Global Network of Women Peace Builders has made localization of action plans on 1325 their signature program, particularly in the Philippines and Nepal. Localization engages local governing authorities, traditional leaders, and women's groups in translating national commitments to WPS resolutions into community-relevant actions. In Nepal, for instance, the focus has been on ensuring that women engage in the local Peace Committees formed across the country to implement the peace agreement, and also to ensure that women participate in decision-making over the distribution of funds from the National Peace Trust Fund, which were supposed to distribute reparations to war widows.

13 UN Women, *Global Technical Review Meeting: Building Accountability for Implementation of Security Council Resolutions on Women, Peace and Security* (New York: UN Women, 2013).

14 Natalie Florea Hudson, *National and Regional Implementation of Security Council Resolutions on Women, Peace and Security: Background Paper for Global Review Meeting* (New York: UN Women, 2013).
15 Hudson, *National and Regional Implementation of Security Council Resolutions on Women, Peace and Security: Background Paper for Global Review Meeting*, 14.

6 Seeing sexual and reproductive health and rights through the eyes of a youth activist

A reflection

Maria Antonieta Alcalde[1]

In 1994, I was a college student in Mexico City, spending much of my time as a volunteer promoting young women's voices and votes in my country's presidential elections. I wanted to change the world for women and girls. I did not know that the world was indeed being changed at the same time halfway around the planet in Egypt.

The International Conference on Population and Development (ICPD), held by the UN in Cairo that year, forged an agreement among 179 countries in a historic event that brought about a paradigm shift in the relationship between mainstream considerations of population and development. The result would be steady movement away from family planning programs grounded in often harshly implemented demographic targets, to a broader understanding of state obligations to protect and advance the sexual and reproductive health and rights of women and girls, and to provide accessible, client-centered services of high quality. This was a landmark achievement. As a young person, I had the opportunity to be part of these exciting times.

Women's movements from around the world were central to the success in Cairo, but it would take a few more years for young people to become involved as well. Leading up to the ICPD+5 review process, the United Nations made a very conscious effort to broaden its outreach. Youth leaders from around the world were invited to bring their perspective to national and international evaluations of the Cairo accords.

By this time in 1999, I had helped found and was leading the Elige Youth Network for Sexual and Reproductive Rights. In that capacity, I was invited to comment on Mexico's official report on progress toward meeting its obligations under the Cairo accords. I soon became fully engaged internationally as well. Prior to the official preparatory meetings and review scheduled for March in New York, civil society met in the Netherlands to develop a common strategy. With funding and technical assistance from the UN Population Fund (UNFPA) a youth forum was convened, and our views were, in turn, incorporated into the Hague Civil Society Forum Declaration, which recognized the need to strengthen youth participation in the ongoing design, implementation, monitoring, and evaluation of all programs. The document also explicitly called on governments and the international community to establish youth councils and increase funding for youth organizations to at least 20 percent of donor funding in the field.

Young people then traveled to New York to organize as a single force. A group of us was again supported by UNFPA, as well as by a number of civil society organizations including, the Center for Development and Population Activities (CEDPA), the International Women's Health Coalition (IWHC), Action Canada for Population and Development (ACPD), the World Population Fund (WPF), and the Latin American and Caribbean Women's Health Network. Recognizing the need to better coordinate our voices, we created the Youth Coalition (YC), later renamed the Youth Coalition for Sexual and Reproductive Rights. By the time of the subsequent UN General Assembly Special Session (UNGASS) review of ICPD, we were an organized and influential group, which played a role in ensuring stronger commitments to young people in the "Key Actions for Further Implementation" (ICPD+5) document. Our gratitude to the women's organization that supported us was enormous. They shared their space and knowledge but also recognized us as a distinct constituency and respected our inputs and decisions as such. They helped us to flourish.

Many more youth-led organizations were created around the ICPD +5 process, including the Latin American and Caribbean Youth Network for Sexual and Reproductive Rights (RedLac) and Choice, for Youth and Sexuality, a youth-led international organization based in the Netherlands. These groups have continued their work ever since, exploring mechanisms to renew leadership and to bring attention to the special needs of adolescents in accessing culturally sensitive, comprehensive sex education and reproductive health services.

The impact of youth participation

The impact of this first generation of youth activism has been significant. Substantively, I believe we have helped reshape thinking about adolescent sexuality from a largely negative framing that focused on the victimization of young women to a far more positive understanding of the rights of young people to healthy and safe sexual expression, and of the need for an enabling environment to help realize those rights. Religious and other cultural institutions had, of course, long stigmatized adolescent sexuality—or any sexuality outside of marriage, for that matter—and had driven it underground. We helped bring about long overdue changes in the willingness of governments and secular civil society institutions to challenge those views. Sadly, however, it may have also required an international health epidemic to accomplish this goal. HIV/AIDS and an explosion of other sexually transmitted diseases galvanized a concerted public policy response to educate and protect adolescents.

Youth movements have also reshaped the institutional dynamics and internal governance structures of many organizations in our field, including the International Planned Parenthood Federation (IPPF), an umbrella organization for many national family planning movements, in whose Western Hemisphere Region office I now work. In 2001, IPPF's Governing Council approved a resolution that strongly urged its member associations to incorporate young people under the age of 25 into their governing structures. IPPF has since included youth participation as one of its standards in accrediting member associations, and all national Planned Parenthood affiliates now include young people on their boards.

Sexual and reproductive health and rights for adolescents remain highly contested, of course, but also a matter of great interest from international agencies, governments, donors and civil society. I participated in the 45th session of the UN's Commission on Population and Development (CPD) in 2012, which focused its deliberation on youth and adolescents. Young people from all over the world gathered in large numbers, and as a former youth activist, I was reassured by how much the movement had grown over the years.

Youth leaders knew their own minds and were willing to take risks not always well received by some of the more experienced activists, but in the end, the results spoke for themselves. The CPD 45th outcome document represents another landmark in its explicit recognition of the right of young people to decide on all matters related to their sexuality. The resolution extends beyond lofty abstract commitment and establishes an international norm for state provision of comprehensive sexuality education and for universal access of adolescents to sexual and reproductive health services, including safe abortion where legal—services that respect confidentiality and do not discriminate. The gains at CPD 2012 were relevant not only to young people but to the larger women's rights agenda in general.

ICPD beyond 2014

We have witnessed growing interest in creating new norms and expanding services to realize the sexual and reproductive health and rights of young people, but as with other promises made since Cairo, we are falling short on implementation. Twenty years later, adolescents and young people in many developed and developing countries still regularly encounter age-based discrimination and barriers to services that leave them in a situation of great vulnerability. Recognizing the enormity of the challenge, the UN extended its 20-year review of Cairo across sectors, involving not only its population and health agencies and constituencies, but also its regional economic commissions.

As a representative of the Western Hemisphere Region of IPPF, I recently had an opportunity to participate in the Economic Commission of Latin America and the Caribbean (ECLAC) conference, which concluded with the adoption of one of the strongest UN documents ever adopted on issues of sexuality and reproduction, now known as the Montevideo Consensus. It is significant for several reasons.

First, although widely used elsewhere, the now standard phrase "sexual and reproductive health and rights" was never incorporated in a consensus UN intergovernmental document until Montevideo. Earlier documents employed language that addresses sexual and reproductive health but explicitly limits the concept of rights to reproduction, where protection from coercion must be guaranteed. Montevideo goes beyond the characterization of "sexual and reproductive health and reproductive rights" established in Cairo in 1994 and is clearly another landmark achievement, especially as this breakthrough has also since been achieved regionally elsewhere in the UN system—with the exception of the Economic and Social Commission of West Asia (ESCWA), where some conservative governments are still opposed.

The Montevideo Consensus recognizes "sexual rights" and "reproductive rights" and also adopts a definition of sexual rights that goes beyond their characterization in Paragraph 96 of the Beijing Platform for Action, by embracing the right of all individuals (not just women) to fully realized and safe sexuality, including the right to make free, informed, and responsible decisions on sexual orientation and gender identity.[2] These advances overcome longtime resistance on these matters. Moreover, at the Economic and Social Commission for Asia and the Pacific (ESCAP), UN member states expressed "grave concern at acts of violence and discrimination committed against individuals on the grounds of their sexual orientation and gender identity," and called attention to the profound impact that law has on consensual adult sexual behaviors and relationships.

All of the regional outcome documents in this process also call on governments to provide quality, youth-friendly sexual and reproductive services and information to adolescents. The strength of this language is remarkable given the continued opposition from some governments in the Middle East and Africa, heavily influenced by conservative Islamist and Catholic religious beliefs. Even so, the West Asian (ESCWA) agreement calls upon governments to ensure that young people can access "high quality affordable, youth-friendly health services including age appropriate sexual and reproductive health services and information, taking into account privacy and confidentiality and free from all forms of discrimination and stigma."[3] And its counterpart elsewhere on the continent, the Economic Commission of Africa (ECA), commits "governments to achieving universal access to sexual and reproductive health services, free from all forms of discrimination by providing an essential package of comprehensive sexual and reproductive health services for women and men, with particular attention to the needs of adolescents, youth, and other marginalized populations".[4]

Although "comprehensive sexuality education" is endorsed by the UN operating agencies UNFPA and UNESCO as appropriate language, only a more vague reference to "education on human sexuality" has been made in UN intergovernmental agreements until now. Again, at all of the regional meetings, except West Asian (ESCWA), member states recognized the need for "comprehensive sexuality education programs," which again represents a significant advancement from existing language. The most progressive language comes from Latin America and the Caribbean (ECLAC), which urges governments to ensure the effective implementation of comprehensive sexuality education programs that "are age-appropriate, gender sensitive, evidence and rights-based, and promote values of respect for human rights, tolerance, gender equality and non-violence".[5] Meanwhile, the ECA commit governments to adopt and implement "comprehensive sexuality education programs," in and out of school, which are directly linked to sexual and reproductive health services and include the active involvement of parents, community, traditional, religious and opinion leaders, and young people themselves.[6]

The regional agreements also call for access to safe abortion but limit the reach of this norm by adding the significant caveat "only where permitted by law". While this is not a new advancement, it also signifies that there has been no regress on abortion rights either, despite major lobbying efforts by the churches and by anti-choice civil society organizations. Indeed, the regional agreements out of Latin America and the Caribbean (ECLAC), Asia and the Pacific (ESCAP), and Europe (ECE) add new language encouraging governments to review and repeal laws that punish women and girls who have undergone illegal abortions. The subsequent UN Commission on Population and Development session in New York, which considered ICPD beyond 2014, could not reach a unanimous agreement by all member states on all of these commitments. However, in an unusual development, the final resolution of the session does take note of the outcome documents of the regional conferences and encourages countries to recognize region-specific guidance as the basis of their national population and development programs.[7]

Conclusion

Over the past 20 years, dedicated international movements of women and youth have helped to secure a global and national understanding that sustainable development is not just a matter of putting the right economic programs in place. It also requires the participation of women and girls who can help grow economies and reverse the chronic drag on stability and prosperity that comes from neglecting their productive potential. This commitment to gender equity in turn requires a positive state commitment to sexual and reproductive health and rights, which are essential to women's empowerment. And it requires continued recognition that sexuality and its attendant risks begin in adolescence, which means that education and services must extend to the young.

Many of these issues are being recognized as key components in ongoing negotiations leading to the adoption of the UN's Post-2015 Sustainable Development Agenda. But rigorous advocacy from young people must continue to assure no backsliding. As a former youth activist, who has long ago aged out of the movement, I am also well aware of the need to keep replenishing the ranks. We need to find better ways to share our experience and knowledge with younger generations, as they emerge, ensuring room for dialogue and disagreement based on the principles of respect and solidarity.

Notes

1 The author gratefully acknowledges Ellen Chesler's editorial assistance.
2 *Montevideo Consensus on Population and Development* (Economic Commission on Latin America and the Caribbean (ECLAC) document PLE-1/EN), 12–15 August 2013, para. 34.

3 Economic and Social Commission for West Asia (ESCWA), *Cairo Declaration: Development Challenges and Population Dynamics in a Changing Arab World*, 24–26 June 2013, para. 49.

4 *Addis Ababa Declaration on Population and Development in Africa beyond 2014* (Economic Commission for Africa (ECA) document ECA/ICPD/MIN/2013/4), 2013, para. 34.

5 *Montevideo Consensus on Population and Development* (Economic Commission on Latin America and the Caribbean (ECLAC) document PLE-1/EN), 12–15 August 2013, para. 11.

6 *Addis Ababa Declaration on Population and Development in Africa beyond 2014* (Economic Commission for Africa (ECA) document ECA/ICPD/MIN/2013/4), 2013, para. 40.

7 Commission on Population and Development Resolution 2014/1, 12 April 2014, para. 17.

7 The evolution of ideas:

A feminist's reflections on the partnership with the UN system[1]

Devaki Jain

In its early years the United Nations struggled valiantly to craft workable international covenants to protect nations and peoples from wars and injustices. It also served as a marketplace for the exchange of knowledge and the building up of transformative ideas, and as such became a critical space for women to form collectives and build strength outside of the state. In collaboration with women's movements, the UN enabled several international covenants to protect and advance women's rights and nurtured various feminist networks organized geographically or around specific subjective identities. These entities have since acted as important voices for change on the global stage and within states and other power clubs.

But with the advent of globalization in recent years and the growing power of the private sector, including international capital and multinational corporations, governments and multilaterals like the UN have increasingly been pushed aside and have lost their power to negotiate justice. In the troubling conditions of the world around us today, the UN's mandates are not working, whether in the context of regional conflicts, or economic crises or even the fulfillment of its own goals, as in the case of the Millennium Development Goals (MDGs). I am especially disheartened by the lack of change in the condition of women and girls in our countries. Yes, there is more awareness of gender and many commitments to rights and equality in high places, but as I will demonstrate, the ground remains largely still.

The UN's role as an effective designer and monitor of development has receded and, therefore, these brief reflections argue that the institution should return to its original role as a marketplace for ideas. It should dismantle its unwieldy development bureaucracy—or, at least, that aspect focused on women—and provide a space for us to rethink basic assumptions, strategies, and goals instead.

I am, of course, aware of and understand the value of the UN in certain spaces, such as the Security Council, however powerless it may also sometimes be. And I applaud its humanitarian limbs. However, on questions of economic and social development, the institutional need to build consensus among so many disparate and often conflicting constituencies no longer well serves the best interests of any one of them. For women, especially, I argue that regional or national affiliations may be more productive. The UN as a whole is just not as effective as it used to be.

Further, I suggest that there is a faultline in the content of the feminist movement where the main headlined argument is for gender equality. As feminists have long maintained,[2] understandings of, and responses to, gender inequality must be situated in the context of other forms of inequality. Efforts to advance women's status should not be divorced from those promoting a more equal world for all. It is not enough to call for the participation of women in existing patterns of market-based production or for gender mainstreaming within existing configurations of institutional power. It is these paradigms—the forms of production, the institutions themselves—that need to be questioned and transformed through social mobilization around new ways of thinking about political economy.

We must begin by redefining and re-evaluating all the terms we use to assess progress, such as GDP or MDG, or even "gender equality" itself. In the old days, we used to argue in these picturesque ways, do we want to eat a part of a poisoned cake? Do we want to swim in a polluted river? Do we want equality within the confines of existing political and economic spaces?

Experience can have value in planning for the future, but it can also be a dampener. I have walked alongside the UN system for 40 years and have also written a history of its efforts on behalf of women. I have been part of many feminist networks and of more expert groups and panels of eminent persons than I can count. But I am, in the end, wondering what all this effort has wrought.

Understanding the politics of place and the difference in "vibrations" North and South

The UN came of age from the 1940s through the 1960s in heady times, especially for former colonies. Emancipation and liberation were the guiding words of the moment. And out of the struggles for freedom and for affirmation of political rights in so many countries of the Global South, many prominent women leaders emerged.

Hansa Mehta (1897–1995), a freedom fighter who was part of Gandhi's famous QUIT INDIA movement, is a good example. As retold by Kamala Devi, here is a description of Mehta's courage in defying British rule:

> The congress decided to hold a mammoth procession ... As all activities had come to be banned at the time, every move had to be in defiance of the law ... very quietly without a murmur, the processionist, Hansa Mehta, sat down on the road. All traffic on the main road of this vast metropolis was stopped ... New history was made that night on a weary road under the dark purple canopy of the heavens. In the early hours of the morning the spell was broken, the siege was raised, the police bowed and passed out. The procession rose and moved on to meet a new dawn, a new life, as silent in its victory as in its adversity.

Later, Hansa Mehta represented India on the UN Commission on the Status of Women and as a delegate to the UN Human Rights Commission where she was responsible for changing the language of the Universal Declaration of Human Rights (1948). The draft formulation of its first article, proposed by Mrs. Eleanor Roosevelt stated that "all men are created equal." Ms Mehta protested this gender opaque language, insisting "that would never do"—that "all men" might be interpreted to exclude women.

My book *Women, Development, and the UN* [3] uncovers many such tensions in intellectual perceptions between North and South in these years, tensions far transcending gender. As the North followed a development trajectory defined by such driving forces as the Keynesian economics exemplified in the Marshall Plan, the South marched along to a different rhythm of state socialism and new experiments in democratic governance. The economic plundering and the effacing of cultural and intellectual identities by the imperial powers were the strong legacies that shaped the history of developing nations like India in these years.

Enabling a global women's movement

Still, as I have said, the UN at this time served as what another volume on its history [4] calls "a marketplace for ideas," a particularly apt description of the role it played for women's movements. Again, I repeat, these were heady times overall and especially for women: the experience of learning from sisters all around the world; the excitement of finding extraordinary similarities of gendered living and identity; the forging of bonds that never broke; arguing, negotiating, merging differences into a collective agenda and recognition of a common claim of power. Women's participation influenced both the politics of the UN and the understanding of development within the institution in these early years.

The institution continued to provide women an especially critical space in the two decades between 1975 and 1995. New national, regional, and global networks emerged from the cluster of conferences the UN sponsored on women, helping to mobilize women's groups and connecting them to private foundations with financial resources, and these networks, in turn, had a palpable impact on the world's broader conversation about development. Some years ago, my colleague Shubha Chacko and I argued:

> Over these decades, women's engagement with the UN's work in development ... has been to challenge the terms of reference, open the door to reveal other contours even of the industrial typology, of the hierarchies in values given to various aspects of social and economic organization, to spaces—the public and private—to the basis of knowledge creation, to the very notions of theory or bounded ideas. Their engagement revealed the variety of inter-pretations and appearances of what can be called difference and the prismatic quality of the concept of equality and its accom-modation by even the basic mandate of the UN, as envisioned in its charter. The dilemmas these concepts pose are summed up as the equal but different debates and also permeate into ideas such as giving of quotas to redress inequality.[5]

Unfortunately, the thinking on women and their engagement with development, as it was perceived in the North, became embedded. The equity principle became enshrined and linked with the utility principle. "Women in Development" became the Decade of Women's overnight catchphrase, a seductive one, which for a time at least, could evade the question of what kind of development women were to be drawn into.[6] And equally important, what is the development that women design?[7]

At the second UN world conference of women, in Copenhagen in 1980, women also began to see the "differences" that characterized the North and the South. In non-official spaces women from the South expressed their discomfort with the patronage of their Northern sisters, expressed in the latter's research, analyses, and conclusions regarding them.

But where do we find ourselves today?

All this effort aside, I am sorry to report that reports on the progress of women in recent years, including those prepared by the UN itself, make disappointing reading. I offer just a few highlights.

- Women continue to be absent from key decision-making forums, which further perpetuates gender inequality. Constraints faced by women include their disproportionate concentration in vulnerable forms of work, occupational segregation, wage gaps, and the unequal division of unpaid domestic work. Women are more likely to be unemployed than men. They dominate the unprotected informal sector, are more likely than men to be in part-time formal employment in most high-income regions, spend more time than men in unpaid care-work globally, have lower levels of productivity and earn less than men for work of equal value, and are poorly represented in public and corporate economic decision-making.[8]
- Women in many parts of the world continue to face discrimination in access to land, housing, property, and other productive resources, and have limited access to technologies and services that could alleviate their work burdens. Unequal access to resources limits women's capacity to ensure agricultural productivity, security of livelihoods, and food security, and is increasingly linked to poverty, migration, urbanization and increased risk of violence.[9] Existing statutory and customary laws still restrict women's access to land and other types of property in most countries in Africa and about half the countries in Asia.[10]
- Despite gains in gender parity in education, women account for two-thirds of the world's 774 million adult illiterates—a proportion unchanged over the past two decades. Gender disparities in adult literacy rates remain wide in most regions of the world.
- Although rates of women exposed to violence vary from one region to the other, statistics indicate that violence against women is a universal phenomenon, and women are subjected to different forms of violence—physical, sexual, psychological, and economic— both within and outside their homes.[11]
- Time use studies in 30 developed and developing countries show that despite women's increasing labor force participation, they devote more time than men to housework and childcare, with differences ranging from about 50 percent more in Cambodia and Sweden to about three times more in Italy and six times more in Iraq. But in no country do women spend as much time as men in

market work.[12] ILO evidence from 83 developed and developing countries shows that women earn between 10 and 30 percent less than men.

Thus, a quick scan of the progress of women in almost all indicators shows little or no change over the last 40 years, especially in the condition, entitlements, and capabilities of women.[13] Papers written by economic statisticians, as well feminist groups reveal that although on certain fronts like education there has been some improvement, others, like work, violence, and survival, leave a lot to be desired.

How did we lose our way?

Let me suggest two major structural problems with the UN that may account for the lack of results—for why, as I have said, the ground is still.

First, over the course of time—in attempting to fulfill its multiple roles as development activist, human rights champion, and negotiator of peace and security—the UN has converted itself into an unwieldy bureaucracy intent on developing goals and frameworks for member countries to adhere to and on monitoring their implementation. By its very nature as a multi-lateral institution, the UN must incorporate the many differences in viewpoints of its member states into this process. Building coherence out of so many differences has wound up having a negative impact on larger goals of peace and justice, to which women's movements are also dedicated.

I would argue that since 1995, the UN's need to build consensus and its reliance on private/public partnerships has actually impeded the progress of feminist efforts and thinking. The UN fosters private investment, but there is often a lack of transparency and accountability of such investment, and it is impossible to have consensus around women's and girls' rights with conservative member states in the mix. Therefore, the time has come for the international feminist movement to reconsider its desire to be involved in the post-2015 UN agenda.[14] In my view, it would be more useful to put our energy elsewhere.

Second, the rights framework, incorporating the UDHR and CEDAW, has been a strong component and enabling tool for uprisings and demands by subordinated or excluded groups, and especially valued by women. The language of rights cannot be questioned for its power and relevance in the fight for justice. It gives access to the legal system, to courts and laws, and that is, in fact, the only and best protection for citizens, especially those who are discriminated against and who are unjustly treated. However, much as I appreciate the value of these tools to promote civil justice and equality, I say again that more advanced and just economic frameworks are a necessary condition for rights to be an effective enabling tool.

Those civil rights that do not require financial outlay or economic change to advance a more society—rights to vote[15] or to expose corruption and other violations, for example, may be working. But social and economic rights, like the right to education,[16] which require vast outlays of state resources for schools and teachers and supplies,[17] or the right to food, which also necessitates public investment, have been reduced to rhetoric. This is precisely what has happened to so much of the women's rights agenda. It has foundered for lack of resources to back it up.

Linking the ebb of the UN to globalization and inequality

Since the 1990s, moreover, a new ogre has arrived in the form of the neo-liberal economic program. Many countries that have accepted the terms of economic restructuring and so-called "advancement" put forth by international financial institutions now find their societies crippled by deep inequalities and the loss of basic livelihoods. Fact-focused arguments are appearing from a whole range of places, UN-led as well as elsewhere,[18] showing that a dramatic increase in national and international inequality of wealth and income has occurred and is responsible for the economic convulsions that began in 2008 and are still shaking the world.

A review of current academic books, papers, and reports from the major economic institutions offers significant lessons for necessary course corrections to prevailing theories of growth and macroeconomic policies. Thomas Piketty's book, *Capital in the Twenty-First Century* [19] has been a powerful addition to these arguments. His basic reasoning is that capital-led modes of engineering economic growth have neglected the other crucial factor of production—labor. He also points out that as developing countries become industrialized, inequalities grow worse, not better. In the developed capitalist world, he warns that "the prospect of slower economic growth in the years ahead, combined with the political domination of the super-rich in our political systems, threatens to make these extreme inequalities even more grotesque."[20]

The contribution of the UN's own International Labour Organization's (ILO)[21] to these domains is most pertinent. Unintentionally, it links to Piketty in arguing: "It is time to reconsider the validity of these pro-capital distributional policies and to examine the possibility of an alternative path, one based on pro-labour distributional policies, accompanied by legislative changes and structural policies."[22] The ILO puts forth a case for wage-led growth, a platform which I believe needs to be moved forward by the feminist movements of the North and South. It resonates to what feminists have been arguing for over many years. We need livelihoods secured by social protection.

Other reports from non-governmental organizations, such as "Working for the Few: Political Capture and Economic Inequality" by Oxfam,[23] argue that such deep inequalities place a very few elites in control, and will as a result lead to policies that naturally support their narrow interests. Feminists[24] had flagged these links between poverty and inequality earlier, but until the big agencies made this construct and Piketty blew the whistle, this was not always noted.

Finding our way again

The Indian economic landscape and many of the other economies of the South offer fertile soil for reversing the current reform process and putting on the ground broad-based growth that does not exacerbate inequality. The Indian economy, despite the prominence given to the corporate sector in public policy, is still tethered in a deeply embedded landscape of small agriculture and entrepreneurship.[25]

Also, there is now a "rising" up of the nations of the South. Groups such as G-77[26] are talking about separating themselves from the UN and defining their own futures. At the recently held African summit in Washington, DC, moreover, Paul Kagame, Uhurru Kenyata, and Yoweri Museveni[27] presidents of Rwanda, Kenya, and Uganda, said:

> While conflict and poverty remain serious problems in many African regions, our continent is not only more stable than ever before; it is also experiencing some of the highest economic growth rates anywhere on the planet. Over the past decade, tens of millions of people across Africa have joined the middle class; our cities are expanding rapidly; and our population is the most youthful in the world.

These countries now request a more "normal" relationship with the US, focused on reciprocity in relationships between business sectors rather than on what Americans can do for them through foreign aid. BRICS—the new economic club made up of Brazil, Russia, India, and China also—"are telling a different tale: one of agency and power,"[28] says an article in *TIME Magazine* from 2011. In 2013 the BRICS countries formed the New Development Bank as an alternative to the existing US-dominated World Bank and International Monetary Fund

(IMF) to foster greater financial and development cooperation among their emerging markets.[29] With $50 billion in initial capital, the bank will primarily finance infrastructure and "sustainable development" projects in the BRICS countries, but other low- and middle-income countries will be able to buy in and apply for funding.[30]

The potential of renewed feminist vitality through regional or transnational networks

I have acknowledged that a large number of regional and international women's networks have emerged in recent years on a multitude of issues ranging from trafficking and legal protections to globally connected trade unions according to occupation. Some of these efforts indeed came directly out of UN gatherings, whereas others were created only as a result of local or regional mobilization.[31] Moving forward I would argue that putting more effort close to home makes more sense.

Women in Informal Employment: Globalizing and Organizing (WIEGO) is an example of a network that grew out of regional mobilization rather than being UN-led, and is now a worldwide coalition of institutions and individuals concerned with improving the status of women in the economy's informal sector, including a branch for home-based workers in South Asia and a waste pickers' network in Latin America and the Caribbean. There are also many other instances of women taking control of resources and managing economic entities in developing countries. A key example in India is the Self Employed Women's Association (SEWA),[32] a trade union of self-employed and home-based workers that owns a bank and provides health insurance and retirement benefits to working women in rural India.

Development Alternatives with Women for a New Era (DAWN), founded in 1984, is a feminist network of women, researchers, and activists from the Global South. The intervention by DAWN into the discourse on women and development not only transformed its intellectual underpinnings but also shifted the creativity and the intellectual leadership from the "patrons" in the North to the "clients" in the South.

Another network called the Casablanca Dreamers, founded in 2006, composed of leaders from UN agencies as well as feminist scholars, authors, and activists from across the world, critiqued the development framework used by the UN, including the goal of gender equality, and came up with a new message—*Getting the Fundamentals Right: Women, Water and Wealth.* These networks support and reinforce each other and provide a formidable defense against powerful agencies. There is increasing regional networking as it is less fund-demanding and also emphasizes the common bonds of geography. Inter-regional networking and advocacy may be more effective than global resolutions. For example, in 2010 a campaign by the WIEGO and Homenet, a group in Thailand, resulted in the ratification of the Homeworkers' Protection Act.[33]

An idea for the future: transacting feminist knowledge with the other

Amartya Sen, who has given feminists so much potent language about agency,[34] brings forth another powerful concept in his extraordinary book, *Identity and Violence.* "Open-minded engagement in public reasoning is quite central to the pursuit of justice," Sen writes. His deviation from the old discourse of participatory decision-making is his use of the term "reasoning." Reasoning leads to the mind, and to Sen the mind is the most important element for establishing and affirming human agency. All of Sen's contributions to vocabulary are embedded in his basic belief that argument, reasoning, and the application of thought are critical in building a just world. Another shift he makes— although in this case not a linguistic or even a hierarchical one, but one of focus—is to use injustice as the fulcrum of his argument, and not justice. Eliminating injustice should take precedence to striving for that perfect goal of justice. He argues that there is so much tangible injustice around us and that focusing on reducing it is itself just.

Taking off from Sen, I would suggest that this is the time for the feminist movement to build on the many ideas born out of our lived experience—our many action-oriented illustrations of engineering change, our work on knowledge, and on our own experience-driven reasoning.

Feminist theorists have given us valuable descriptions of how this should work. Helen Longino has this to say: "The problems of knowledge are central to feminist theorizing, which has sought to destabilize andocentric, mainstream thinking in the humanities and in the social and natural sciences."[35] Christine Sylvester suggests: "The feminist agenda raises questions on what constitutes knowledge and how the disciplinary divisions are created. This questioning creates a politics of disturbance." It unsettles the given and starts to "plough up inherited turfs without planting the same old seeds in the field."[36]

In *Harvesting Feminist Knowledge for Public Policy: Rebuilding Progress,*[37] a book published by the Casablanca Dreamers, we argue that combating poverty can itself be an engine of growth. This growth is driven by empowering women at the poorest level by guaranteeing employment, in turn powering production and moving the economy in a broad-based, socially equitable direction. We ask for economic democracy and social and economic transformation that "bubbles up" rather than "trickles down." The book points out that we feminists have "ghettoed" ourselves and that feminist knowledge has not been able to cross the barriers into mainstream economic thought. How then can we better transform feminist knowledge into feminist policy?

After almost four decades of research related to public policy and feminist movements in India and around the world[38]—including many forays with the UN—I agree with this assessment. Our knowledge of lived experience, as well as our research, has not crossed barriers into the mainstream. I have also come to the view that we have spent too much time emphasizing demands arising out of our bodily differences—biologically and socially defined. Another faultline, perhaps, has been that our engagement with activism has been so intense and wearying that it has sidelined intellectual work. Women who are true public intellectuals must be more visible and influential.

Conclusion

Seen with the perspective of many years, I cannot help feeling that the UN system needs a very revolutionary overhaul. The roles it is now able to play do not justify the kind of high levels of expenditure that the structure and its employees absorb. It needs a thinning down to reflect contraction elsewhere in the economy. A sharpening and a selective re-assembling are crucial.

The feminist movement should convince the UN to take up the challenge of the overall increase in inequalities—not limit ourselves to gender equality—and we should take note of the "rising" in the South and of new ideas of wage-led growth, instead of only batting for gender equality. This could be a great leap forward. We need new macro-economic theories built and transacted by women. Mild modifications will not suffice—as Joseph Stiglitz says in his latest paper, the financial meltdown after September 2008 was not just a crisis for economic policy, but also for economic theory.[39]

I end by emphasizing that our struggle and our fact-based arguments should be directed towards reconstructing growth theories and developing broad-based growth measures. The UN could return to its valuable role as a marketplace for ideas and as a builder of the strength of social and economic movements against injustice and move away from attempting to put together development agendas and frameworks to monitor countries' progress. Then indeed women and girls—all of us together—will rise.

As the feminist theorist, Amina Mama, has said: "We women are in no position to deprive ourselves of the intellectual tools that can assist us in pursuit of gender justice. The arena of the intellect has been used to suppress us. We cannot afford to ignore the importance of intellectual work, especially in the 21st century when knowledge and information define power more than ever before."[40]

Notes

1 The author gratefully acknowledges the research assistance of Divya Alexander and Smriti Sharma and the editorial support of Ellen Chesler and Terry McGovern.
2 Sakiki Fukuda-Parr, James Heinz, and Stephanie Seguino, "Critical Perspectives on Financial and Economic Crises: Heterodox Macroeconomics Meets Feminist Economics," *Feminist Economics* 19, no. 13 (2013).
3 Devaki Jain, *Women, Development, and the UN* (Bloomington and Indianapolis: Indiana University Press, 2005).
4 Louis Emmerij, Richard Jolly, and Thomas Weiss, *Ahead of the Curve: UN Ideas and Global Challenges*, first edn (Bloomington: Indiana University Press, 2001), 10.
5 Devaki Jain and Shuba Chacko, "Unfolding Women's Engagement with Development and the UN: Pointers for the Future," *Forum for Development Studies* 35, no. 1 (June 2008): 5–36.
6 Lucille Mathirun Mair, "International Women's Decade: A Balance Sheet," Third J.P. Memorial Lecture, Centre for Development and Women's Studies, New Delhi, 15 December 1984.
7 Devaki Jain, *Women, Development, and the UN: A Sixty-Year Quest for Equality and Justice* (Bloomington: Indiana University Press: 2005).
8 UN Women and ILO, "Decent Work and Women's Economic Empowerment: Good Policy and Practice," 2012, www.ilo.org/wcmsp5/groups/public/—ed_emp/—emp_ent/—ifp_seed/documents/genericdocument/wcms_184878.pdf.
9 Department of Economic and Social Affairs, Division for the Advancement of Women, "2009 World Survey on the Role of Women in Development: Women's Control over Economic Resources and Access to Financial Resources, including Microfinance," United Nations, 2009.
10 United Nations Statistics Division, "The World's Women 2010: Trends and Statistics," 2010.
11 United Nations Statistics Division, "The World's Women 2010: Trends and Statistics," 2010.
12 UN Women and ILO, "Decent Work and Women's Economic Empowerment: Good Policy and Practice," 2012, www.ilo.org/wcmsp5/groups/public/—ed_emp/—emp_ent/—ifp_seed/documents/genericdocument/wcms_184878.pdf.
13 Devaki Jain and C.P. Sujaya, eds, *Indian Women Revisited* (New Delhi, India: Publications Division, Government of India, 2014).
14 UNDP, *Post-2015 Development Agenda*, www.undp.org/content/undp/en/home/mdgoverview/mdg_goals/post-2015-development-agenda/.

15 Aruna Roy, "Time to Move Ahead of RTI," *The New Indian Express*, 10 November 2013, www.newindianexpress.com/states/odisha/Time-to-move-ahead-of-RTI-Aruna-Roy/2013/11/10/article1882625.ece.

16 Vimala Ramachandran, "Gendered Inequality and Education—Advocacy Brief," UNESCO Bangkok Asia-Pacific Programme of Education for All, 2010, http://unesdoc.unesco.org/images/0018/001898/189825e.pdf.

17 Vimala Ramachandran, "Right to Education Act: A Comment," *Economic and Political Weekly*, 11 July 2009.

18 UNDP, "Humanity Divided: Confronting Inequality in Developing Countries," 2013; Department of Economic and Social Affairs, "Inequality Matters: Report of the World Social Situation 2013," United Nations, 2013; "The Reshaping of the World: Consequences for Society, Politics and Business," World Economic Forum Annual Meeting 2014, Davos, Switzerland; ILO, "Wage–led Growth: An Equitable Strategy for Economic Recovery," 2013; Oxfam, "Working for the Few: Political Capture and Economic Inequality" Oxfam Briefing Paper 178, 2014; World Bank, "Inequality in Focus," www.worldbank.org/en/topic/isp/publication/inequality-in-focus.

19 Thomas Piketty, *Capital in the Twenty-First Century* (Cambridge, Mass.: Harvard University Press, 2014).

20 John Palmer, "Book Review: Capital in the Twenty-First Century by Thomas Piketty," *Red Pepper*, April 2014, www.redpepper.org.uk/book-review-capital-in-the-twenty-first-century-by-thomas-piketty/.

21 ILO, 2014, http://www.ilo.org/global/lang–en/index.htm.

22 Mark Lavoie and Engel Stockhammer, "Wage-led Growth: Concepts, Theories and Policies" ILO, 2013, www.ilo.org/wcmsp5/groups/public/—ed_protect/—protrav/—travail/documents/publication/wcms_192507.pdf.

23 Ricardo Fuentes-Nieva and Nicholas Galasso, *Working for the Few: Political Capture and Economic Inequality*, Oxfam International, 20 January 2014, www.oxfam.org/en/research/working-few.

24 Devaki Jain, "Growth, Poverty and Inequality: the Linkages and Relevance of Macroeconomic Policies," UNDP Gender Equality, Economic Growth and Poverty Reduction Expert Group Meeting, Essex University, UK, 21–22 June 2007; Devaki Jain, "This Thing Called 'Poverty,'" Presented at UNDP, New York, 20 May 1997.

25 Devaki Jain, and Deepshikha Batheja, "Using Inequality to Engineer Growth," *LiveMint*, 13 June 2014, www.livemint.com/Opinion/HC2XT2gQSdtck73VsP6e7H/Using-inequality-to-engineer-growth.html.

26 "Algiers Ministerial Conference of the Non-Aligned Movement (NAM) Reviews Existing, New and Emerging Challenges to the Developing World" *South South News*, 16 June 2014.

27 "The Dream of An African Century," *LiveMint*, 8 August 2014.

28 Sylvia Ann Hewlett, "Is a Woman in Brazil Better Off than a Woman in the U.S.?," *TIME*, 24 October 2011, http://ideas.time.com/2011/10/24/is-a-woman-in-brazil-better-off-than-a-woman-in-the-u-s/.

29 "The BRICS Bank: An Acronym with Capital," *The Economist*, 19 July 2014, www.economist.com/news/finance-and-economics/21607851-setting-up-rivals-imf-and-world-bank-easier-running-them-acronym.

30 Raj M. Desai and James Raymond Vreeland, "What the New Bank of BRICS is All About," *The Washington Post*, 17 July 2014, www.washingtonpost.com/blogs/monkey-cage/wp/2014/07/17/what-the-new-bank-of-brics-is-all-about/.

31 Peggy Antrobus, "*DAWN, the Third World Feminist Network: Upturning Hierarchies,*" Oxford Handbooks, April 2014.

32 Self Employed Women's Association, www.sewa.org/.

33 The Homeworkers' Protection Act in Thailand provides for protection of wages, occupational health and safety, and the responsibility of employers towards homeworkers. This legislation impacts about two million workers in Thailand. See Home Workers Protection Act, B.E.2553 (2010).

34 Amartya Sen, *Identity and Violence: The Illusion of Destiny* (New Delhi, India: Penguin Group, 2007).

35 Helen E. Longino, "Feminist Standpoint Theory and the Problems of Knowledge," *Signs* 19, no. 1 (Autumn 1993): 201–212.

36 William Connolly, "Democracy and Territory" in *Reimagining the Nation*, ed. Marjorie Ringrose and Adam J. Lerner (Buckingham: Open University Press, 1993), 61.

37 Diane Elson, and Devaki Jain, eds, *Harvesting Feminist Knowledge for Public Policy: Rebuilding Progress* (New Delhi, India and Ottowa, Ontario: SAGE Publications India Pvt Ltd and International Development Research Center, 2011).

38 "Women's Participation in the History of Ideas: The Importance of Reconstructing Knowledge," paper presented at the National Institute for Advanced Studies, Bangalore, India 6 February 2004; Devaki Jain "Feminism and Feminist Expression: A Dialogue" in *Culture and the Making of Identity in Contemporary India*, eds Kamala Ganesh and Usha Thakkar (New Delhi, India: SAGE Publications India Pvt Ltd, 2005), 184; Devaki Jain, ed., *Indian Women* (New Delhi, India: Publications Division of Ministry of Information, 1975).

39 Geroge Akerlof, Oliver J. Blanchard, David Romer, and Joseph E. Stiglitz, eds, *What Have We Learned? Macroeconomic Policy After the Crisis* (Washington, DC and Cambridge, Mass.: IMF and MIT: 2014).

40 "Talking About Feminism in Africa," *Women's World*, www.wworld.org/programs/regions/africa/amina_mama.htm.

Part II
Realizing rights at the national and local level

8 Women's human rights and the political arena of Brazil

From dictatorship to democracy

Jacqueline Pitanguy

This chapter considers how women's human rights impacted the political arena of Brazil in different periods of its contemporary history. It highlights the efforts of feminists emerging as political actors in the 1970s, who brought the women's rights agenda into the struggle against the then-ruling dictatorship. It analyzes the role of feminism in making gender equality a central component of the democratization of Brazil in the 1980s. It focuses on the advocacy process developed by women to guarantee their rights in the country's new constitution.

The chapter also considers the participation of women's movements in the United Nations (UN) conferences during the 1990s and the impact these conferences, in turn, had in Brazil, including the reform of discriminatory legislation, the creation of new legislation, and as intellectual and political reinforcement around our advocacy for, and implementation of, improved public policies to benefit women. Finally, it assesses current challenges and achievements in gender equality and references the interconnection between national and global scenarios, with a specific discussion of the paths of two main areas of the feminist agenda: violence and reproductive rights. The roles of cultural values, traditions, religious forces, and the authoritarian or democratic character of the political institutions in place at the time—and their relevance to changing power dynamics over time—is also considered.

Human rights, advocacy, and democracy in Brazil

As advocacy has been, and still is, a main feature of Brazilian feminism, I will first say a few words about it. To develop advocacy work means to be part of a political process in which three elements can be distinguished: the context, the field, and the agenda. These elements are interconnected, and the success of the advocacy depends on their interplay.[1] By "context," I refer to the macro level on which the advocacy takes place—the structural characteristics of the country, including the more-or-less authoritarian or democratic character of its political institutions, its cultural values, and its social and economic policies at the national and international level. By "field," I suggest a dynamic concept, encompassing such actors as social movements, NGOs, churches, unions, the media, governments, academia, the private sector and foundations, among others, who are involved in the advocacy process. These actors may have conflicting or similar views and goals, and their relative weight and influence in the scale of power differs. By "agenda," I mean to uncover where goals and strategies are concretely defined and then subjected to constant review, to respond to fluctuating elements of the context and/or the field.

An advocacy process from civil society organizations usually aims to denounce public or private initiatives seen as harmful or discriminatory, to propose new legislation or policies, and to monitor their implementation. Different skills and strategies are required at different stages. The success of the advocacy effort depends largely on the capacity to build alliances and coalitions and to define clear parameters of what is and what is not negotiable in terms of substance and tactics. Gaining the support of key, influential sectors and individuals, even if they are not directly involved, is critical. It is also important to reach the hearts and minds of the population at large, and to address international spheres of influence.

The process of advocacy is always dynamic and requires flexibility to adjust to new circumstances that may present unexpected opportunities or obstacles. The development of an advocacy campaign plan usually involves conflicts of vision and interests, leading to the struggles, negotiations, and necessary compromises that characterize all meaningful political action.

Because advocacy is a collective process, its success requires leadership with integrity and vision, but also with strong alliance-building skills. Creating a sense of common responsibility is important if the goals achieved are to be sustainable especially after pioneering leaders step down.

The instruments used by advocates obviously vary depending on the degree of visibility appropriate for the cause and the human and financial resources available. Solid research to provide data and analysis of an issue almost always precedes any successful action by providing compelling arguments to use in public campaigns through the media, as well as in direct conversations with allies and with opponents. The use of appropriate language and slogans is critical, especially for news stories and advertising on billboards, television, and radio. In recent years, the Internet has also become a formidable instrument of advocacy, and social media is essential. Public demonstrations may also be important and, today, using digital networks, they are easily and rapidly organized. However, while mass demonstrations may be necessary, they are just one component of a much longer process. In fact, it is only through determined follow-up, interlocution, and negotiation with the institutional channels of power that demands are effectively translated into law and public policy. Finally, it is also important to remember that there is never a linear path towards progress because rights are historical conquests subject to backlash—sometimes even temporary paralysis—before they are fully realized.

We can distinguish two moments in contemporary Brazilian history—the periods of dictatorship and democracy—that have defined the parameters for advocacy work around women's human rights. In both contexts, the feminist movement has been crucial. Under the 21-year dictatorship from 1964 to 1985, including its last years of transition to democracy, feminists emerged as political actors questioning the power relations, inequalities, and hierarchies that define our society. Working in alliance with the social forces that were then struggling against an authoritarian regime, they expanded the democratic agenda to include equal rights for women as a central value. The other relevant period is after the enactment of the 1988 Constitution, in a democratic context, where fundamental women's rights had already been formally assured in legal terms, but growing conservative forces, largely supported by the political power of conservative religions, threatened their implementation and sustainability.

Period of dictatorship

In 1964, when the Cold War between the United States and the Soviet Union inspired growing fear that Communism would overtake Latin America, a military coup overturned Brazil's democratically elected government. For the next 21 years, with varying degrees of violence and coercion, the country lived under a dictatorship characterized by ongoing conflict between the state and civil society. The state suppressed basic civil rights such as habeas corpus, freedom of association, freedom of the press, and free elections. Consequently, civil society mobilized an intense anti-dictatorship movement. Civil society denounced the dictatorship's violations of human rights, including arbitrary imprisonment, torture, and assassination, and found support in international human rights organizations such as Amnesty International. The democratic forces were organized under the slogan: "the people united will never be defeated," and there was little room to deconstruct the concept of "people" by categories of sex, race, ethnicity, and/or sexual orientation.

But that is precisely what the feminist movement did. By the early 1970s, women were already meeting and pointing out the need to fight for an expansive definition of democracy, which among its central components recognizes women's equality with men and advances women's full citizenship rights as core human rights. From 1975 to 1979, feminism became visible in the public arena, building alliances with other movements and associations, such as lawyers and professional associations, labor unions, and universities that created the first academic initiatives on women's studies. The feminist agenda included fighting domestic violence, ending discriminatory legislation (with an emphasis on family law), demanding equal pay in the labor market, and claiming such social benefits as reproductive health and rights, including the right to abortion. These issues were disseminated by an ambivalent, often skeptical media, which gave visibility to some demands but also exhibited considerable prejudice overall.

In this period the first feminist organization in the country, the Center of Brazilian Women, was established. Many informal women's groups also flourished, and an alternative feminist press emerged. Feminism gained visibility despite substantial barriers imposed by the authoritarian regime, including the formal prohibition of freedom of association. The movement also faced resistance from certain sectors working against the dictatorship who argued that our agenda was diverting attention from and weakening the resistance movement. Nonetheless, the feminist movement, with which I was deeply involved in this period, refused to isolate itself from the democratic forces. We would never concede that our agenda ought to be an addenda, only to be considered after the consolidation of the democratic institutions. And this was one of the main reasons for our success. A key strategy was to reach other existing organizations. We brought the issues of equal rights in the family and in the labor market—of social benefits for rural women and domestic workers, of ending impunity to domestic violence perpetrators, of reproductive rights—to labor unions, professional associations, neighborhood associations, political parties, reaching a large number of women who, even if not defining themselves as feminists, did embrace our agenda.

Democracy

From 1979 to 1985, when the first civilian president was elected and the restoration of civil and political liberties took place, important political events occurred as part of the transitional process: the opposition won legislative elections; the state granted amnesty to those in exile, and they returned home; elections were held for governors; and there were huge public demonstrations demanding the election of a civilian president. These events transformed the authoritarian context, bringing new possibilities, as well as new challenges, for women's advocacy work. Civil society grew more complex as other actors, such as environmentalists and movements for the rights of black and indigenous peoples, also gained greater public visibility. As early as 1979, feminists presented candidates for legislative elections with a platform of demands called Feminist Alert for the Elections. It was the first time the political parties became aware of women as a distinct constituency and understood that we are capable of influencing electoral results.

Important political changes took place in the early 1980s, when the democratic opposition won a significant number of seats in Congress, and reform governors were elected in key states. Feminists understood that, given those contextual changes, it would also be necessary to create government spaces in which public policies addressing our demands could be designed and implemented. We needed to move inside the system. Building consensus within the women's movement about this new agenda was not easy. There was fear that, given the fragility of democracy, the agenda could be co-opted by conservative sectors. There was also resistance to participation in a state that had been dominated by the military for years. After endless meetings and discussions, however, women's movements began to focus on building alliances with other social forces to push for the creation of such spaces.

Gender rights architecture

Our advocacy work led to two important victories: the creation of special police stations to attend to women victims of domestic violence (DEAMs) and of state-level machineries for women. DEAMs were a central demand of the feminist violence against women (VAW) agenda and were urgently needed. The advocacy work involved in achieving these police stations was difficult because the official security apparatus was initially opposed. Research was disseminated by advocates and the media showing how often the security system failed in cases of domestic violence, leading to the death of the victim and impunity for the aggressor. The advent of the stations was the result of a *tour de force* of women's groups working in alliance with lawyers' associations and professionals within the criminal justice system, including women who advanced to important positions there. With the support of women from a broad spectrum of society, we demonstrated the inadequacy of traditional responses by police officials to complaints on domestic violence. The context was also favorable as the police were being held accountable for prior human rights violations of all sorts during the years of dictatorship and were pressed to redeem themselves in the eyes of the public.

There are currently more than 450 DEAMs around the country. The creation of the first one had two immediate effects: it increased attention to victims and had a pedagogical effect on the police system, making clear that domestic violence is a matter of public security and not a private affair. DEAMS are now an organic part of the security system; however, they are still seen as secondary to other policing interventions that deal with perceived "real crime," such as homicides, drugs, robberies, etc., and they require constant support from women's rights activists to be respected and supported fully.

With the election of Brazil's first civilian president in 1985, a federal entity, the National Council for Women's Rights (CNDM), was also created. CNDM has a mandate to promote public policies at the national level and to propose legislation to eliminate discrimination against women and guarantee their equal rights and equal opportunities in all spheres of life. This agency has been crucial in advocating for gender equality within the state.[2]

I headed CNDM for four years, working with activists to advance the feminist agenda from within. CNDM played a key role in assuring women's rights in the new federal constitution enacted in 1988. Our campaign "A Constitution to be worthy has to guarantee women's rights" is considered one of the most successful advocacy processes in the country's history. It resulted in the inclusion in Brazil's "Magna Carta" of the vast majority of our demands on labor, social rights and benefits, social security, family relations, reproductive rights, property rights, and violence.[3]

In 1985, CNDM launched a national campaign during which we visited all 26 states of the country and together with local women's groups raised awareness of the importance of the upcoming election of a new Congress that would be in charge of writing a new constitution and of the need to incorporate women's rights in that essential document. The local movements were encouraged to organize consultative meetings with women's groups and associations and send CNDM their proposals and demands for the new constitution. These suggestions came by the thousands to our offices, via fax, letters, and telegrams, as the Internet was not yet available. They were analyzed first by our own staff, organized according to the various chapters of the constitution that were being debated in Congress and then analyzed by a group of pro bono lawyers and jurists committed to our cause.

CNDM then held a huge conference of representatives from NGOs and women's movements from all over the country, where a condensed version of these inputs was presented. A document called *Letter of Brazilian Women to the Constituents* was approved and delivered to Congress.[4] For the next three years, we made repeated visits to political party leaders. We launched campaigns on TV and with the written press. We held public marches and distributed folders containing our proposals all over the country. Organized as both a key local electoral constituency and as a national movement, advocates for women created massive pressure on parliamentarians to include our demands. Through this process, more than 100 proposed amendments were sent by CNDM to the Constituent Assembly.

It is important to note that the political context at the time was very favorable to our work. Brazil's democratic forces were demanding that the new constitution have a human rights framework as its axis, and that the state be obligated to fulfill and implement that framework. This stood in sharp contrast with the authoritarian matrix of the prior regime.

In this larger human rights context, we were able to build consensus on goals and strategies beyond feminists by working with a number of organizations, such as labor unions, domestic workers associations, lawyers associations, medical doctors and nurses (engaged in bringing the parameters of health as a human right to the new charter), indigenous peoples, black movements, and rural women's organizations, among others. Some actors would only support parts of our agenda. For example, the Catholic Church agreed with our demands for social and labor rights but strongly opposed reproductive rights and abortion. Sectors representing private corporations held the reverse position, endorsing reproductive rights but strongly opposing the enlargement of social benefits, particularly our demand for four months of paid maternity leave and the extension of labor rights and social benefits to rural women and domestic workers. The media, after years of censorship, supported our values of freedom and liberty and moderated their historic antagonism to women's rights. CNDM also worked closely with the newly elected female constituents proposing joint efforts that, in spite of political differences, would allow for support to some, if not all, propositions.

However, it was then, and still remains, clear to women's rights defenders working in both national and international contexts that the agenda of feminism encompasses issues ranked differently in importance and enjoying varying degrees of legitimacy and social acceptance. Some elicit much greater resistance than others, and this necessitates issue-specific advocacy strategies.

I would like to compare two feminist issues—violence against women, and sexual and reproductive rights—and point out how their political trajectories have been markedly different. In Brazil, our advocacy work against VAW has advanced significantly, whereas simultaneously reproductive and sexual rights, particularly abortion, have stalled and are constantly threatened.

In Brazil, violence against women was long part of the platform of women's rights defenders but became a major issue in the1970s, when a number of women were killed by spouses or partners who were then acquitted at trial or received minimal penalties. In their defense, lawyers often argued that the perpetrator had a "legitimate defense of honor," which had been compromised by the victims' behavior, usually through alleged adultery.[5] For the feminist movement, it was clear that when the victim was a woman who had an intimate relationship with the killer, he almost always got away with total impunity. The prevailing cultural patriarchy and devaluation of women, our subordination to men in existing family law and our absence from power positions in politics and in the economic sphere—all were factors in making it possible to condemn the victims of domestic crimes instead of the aggressors.[6]

The advocacy work of feminists around this issue was wide-ranging, from street manifestations and public opinion surveys to academic studies on how the justice system was riddled with inherent discrimination. The 1988 Constitution's recognition of equal rights for men and women in the family—and its claim of state responsibility to prevent and respond to violence within the family—was a landmark.[7] In fact, this constitutional provision represents a paradigmatic shift in the realm of human rights, which had traditionally been narrowly circumscribed to address the relationship between individuals and the state and was expanded to consider the relationship between private individuals within the walls of the home. In 1991, feminists celebrated another important victory when Brazil's Superior Tribunal of Justice rejected the use of the "defense of honor" argument in so-called crimes of passion, stating that male honor inheres in the individual alone and should not be defined by the behavior of others, including his wife who enjoys autonomous rights of her own and cannot be treated by the law as his property.[8]

Recognizing that practical application of law is determined by social inequalities and hierarchical value systems—and that traditional values are slow and difficult to change—advocacy against VAW has been successful in Brazil. In addition to overseeing local services such as special police stations and shelters, the federal governmental entity in charge of women's issues, the "Secretaria de Politicas para as Mulheres" (SPM), is responsible for conceptualizing national strategies to combat VAW. These plans comprise a number of different initiatives, including improved collection of data, the training of security officers, the expansion of services to remote rural areas such as the Amazon, and the regular monitoring and evaluation of existing services. As a result of earlier reviews that found inadequacies in the service model, the "Casa da Mulher," a physical space that brings security and judicial services together for the victims, has recently been introduced as a programmatic innovation.

Since 2006, Brazil has had a special law on VAW, the "Maria da Penha," which addresses domestic violence in a broad sense, including psychological violence. It also stipulates protective measures for the victim and creates special justice courts for domestic violence crimes among others measures (Law 11340/2006). This legislation is the result of the combined advocacy effort of a coalition of NGOs working with progressive parliamentarians and the SPM, which lobbied for the legislation and its approval by the National Congress.[9] The legislation is well known in the country and generally accepted by the population at large. Although there have been several attempts by conservatives to overthrow it with allegations that it favors women and is therefore unconstitutional, Brazil's Supreme Court has steadfastly rejected these arguments. The advances in both law and public policy on VAW are a success story of the advocacy work of feminists in alliance and negotiation with other sectors.

Reproductive and sexual rights have not followed the same pattern. They were also part of the feminist agenda of the1970s and a CNDM programmatic priority during the 1980s. They are recognized rights in the 1988 Constitution, intended to be implemented and regulated by specific family planning legislation passed shortly thereafter. Still, the context for their realization has always been very difficult, the field of allies and partners, complex. Whereas family planning has been incorporated into governmental policies and programs and generally accepted as a legitimate health concern, abortion has been essentially ignored by most of the relevant actors in the field, including doctors and health professionals, lawyers and bar associations, politicians and policymakers, social movements and others with the capacity to influence public opinion. Brazilian feminists, with very few exceptions, have been isolated in the struggle for decriminalization and regulation of access to abortion in a country whose penal code of 1940 still stands and permits pregnancy termination only in cases of rape or risk of death to the mother. The single advance of recent years is a 2012 ruling of the Supreme Court, allowing the interruption of the pregnancy when there is a severe fetal malformation incompatible with life.[10]

The international and national contexts for abortion reform are adverse, with intensifying religious fundamentalism fueling conservative perspectives on sexuality and reproduction. Newly expanding Evangelical churches and the ever-present Catholic Church are playing more and more of a political role in Brazil and impeding the full realization of reproductive rights. Whereas more than 450 police stations attend to victims of domestic violence around the country, only about 60 centers, in a nation of 200 million, provide abortion to victims of rape, and they are under constant attack from religious conservatives. Abortion, an issue that pertains to women only, faces much stronger opposition from conservatives than the sexual rights of gays and lesbians, which have strong advocacy by the LGBT movement. The struggle for abortion rights faces the combined antagonism of religious dogmas and patriarchal values and also suffers because as abortion is a crime, many potential allies remain silent because of fear and shame. Sexual orientation is not a crime, and it is a new agenda, and although prejudice and discrimination exist, the demand that rights accorded to heterosexuals, by law actually be ascribed to them, seems to face less resistance than abortion.

Local challenges in the implementation of global norms

The Universal Declaration of Human Rights (1948) served as a foundational norm for the democratic opposition to dictatorship in Brazil. For feminists, struggling at the same time to bring gender equality within a human rights frame, the UN's First World Conference on Women in Mexico City in 1975, with its declaration of 1975 as the International Year of Women, also had an important impact and gave legitimacy to our movement. In 1975, we organized the first national meeting on women's rights, which is now seen as a landmark in our struggle. The Convention on the Elimination of All Forms of Discrimination Against Women (CEDAW) also served as an important point of reference for us, although limited as in its initial 1979 version, CEDAW did not address domestic and sexual violence. Brazil's constitutional provision obligating the state to intervene to protect women from violence within the family (Article 226 paragraph 8) anticipated later recognition by the 1993 UN Human Rights Conference in Vienna that domestic violence is not just a private matter but a human rights abuse worthy of adjudication. This led to the amendment of CEDAW so that it also encourages state obligation to protect women.

The political role of civil society in the last decades of the twentieth century, in both national and international arenas, constitutes one of the most outstanding characteristics of active citizenship as defined by

Hannah Arendt (1993).[11] Feminism has had a major impact in the political sphere. Women's rights advocates developed national and transnational coalitions that share solidarity and a common identity transcending class, race, cultural, and ethnic diversity. Indeed, the last century is marked by the presence of feminism in the public arena, by its remarkable success in claiming equal rights for women, but also in creating new rights pertaining to domestic violence, sexuality, and reproduction. Women's movements questioned the traditional meaning of citizenship from which hierarchies derived from sex, race, and ethnicity are absent.[12]

Brazilian women's movements participated forcefully at the UN Conferences of the 1990s, particularly the Human Rights Conference of 1993, the International Population and Development Conference (ICPD) of 1994, and the Fourth World Conference on Women in Beijing the following year. For the first time in the history of UN thematic conferences, women from different countries built transnational coalitions, developed consensual agendas and strategies, and became the most influential civil society actors in these forums, the results of which were key to redefining and enlarging women's rights in national scenarios. Beijing was also a major achievement, having incorporated the achievements of the other conferences and expanded on them.[13]

There are distinct synergies between national and international advances in women's rights, but regrettably there are also patterns of backlash. A country will only agree with an international convention or with a UN Plan of Action if doing so does not threaten its own national legislation. On the other hand, advances in global human rights have a direct effect on national scenarios as a formidable advocacy tool for local activists. The tensions between universality and national or cultural sovereignty are always present in this dynamic.

Reproductive rights reflects this tension. During ICPD there was a convergence of Islamists and Catholics in opposition to the inclusion of such rights in a UN document. Reproductive rights are directly linked to autonomy of decision, and in many Islamic countries this autonomy is denied to women. The Vatican, as a member state of the UN voiced its opposition all along the preparatory process for the Conference and in Cairo itself. The Catholic Church also influenced many governments to oppose such rights, particularly in Latin America. Members of OPUS DEI, a very conservative organization within Catholicism, were part of many official Latin American delegations. While traditionally working together with these countries in other UN Forums, Brazil stood apart in ICPD, in compliance with our new constitution.

These synergies in progress and resistance are even stronger today, as the world shrinks with the technological revolution in communication and the massive potential of transportation. In Brazil, the connection between local and global policies was still limited in the1970s, the interconnectivity being more on an intellectual than a practical order. The following decade the UN Second World Conference on Women in Nairobi and its Forward Looking Strategies, recommended the creation of governmental machineries for the improvement of women's conditions, but this did not resonate much in Brazil, where feminists were already involved locally in advocating for such reforms. CEDAW (1979) has always been a main reference for activists and was ratified in 1982 by the Brazilian government with reservation on the provisions around the family, as at that time men were still considered lawful heads of households. After the 1988 constitutional reform, however, this reservation was dropped.

Other examples of synergy are the UN International Conferences of the 1990s. The Vienna Human Rights Conference of 1993, which consecrated principles of universality and indivisibility in human rights, is a landmark for the recognition that domestic violence against women is a human rights violation. As Brazil's constitution had already recognized these rights and the state's responsibility over such violence, the Brazilian delegation was able to support the Declaration and Plan of Action of the Vienna Conference, which brought international legitimacy to our constitutional provision. The UN Declaration on the Elimination of Violence Against Women (1993) broadened the definition of VAW, and the Belem do Para Convention on the Elimination of all Forms of Violence against Women (1994) was a key regional instrument that expanded on Vienna and influenced national laws, and has given legitimacy to continued advocacy work around VAW.

The Cairo Conference (ICPD) of 1994 was very important in providing global reinforcement for local recognition of reproductive rights and influenced Brazil's 1996 Family Planning Law. The ICPD provisions addressing abortion, in which the state is held responsible to attend to cases of abortion in circumstances that are legal and to provide post-abortion health care even where abortion is not legal, have been key to providing a legitimate parameter for our "Technical Norms to Attend Victims of Sexual Violence," enacted by the Ministry of Health in 1999. While in Brazil abortion is legal in cases of rape, there were no norms regulating its access in this circumstance. This technical norm provided guidelines for treating the victims, including emergency contraception and abortion. They are directly related to the Cairo Conference Plan of Action and Declaration, which was, and still is, a powerful advocacy tool in the country.

Today the global scenario is clearly more conservative, and fundamentalist religious values are influential in national and international spheres. Such influence is centered on the position of women in the family, in education, in the labor market, in politics, and in the control of sexuality and reproductive life. Restrictive policies are ascendant—from extreme prohibitions based on Sharia law in the Middle East, to the infiltration of Christian conservative values in the legislative process of countries like Brazil—where efforts to ban abortion and emergency contraception, as well as against sexual rights, remain a fixture of our politics. The recent 47th Session of the Commission on Population, of the UN (2014), is an example of the intensifying international power of conservative sectors grouped in coalitions that impede any progress in relation to the Cairo Conference, including the mention of sexual rights. These forces embrace regression by denying even the recognition of the existence of a variety of forms of family—language already approved in the ICPD, Chapter 5 paragraph 5.1. A group of countries, including Brazil, defended the recognition of ICPD language in relation to families but were opposed by Arab and African countries, which along with the Vatican and other allies, also evidenced a growing rejection of LGBT rights.

The current situation demands new strategies to create consensus among different sectors on fundamental principles of separation of church and state that locate the regulation of sexuality and reproduction in the secular realm of rights and policies, not in faith and theology. Feminists in Brazil and elsewhere have gone a long way in affirming women's rights. It is crucial that we now expand our allies, including youth, and accept that "women" are not a homogeneous category. Our diversity in terms of social class, race, ethnicity, culture, age, and sexual orientation, was a source of strength for alliances and coalitions in the 1990s. Today there is a growing presence of culture and religion in power arrangements of different governments, not only in Islamic countries but also in Western societies. This influences women's identities and tends to divide them, presenting a difficult challenge that requires building bridges between religious and non-religious women from different cultures, to find common ground for advocacy in national and international arenas, and to guarantee and advance the agenda of women's human rights.

Historical examples and current challenges highlight the long, difficult, and non-linear path of women in different moments and societies towards human rights and equality. Every day in all parts of the world, women advocate for their rights. Sometimes they do so, unaware that they are performing a political action and that by claiming their rights in their family, their work place, their community, and their political institutions, they are protagonists of this long march that makes women, in spite of our differences, a universal political category.

Notes

1 Jacqueline Pitanguy, "Advocacy and Human Rights," in *The Progress of Women in Brazil* (Rio de Janeiro: CEPIA and UN Women, 2011): 20–578 (in Portuguese).

2 Responding directly to the President, CNDM had its own budget, approved by the National Congress, and was organized in thematic departments such as legislation, the constitution, labor rights and social benefits, rural women, education and culture, reproductive health, violence, black women, communication and media. Its board had representatives from various sectors of civil society, from feminist groups, academicians, writers, activists from the black movement, labor union leaders.

3 For an analysis of this advocacy work, see Jacqueline Pitanguy, "Bridging the Local and the Global: Feminism in Brazil," *International Human Rights Agenda in Social Research* 69, no. 3 (2002): 805. Women have come a long way since the Constitution was enacted. Fertility rates have decreased from an average of six children in the 1960s to 1.9 in 2010, thanks to growing access to family planning; education levels are today higher among women than men (in 2007 39% of women had more than 9 years of education in comparison with 35% of men) reverting, since the 1980s, a historical trend of male predominance. In 2010, 15.1% of women aged between 18 and 24 years attended the university versus 11.3% of men; female presence in the labor market rose from 26.6% in 1980 to 48.9% in 2010, whereas the male labor force decreased from 72.4% to 67.1% (Instituto Brasileiro de Geografia e Estatistica, *Demographic Census 2010*, www.ibge.gov.br/english/estatistica/populacao/censo2010/.) However, progress is not even among women, as race and ethnicity also are responsible for inequalities. Black women have lesser access to education, and, although women in general still receive 70% of what men make for equal work, this gap is larger among black women.

4 Most of the Constitutions from after the Second World War are extensive and comprehend more dimensions of political, economical, and social life.

5 The Legitimate Defense of Honor is not inscribed in our penal code. It is an argument, created by defense lawyers, but accepted in the courts (popular jury). A friend from my childhood, Angela Diniz, was killed in 1979 by her partner, who was acquitted. The case was appealed and, thanks to the advocacy work of feminists who held the justice system responsible for her institutional murder, he was condemned at the second trial. The use of the argument of legitimate defense of honor started then to be questioned in the courts.

6 See Jacqueline Pitanguy, "Reconceptualizing Peace and Violence against Women: A Work in Progress" in *SIGNS*, no. 1 (Spring 2011): 561, for a discussion on the redefinition of peace by feminists by including domestic and sexual violence in its realm.

7 Paragraph 6, Article 228 of the Federal Constitution of Brazil.

8 On the Superior Tribunal of Justice ruling, see Human Rights Watch, "Violence Against Women in Brazil," *Americas Watch Report*, 1992.

9 CEPIA, the NGO that I coordinate, was part of the coalition that proposed and drafted the new law and is now involved in its full implementation.

10 This ruling was the result of advocacy action initiated by a feminist NGO. ANIZ, along with an association of health workers and the field of allies, was expanded to include other NGOs like CEPIA, who developed a national campaign, the SPM, and some medical associations.

11 What I would like to retain from her understanding of this concept is the relevance of agency in building a dynamic concept of citizenship, for which political action is crucial; Hannah Arendt, *La Condición Humana* (Barcelona: Paidós, 1993).

12 Nancy Frazer and Linda Gordon, "Contract Versus Charity: Why is There no Social Citizenship in the US?," *Socialist Review* 22 (1992): 45–68.

13 History is made by collective processes but also by individual actors. I would like to recognize the major role played by the Center for Women's Global Leadership and the leadership of Charlotte Bunch on the Human Rights Conference of 1993, as well as the role of the IWHC and the leadership of Joan Dunlop and Adrienne Germain on the ICPD of 1994 and of WLP, and Mahnaz Afkhami in coalition building in this millennium.

9 Tackling history and culture: building the women's rights movement and leveraging global conferences for local realities in Pakistan

A reflection

Farida Shaheed

I have a passion for history. This is not so much because of what actually happened, which interests me in its own right, but also because of how profoundly the narratives of the past influence contemporary reality. Our stories—his stories and her stories—heard at home, imbibed in traversing and engaging in public spaces, taught in schools, related in literature, conveyed in myriad entertainment and news media—fundamentally shape our sense of who we are individually and collectively.

Historical narratives are inextricably linked to identity and hence to culture. They tell us who is to be valorized and who condemned, who to socialize with, shun, praise, or treat as the enemy. Historical narratives—far too frequently *his* stories rather than *hers*—help to shape how we conceive of ourselves; they serve as the springboards of future desires, selectively illuminating and obscuring potential pathways to explore. From the perspective of women's rights and gender equality, the history-culture nexus is crucial enough that it should compel us to engage with it in all its facets.

The importance of overturning dominant narratives, which in general dismiss women as weak helpless beings and address as exceptions only martyrs or ruthless men-like warriors, cannot be overstressed. The end of the twentieth century saw renewed efforts by feminist scholars and some activists to retrieve women from history's footnotes. My personal contribution has been to prepare a training module, Great Ancestors: Women Asserting Their Rights on behalf of the international solidarity network, Women Living Under Muslim Laws. Its express purpose is to debunk the dual myths that Muslim women are acquiescently subservient, on the one hand, and that women's rights are a foreign idea imported from the West, on the other.

Unfortunately, even women start to believe in these myths. Each time we run the training module, whether for an international group of activists or in a remote Pakistani jail, I am struck by the intensity of relief women express at learning of a past full of strong women from their "own context" (however this is defined). Narratives of Muslim women who have mounted resistance, led rebellions, and dared to combat the unjust status quo have the power to release women's agency, enabling them to say "Yes, this is also our history. This is my legacy and I can take it forward to fight against the injustice I confront in my own life." The past has long been deliberately constructed to project disempowering myths; but the myths wield real power and need to be vigorously contested.

History as a vital key for unlocking women's agency was confirmed in an Asia-based action-research project: Women's Empowerment in Muslim Contexts: gender, poverty and democratization from the inside (WEMC) (2006–2010). Carried out in countries with divergent histories, socio-political and economic frameworks from China to Iran, WEMC teaches us that it is not only the history of women's resistance and actions in one's own village, community, or country that makes a difference. The knowledge of struggle and resilience elsewhere galvanizes women; it breaks the crippling impact of feeling isolated, of seeing oneself as a maverick or as just plain different. It affirms that women are a part of something bigger—of a collective experience of injustice and discrimination that demands our defying and challenging the status quo—frequently against huge odds and sometimes at the cost of our lives or liberty. A further insight from this study is that tales of social justice movements that are not women-specific can be just as inspiring as those focused on gender justice.

The plethora of practices and norms that discriminate against women are so frequently justified by reference to culture, religion, and tradition that it seems fair to say that "no social group has suffered greater violation of its human rights in the name of culture than women."[1] In this day and age, it is "inconceivable" that such practices "would be justified if they were predicated upon another protected classification such as race."[2] The tendency to view culture as largely an impediment to women's human rights is, however, both oversimplistic and problematic. Gender, culture, and rights intersect in intricate and complex ways. By definition, culture is about what *people* do and create, but too often "culture" is attributed a self-propelling agency, as if it were an autonomous actor with a volition and mind of its own.

This myth too should be put to rest. Culture cannot—and must not—be disconnected from the actions of human beings. Speaking of culture as if it has independent volition diverts attention from the real problem—the specific actors, institutions, rules and regulations that keep women subordinate within patriarchal systems and structures. This false construct of a culture that directs human action like a puppeteer feeds into the agenda of those who use discourses of cultural relativism to challenge the universality, legitimacy, and applicability of human rights and gender equality. It also renders invisible women's agency in terms of reproducing, or contrarily challenging dominant cultural norms and values.

Culture, permeating all human activities and institutions, including legal systems in all societies across the world, is created, contested, and recreated within the social realities of diverse groups interacting in economic, social, and political arenas. Expressed, understood, and practiced individually and collectively, cultures embody particular worldviews. They function as a prism through which we view, understand, relate to, and engage with the world around us—human, natural, and constructed. Delinking culture from the historical processes and contexts in which it is embedded, essentializes cultures, which are then presumed to be static and immutable, homogenous and monolithic, apolitical and detached from prevailing power relations.[3] Nothing could be farther from the truth. Cultural and historical narratives are both sites of contestation over meanings and perspectives of the past, present, and future. It is imperative that advocates for women's rights vigorously oppose patriarchal systems, structures, and actors in all ideological hues, shapes, and sizes, and energetically pursue and promote our agenda in all possible arenas we access, from local households and communities to national and international forums.

Dealing with culture has been a particularly knotty issue for women's rights activists everywhere, leading to heated debates on how best (and whether) to address the challenge in theoretical terms and, especially, in practice. On being appointed the first mandate holder for cultural rights by the United Nations' Human Rights Council, I grappled with what an effective strategy to counter states' cultural excuses for non-compliance or lack of progress on their commitments under the almost universally ratified Convention to Eliminate all forms of Discrimination against Women (CEDAW) could be. Aside from some blatant abuses, it is in fact quite difficult to classify exactly which cultural practices are to be rejected as harmful. In any case, the constantly evolving nature of cultures makes it impossible to list them all. To avoid falling into the trap of essentializing, condemning, or patronizing "others" as lesser, and still be able to effectively address the complex subject of gender, culture, and rights, demands an entirely different approach—making states accountable in tangible terms rather than fruitlessly trying to impose cultural change from afar.

This requires a paradigm shift from seeing and engaging with culture solely as an obstacle to women's human rights, to demanding that women and girls enjoy the full compendium of cultural rights on a basis of equality with men and boys.[4] Instead of trying to itemize all that is wrong in every culture—and thereby engage in a discourse disturbingly akin to that of the colonial "civilizing mission"—we must hold states accountable for ensuring that girls and women have resources, opportunities, and recognition equal to boys and men in all aspects of life. In tangible terms this translates, for example, into whether equal resources are devoted so that girls and women have opportunities to develop their creativity in terms of the arts and sciences, as well as in physical sports, just as men do; whether they are equally represented in performances, air-time, exhibitions, science projects, etc. Just imagine, for example, the difference it would make to our world if gender parity were actually achieved in the lucrative world of competitive commercial sports.

Moreover, cultural rights are inextricably linked to participation and hence to all decision-making in society—formal and informal, public and private. The marginalization of women and the silencing of our voices must be overcome, obstructions to our equal participation in public life eliminated, and our underrepresentation in the institutions and processes defining the culture of our communities, surmounted.

From the start I have also stressed that the right to take part in cultural life includes the right *not* to participate in any practice or ritual that undermines human dignity; to freely be part of, leave, rejoin, and create new communities of shared cultural values; and to reshape cultural heritage, without fear of punitive action by the state.

Women should not be confronted with binary choices—either accepting the culture of their communities as is, or being altogether jettisoned. To insure gender equality, women's perspectives and contributions must move from the margins of cultural life to the center of the processes that create, interpret, and shape culture. Women must be recognized and supported as equal spokespersons vested with the authority to identify and interpret cultural heritage, including historical narratives, and to decide which cultural values and practices are to be kept, recast, modified, or discarded altogether.

There is overwhelming evidence that social practices and attitudes are stubbornly resistant to legislative, policy, and administrative actions intended to guarantee gender equality. To reorient all cultures to support women's human rights, societal actions are indispensable. Human rights can only be realized within, and are therefore contingent upon, the factors and dynamics operative on the ground, which are steeped in cultural specificities. This makes it imperative for human rights to be "vernacularized"[5] through "initiatives that ground human rights concepts in diverse cultural traditions, in a culturally relevant lexicon and philosophical vocabulary."[6] Revising and making known historical narratives that reflect the multiple narratives and pluralism of the past and highlight women's contributions is one strategy. It may also be possible for women to retrieve and build upon elements from cultural heritage that have fallen into disuse to their advantage.[7] For all these reasons, I am convinced that women's cultural rights provide an important and essential new framework for promoting all other rights.

The ultimate effectiveness of a human rights agenda is dependent on a number of factors, starting with women (as well as men) being convinced that they have the right to be right holders. This implies an understanding of the citizen-state relationship, a knowledge of legal rights and how these differ from prevalent cultural norms and practices, as well as practical knowhow and support to access legal entitlements and state benefits. Finally, our experience in Pakistan of the multi-country Women's Empowerment and Leadership Development for Democratization project (WELDD) (2012–2015) underscores the vital pivotal role of solidarity. Forging a collective identity enables women to engage in concerted actions for sustainable change; it provides support systems and reference points beyond immediate family, friends and community; it validates a sense of self and replenishes flagging energies. Having spaces to share experiences and analyze the problems and dynamics at work facilitates the formulation of effective change strategies. The dividends of being part of a movement are very real, even if intangible in quantitative terms.

The UN conferences on women from 1975 to 1995, in my view, were critical sites for movement building—for negotiating and establishing international consensus on an effective agenda for women. My understanding from women who attended[8] is that the main demand in 1975 in Mexico City was for women to be given a seat at the table. Ten years later in Nairobi, some women had managed to be seated, and their demand was for an equal share of the fruits or food on offer. Beijing in 1995 marked another crucial shift. No longer content just to be seated and enjoy the repast, women demanded to design the shape of the table and fashion the menu offered there: to be architects and chefs, not just beneficiaries.

This evolution and the gains achieved between 1975 and 1995 were the result of an energetic global alliance, which brought together and learned from the experiences of women engaged in diverse struggles, with sometimes conflicting priorities across the globe. Importantly, however, the movement incorporated these experiences and concerns into an overarching analysis that showcased the universality of gender discrimination and therein demanded a concerted global response. The movement derived its ideology from a comprehensive and incisive analysis of the realities of women's lives on the ground and how these realities interconnect with, and are inextricably linked to, broader social and economic dynamics. This analysis translated into concrete recommendations for the Beijing Platform for Action.

Few women from Pakistan attended the Mexico conference. A largely male delegation was led by our then-First Lady, Nusrat Bhutto, and the government did try to act on the agenda of women's equality, development, and peace. The International Year of the Woman in 1975 was followed by conferences, seminars, and institutional initiatives at home. It provided an impetus for new women's organizations (although Shirkat Gah—Women's Resource Centre was probably the only feminist one). It put gender squarely on the national agenda and moved away from an earlier welfare approach to women's rights and development. The year culminated with a Declaration on the Rights of Pakistani Women, which enshrined the principle of gender equality in our secular constitution, insisting that this is not in contradiction with religion. Unfortunately, the document was then lost in the political turmoil and fallout of Zia-ul-Haq's military coup in 1977. (I have since had to personally supply copies of the declaration to various government institutions on numerous occasions.)

Very few Pakistani women attended Nairobi either. In 1985, Pakistan was still suffering under its worst spell of martial law, which saw the military using a religiously projected political agenda to systematically rescind rights, especially those of women and minorities. Women's rights activists were too busy safeguarding rights at home to think of international engagements. Most activists also refused to accept funding to attend Nairobi, wary of the potential strings attached.

The Beijing conference process provided an unprecedented opportunity for Pakistani activists who, after the fall of the military regime in 1988, had started to develop new skills and adopt new strategies—from oppositional street protests to advocacy and negotiations in a democratic set-up. In 1995, for the first time, civil society organizations, activists, academics, and the government came together to prepare a

"National Report for Beijing." Half of the official delegation, led by Prime Minister Benazir Bhutto who was willing to speak out for women's rights, consisted of non-government women. Collaboration was facilitated by the presence of women in parliament who had been active on the streets under martial law. It always helps to have women in the political process and decision-making who support gender equality and women's rights. Engaging with the civilian government in the Beijing process helped bring home the agenda. The resultant "National Plan of Action for Women" was jointly prepared by women's rights activists, experts, and government representatives. A second vital task was ensuring that the agenda reached the grassroots for Zia's martial law had demonstrated just how easy it is to rescind rights when so few women know they have them and even fewer enjoy them.

This led to numerous interventions on the ground to bolster women's knowledge and understanding of gender and rights as well as expand the voices demanding gender justice in the country. A few key learnings from our current work are as follows. The vitality of public discursive spaces for women's practical needs, as well as for movement building, had been highlighted in the work of the WEMC action research in which Shirkat Gah was a main partner.[9] The need for such spaces was reaffirmed in our humanitarian work in post-disaster situations. Shirkat Gah therefore set up Women Friendly Spaces (WFS). Introducing leadership capacity-building, supportive networks and old-fashioned consciousness-raising about gender, complemented by a wider understanding of state–citizenship relations, critical thinking and communication, and negotiation skill-building. WFS have become springboards for women's empowerment and for practical local initiatives conceived of and prioritized by the women. Our work has a greater focus on youth and has started to engage men more, especially young men. Working with men helps to mitigate the possible backlash when women start demanding rights; it also helps to ensure that the agenda of gender equality is owned by men as well as women.

The impact has been striking and women's transformation, notable. "We were sleeping in the darkness before, now we have come into the light," says one woman; "Yes, we help women resolve their issues, this is why the men are also scared of us," says another. Men too have changed, as one confessed:

> We were always fighting in my house. I used to hit my girls ... I used bad language and was very abusive. ... I initially did not give them permission to go [to the WFS] as people don't think well of

NGOs ... [who they think are] spoiling the women ... My daughters used to tell us everything they learned there and slowly the environment in our house began to change. We started fighting less as I learned that beating women, abusing women is an injustice and violence. They are also equal to us—the way we worry about poverty so do they. There is peace in our house now.

In the final analysis, however, discursive spaces for open-ended discussions, sharing, and learning are not only essential for village women. Such spaces are critical for the movement as a whole. There are far too few such spaces and opportunities from the grassroots right through to the international forums. It seems that such spaces have diminished since 1995. Women's engagements today tend to focus on siloed aspects of the gender agenda, for example violence against women, sexuality, environment and economics, political participation, etc.

Twenty years after Beijing, it is time to step back, reconsider and reshape the feminist agenda within a wider framework of global dynamics and developments, and in the light of the new experiences women have gained on the ground. We should learn from and link up with other social change movements. In short, we need to revitalize the global women's movement by enriching it once again with the diverse experiences and analyses of women engaged in struggles on the ground across the world. We must refresh our common thinking and our collective agenda, while still acknowledging sufficient diversity within it.

Notes

1 Arati Rao, "The Politics of Gender and Culture in International Human Rights Discourse," in *Women's Rights, Human Rights: International Feminist Perspectives*, ed. Julie Peters and Andrea Wolper (New York and London: Routledge, 1994), 167.
2 Berta Esperanza Hernández-Truyol, "Out of the Shadows: Traversing the Imaginary of Sameness, Difference and Relationalism—A Human Rights Proposal," *Wisconsin Women's Law Journal* XVII, no. 1 (2002): 142.
3 See, in particular, Uma Narayan, "Essence of Culture and a Sense of History: A Feminist Critique of Cultural Essentialism," *Hypatia* 13, no. 2 (1998).
4 See the report of the Special Rapporteur in the field of cultural rights, *Ensuring Cultural Rights for Women on a Basis of Equality with Men* (A/67/287), 30 October 2012.
5 See, for example, P. Levitt and S. E. Merry, "Vernacularization on the Ground: Local Uses of Global Women's Rights in Peru, China, India and the United States," *Global Networks* 9, no. 4 (2009): 441–461; and M. Goodale, "Locating Rights: Envisioning Law Between the Global and the Local," in *The Practice of Human Rights: Tracking Law Between the Global and the*

Local, ed. M. Goodale and S. E. Merry (Cambridge: Cambridge University Press, 2007).

6 Farida Shaheed, "Reflections on Human Rights, Traditional Values and Practices," contribution circulated at the workshop on the traditional values of humankind (A/HRC/16/37), 5.

7 Oral information provided by anthropologist Jeanette Kloosterman, Oxfam Novib.

8 In particular Miriam Habib, a renowned journalist and women's rights activist in Pakistan.

9 WEMC: the "Women's Empowerment in Muslim Contexts: gender, poverty and democratisation from the inside out" was a four-year programme, jointly run by seven partners, Shirkat Gah—Women's Resource Centre, under the leadership of the Kong City University, Social Science Department. The project ran from 2006 to 2010 focusing principally on women in Indonesia, China, Pakistan, and Iran.

10 Women's human rights in Iran

From global declarations to local implementation

Mahnaz Afkhami

Since the adoption of the United Nations Universal Declaration of Human Rights in 1948, the effect of international conferences, resolutions, documents, and consequent laws on the struggle for women's human rights at regional, national, and local levels has been a matter of debate and controversy. In my view, they have been and continue to be indispensable to promoting women's human rights, but to be made practicable they must have popular support; that is, the ways and means of using them must be based on the exigencies of the social and cultural contexts in which they are to be applied.

In this article I recount the story of our work for women's rights in Iran in the 1970s, partly as an historical reflection—because I believe we cannot go forward without understanding the past—but also as a case study of the Women's Organization of Iran (WOI) and its role before, during, and after the First UN World Conference on Women in Mexico City in 1975. I describe how the WOI developed and mobilized itself to dialogue with national policymakers in Iran and with the international community, how this grassroots to national to international-level decision-making effort had a major impact on the 1975 First World Conference on Women and, in turn, how that impact filtered back to the national and grassroots levels in Iran.

The history of the Iranian women's movement has been distorted by post-1979 revolutionary propaganda and sometimes left invisible because of the proximity between the major events in which the WOI played a decisive role and the upheaval that resulted in the Iranian Revolution. However, it is important to recall that history because despite what followed, the WOI's struggle for women's rights in Iran remains a powerful and potentially replicable example of how local concepts and norms move up, and how international agreements based on local ideas can move back down, to act as a powerful tool to help raise community ownership and become more easily implemented at the local levels.

The Women's Organization of Iran

In 1967, after living and studying in the United States for 12 years, I returned to Iran to teach English literature at the National University of Iran. There I found that my female students were energized by stories describing the liberties and rights that Western women enjoyed. However, I also found that my students did not want to *replicate* those rights exactly. They wanted to find a way to define and position these rights within their own culture. Our discussions and the challenge of negotiating our demands for independence, autonomy, and agency within a male-dominated structure, culture, and religion led to the founding of the Association of University Women, which focused on probing the contradictions and finding solutions to the discrepancies between the impulse toward modernity and freedom and the exigencies of culture, religion, and tradition.

The association's success and growth led to my being drafted as Secretary General of the WOI in 1971.[1] As such, I traveled throughout Iran to hear what women from all types of backgrounds wanted and worked to help them discover and articulate their needs and priorities, to arrive with them at a shared vision of rights and to map out an efficient strategy to gain these rights.

The WOI had been founded in 1966 by a 5,000-member assembly of Iranian women from diverse backgrounds and regions, gathered through consultation, brainstorming and negotiation, and initiated by a 50-member advisory group tasked by the High Council of Iranian Women's Associations and its president, Princess Ashraf Pahlavi. Its mission was "to raise the cultural, social and economic knowledge of the women of Iran and to make them aware of their family, social and economic rights, duties and responsibilities." Initially, much of the WOI's rhetoric stressed women's responsibilities as good mothers, good wives, and pleasant companions for their mates. However, rapid changes in the circumstances of women, especially the increasing number of trained and educated professional women entering into the workforce, made it apparent that carrying the double burden of home and profession without changes in men's behavior or in society's structures and attitudes would be almost impossible for most women. The ideological turning point came at the WOI's 1973 General Assembly, which led to amending the WOI Constitution.

At the General Assembly's opening session some activists spoke about the beneficial effects of women's education and employment for the family and women's proven ability to perform simultaneously as traditional wives and mothers and as modern professionals. One WOI Central Council member argued that the role of woman is complementary to that of man, using the image of an apple—the woman being the half that completes the whole. I walked to the podium after my colleague, looked at the gathering, wondered whether I had sensed their feelings correctly from conversations in preparation for the assembly and said:

> Sisters, it is time to name our problem and its solution. We know that we are not all superwomen. It is unfair to expect us to be superwomen. No one can function in so many different and demanding roles. We ought not to be asked to accept total responsibility for the home while holding a full-time job outside the home. Women should not be asked either to do both jobs or to give up life outside the home. We are each a whole human being, complete in ourselves. We are half of nothing and no one.

There were a few seconds of silence, then applause and shouts and loud ululation[2] from our colleagues from the southern part of the country. We had reached a point where we were able and willing to express our thoughts freely and to insist that our condition, roles, and needs had changed. We no longer begged for a chance to do everything under rules that were not of our making. We demanded that the structure of society and the relations among members of the family change, so that an equitable distribution of rights and responsibilities would occur.[3] The WOI's constitution was then amended to include the goal of "defending the individual, family and social rights of women to ensure their complete equality in society and before the law."

The WOI grew in size, membership, and function during a period of rapid economic and social development in Iran, and during its 12-year existence became one of the most vibrant and effective agents of change in the status of women in the Global South.[4] In our approach to the unequal status of women in Iran and the ways we developed our strategies, we went from evidential experience to theory—we did not start with a theoretical assumption and try to fit reality to it. Our only presupposition was that the status of women in our country was unequal and that the condition of women, especially poor women, was brutal. We sat with groups of women around Iran, listened to their stories and asked them about their hopes for their daughters, about what frustrated and saddened them and what would change their lives for the better. Overwhelmingly, women told us that economic self-sufficiency was their highest priority. For example, one woman said, "What good is equal right to divorce to me, if all it means is that I go from my husband's house back to my father's house?" Local women helped decide what services would be offered at WOI centers,[5] which typically focused on education, including literacy skills and vocational training. Trial and error showed that the most effective centers were those that were small, centrally located, unassuming, and an integral part of the community. Our programs grew from the ground up and were adapted and altered depending on the neighborhood, the city, and the focus of the particular activists in a given locality. Our programs all had one thing in common—encouraging and enabling women to develop their capabilities and their self-reliance.

My work at the WOI had convinced me that it would be helpful to become familiar with other ways of seeing the world and the place of women in it, so in the early 1970s my colleagues at the WOI and I planned a series of travels and dialogues to learn about women in other parts of the world and about their challenges and strategies. Each of these trips brought us lessons of what would or would not work for us. We developed a reading list for our WOI board and other colleagues and discussed the contents in diverse settings. In the process we learned that the language and concepts that Western feminists like Kate Millet used in books such as *Sexual Politics* were less appealing to women in our region—perhaps even counterproductive. Betty Friedan's *The Feminine Mystique*, on the other hand, seemed more familiar, not so much in its particulars, but in the way she looked at a situation, saw it within its own context and tried to understand the problem. Betty had an important message based on the realities of middle-class women in suburban America that reflected universal problems of patriarchy. She did not focus on sexuality in studying the challenges women face.

I thought it would be good for Iranian women to hear these experiences and opinions first-hand, just as we had already heard from women elsewhere on our travels. Although none presented models that would work for us, talking to women in these countries—textile workers, teachers, political leaders—had taught us that the underlying structures that affected the status of women were essentially the same across the world. The universality of women's condition around the world suggested that we need to look at the roots of the problem of inequality across diverse circumstances, build solidarity around that understanding, nurture the capability to understand and respect the other, and base our solidarity on our shared experience and respect for the ability of each of us to find our own solutions. It also taught us that although women's aspirations were very similar, the priorities and the strategies to reach these aspirations had to fit the specific circumstances on the ground. We had to find our own way in the world, based on our own cultural roots and our own way of life.

Western feminists visit Iran

In 1973 I talked with my WOI colleagues about inviting a few Western feminists to Iran to give lectures, visit our centers and give us feedback on our work. Some of my colleagues loved the idea and thought it would be useful to have this dialogue. Some were worried that the publicity around the visit might further typecast us as "Westoxicated," a nebulous concept in vogue among Iranian intellectuals at the time. Others were concerned about what the speakers would say and the ramifications of their opinions for us. In the end, we decided to move ahead. I suggested we invite Betty Friedan as the founder of the National Organization for Women, Kate Millet as one of the main theoreticians of radical feminism, and Helvi Sipilä as the UN's first female Assistant Secretary General, the highest ranking woman at the UN. Kate could not come,[6] so I invited Germaine Greer as a representative of the more radical wing of the feminist movement.

Our visitors demonstrated varying levels of understanding of the complexities of our situation, the cultural context and the limitations it placed on our work. For example, on a visit to a WOI center in south Tehran's slum area, Betty asked one woman, "Why are you studying hairdressing? That's such a traditionally female skill." We couldn't expect her to understand the immense effort it took for a semi-literate, poor woman from the slums to gain the self-awareness just to want to leave her house and come to a class, nor could she realize what such a woman must do to gain agreement from the menfolk in her household to do so.

Germaine was brilliant but emotionally volatile. She was younger, with much less exposure to any but the Western liberal-left academic milieu. In Shiraz we organized a meeting at her request with women students at Pahlavi University. She began in a relaxed tone, talking about women's problems and needs, as though these young women were very much like those in her own classrooms. But what had worked at home did not work here. The young women began whispering to each other. It was unusual for the students to challenge a speaker, especially a guest from far away, but one said, "How can you presuppose what we want or need? Why are you preaching to us about our life choices?" Germaine was taken aback. It was not that she was saying something terribly radical. It was the impression she gave that they were somehow in need of Western direction and guidance. To her credit, Germaine explained that she had no such intention, the young women relaxed, and the conversation resumed.

Helvi, on the other hand, was an experienced diplomat and had been a leader in several women's organizations in Finland. Her work at the UN had brought her into contact with a wide variety of cultures and life experiences. She had been exposed to many approaches to women's issues across the globe and had a good experiential basis for comparison.

At this time (1974), we had 80 women's centers around the country. We secured a grant from the Iranian government to build new centers provided that the local community paid half of the cost. Our provincial activists were able to raise the matching funds from individuals, and more often from the local governments. In those years there was no tradition of grants from international organizations, as there is today. Local philanthropy in Iran, then as in most cases even today, was limited to religious endowments or charities catering to the needs of the poor. It was through the UN conferences of the 1970s and 1980s that NGOs began to flourish in the developing as well as the developed worlds, and women from across the globe came into contact with and began to learn from one another. Thus at that time, other than Helvi Sipilä, our foreign visitors had little contact or information available to them about our world, just as most of our population knew little about theirs. Nonetheless, their response to the centers was very positive.

Helvi was especially impressed with the potential of the work and the possibility of using it as a model elsewhere. During the visit she and I discussed possibilities for the upcoming UN World Conference on Women scheduled for June 1975 in Mexico City, for which she had been appointed Secretary General. I inquired about the possibility of a regional research and training center on women in Tehran for the ESCAP[7] region, similar to those already launched in Latin America and Africa. We also discussed the outlines of a proposal to create a UN institute located in Tehran that could serve as a clearinghouse and research and documentation center for the global women's movements (this later became INSTRAW).[8] I thought I might be able to interest the Iranian government in supporting these initiatives. Sensitive as it then was to international public opinion, the government, we thought, would be responsive to UN resolutions, declarations, and documents, and we, in turn, could use international pressure to support our national goals and plans. At the same time Iran's position as a nation rich in human and natural resources, with a government committed to modernization, and with ties to East and West as well as to the developing world, might help us push some of our ideas and projects through the UN General Assembly.

In the end, the Western feminists' visit was very helpful for us at the WOI. We translated their presentations into Persian and published a booklet that reached all our WOI members and many others across Iran. It also resulted in our becoming important players in the planning for the UN's Mexico City conference.

The UN World Conference on Women in 1975 in Mexico City

While the WOI created new local centers throughout Iran, the WOI Center for Research on Women conducted studies[9] on women in various socio-economic and geographic sectors and sought to identify solutions to their problems. Throughout 1975 the International Women's Year, the WOI held a series of seminars on such key issues as the status of women in decision-making, law, economic and political participation, education, employment, and health, among others. We compiled statistics, commissioned research from various universities and used it to prepare what we considered to be an accurate account of the situation of women in our country.

In modernizing patriarchal societies, international connections and support are particularly important for promoting women's human rights, and in the WOI's case they proved critical. In March 1975, we presented a working paper[10] to the UN Consultative Committee in New York, which was the starting point for preparing the World Plan of Action (WPA) for the improvement of the status of women. The committee, with representatives from 23 nations, was chaired by Princess Ashraf Pahlavi, a career diplomat serving as head of Iran's delegation to the General Assembly. She would lead our delegation to Mexico City later that year. The committee used our working paper in formulating the key concepts and policies and preparing the draft WPA for Mexico City. The WPA final draft adopted by the UN General Assembly in 1975 reflected many of the ideas we had researched and tested in Iran, and was based essentially on the following concepts:

- Regardless of the socio-political, cultural, and economic differences among nations, there are similarities in the situation of women throughout the world.
- Problems of development cannot be solved efficiently and in any real sense without a thorough change in the status of women in the developing world.

- The involvement and total commitment of governments to initiate, implement, and monitor change are essential in bringing about women's full participation.

At the conference the Iranian delegation also initiated and lobbied for the resolutions to create the two important UN research, training, and policy organizations for women that we had conceptualized earlier with Helvi Sipilä. The first, the Economic and Social Commission for Asia and the Pacific (ESCAP) Center for Women and Development, was inaugurated in Tehran in February 1977 and was headed by Elizabeth Reid.[11] Iran supported the ESCAP Center with substantial financial contributions and in-kind support for facilities, support services, and some personnel. The second, INSTRAW, could not be established in Iran because of the revolution, but it is still a vital part of the network of gender initiatives at the UN.

Subsequently several governments used the WPA to develop their own plans of action. Iran's WOI used it to formulate and implement a National Plan of Action that called for the full interaction of women in the process of development and that allowed women to become an integral part of the political decision-making process, not only in matters traditionally considered women's issues, but in all governmental decisions impacting women's lives. At that time, perhaps even today, this was a feat quite unmatched anywhere else in the world.

In December 1975, I was appointed as Iran's first Minister for Women's Affairs,[12] and I presented our findings to the Iranian cabinet.[13] The picture I drew for the ministers was rather dismal:

The stated position of the government of Iran is to reach equality between men and women in all areas of endeavor. The real situation of women in the country is, as you have seen, quite far from that goal. For centuries women have been relegated to the private sphere in this country as in almost all others. Their subservient position has been reinforced by societal arrangements across all fields of endeavor and has been strengthened by the subtle support of literature, myth and the arts. To change this, there needs to be a commitment to change that covers the entire range of human relationships. We need to examine all aspects of our development planning, from skills building, job distribution, family support systems and school curricula to city planning and legislative reform. Achievement of the goal of equality takes a revolutionary stance on the part of the government.

Prime Minister Amir Abbas Hoveyda dismissed my comments and the report, claiming instead that Iranian women had made significant progress and that the report gave an unrealistic picture. He was acutely aware of the influence of the traditional groups in society and especially mindful of the power of the clergy. The clergy had fought women at every step for every reform, especially after we passed the expanded Family Protection Law in 1975, which granted women more rights in the family[14] and gave Iranian women the most far-reaching rights in the MENA region, with the exception of Tunisia. The changes angered and threatened the clerics because they lost not only on a most important ideological front but also in the area of their own power and financial gain, as matters related to family affairs, such as marriage, divorce, the custody of children, etc., were moved from the religious to the civil courts.

Hoveyda had been prime minister for 10 years and was a knowledgeable, deeply connected, highly skilled politician. He was well aware of the backlash building against the radical changes we had initiated. He was afraid of the consequences of too much visibility and too strong a movement toward rapid change in the contested terrain where the private and public intersect and relations between family, community, and society are negotiated. This is the area where the deep-rooted beliefs of the population were skillfully manipulated by the conservative clergy.

We decided that we needed strong support from women—at the top, as well as at the grassroots. The simpler task was to seek support from the Queen, who was sympathetic to our cause, regularly supported our efforts, and often lobbied for us with the Shah and the Prime Minister. I called her office, which immediately responded with an appointment. In the meantime, I called a meeting with my colleagues to discuss an action plan. We had a built-in constituency in our membership and the hundreds of thousands of women who regularly attended the WOI centers. We had focused on building the foundations and venues for advocacy, but we had not developed a clear-cut national action plan. We realized that if we found a way of involving the grassroots and other stakeholders in formulating a shared vision, we would have a roadmap for the future.

Our final document, the "National Plan of Action for the Improvement of Women's Status in Iran," included the goals of improving the status of women and involving them fully in the process of development along with specific mechanisms for implementing and monitoring this agenda. The draft plan was discussed and debated in 700 gatherings of activists and policymakers throughout the country during 1976–1977. It covered all relevant areas of development and rights to be achieved through legislative reform—education, employment, culture, the media, agriculture and rural cooperatives, health and reproductive rights, etc. The implementation mechanism was to be a high council of 12 cabinet ministers tasked by the prime minister to meet annually to plan the ways and means of integrating women in all fields of development and, periodically, to review the progress made. In the interim senior deputy ministers would meet monthly to monitor and evaluate the challenges and the progress made in each ministry's domain, a meeting which I as Minister of Women's Affairs chaired. This internal monitoring system, aligning the expressed goals of the women's movement and national development policy, was an innovative structural accomplishment.

The Iranian cabinet approved the National Plan of Action in May 1978. The momentum we had achieved through widespread consultation and interaction among the women, and between various NGO and governmental participants, transformed what would have otherwise amounted to no more than a plea from a pressure group into an essential part of the national agenda and became the most important accomplishment of the women's movement. If the subsequent failure of the political system had not made it irrelevant, Iran's experiment in the interaction of the women's movement and the national decision-making apparatus could well have provided a model for many developing (and perhaps other) countries.[15]

As the WOI became more influential and more successful in helping secure increased legal rights for women, however, so the opposition became stronger and more overt. To appease the fundamentalists, my position as Minister for Women's Affairs was eliminated in August 1978. However, even though the revolution prevented implementation of the National Plan of Action, we considered our successes to that point, especially the integration of elements of women's participation into the work plan of 12 ministries of government under the direct supervision of the prime minister, to be a major victory.[16]

The Iranian revolution

The WOI was one of the first organizations to feel the brunt of the early revolutionary rage. It became a focal point not only for the revolutionaries but also for others who feared and hated the accelerating change we were helping to bring about in the status of women and their role in the family.

I left Iran for New York in late 1978 to negotiate the final contract to establish INSTRAW. The negotiations with the UN took a few weeks longer than anticipated. By the time they concluded, I was warned by my colleagues at home that the Islamic revolutionary movement was gaining momentum, and as a gesture of appeasement the government was arresting some of those who were targeted by the revolutionaries. Thus it would be dangerous for me to return. My work for women had put me on the death list of the fundamentalist revolutionaries, who condemned me as "corrupt of the earth and a warrior with God." My mission took me out of the country during the worst of the revolution and thus saved my life, sparing me the fate of others. Several of those arrested, such as former Prime Minister Hoveyda, would be executed a few months later when the revolutionary government came to power. The first female political prisoner executed was Farrokhru Parsa, who had been the first woman to hold a cabinet post in Iran.[17] She was hanged in Tehran's red-light district, alongside a woman accused of prostitution and a man accused of drug dealing. She was executed not for her political role, but because her political role by being public and visible was seen as the same as prostitution. To Khomeini, the very fact of a woman being in the public sphere, and unveiled, made her a criminal and a sinner.

The Iranian Revolution was a watershed moment in contemporary Middle East history in general, and for the status of women in the Middle East in particular. The Islamist movement conceptualized and organized by Khomeini and his followers had begun in 1963, when the franchise for women was first announced as part of Iran's White Revolution. This movement spread across the MENA region and changed the nature of politics, international relations, and the role of the citizen in society. The central tenet of Khomeini's worldview was his vision of human relationships rooted in the family as the foundational unit of society. At the center of this vision stood woman as wife, mother, and daughter—always dependent, always protected, always controlled. The status, place, and behavior of women in the "community of Muslims" were focal points in his delineation of good and evil.

By 1975, the International Year of the Woman, the WOI had successfully established 349 branches and 120 centers and had 55 affiliates among independent organizations. In 1977 alone, over one million women used WOI services. On the eve of the Iranian Revolution, nearly two million women in Iran were gainfully employed in the public and private sectors; 187,928 women were studying in various branches of Iran's universities; nearly 150,000 women were government employees, including 1,666 in managerial positions, 22 Majlis deputies, two senators, one ambassador, three deputy ministers, one provincial governor, five mayors, and 333 municipal council members.[18] Despite or perhaps because of our success, all of the WOI centers were dismantled or trashed after the revolution.

The laws we were able to pass by 1978 had given women nearly equal rights to divorce, raised the minimum age of marriage for girls to 18, increased women's rights in cases of child rearing and child custody, and supported women's employment outside the home, including extended paid maternity leave, part-time work with full-time benefits for mothers, and childcare on work premises.

Khomeini returned to Iran in February 1979. His first act, before there was a new constitution or government, was to annul the Family Protection Law we had worked so hard to achieve. His next command was to require the sexual apartheid in public places and veiling for women that remains the law in Iran even today. Women activists who had joined the revolutionaries in the hope of expanding their rights were the first among the progressive groups to realize the anti-historical nature of the new regime, and on 8 March 1979 they were the first to demonstrate against these commands. They were met with brutal force, beaten and imprisoned. The legal status of women regressed a century: polygamy was reinstated; the right to divorce and to custody of children became the sole prerogative of the husband; the minimum age of marriage for girls was set at nine years; gender apartheid became the rule at universities and all public spaces, and over 100 majors were closed to women; family planning was banned and the population doubled in the following decade; female government workers were forced into early retirement; women were forbidden to serve as judges; adultery by women became punishable by stoning; and women's testimony was valued at half of a man's.

Women resisted the Islamic government at every step, and gradually their efforts met with some success. The need for their skills and talent forced the government to rehire women, and their numbers in the private sector inched back closer to what they were in pre-revolutionary times. The trend toward the increase in women at institutions of higher learning accelerated. As the government realized the negative economic impact of the population explosion, it resumed the aggressive family planning policies of the past, and population growth was reduced substantially, although unfortunately, this policy was recently reversed by the supreme leader, the Ayatollah Khamenei.

In the 35 years since the revolution, and despite the able and vociferous advocacy attempts of women activists, the repressive laws affecting women and the family have remained intact. Even President Mohammad Khatami, who enjoyed considerable public support and made several attempts at introducing modest changes in the laws on the status of women, did not succeed. Increasing the minimum age of marriage from nine to 13 was his most important achievement in this area.

Iranian women have excelled in creative endeavors where government involvement is less intrusive, such as in the arts and literature, and also in private business and fields where the edicts on segregation of services require female professionals to serve women. Women have been pushed back, but they have not been defeated.[19] They have found ways around the limitations on their rights and shown their creativity and resilience. However, the cost of the Iranian Revolution has set back their trajectory of change and growth, just as it has retarded the country's overall development considerably.[20]

Conclusion

What then can we take away from this case study? First, Iranian women achieved the rights they possessed before the Iranian Revolution by their own hard work and persistent effort. It took them almost a century to move from total public invisibility to a position of visible political, social, and economic presence. Second, once rights have been achieved, they settle in a society's collective psyche, creating a new set of historical conditions that thereafter cannot be easily dislodged. The obverse of this statement is that lasting social change involves hard infrastructural transformation resulting from persistent and diverse economic, social, and intellectual stimuli, and support.

Third, securing rights depends on achieving and dispensing political power, and this requires widespread consciousness-raising based on dialogue that is focused on a variety of constituencies, from the grass-roots to academia, from school curricula to the media, from community centers to governmental offices.

Fourth and finally, the will of the international community expressed in the United Nations documents that resulted from the interactions of local, national, and international private and public institutions is indispensable to improving the status of women and creating inclusive and just societies.

Notes

1 Much of the information presented here about the WOI comes from my article, *An Introduction to the Women's Organization of Iran*, Foundation for Iranian Studies, www.fis-iran.org/en/women/organization/introduction; and from my article, "The Women's Organization of Iran: Evolutionary Politics and Revolutionary Change," in *Women in Iran from 1800 to the*

Islamic Republic, ed. Lois Beck and Guity Nashat (Champaign: University of Illinois Press, 2002).

2   Ululation is a long, wavering, high-pitched trilling of the tongue, used by Middle East women to express approval or celebration.

3   Mahnaz Afkhami, *An Introduction to the Women's Organization of Iran.*

4   Parvin Paidar, *Women and the Political Process in Twentieth-Century Iran* (New York and Cambridge: Cambridge University Press, 1995).

5   We created these centers to increase grassroots women's ability to achieve financial independence, without which all rights and legal protections were irrelevant. The centers grew to include other crucial services, such as childcare, job counseling, family planning, and consciousness-raising gatherings.

6   In 1979, soon after the Shah's departure, Kate did travel to Iran under the auspices of the Committee for Artistic and Intellectual Freedom to participate in demonstrations for Iranian women's rights, a trip that ended disastrously (as she describes in her book *Going to Iran*).

7   Economic and Social Commission for Asia and the Pacific.

8   INSTRAW (International Research and Training Institute for the Advancement of Women) is today the leading UN institute devoted to research, training, and knowledge management to achieve gender equality and women's empowerment.

9   See, e.g., Cyrus Elahi, *A Comparative Study of the Socioeconomic Situation of Working Women in Tehran, Qazwin, and Kashan* (Tehran: WOI, 1977); Sekandar Amanalahi, *Status of Women in Tribal Society* (Tehran: WOI, 1977); and Nikchehreh Mohseni, *Images of Women in Elementary School Textbooks* (Tehran: WOI, 1976).

10 United Nations Economic and Social Council, *Draft International Plan of Action, working paper submitted by Iran with a view to facilitating discussion of the Draft Plan of Action* (E/CONF.66/CC/L.1/, 75–04559), 3 March 1975, Item 3 of the provisional agenda.

11 In 1973 she had been appointed the world's first advisor on women's affairs to a head of government (Australia); after heading the ESCAP Center (1977–1979), she was later Director of the UN Development Program Division for Women in Development (1989–1991).

12 After France, this office was only the second of its kind in the world.

13 As Iran's first Minister of Women's Affairs and the only woman in a cabinet of 20 men, I had yet to build meaningful alliances.

14 For example, prior to the law's passage, the right of divorce had belonged solely to the husband, after passage, both men and women could ask the courts for divorce under specific circumstances; while earlier, a man could marry four wives and have many temporary marriages, after the law's passage, a man could marry a second wife only after obtaining the express consent of his first wife and the first wife was given the right to obtain a divorce from her husband in case he took a second wife. Although the Family Protection Law was annulled in 1979 after the Iranian Revolution, it still stands out today for having been ahead of its time, particularly in a Muslim-majority country.

15 Mahnaz Afkhami, *Iran's National Plan of Action: Ideology, Structure, Implementation* (Tehran: Manuscript prepared for publication for the Center for Research, WOI, 1978).

16 *Faith and Freedom: Women's Human Rights in the Muslim World (Gender, Culture, and Politics in the Middle East)*, ed. Mahnaz Afkhami (Syracuse, NY: Syracuse University Press, 1995); my oral history interview at The Foundation for Iranian Studies, *Afkhami, Mahnaz*, http://fis-iran.org/en/oralhistory/Afkhami-Mahnaz; Interview with Mehrangiz Dowlatshahi, the Oral History Archives of the Foundation for Iranian Studies, *Women, State, and Society in Iran: 1941–1978*, ed. Gholam Reza Afkhami (Bethesda, Md.: MFIS, 2002), 82–88; and Mahnaz Afkhami, "Iran: A Future in the Past—The Prerevolutionary Women's Movement," in *Sisterhood Is Global: The International Women's Movement Anthology*, ed. Robin Morgan (New York: Anchor Books Doubleday, 1984). See also Noushin Ahmadi Khorasani, *Senator: Struggles of Mehrangiz Manouchehrian in the Context of Women's Activism in Iran* (Tehran: Towse'e Publications, 2003), which offers further information on the WOI and several of the topics discussed in this chapter.

17 Mrs. Parsa had been a teacher and headmistress of one of the best girls' high schools in the country. When women gained the right to vote in 1963, she was among the first group elected to serve in Iran's parliament. Subsequently, she was appointed as the first woman cabinet minister (education) in Iran's history.

18 *Iranian Women in the Era of Modernization: A Chronology*, www.fis-iran.org/en/women/milestones/pre-revolution.

19 *Iranian Women's One Million Signatures Campaign for Equality: The Inside Story, Women's Learning Partnership Translation Series* (Syracuse, NY: Syracuse University Press, 2010). Khorasani describes how the founders of the One Million Signatures Campaign were able to gain legions of supporters and form a nimble coalition of women's groups to successfully pursue and promote women's issues prior to Iran's disputed 2009 presidential election.

20 *Reconstructed Lives: Women and Iran's Islamic Revolution* (Baltimore, Md.: The Johns Hopkins University Press, 1997), and Haleh Afshar, *Islam and Feminisms: An Iranian Case-Study* (New York: St. Martin's Press, 1999).

11 Crossing the bright red line

The abuse of culture and religion to violate women's sexual and reproductive health rights in Uganda

Sylvia Tamale

The specter of cultural and religious relativism has dogged African women's rights activists for decades, particularly in the area of sexual and reproductive human rights. In this respect, recent developments have stimulated considerable debate and tension in Uganda. They include the passing of the Anti-Homosexuality Act (AHA), the Anti-Pornography Act (APA), and the HIV and AIDS Prevention and Control Act (HAPCA), all in rapid succession, along with a policy adopted by religious-based private universities to suspend or expel female students who conceive out of wedlock. In all these cases, a fusion of African culture/morality and a wide array of religious values have been invoked to justify the actions and to legitimize overtly political agendas, clearly linked to much deeper and more invasive structures of governance, social control, and exploitation. This chapter exposes how patriarchal agents reinvent and misinterpret culture and religion to further their interests and argues that recent developments in Uganda reflect a new stage of overt struggle over the recognition of sexual and reproductive rights as duly established fundamental rights belonging to women.

Talking about sexual reproductive rights invariably means stepping over a bright red line of social taboos, moral restraints, and cultural boundaries. That is why it took the international human rights community almost 50 years after passing the Universal Declaration of Human Rights (UDHR) to place these topics firmly on the global agenda during the 1994 fourth International Conference on Population and Development (ICPD) in Cairo and again at the 1995 Fourth World Conference on Women in Beijing.[1] The paradigm shift that took place in Cario and meant that sexuality and reproduction were discussed within a human rights framework for the first time at UN forums. But crossing the bright red line came with a price; it immediately triggered a backlash.

In the last three decades or so, the women's movement in Uganda has made significant strides. Women have resiliently marched forward through civil strife, violence, structural adjustment programs, famine, poverty, HIV/AIDS, and religious fundamentalisms. Ugandan women have been pivotal to the subsistence and survival of entire communities, acting as shock absorbers, unpaid caregivers, innovators, organizers, and change agents. Although there is still considerable distance to cover before we achieve full economic independence, political participation, dignity, and social justice, there is a notable increase in the visibility and voice of women in all sectors of Ugandan society.

Today, however, we see a resurgence of forces determined to reverse these gains in the name of religion and culture. This backlash manifests as a call for moral regeneration and the protection of "traditional cultural values." The state provides a platform for Christian and Muslim fundamentalists to preach essentialist "natural law" doctrines that promote male dominance, female subordination, and heteronormativity. Sexual and reproductive rights are fundamental for women as they speak to broader issues of health, autonomy, self-determination, bodily integrity, pleasure, privacy, and life itself. They are the avenues to autonomy and gender equality, and therefore are highly contested.

Sexuality is thus the vulnerable heel of Africa's Achilles—particularly susceptible to exploitation, control, and regulation. The rolling back of sexual and reproductive rights in Uganda emerges against a backdrop of difficult times and declining socio-economic indicators. Unprecedented rates of unemployment, below-average wages, high taxes, an extremely high cost of living, and the poor state of health care translate into an agitated, distressed, and angry population. History teaches us that in periods of turmoil, when governments are called to account, they routinely look for "red herrings" to try to deflect the pressure. They make defenseless social groups the targets of state persecution, in this case women and sexual minorities.

Karl Marx's classic dictum that "religion is the opiate of the masses" holds more than a grain of truth in Africa.[2] Marx was referring to the "false consciousness" of the working classes in mid-nineteenth century Europe. He argued that poor people dissatisfied with exploitation and oppression found refuge in religion, which reconciled them to their condition.

Religion need not always align with vested interests and dominant groups. Indeed, liberation theology has been used to effect transformative change. For example, Buddhism counsels inner peace and enlightenment. In Africa, however, as elsewhere in the past, religion is increasingly becoming a haven for conservatives and reactionaries seeking to mask structural oppression by deflecting attention to other matters.

In Uganda, 42 percent of the population are Catholics, 37 percent Anglicans, and 12 percent Muslims.[3] These statistics belie the often violent and divisive role that religion has long played in the country. Religious wars that pitted British-supported pro-imperialists against contenders from France and Germany determined whose sphere of influence Uganda fell under during the era of early colonialism. Political affiliations thereafter followed religious divisions and also explain some of the major cataclysmic events that marked the country's history, even as religious faith provided effective solace for many Ugandans during the post-independence period of turmoil.[4]

Religious forces teamed up with other actors in the Ugandan political economy have played a significant role in the enactment of the laws under scrutiny—the anti-gay evangelical lobby on the AHA, Christian moralists and neo-traditionalists and nationalists on the APA, and moral majoritarians and sexual abstemists on the HAPCA. An analysis of this recent crackdown on sexuality in Uganda constitutes another example in a long global history of collusion between religious and political actors to find scapegoats in minority groups as a cover-up for their broader governance problems.

Understanding the place of religion in Ugandan politics

The alliance between messianic religions and the state is crucial for maintaining the status quo. Although its constitution declares Uganda a secular state,[5] in practice the opposite has been true. The country's motto: "For God and my Country" and the first line of the national anthem—"Oh Uganda, may God uphold thee"—speak volumes about the centrality of religion in its culture and politics. Although Uganda is not officially governed by religious law, religious principles find expression in its laws and policies and are often used to justify and legitimize them. Religion is effectively incorporated into Uganda's legal and policy framework.[6] Nowhere is the effective incorporation of religion in Uganda's legal system more apparent than in the area of women's sexuality and reproductive control. By controlling these facets of women's lives, their domestication and subordination is guaranteed. Many scholars have demonstrated how the intersection between gender inequality and women's roles in the unpaid care economy are crucial in the sustenance of patriarchal-capitalist systems.[7] In all of these cases, a fusion of African culture/morality and a wide array of religious values have been invoked to justify the actions and legitimize such overtly political agendas.

Although African cultural norms and traditional religions were generally not strong expressions of egalitarian gender ideologies, most celebrated and valorized the female body as a reproductive or sexual icon.[8] With the introduction of the Abrahamic religions, the positive conceptualizations of African sexualities (including the African female body) were largely negated and overtaken by the state-supported advocacy of the messianic religions.[9] Mutua explains how African traditions were delegitimized by a new socio-political and religious order:

> Africa—from top to bottom—was remade in the image of Europe complete with Eurocentric modern states. Christianity played a crucial role in this process: weaning Africans from their roots and pacifying them for the new order. Utilizing superior resources, it occupied most political space and practically killed local religious traditions and then closed off society from other persuasions... Islam, which had invaded Africa at an earlier date, was equally insidious and destructive of local religions. Its forceful conversions and wars of conquest, together with its prohibition of its repudiation, were violative of the rights of Africans as well... Progress, culture and humanity were identified entirely in Islamic or Christian terms, never with reference to indigenous traditions.[10]

Through the processes of proselytization and acculturation, many sexual practices that had been acceptable in pre-colonial, pre-Islamic, and pre-Christian Uganda were transformed into "sinful," "deviant," "illegitimate," and even "criminal."

Unlike the Abrahamic religions where God is defined as male, in African Traditional Religions (ATR) neither the Supreme Being nor the divinities are necessarily male. The status of women in the Abrahamic religion is also mirrored in the positions they hold in their ministrations. Leadership and ministration in both the Catholic and Muslim religions remains the preserve of men to this date. And although Anglicans allowed women into priesthood more than 20 years ago, the question of whether they could be ordained as bishops was a subject of great controversy until very recently (July 2014), when the Church of England voted to allow it. Uganda's Anglican Church, which takes its cue from its former colonial master, will most likely vote to endorse the decision of the Church of England.[11]

Fundamentalist Christianity and Islam in the United States and the Middle East, respectively, have infiltrated Africa through a highly organized born-again evangelical movement as well as conservative branches of various Islamic sects.[12] Several scholars have examined the role of these fundamentalist religious teachings to the politics of gender and sexuality in Africa.[13] There is an unprecedented flow of resources from outside, particularly the US, into Uganda to promote propaganda, laws, and policies against sexual and reproductive rights.[14] For instance, Uganda is bombarded with billboard and media messages that promote abstinence.[15] Some of the financial resources that flow in from foreign conservative and religious sources are often misappropriated by the Ugandan-based partners for personal enrichment. Other scholars have long erased the mythical line that attempts to separate religion from the secular in Africa.[16]

Excavating the religious impulses behind recent laws

The Anti-Homosexuality Act (AHA)

Same-sex sexual relations have been outlawed in Uganda since 1956.[17] Therefore the anti-homosexuality law that was first tabled in parliament in 2009 as a private member's bill and signed into law in February 2014, was essentially re-criminalizing the offence of homosexuality by expanding its scope. Its stated objectives did not mince words:

> ... providing a comprehensive and advanced legislation to protect the cherished culture of the people of Uganda, legal, religious and traditional family values of the people of Uganda, against the attempts of sexual rights activists seeking to impose their values of sexual promiscuity on the peoples of Uganda. There is also need to protect the children and youths of Uganda who are made vulnerable to sexual abuse and deviation as a result of cultural changes ...[18]

State-orchestrated "moral panics" have always served as an effective decoy to distract attention from the more significant socio-economic and political crises afflicting society. This was as true of the targeting of Jews and homosexuals by the German Nazis as it was true of the McCarthyist witch-hunt of homosexuals and Communists in the US. Conflating homosexuality with pedophilia, promiscuity, immorality, and bestiality is an effective way of whipping up moral panic and galvanizing support for regulatory legislation. Preachers continuously used the discourse of child-molestation, recruitment of children, satanic acts, sexual perversion, and spiritual warfare to denounce homosexuality and lobby parliament for the AHA. Hence, homosexuality is one of the hot-button policy issues in Uganda and the overwhelming majority of Ugandans supported the AHA.[19] When the law was passed, the Archbishop of Uganda called on all Ugandans to commend and support parliamentarians.[20]

In 2007, a number of religious groups together with the government Minister of Ethics and Integrity, formed a coalition, ironically called the Interfaith Rainbow Coalition against Homosexuality. Backed by powerful US conservatives and religious leaders, this coalition has systematically and successfully influenced policymakers and the general public against Ugandan homosexuals,[21] by organizing national prayer days and nights, petition drives, fasting campaigns, protest rallies, and street marches to denounce homosexuality. It is not a coincidence that the Anti-Homosexuality bill was tabled just weeks after a conference to expose the "dark and hidden" agenda of homosexuality.[22]

Recently Uganda's Constitutional Court overturned the AHA on the grounds that parliament passed it without the requisite quorum.[23] Still, it has not been erased from the legal landscape. The state's Attorney General immediately filed a notice of appeal against the decision and members of parliament have indicated that they will re-table the bill and pass it with the requisite quorum.[24] The caucus of the National Resistance Movement party also set up a committee to review the matter and report back within a short time.[25] Moreover, as the law was invalidated on a legal technicality, the Constitutional Court is yet to deliberate on whether its substantive provisions conflict with Uganda's international and regional human rights obligations.[26]

The Anti-Pornography Act (APA)

The Anti-Pornography Act (APA) was first drafted in 2005 by the then-Minister of Ethics and Integrity, Nsaba Buturo. At one press conference he told journalists that miniskirts are one of the vices facing Ugandan society because they distract drivers and "can cause an accident because some of our people are weak mentally."[27] In 2009, Buturo was replaced by former Catholic priest Father Simon Lokodo. The draft bill underwent several revisions before it was finally passed and signed into law by President Museveni on 6 February 2014. The stated objectives of the APA are to define what constitutes the offence of pornography and to establish a Pornography Control Committee.[28] Supporters argued that pornography fuels sexual violence against women and girl children and offends public morality.[29] The legislation does indeed include several good provisions that protect children against predatory sexual behavior such as child pornography.[30] However, the definition of pornography in the law is vague, and it fails to delineate the parameters of the offence. Section 2 defines "Pornography" as "any representation through publication, exhibition, cinematography, indecent show, information technology or by whatever means, of a person engaged in real or stimulated explicit sexual activities or any representation of the sexual parts of a person for primarily sexual excitement." The vagueness in this definition allows its scope to extend from something read or seen on screens and stages to something seen on the streets. Such ambiguity resulted in the APA being dubbed the "Miniskirt Law," despite the fact that the term "miniskirt" is never mentioned. That nickname resulted from the popular interpretation of the law's prohibition of *inter alia*, "any representation of the sexual parts of a person for primarily sexual excitement." Father Lokodo said as much:

> Anything related to indecent dressing, exposing certain parts of the anatomy of a person, I call it pornographic and therefore condemn it … I don't like this question of saying human rights, maturity, et cetera. This is not correct … because when you go indecently on the streets of Kampala you'll become … a cinema … Say what you want to say, but we're coming out with a law that people should go back to their decent way of covering their bodies.[31]

The bill version of the law had also explicitly banned the depiction of "sexual parts of a person such as breasts, thighs, buttocks or genitalia." As soon as the bill was signed into law, several vigilante groups largely made up of young men started publicly undressing women they saw as violators.[32] Police officers also started ordering women on the streets to return home and "dress decently." There was even a case where a magistrate summarily sentenced two women in her courtroom to a three-hour confinement for wearing miniskirts.[33] Ironically, the law that was passed to protect women from violence is in fact fuelling it. It emboldens Ugandans to abuse women's right to bodily integrity, privacy, equality, and non-discrimination.

Infuriated women's rights groups protested at the National Theatre grounds holding placards with messages such as, "Don't sexualize *my* body," "Give us maternal health care; don't undress us on the street!," "Keep your eyes off my thighs and fix the economy," "Thou shall not touch my miniskirt," and "My body, my closet, my money, my rules." The police were quick to invoke another recently passed draconian law—the Public Order and Management Act—to suppress the protestors.[34]

Police officials then issued a statement condemning those engaging in "mob undressing." The Minister of Information and National Guidance then clarified that the law was being misinterpreted, as it does not prohibit short skirts. She said the government was ready to make adjustments to the law in case genuine concerns were raised.[35] Even Father Lokodo retracted his words about the "miniskirt law."[36] The Prime Minister and the Attorney General told parliament that they would recall the law and review it.[37] But so far, nothing has happened. Instead there has been a marked up-surge in sexual harassment and a *de facto* dress code.[38] Although three ministers (Ministers of Ethics and Integrity, of Information, and of Gender, Labor and Social Development) went on record to deny that the law imposes a dress code for women, the gendered subtexts of the APA had been constructed as far back as 2005.

It is important to place the "mob undressing" that followed the passing of the APA in the wider context of violence against women in Uganda. For the majority of Ugandan women, violence is not an isolated act but an unfortunate fact of life. The 2006 Uganda Demographic and Health Survey (UDHS) estimated that up to 60 percent of women in Uganda aged 15 and above have experienced gender-based violence.[39] An earlier nationwide study conducted by the Uganda Law Reform Commission yielded similar statistics.[40]

The objectifying language that defines "pornography" in the APA, particularly the phrase, "representation of the sexual parts … for primarily sexual excitement" echoes the linking of women's bodies to sexuality by the two Ethics and Integrity ministers mentioned above. The language in the law unfairly harms women, particularly young women and sex workers who already face harassment and discrimination.[41] The direct violation of women's right to bodily integrity, privacy, equality, and non-discrimination is the consequence of the indirect suggestions and implicit marking of women's bodies as sexual and erotic within the APA.

The HIV and AIDS Prevention and Control Act (HAPCA)

The HIV and AIDS Prevention and Control Act (HAPCA) was passed by parliament on 13 May 2014 and signed into law by President Museveni on 31 July 2014. In enacting HAPCA, the government ostensibly sought a legal framework for the prevention and control of HIV and AIDS. The HAPCA contains several punitive provisions that have been described as "regressive" and "antiquated."[42] Several executive entities including the Ministry of Health and the Uganda AIDS Commission issued public critiques.[43]

The HAPCA imposes a maximum 10-year custodial sentence for "intentional transmission" of HIV and five years for "attempted transmission" of the virus. In addition, the law subjects pregnant women and their partners to mandatory HIV testing. It allows for the disclosure of a person's HIV status by a court order without their consent in certain cases.[44]

The National AIDS Commission has reported that the overwhelming majority of Ugandans are unaware of their HIV status[45] and has for decades been promoting the strategy of voluntary counseling and testing (VCT) as the most effective way to reduce transmission and increase treatment. By reversing course and mandating testing, the Ugandan government is negating the recommendations of its own professional agencies and a fundamental right to privacy guaranteed in its constitution and in international treaties it has ratified.

However well intentioned the law may be, available evidence demonstrates that laws criminalizing HIV transmission, exposure, or non-disclosure ultimately cause more harm than good.[46] Criticizing the punitive provisions of the law, the Global Commission on HIV and the Law stated:

> While the desired aim of such punitive laws is to protect people from HIV infection, they often have the opposite effect. Laws which criminalize HIV transmission and exposure widen the net of criminal liability and turn people living with HIV into potential criminals. They shift the responsibility for HIV prevention solely onto people living with HIV, in direct contrast to effective HIV prevention messages that call for everyone to practice safer sex. Most damagingly, the fear caused by the criminalization of HIV transmission and exposure isolates people living with HIV. Misdirected criminal laws discourage people from accessing HIV testing and other HIV prevention and care services. Ultimately these laws undermine investments and corrode hard-fought gains in HIV prevention, treatment and care.[47]

UNAIDS has also noted that national responses to HIV continue to fail to deal with the main drivers of the epidemic, including gender inequality and criminalization of populations at risk.[48]

The fact that the prevalence rate of HIV is higher in women (8.3 percent) than the national average (7.3 percent) has been linked to women's *de jure* and *de facto* inequality.[49] Such issues go beyond the biomedical or epidemiological aspects of the disease and expose the socio-economic and cultural facets of the pandemic, which HAPCA seems to have ignored, such as the increasing feminization of poverty.

The response to HIV/AIDS in Uganda cannot afford to neglect these structural issues. Women are usually the first to know their sero-status (through their connection to antenatal care) and are hence often presumed to be transmitters of the virus, not recipients.[50] Criminalizing HIV transmission thus makes women even more vulnerable, and it also deters their seeking HIV testing and antenatal care. If an HIV-positive mother breastfeeds her baby, she may now be charged with intentional transmission. Routine mandatory testing of pregnant women and their partners is a breach of their right to privacy.

Sex workers—who are recognized among the most at-risk popula-tion (MARP) group in Uganda—are also affected by the passage of HAPCA.[51] By criminalizing transmission, the law further opens the door to the violation of the rights of sex workers, the majority of whom are women.[52] First, the law acts as a disincentive for sex workers to test for HIV and avoid the criminal net of "intentional transmis-sion." Secondly, and most importantly, HAPCA effectively shifts the responsibility of engaging in safe sex exclusively to the sellers and lets purchasers off the hook. Street-based female and transgender sex work-ers are bound to suffer the most. The policies enacted in the HAPCA are in line with the abstinence-only stance that the government adopted in recent years, moving away from the earlier, more effective HIV response strategy of "**A**bstention, **B**e faithful and **C**ondom-use"—ABC.[53]

The link between these policies and the new-fangled religious mor-ality is clear. Although Uganda pioneered the now globally acclaimed ABC strategy in its early public health approach to HIV/AIDS, fund-ing under US President George Bush's PEPFAR in the mid-2000s was premised on religion-based policies of abstention and faithfulness. The result was an upward spiral in infection rates, which, ironically, in turn, encouraged the enactment of HAPCA.

Policy against unmarried pregnant students

Several universities, particularly faith-based ones, have adopted policies forcing pregnant students to leave school by either suspending or expelling them.[54] The same policy does not target the men who impregnate them. This obvious double standard reflects a patriarchal obsession with female sexual purity but leaves untamed the unbridled sexuality of men, again a view strongly rooted in religious dogma.

Faith-based universities say they cannot condone the sin of fornication in their community and argue that as private institutions they have a right to impose their moral values on their students. These restrictions on women's sexual behavior and the high cost imposed on them for being sexually active in the name of religion plainly violate international human rights standards enumerated in several international treaties and in Uganda's 1995 constitution, which establishes equality between the sexes and outlaws any form of discrimination based on sex.[55]

These religious universities also exhibit double standards and hypocrisy in penalizing women for exercising their reproductive rights while, at the same time, offering a legal curriculum that includes constitutional law and international human rights law, and a course on women's rights including their right of access to family planning methods that give control over the number, spacing, and timing of children.

Finally, the law defines a private university as one whose "proprietor is a person, firm or organization other than government and basically maintained out of funds other than a public fund," and clearly states that any accredited private university is treated as a corporate body suffering the same fate as any other corporations. However, these religious universities are exempt from certain taxes like corporation tax. By offering them such exemptions that constitute subsidies, the government is footing the bill for discrimination and the violation of its own constitution.

Conclusion

If we bend the arc of Ugandan history towards women's rights, then we will have achieved a significant landmark in achieving freedom for all. Those promoting laws and policies in opposition valorize religious and cultural pluralism. But deference to the values of Ugandan society cannot be absolute. Indeed, Uganda's constitution extends international human rights standards to minorities against the will of the majority culture.[56] In other words, the majority does not have a political right to legislate against what it deems immoral at the expense of the minority.

But we do not have to rely exclusively on international human rights standards in responding to the arguments of religious and cultural relativists. One of the unique features of the African regional human rights instrument—the African Charter on Human and Peoples Rights (Banjul Charter)—is its emphasis on group (people's) rights and on the indivisibility of rights.[57] This means that socio-economic rights and group rights are unequivocally as justifiable as civil and political rights.[58] In this case claims of sexual and reproductive freedom by the social group of women stand at par and are interrelated with their civil rights to work, vote, or exercise freedom of speech.

Hence African cultural and religious relativists who revere "group rights" above "individual rights" must acknowledge the rights of women as a significant social group in society.[59] Just as they argue that there is no such thing as universal "moral truths" and that the structure of human rights needs to recognize cultural differences when applying human rights norms, so too must the relativists realize that their "moral truths" are not universal to women in their diversity. Ironically, the contemporary religious morality being parroted by these relativists is steeped in Abrahamic religions, which are alien to African culture and therefore can lay no legitimate claim to traditional values.

The sexual laws and policies discussed in this chapter are embedded in and shaped by the "moral panics" associated with a socio-political crisis brewing in Uganda. They are a consequence of exaggerations and misinformation on HIV/AIDS, same-sex desire and youth sexuality, and are fuelled by religious, cultural, and political leaders for self-serving agendas. They signify an attempt to perpetuate patriarchal notions of female sexual purity and the confinement of sexuality within a hetero-normative marital and coital framework. However, being inherently discriminatory and exclusionary, they can never succeed. To borrow an old religious mantra: we shall overcome!

Notes

1 *CEDAW General Recommendation No. 24: Article 12 of the Convention (Women and Health)*, UN Committee on the Elimination of Discrimination Against Women (CEDAW), (A/54/38/Rev.1), 1999.
2 Danoye Oguntola-Laguda, "Religion and Politics in a Pluralistic Society: The Nigerian Experience," *Politics and Religion* 2, no. 2 (2008): 123–33.
3 UBOS, *2002 Uganda Population and Housing Census: Analytical Report* (Kampala: Uganda Bureau of Statistics, 2002).
4 Astrid Schau-Larsen, "In God We Trust: Christianity, Uganda and AIDS Epidemic," MA Dissertation (Concordia University, Montreal, Quebec, Canada, 2011); Adrienne Silnicki, "Aid for AIDS: The Policies and Performance of PEPFAR in Uganda," MA Thesis (St. Mary's University, Halifax, Nova Scotia, 2014).
5 Article 7 of the 1995 Constitution clearly states: "Uganda shall not adopt a State religion." Constitution of the Republic of Uganda. Art. 7. (1995).
6 Sylvia Tamale, "Exploring the Contours of African Sexualities: Religion, Law and Power," *African Human Rights Law Journal* 14, no.1 (2014): 150–177
7 For example, see Nancy Folbre, "The Care Economy in Africa: Subsistence Production and Unpaid Care," *Journal of African Economies* 23, Supplement 1 (2014): 128–156; Mónica Serrano, *Unpaid Care Work in Africa,*

(Bilbao: Fundación BBVA, 2012), Documento de Trabajo 6, available at: http://w3.grupobbva.com/TLFU/dat/DT_06_2012_web.pdf; Debbie Budlender, *A Critical Review of Selected Time Use Surveys. Programme on Gender and Development*, Paper No. 2. (Geneva UNRISD, Geneva, 2007); Diane Elson, ed., *Male Bias in the Development Process*, second edn (Manchester: Manchester University Press, 1995).

8   Nkiru Nzegwu, "'Osunality' (or African Eroticism)," in *African Sexualities: A Reader*, ed. Sylvia Tamale, (Oxford: Pambazuka Press, 2011), 253–270; Izugbara Chimaraoke, "Sexuality and the Supernatural in Africa," in *African Sexualities: A Reader*, ed. Sylvia Tamale (Oxford: Pambazuka Press, 2011), 533–558; Bibi Bakare-Yusuf, "Nudity and Morality: Legislating Women's Bodies and Dress in Nigeria," in *African Sexualities: A Reader*, ed. Sylvia Tamale (Oxford: Pambazuka Press, 2011), 116–129.

9   Tamale, "Exploring the Contours of African Sexualities: Religion, Law and Power," 150–177; Ikechukwu Kanu, "African Traditional Religion in a Globalizing World," *International Journal of Humanities Social Sciences and Education* 1, no. 8 (2014): 4–12.

10 Makau Mutua, *Human Rights: A Political and Cultural Critique* (Philadelphia: University of Pennsylvania Press, 2002), 109–110

11 The Archbishop of the Church of Uganda, Most Rev. Stanley Ntagali released a statement soon after the Church of England's decision, welcoming the latter's vote.

12 Tamale, "Exploring the Contours of African Sexualities: Religion, Law and Power," 155–159.

13 Kapya Kaoma, *American Cultural Warriors in Africa: A Guide to the Exporters of Homophobia and Sexism* (Somerville, Mass.: Political Research Associates, 2014); Ayesha Imam, "The Muslim Religious Right ('Fundamentalists') and Sexuality," in *Women and Sexuality in Muslim Societies*, ed. Pinar Ilkkaracan (Istanbul: Women for Women's Human Rights (WWHR)/Kadmin Insan Haklari Projesi, 2000) 15–30; Paul Gifford, *The New Crusaders: Christianity and the New Right in Southern Africa* (London: Pluto, 1981).

14 The Oscar-nominated movie, *God Loves Uganda* vividly demonstrates these links. Renee Fabian, "'God Loves Uganda' makes Academy Awards Short List," *Glaad.org*, 3 December 2013, www.glaad.org/blog/god-loves-uganda-makes-academy-awards-short-list.

15 Monica Twesiime, "'Until Marriage' or 'Until Graduation': Abstinence-Only Strategies and their Impact on University Students in Uganda and Kenya," *Working Paper* No. 1 (Kampala: Law, Gender and Sexuality Research Project, 2008).

16 John D. Y. Peel, "The Pastor and the *Babalawo*: the Interaction of Religions in Nineteenth Century Yorubaland," *Africa* 60, no. 3 (1990): 338–69; John Comaroff and Jean Comaroff, *Of Revelation and Revolution: Christianity, Colonialism, and Consciousness in South Africa*, Vol. 1. (Chicago, Ill.: University of Chicago Press, 1991); Norman Etherington, "Recent Trends in the Historiography of Christianity in Southern Africa," *Journal of Southern African Studies* 22, no. 2 (1996): 201–19.

17 See Section 145 of the Penal Code Act which criminalizes sex "against the order of nature" punishable with life imprisonment.

18 The Ugandan Anti-Homosexuality Bill. Principle 1.1. (2009).
19 Its popularity is based on opinion polls published in the local media and the turnout at the National Thanksgiving Prayer Rally held in Kololo Independence grounds in the wake of the passing of the AHA.
20 Paul Aruho, "Homosexuality Threat to Mankind, Says Archbishop," *Daily Monitor*, 13 January 2014, 13.
21 Kaoma, *American Cultural Warriors in Africa: A Guide to the Exporters of Homophobia and Sexism*.
22 The conference was organized by a fundamentalist religious NGO called the Family Life Network with keynote speeches delivered by several American evangelicals. See Kaoma, *American Cultural Warriors in Africa: A Guide to the Exporters of Homophobia and Sexism*; Tamale, "Exploring the Contours of African Sexualities: Religion, Law and Power."
23 See judgment in the case of *Oloka-Onyango and Ors v. Attorney General* Const. Petition No. 8 of 2014 (Unreported), dated 1 August 2014. The speed with which the case was decided led pundits to speculate that government had responded to international pressure and sanctions in repudiating this law.
24 Solomon Arinaitwe, "MPs Begin Drive to Return Law on Homosexuality," *Daily Monitor*, 6 August 2014, 5; Umaru Kashaka, "Legislators Want the Anti-Gay Bill Back," *New Vision*, 5 August 2014, 7; Solomon Arinaitwe, "More MPs Want Gay Law Back," *Daily Monitor*, 7 August 2014, 5.
25 In the midst of all this, President Museveni cautioned the NRM Parliamentary Caucus to handle the overturned law with care: "This law is now an issue of *Semusota guli mu ntamu* [a snake in a cooking pot]. If we try to kill the snake, we may break the pot, if we don't we won't." Henry Sekanjako and Moses Walubiri, "Gay Bill: Museveni warns MPs," *New Vision*, 12 August 2014, 6.
26 Uganda has ratified all the major international and regional human rights treaties and even incorporated their basic principles into its constitution.
27 "Uganda Seeking Mini-Skirt Ban," *BBC*, 17 September 2008, http://news.bbc.co.uk/2/hi/7621823.stm.
28 The Uganda Anti-Pornography Act (2014).
29 See Official Hansard, 19 December 2013.
30 The Ugandan Anti-Pornography Act. Section 14. (2014).
31 NTV Uganda. "Ethics Minister Proposes Law to Ban Mini-Skirts," *Youtube* video, 4:08, 5 April 2013, www.youtube.com/watch?v=jCuxFJipQUk.
32 Yazid Yolisigira, "Mob Undresses 10 People Over Indecent Exposure," *Daily Monitor*, 26 February 2014, 26; Tina Musuya, "Activist Vows to Wrestle Anti-Porn Law," *Daily Monitor*, 28 February 2014, 22.
33 Malik Fahad Jingo, "Women Get Three-hour Jail Term for Wearing Miniskirts" *Daily Monitor*, 7 March 2014.
34 J. Oloka-Onyango, "Understanding the Genesis and Impact of Recent Legislation in Uganda," *Pambazuka News*, Issue 676 (2014), available at: www.pambazuka.org/en/category/features/91567.
35 Dan Wandera, "Anti-Pornography Law was Misunderstood, Says Minister," *Daily Monitor*, 5 March 2014, 13.
36 Stephen Otage, "Women Free to Wear Miniskirts—Lokodo," *Daily Monitor*, 17 January 2014, 3.

37 Joyce Namutebi and Umar Kashaka, "Cabinet to Review Anti-Pornography Law," *New Vision*, 26 February 2014, 5.

38 J. Oloka-Onyango, "Understanding the Genesis and Impact of Recent Legislation in Uganda," *Pambazuka News* 676, 1 May 2014.

39 UBOS, *2002 Uganda Population and Housing Census: Analytical Report.*

40 Also see Lillian Tibatemwa-Ekirikubinza, *Women's Violent Crimes in Uganda: More Sinned Against than Sinning* (Kampala: Fountain Publishers, 1998).

41 Sex worker organizations have joined other human rights defenders to petition against the APA in the Constitutional Court.

42 Deborah Birx, "Statement from Ambassador Deborah Birx, M.D., U.S. Global AIDS Coordinator, on the Passage of the HIV Prevention and Control Act by the Ugandan Parliament," *PEPFAR*, 14 May 2014, www. pepfar.gov/press/releases/2014/226095.htm; "Will Criminalisation of HIV Transmission Help Prevention Efforts?" *New Vision*, 7 July 2014, 14.

43 International Community of Women Living with HIV & AIDS Eastern Africa, *Uganda's President Yoweri Museveni Signs HIV Prevention and Control Bill into Law, Contradicting Evidence, Human Rights*, 20 August 2014, www.icwea.org/ 2014/08/ugandas-president-yoweri-kaguta-museveni-signs-hiv-prevention-and-c ontrol-bill-into-law-contradicting-evidence-human-rights-2/; Mercy Nalugo, "Rights Bodies Protest HIV/AIDS Bill," *Daily Monitor*, 15 May 2014, 3.

44 The Ugandan HIV and AIDS Prevention and Control Act. Sections 41, 13, 18. (2014).

45 Uganda AIDS Commission, *Global AIDS Response Progress Report: Country Progress Report, Uganda* (Kampala: Uganda AIDS Commission, 2012). Available at: www.unaids.org/en/dataanalysis/knowyourresponse/coun tryprogressreports/2012countries/ce_UG_Narrative_Report[1].pdf.

46 Global Commission on HIV and the Law, *Risks, Rights and Health* (New York: UNDP, 2012) available at:www.hivlawcommission.org/index.php/report.

47 Ibid.

48 UNAIDS, *Recommendations Brief to Michel Sidibe, UNAIDS Executive Director* (Geneva: UNAIDS Reference Group on HIV and Human Rights, 2009).

49 Christine Obbo, "Gender, Age and Class: Discourses on HIV Transmission and Control in Uganda," in *Culture and Sexual Risk: Anthropological Perspectives on AIDS*, eds Han ten Brummelhuis and Gilbert Lerdt (Luxemburg: Gordon and Breach, 1995).

50 Global Commission on HIV and the Law, *Risks, Rights and Health.*

51 Uganda AIDS Commission, *Global AIDS Response Progress Report: Country Progress Report.*

52 Anna Forbes, *Sex Work, Criminalization and HIV: Lessons from Advocacy History* (San Francisco, Calif.: BETA, 2010) available at: www.sfaf.org/hiv-info/hot-topics/beta/2010-beta-sumfall-sexwork.pdf.

53 Human Rights Watch, *The Less They Know the Better: Abstinence-Only, HIV/AIDS Programs in Uganda* Report Volume 17, no. 4 (2005); Schau-Larsen, "In God We Trust: Christianity, Uganda and AIDS Epidemic."

54 Such Universities include Uganda Catholic University and the Islamic University in Uganda. Christine Wanjala, "Varsity Suspension Over Pregnancy: Punishing Sin or Girls?" *Daily Monitor*, 7 May 2014.

55 Sylvia Tamale, "Women Have a Right to Reproduce," *Sunday Vision*, 11 May 2014.

56 See, for example, Articles 32, 33, 36 of the Constitution. Also see the case of *Atala and Daughters v. Chile* [IACHR (23 July 2008) Ser L/Doc 22 Rev 1], where the Inter-American Court of Human Rights refuted the common objections to sexual orientation as a ground for non-discrimination, cementing LGBT rights under the concept of *jus cogens* (Rudman 2014).

57 Traditionally, human rights are hierarchically divided into "first generation" (civil and political rights), "second generation" (economic and social rights), and "third generation" (group rights).

58 Oji Umozurike, *The African Charter on Human and People's Rights* (The Hague: Martinus Nijhoff, 1997) 46; Frans Viljoen, *International Human Rights Law in Africa* (Oxford: Oxford University Press, 2007) 237.

59 This argument is made with full knowledge of the differences among women and the intersectional discrimination that such heterogeneity engenders. Reference to the social group "women" is used here politically and strategically to spotlight the gender injustice suffered by all women.

12 Negotiating gender mainstreaming in China

Cai Yiping and Liu Bohong

The last decade of the twentieth century witnessed the emergence of a global women's movement, which fought for and won recognition of women's human rights in a series of international conferences around issues of environment (Rio, 1992), human rights (Vienna, 1993), population and development (Cairo, 1994), poverty (Copenhagen, 1995), habitat (Istanbul, 1996), and food (Rome, 1997). However, the spread of neo-liberalism and fundamentalism in the years since threatens to erode the gains women envisioned two decades ago.[1] Marked by two unprecedented critical events: the "war on terror" and, more recently, the global financial crisis, the first decade of the twenty-first century gave birth to "the fierce new world"—a world full of shaken premises, complicated contradictions, serious fractures, severe backlash, broken promises, and uncertain outcomes for the world's women, especially those of us from the economic South.[2]

Situated in the Asia Pacific region, arguably the most dynamic in recent years, China has become a vital player in this new world order. When the government initiated reforms and opened the country to the world in the late 1970s and early 1980s, new challenges arose to Chinese women's rights. Social and economic transformation often enforced patriarchal gender norms, and job discrimination flourished in the market-oriented economy. At the same time, however, a Chinese women's movement re-emerged and reconnected with the global women's movement, especially at the United Nations Fourth World Conference on Women in Beijing in 1995.

The conference and its non-governmental organization (NGO) forum provided "a historic turning point for the women's movement in China."[3] Some Chinese participants describe it as "eye-opening," ending their intellectual isolation and pushing the boundaries of national critical feminist reflection. More than 5,000 Chinese women attended the NGO forum in Huairou, among more than 30,000 participants from all over the world.[4] The event had an immense and profound impact on the development of women's civil society, especially through the introduction of new concepts such as "gender mainstreaming." The forum enhanced our understanding of the role of NGOs generally, and of the international women's human rights framework and global feminist movements more specifically.

The concept of gender mainstreaming had first been proposed to the international community at the 1985 Third World Conference on Women in Nairobi, Kenya, and was formally featured again in Beijing.[5] The United Nations Economic and Social Council defines the concept as:

> The process of assessing the implications for women and men of any planned action, including legislation, policies or programs, in all areas and at all levels. It is a strategy for making women's as well as men's concerns and experiences an integral dimension of the design, implementation, monitoring and evaluation of policies and programs in all political, economic and societal spheres so that women and men benefit equally and inequality is not perpetuated. The ultimate goal is to achieve gender equality.[6]

This chapter will assess the trajectory of "gender mainstreaming" in China since 1995, examining how it has been officially interpreted, its impact on policies and programs, and its overall effect on women's rights and development. We will examine the main actors currently driving China's gender mainstreaming agenda, weigh progress and setbacks, and set forth possible future strategies. China has incorporated principles of gender equality into its legal frameworks, thereby quite literally mainstreaming gender into public policy so as to conform with the Beijing Platform for Action. However, concurrent neo-liberal policies that have vastly expanded China's privately held economy have overwhelmed the capacity of government to monitor and enforce the gender commitments it has made—giving rise to vast differences between rhetoric and reality, and leaving Chinese women vulnerable to work-based discrimination and disparities. There is a gap between the officially sanctioned gender policies and the actual circumstances of women in China.

From "women can hold up half the sky" to gender mainstreaming

"Gender" as an important analytical category was first introduced to China in 1993 by a group of overseas Chinese women scholars who had studied in the United States under the auspices of the Gender and Development Seminar of Tianjin Normal University.[7] The concept took root and was then widely disseminated after the UN conference by academic Chinese feminists and women's rights advocates.[8] Before the concepts of "gender" and "gender equality" landed in China in the 1990s, "equality between men and women" had been the prevailing discourse, enshrined in China's constitution since 1954[9] and manifest in Chairman Mao's well-known quote "women can hold up half the sky."[10] Together with the fact that China hosted the UN summit in Beijing, this should have made the introduction of "gender equality" relatively straightforward. However, the concept was co-opted immediately, and "gender mainstreaming" was translated into Mandarin to mean "mainstreaming gender into policymaking." This phrase became a resounding slogan after 1995, promoted by the All China Women's Federation (ACWF).[11]

In the 20 years since, China has made a great deal of progress mainstreaming gender into policymaking. First, the government has made a political commitment to promote gender equality at the highest levels. In 1995, at the welcoming ceremony for the UN summit, President Jiang Zemin announced that the country "has made equality between men and women a basic national policy in promoting Chinese social development."[12] And in 2012, the *Report of the Eighteenth Congress of the Chinese Communist Party* reaffirmed this "basic national policy of equality between men and women."[13] Although the explicit language guarantees "equality between men and women," not "gender equality," these terms are seen as equivalent and used interchangeably in many Chinese documents when translated into English.

However, the precise meaning of "equality between men and women" has yet to be defined in the Chinese context. In 2004, preparing to commemorate the ten-year anniversary of the UN summit and the "National Policy of Equality between Men and Women," ACWF launched a media campaign promoting gender equality. More recently, in a meeting with new ACWF leadership in 2013, President Xi Jinping further elaborated that "equality between men and women" includes equality in rights, opportunities, and outcomes between men and women.[14]

Second, China has established formal governmental machinery for the advancement of women at national and local levels. The National Working Committee on Children and Women under the State Council (NWCCW) is the government agency that coordinates the promotion of gender equality and facilitates women and children's development in China. Its membership consists of various government ministries and community-based organizations and has grown from an initial 19 members to 33 today. In recent years increased resources have strengthened the NWCCW and its local affiliates, enabling the agency to promote the enactment and enforcement of laws and regulations protecting women's human rights. NWCCW also promotes compliance with the Convention on the Elimination of All Forms of Discrimination against Women (CEDAW), the Convention on the Rights of the Child (CRC), and other international conventions.[15]

Since 2008, the Chinese government has also required the National Bureau of Statistics to disaggregate social and economic data by gender and publish the findings annually. The government also conducts national surveys on the status of Chinese women and other research relevant to women.

Third, laws and policies on gender equality have been promulgated and implemented. In March 2004, China's constitution was amended to declare that the "state respects and safeguards human rights," which allows for the further protection of women's human rights.[16] The addition of "human rights" to the constitution broadens protection for women beyond equality to include an array of economic, cultural and social rights, and international norms. Since 1995, the country's formal system of laws and regulations for the protection of rights and interests of women has become more robust, built around the Law on the Protection of Rights and Interests of Women. Numerous laws and regulations have been formulated or amended to further protect the rights of women.[17] For example, at the local level, the Regulation on Promotion of Gender Equality adopted by the Shenzhen Municipal People's Congress in June 2012 became the first gender equality regulation on mainland China.[18] In July 2008, the state also promulgated Opinions on Preventing and Deterring Domestic Violence, which specifies responsibilities of various departments in preventing and intervening to prevent the problem.[19] Twenty-eight of 31 provinces/municipalities/ autonomous regions have since promulgated laws and policies against domestic violence. Currently, the national Anti-Domestic Violence Act is being proposed to the legislators and the public for consultation.[20] In December 2007, the government issued the China National Plan of Action on Combating Trafficking in Women and *Children* (2008–2012).[21] The plan covers various aspects of the problem—namely prevention and suppression of trafficking, victim rescue, repatriation and rehabilitation, and international cooperation—and provides a long-term anti-trafficking enforcement mechanism. To safeguard the rights of women, all courts have set up collegial panels for women's rights or against domestic violence, with nearly 8,000 cadres from women's confederations acting as people's jurors. By 2010, more than 2,800 counties nationwide had opened a "12338" women's rights hotline in the country's 31 provinces/autonomous regions and municipalities.[22]

Fourth, women's development and gender equality are integrated into China's economic and social development plan and its national human rights action plan, in compliance with the state's commitments to the Beijing Platform for Action and CEDAW. Since 1995, the Chinese government has developed and implemented the National Program on Women and Development, and according to the assessment of the first two national "programs," the main goals have been achieved.[23] In the Outline of the Eleventh Five-Year Program for National Economic and Social Development (2006–2010), promulgated in March 2006, there is a chapter dedicated to "Guarantee Rights and Interests of Women and Children," which incorporates the needs of women into national development. Chapter 36 of the Outline of the Twelfth Five-Year Plan for National Economic and Social Development (2011–2015), issued in March 2011 also contains a section that emphasizes promoting women's development and outlines specific requirements for the advancement of women. In April 2009, the State Council released the National Human Rights Action Plan (2009–2010), the first-ever programmatic document of this kind in China. A second National Human Rights Action Plan (2012–2015) promulgated in June 2012 outlines seven focus areas to protect women's legal rights, including (1) promote women's equal participation in the management of state and social affairs; (2) eliminate gender discrimination in employment; (3) guarantee women's rights to have equal access to economic resources; (4) improve reproductive health services for women; (5) prevent and prohibit domestic violence against women; (6) combat trafficking of women; and (7) strengthen the gender statistics and gender segregated data.

Fifth, training and capacity building on gender mainstreaming has been conducted for government officials, and a group of "gender experts" were invited to provide their expertise in the policymaking process.[24] NWCCW and relevant government departments collaborate with UN agencies and other development agencies to conduct capacity training on gender mainstreaming for policymakers, women's federation staff, and development practitioners, as well as to familiarize them with the international human rights framework. For example, the Jiangsu, Anhui, Zhejiang, and Gansu provinces, and the Beijing municipality have established an inter-sectoral "Gender Equality Evaluation Mechanisms for Laws and Policies," a body composed of government officials, researchers, and women's federation staff, to ensure equality and justice in legislation and policymaking. Some local Party

Schools, where local government officials are trained, offer courses on gender mainstreaming in their curriculum. In 2005, supported by Action Aid's China office, Zhangjiakou municipality of Hebei Province initiated an experimental project on gender-responsive budgets.[25]

Finally, women's/gender studies programs in education and research institutions have increased throughout the country. In 1999, a membership-based national network—the Chinese Women's Research Society—was founded, and it has carried out research and advocacy on various gender issues. In the last two decades, there have been more than 100 women/gender studies centers/programs established in universities, women's federations, and social science academies across the country.[26] The National Fund on Social Sciences lists women/gender studies in its catalogue and encourages young scholars to apply. Increasing numbers of students and young scholars choose gender studies as a major or area of research.[27]

Feminist criticism and reflection on gender mainstreaming in China

Despite the progress on gender mainstreaming made in the last two decades in China, gender inequality continues to grow in the country.[28] Numerous studies on Chinese economic transition indicate that three decades of market-oriented reform have had far-reaching implications for women. In 2010, China became the world's second-largest economy after the United States.[29] Against this backdrop is the glaring reality that gender gaps are widening, as are regional and rural-urban disparities. According to three surveys on the status of Chinese women conducted in 1990, 2000, and 2010, the income gap between men and women has increased both in urban and rural areas, despite relatively high rates of female labor force participation (about 40 percent higher than the world average).[30]

With the state withdrawing from the area of social security, women have faced new obstacles to participation in the labor market. There is evidence that women were more likely to be laid off than men during the restructuring of state-owned enterprises (SOE), giving women, especially married women, higher rates and longer spells of unemployment.[31] Women have also withdrawn from the labor force at much higher rates than men since the 1990s, and a growing number of urban workers, predominantly women, have been pushed into informal types of work that are temporary, insecure, and low-paying.[32] The gender wage gap has also widened in the post-reform period. For example, in Guangdong province, which is in the forefront of the country in per capita income and per capita gross national product (GDP), women's annual incomes are only 60 percent of men's, according to the Third Survey on Status of Women in China conducted in 2010.[33]

In China, as elsewhere in the developing world, migration to the cities is the most common path taken by rural residents in search of higher incomes. According to China's Sixth National Census in 2010, there are 220 million migrants in China, and women comprise almost 47 percent of them (about 100 million). As "second-class" citizens without urban registration (*hukuo*), they have limited access to social services and other social provisions.[34] Nor are they able to take their children with them, as the children would not be granted permission to attend urban schools. Those women "left behind" when their husbands seek work beyond the village often have to perform farming tasks, manage household chores, and provide care for young and old dependents.

Women's political participation is also still low, with women comprising only 21 to 23 percent of the National People's Congress (NPC) and only 21 to 22 percent of the villagers' committee.[35] Although these figures are higher than in many other countries, Chinese feminists are disappointed by the slow pace of progress given the vast political and financial resources dedicated to the problem.

In the field of education, China appears to have achieved the targets set in the UN's Millennium Development Goals (MDGs).[36] However, gender parity as measured by overall national enrollment rates masks sub-national, regional, and rural/urban inequalities. Given the tremendous regional disparities that exist, especially among the coastal, interior, and western provinces, the national average is misleading. Moreover, as some NGOs have discovered, there are a number of policies that are making it difficult for female students, such as a recent government directive on "closing and merging schools," which has resulted in long-distance travel to schools in many areas.[37] This has produced gender-differentiated outcomes in access to education, as parents are often reluctant to allow their daughters to travel long distances. Another discriminatory policy is the government authorization of universities to introduce gender-differentiated criteria for college admissions. Several universities require higher university admission exam scores from female students than from their male counterparts, imposing a ceiling on the proportion of female students enrolled in certain subjects and disciplines.[38]

China has also met the target of MDG5 on reducing maternal mortality.[39] Maternal mortality and safe delivery are clearly important outcome indicators for many women, but women's health needs vary over their life cycle and are not limited to pregnancy and delivery.

Therefore, these require more comprehensive policy interventions. The Chinese family planning program, for example, which began in the early 1970s, has been both beneficial and detrimental to gender equality. The program clearly released many women from family pressure to give birth to sons and also reduced the risk of maternal mortality. But the policy implementation was heavy-handed with continued imposition of non-consensual abortion and sterilization, inadequate counseling and choice about contraceptive methods, and little medical follow-up. The policy has also distorted the sex ratio at birth in favor of boys, leading to higher mortality of girls and higher abandonment of infant girls.[40]

The potential long-term negative effects of the One Child Policy on aging, the labor market, social security costs, and, most principally, economic growth has led the state to reassess its stance. The central government announced in November 2013 that the One Child Policy will now be eased, and couples fulfilling certain criteria will be allowed to have a second child.[41] It is too early to evaluate the effect of this policy shift.[42] Some worry, however, that it could exacerbate discrimination against women in the job market.[43] While all these changes are welcome, full reproductive rights, defined by the UN at Cairo and in Beijing as including the right to decide freely on a desirable number of children remain out of reach in China.

Second, there remain critics of gender mainstreaming in China who question the approach, effectiveness, and ultimate goal. Some feminist scholars argue that the gender mainstreaming promoted by the feminist movement has become a strategy of transnational capital to serve its own interests in neo-liberal led globalization—that it is a mechanism through which women's production and reproduction are instrumentalized and exploited, thereby perpetuating gender inequality.[44] Others comment that top-down approaches to gender mainstreaming do not tackle the root causes of gender inequality and its inter-sectionality with class, ethnicity, disability, migration status, and age—and that they fail to address the multiple structural inequalities and disparities in society.[45] A recent academic review of gender mainstreaming and of the role of the ACWF in promoting it points out,[46] as we have suggested, that current efforts on gender mainstreaming focusing on policymaking, law, and legislation are weak on implementation and enforcement.[47]

Furthermore, there remain no accountability mechanisms in Chinese gender policies related to women's participation. Without the broad participation of women's groups, especially grassroots women, we will never fully transform social structures or society. For instance, with the influence of the UN summits in Cairo and Beijing, and with support from the United Nations Population Fund's (UNFPA) country program, China's population and family planning policy has undergone a welcome shift or "re-orientation" from target-driven demographic control to the improvement of reproductive health services, informed choices, and quality of care, an undoubtedly positive change. However, as Joan Kaufman correctly points out, the progress of government-led reform without the full participation of women is limited, and women's sexual and reproductive health and rights have still never been fully integrated into the practice of China's family planning policies.[48]

The relationship between NWCCW and ACWF, as well as the respective roles they play, has also been criticized and is very tricky. As the country's national machinery for the advancement of women, NWCCW is a coordinating agency without a mandate or budget to implement policies or undertake gender-assessments of laws and policies. There is limited cooperation between the NWCCW and a broad range of civil society organizations working on women's rights issues except for ACWF, which administers the NWCCW program. The ACWF is actively involved in women's lives. However, the fact that it functions as a "mass organization," administering the government's official gender policies, can be confusing and reinforces the perception among government officials and the general public that advances toward gender equality are the mandate of woman's organizations, rather than the obligation of the state, to address.

Third, as in many other countries, gender mainstreaming in China faces the challenge of prevailing and dominating gender stereotypes,[49] which affect legislative decision-makers at all levels and also influence women and girls themselves. Advocacy on gender equality always risks regression. Chinese society includes multiple forms of conservatism, including neo-liberal market economic policies that appear to be discriminating against women in development and economic growth, and the revival of so-called traditional culture and values—a discourse that defines women as good mothers, wives, and daughters without affirming women as rights holders in either the public or private domain.

Conclusion

The 20-year review of the Beijing Platform for Action provides an opportunity to re-negotiate the terms of gender mainstreaming and introduce broader women's human rights concepts in China. As a matter of normative public policy, China embraced gender mainstreaming after 1995 by translating it into a "national policy of equality between men and women." Women's human rights, substantive equality, non-discrimination, and the state obligation for such, however, are being lost in translation of this concept.

We need to redefine the national policy of equality between men and women as a "national policy of gender equality," in accordance with CEDAW, the Beijing Platform for Action and other international commitments, to include substantive equality, non-discrimination, and state obligations. We also need to review and repeal the laws and policies that allow for discrimination against women and other marginalized groups, such as unequal retirement age for women and men[50] and unequal opportunity in education.[51]

The government should also live up to its commitment to mainstream gender in all policies and national development plans by including clear monitoring and accountability mechanisms. Coordinated gender mainstreaming policies should tackle the deep roots of gender stereotypes and inequality to create transformative change in the society. There are successful models for shifting culture, policy and practice. For example, the Gender Equality Policy Advocacy Project, led by feminist scholars of the Central Party School, brought together policymakers, scholars, grassroots NGO activists, and women's federation cadres to address one of the most pressing issues in current China—imbalanced sex ratio at birth (SRB).[52] This initiative applied a holistic approach to identify strategies to change the deep-rooted culture of son preference via community mobilization, raising gender awareness, and policy intervention.

Finally, the critical role played by NGOs, women's rights and feminist groups must be recognized. Those charged with implementing gender mainstreaming policies can and should build synergy with NGOs to create a better enabling environment for achieving gender equality. Despite many legal and financial challenges, NGOs in China are flourishing. This decade has seen a revitalization of the women's movement through grassroots women's groups and innovative youth-led feminist activism. Using the Internet for dissemination of information, networking, alliance building, and advocacy, activism is thriving.[53] Well-known cases include the "occupying men's toilet" campaign by various groups of young activists throughout the country in 2012,[54] and the webcast and comprehensive coverage of the China CEDAW report review in Geneva in 2014 by the feminist independent media "Women's Voice." The trajectory of women's rights advocacy shows that women's NGOs represent the vanguard of women's human rights. Official women's federations, on the other hand, have brought legitimacy and accessibility to the policymaking process. These federations should use their access to connect the NGOs to policymakers so that effective interventions can be identified and brought to scale.

Over the past 20 years, by participating in the UN summit in Beijing in 1995 and other global forums, Chinese feminists have played the global/nationalist card skillfully to hold the government accountable for creating new norms for gender mainstreaming. Whether gender mainstreaming will continue to be a useful strategy to actually promote gender equality and women's rights in China, however, will largely depend on ongoing dynamic negotiations to realize promises that have been made—to prioritize women's rights in the development agenda, democratize policymaking processes and spaces, create more mean-ingful participation of women's rights advocates in policy, and build collaboration and synergy-building among policymakers, academia, the ACWF, and other official women's organizations and stakeholders. No matter the means, women's rights activism in China continues to accelerate as we approach the 20th anniversary of Beijing.

Notes

1 Peggy Antrobus, ed., *The Global Women's Movement: Origins, Issues and Strategies* (New York: Peggy Antrobus, 2004).
2 Gita Sen and Marina Durano, eds, *The Remaking of Social Contracts: Feminists in a Fierce New World* (London: Zed Books, 2014).
3 Wang Zheng, "A Historic Turning Point for the Women's Movement in China," *Signs* 22, no. 1 (Autumn 1996): 192–199.
4 The total number of NGO participants was 31,549 and 5,000 were Chinese. See Office of the Commission of the Ministry of Foreign Affairs to the People's Republic of China in the Hong Kong Special Administrative Region, www.fmcoprc.gov.hk/chn/topic/zgwj/wjlshk/t8963.htm.
5 United Nations, *Beijing Platform for Action*, adopted at the Fourth World Conference on Women, paragraph 189, www.refworld.org/docid/3dde04324. html.
6 United Nations, *Report of the Economic and Social Council for 1997*, Document No. A/52/3, 18 September 1997.
7 Du Fangqin, *Chinese Women and Development: Status, Health and Employment* (Tianjin, China: Henan People's Publisher, 1993).
8 Du Fangqin and Wang Jun, "Women's Studies in Mainland China: the Construction and Adoption of Knowledge—To Review and Rethink of the Last 30 Years and to Prospect for Future," paper presented at the Sympo-sium on Mobilized Asia and Asia Women's Studies in Seoul, South Korea, February 2009.
9 Since the People's Republic of China was founded in 1949, there have been four Constitutions adopted in 1954, 1975, 1978, and 1982. The current Constitution was adopted in 1982 and amended in 1988, 1993, 1999, and 2004. Women and men being equal has been mentioned in each of the four constitutions.

10 Based on Zhong Xueping's study, even though "women can hold up half the sky" was largely believed to be Chairman Mao's quote, there is no evidence on when and where he said it. However, there is another famous quote from Mao, which is "it is a different era and women and men are the same, whatever men can do, women can do as well" (Mao Zedong, June 1964). See Zhong Xueping, "Women Can Hold Up Half the Sky—Four Told Tale," in *Nankai Journal (Philosophy, Literature and Social Science Edition)*, 5 (2009): 55–62; Mao's citation can be found in All China Women's Federation, ed., *Citations of Mao Zendong, Zhou Enlai, Liu Shaoqi, Zhude On Women's Liberation* (Beijing, China: People's Press, 1988): 67.

11 According to the Statute of All China Women's Federation, the ACWF is "a mass organization of women from all ethnicities from all sections seeking the further liberation of women under the leadership of the Communist Party of China. It is a bridge and link of the party and government with the masses of women, and an important social pillar of the State." Critics call the Women's Federation a puppet under the control of Party and State, while others believe that it has unique advantages given its status in political structure. It is the biggest NGO in China and with UN ECOSOC consultative status; it is an umbrella organization with a large national network, from the provincial and township level down to the villages. Given its nationwide network, legitimacy, and leverage, it influences the decision-making process, plays a pivotal role in mobilizing women to participate in development, and influences policies on women's rights and gender equality.

12 Jiang Zemin, "Welcome Address at the Opening Ceremony of UN 4th World Conference on Women," in Beijing, China, 4 September 1995.

13 *The Report of the Eighteenth Congress of the Chinese Communist Party*, 2012.

14 Xi Jinping, "Adhere to National Policy of Equality between Men and Women," *Xinhua Daily Telegraph* 1 (November 2013): 1.

15 CEDAW Committee, *Consideration of Reports Submitted by States Parties under Article 18 of the Convention on the Elimination of All Forms of Discrimination against Women, Combined Seventh and Eighth Periodic Report of States Parties China*, Document No. CEDAW/C/CHN/7–8, 20 January 2012.

16 Amendment of Constitution of the People's Republic of China, art. 33, adopted at the second session of Eleventh National People's Congress, 13 March 2004.

17 These include Adoption Law (1998, amended), Population and Family Planning Law (2001, formulated), Marriage Law (2001, amended), Rural Land Contract Law (2002, formulated), Security Administration Punishment Law (2005, formulated), Law on Promotion of Employment (2007 formulated), Property Law (2007 formulated), Electoral Law (2010, amended), The Social Insurance Law (2010, formulated), Labor Protection of Female Workers Special Provisions (2012, amended), etc.

18 Shenzhen Municipality Regulations on Promotion of Gender Equality, June 2012.

19 Opinions on Preventing and Deterring Domestic Violence, July 2008.

20 Legislative Office of the State Council of the People's Republic of China, www.chinalaw.gov.cn/article/cazjgg/201411/20141100397718.shtml.

21 China National Plan of Action on Combating Trafficking in Women and Children (2008–2012), December 2007.

22 CEDAW Committee, *Consideration of Reports Submitted by States Parties under Article 18 of the Convention on the Elimination of All Forms of Discrimination against Women, Combined Seventh and Eighth Periodic Report of States Parties China*, Document No. CEDAW/C/CHN/7–8, 20 January 2012.

23 NWCCW, "End-of-term Monitoring and Evaluation Report on National Program on Women and Development 1995–2000," 2001; NWCCW, "Midterm Monitoring and Evaluation Report on National Program on Women and Development (2001–2010)," 2007.

24 Rong Weiyi, "Participatory Gender Training and Gender Mainstreaming," in *Report on Gender Equality and Women Development in China (1995–2005)*, Women's Studies Institute of China, ed., (Beijing, China: Social Sciences Academic Press, 2006): 331–336.

25 Institute of Finance of Liaoning Province, "On Gender Responsive Budget," *Finance Booklet* 8 (2010): 1–12.

26 China Women's Research Society, "Information Kit for the Third Session of Steering Committee Meeting of China Women's Research Society," 2010.

27 Wang Chunxia, "Fourteen Women's Studies Projects Received Grants from National Fund for Social Sciences," *China Women's Daily*, 13 January 2013.

28 United Nations, *Equity in China: Chapeau Paper*, December 2013.

29 Malcolm Moore, "China is the World's Second Largest Economy," *The Telegraph*, 14 February 2011.

30 Shahra Razavi, "Women's Organizations in Asia and the Post-2015 Development Agenda," UNRISD, August 2012.

31 Shahra Razavi, "Women's Organizations in Asia and the Post-2015 Development Agenda," UNRISD, August 2012.

32 Sarah Cook and Xiaoyuan Dong, "Harsh Choices: Chinese Women's Paid Work and Unpaid Responsibilities under Economic Reform," *Development and Change* 42, no. 4 (2011): 947–966.

33 "In Guangdong Women Annual Income is Only Sixty Percent of Their Men Counterpart," *Guangzhou Daily*, 2 March 2012.

34 National Heath on Family Planning Commission, "Report on Migration and Development 2013."

35 National Bureau of Statistics, "Statistics on Status of Women and Children," 2013, 68.

36 The Ministry of Foreign Affairs of the People's Republic of China and United Nations System in China, "The Implementation of the Millennium Development Goals (MDGs) Progress Report (2008)."

37 Liu Yanying, "Negative Impacts and the Resolution on Closing and Merging Schools in Rural Areas," http://wenku.baidu.com/link?url=d-DheQNYiIIJlcbNliPW7-V8StGXKSi0b9qG72gr3X2yMN0uIyQPPpAUIBbl5SM37KJ3nrnCcVVEFUAR2VbeERVLYT3m9vGeq_S85LhKtSlO.

38 *Mapping Gender Discrimination in Universities Admission*, http://lady.163.com/14/1013/10/A8EAUH4G00264NQN.html.

39 The Ministry of Foreign Affairs of the People's Republic of China and United Nations System in China, "China's Progress towards the Millennium Development Goals 2010 Report."

40 The sex ratio at birth (SRB) is usually expressed as the number of boys born alive per 100 girls born alive. The biologically normal sex ratio at

birth ranges from 102 to 106 males per 100 females. In China, as a result of preference for sons, the sex ratio at birth increased from 107 in 1982 to 120 in 2005 based on data from the 1982 population census and from the One percent Population Sample Survey (2005). The "Care for Girls Campaign" was launched in 2003 by the National Population and Family Planning Commission in a selected region where the SRB is high. This campaign aims at reducing the high SRB by providing social and economic incentives to families that implement the family planning policy.

41 Xinhua News Agency, "China to Ease Family Planning Policy," 15 November 2013, http://usa.chinadaily.com.cn/china/2013-11/15/content_17109519.htm.

42 China Daily, "Second-child Policy Having Limited Effect," 11 July 2014, http://www.china.org.cn/china/2014-07/11/content_32919208.htm.

43 Chinanews.com, "2nd-child Policy Causes Discrimination Against Working Women," 25 March 2013, www.ecns.cn/cns-wire/2014/03-25/106455.shtml.

44 Bai Di, "Gender Politics: On the Uncertainty of 'Social Gender,'" *Journal of Women's Academy of Shandong* 5 (October 2013): 1–6.

45 Zhang Liming, "Reflection on Gender Mainstreaming in China in the Context of Globalization," *Journal of Shandong Women's University* 1 (2010): 8–11.

46 Li Bin, Han Lian, and Wang Hongyan, "Gender Mainstreaming: New Stage in the Legislation of Women Employment in China," *Journal of Jiangxi Normal University (Social Sciences)* 40, no. 2 (April 2007): 73–78.

47 Zhang Yongying, "Responsibilities of Women's Federation in Promoting Gender Mainstreaming in China," *Journal of Women's Academy of Shandong* 2 (April 2010): 15–19.

48 Joan Kaufman, "The Global Women's Movement and Chinese Women's Rights," *Journal of Contemporary China* (2012): 1–18.

49 United Nations, *Progress in Mainstreaming a Gender Perspective into the Development, Implementation and Evaluation of National Policies and Programmes, with a Particular Focus on Challenges and Achievements in the Implementation of the Millennium Development Goals for Women and Girls: Report of the Secretary General*, Document no: E/CN.6/2014/4, 24 December 2013.

50 China's retirement policymaking process began in 1951 and took shape in 1978. According to the provisions issued at that time, including the Provisional Measures of the State Council on the Resettlement of Sick, Venerable, Senior and Handicapped Cadres, and the Provisional Regulations of the State Council on Retirement and Resignation of Workers (GF No. 104 [1978]), the retirement age of enterprise employees is 60 for males, 50 for female workers, and 55 for female cadres. Since 1989, there have been proposals from representatives in the National People's Congress (NPC) and Chinese People's Political Consultative Conference (CPPCC) proposing the same retirement age for men and women civil servants/technical professionals, but the NPC or the relevant government departments have not accepted this proposal, nor have they taken any remedial actions.

51 There is the sex-segregation of majors at university programs and lower minimum entrance-exam score required in certain subjects specifically for boys at some colleges. See CEDAW Committee, *Consideration of Reports Submitted by States Parties under Article 18 of the Convention on the Elimination of All Forms of Discrimination against Women, Combined*

Seventh and Eighth Periodic Report of States Parties China, Document no: CEDAW/C/CHN/7–8, 20 January 2012.

52 Zhang Lei and Wang Junxiu, "Protection of Women Starts with Revising Village Rules and Regulations" *China Youth Daily*, 25 December 2012.

53 Cai Yiping, "Re-vitalize, Re-strategize and Re-politicize: the Chinese Women's Movement in the New Era," *Asian Journal of Women's Studies* 19, no.1 (2013).

54 China Daily, "Occupation of Men's Toilet Group is Flushed with Success," 10 December 2014, http://news.xinhuanet.com/english/indepth/2012-02/27/ c_131432741.htm.

13 At once and for all

Human rights, American exceptionalism and women's status in the United States

Dorothy Q. Thomas

> I knew from the beginning that feminism is global.
>
> Gloria Steinem[1]

When then-First Lady Hillary Clinton said in Beijing that "women's rights are human rights," she referenced women worldwide, including in the United States.[2] Since then, women's global reality has both justified and belied Clinton's rhetoric. Women's human rights are more widely recognized, and our political and economic power is expanding, even as the actual circumstances of women and girls remain bleak in many places. These international trends have parallels in the United States, where accountability to global standards of women's status has shown some improvement. Yet entrenched US exceptionalism to human rights norms and persistent domestic inequalities continue to confound American women's progress and hinder local implementation of the Beijing Platform for Action (BPFA).

This chapter reviews the historical nexus between human rights exceptionalism and domestic inequality in the United States, charts post-Beijing shifts in this dynamic and assesses the current status of US women in three BPA areas—political participation, economic opportunity, and freedom from violence. It concludes that further progress requires the US government to enhance both human rights accountability and women's equality—and depends on the US women's movement broadening its agenda and fortifying its collective power.

Historical context: exceptionalism and inequality

> I felt more and more the need to draw a line between official United States policy and the voice of an independent private citizen speaking out on behalf of human rights.
>
> The Reverend Dr. Pauli Murray[3]

No struggle for the local implementation of human rights can avoid doing battle with its host country's usually inflated self-image. Still, it is worth remembering that the United States oft-touted superiority to other countries—particularly on issues of rights—actually masks a troubling legacy of white, male, and propertied supremacy in its own history. As the critical race theorist, Patricia Hill Collins, wrote in 2009, "[i]n the United States, because affluent white men control government and industry, public policies usually benefit this group." America's founding commitment to "unalienable rights" deserves acclaim, but as the journalist Ta-Nehisi Coates recently wrote, "to celebrate freedom and democracy while forgetting America's origins in a slavery economy is patriotism a la carte."[4] Continued US exceptionalism to human rights represents the outward face of its inner resistance to full equality.[5]

Historically, defenders of American supremacy abroad openly protected racial privilege at home. In the 1920s, in opposing US participation in the League of Nations, a defiantly racist Senator James Reed of Missouri scoffed at the prospect "of submitting questions involving the very life of the United States to a tribunal on which a ni__er from Liberia, a ni__er from Honduras, a ni__er from India ... each have votes equal to that of the great United States."[6] In 1945, at the UN's founding conference, the lead US delegate, peppered with demands from American civil rights activists like W. E. B. Du Bois and Mary Church Terrell to include human rights in the organization's mandate, said his role "was to create a charter, not to take up subjects like 'the Negro question.'"[7] His co-delegate, John Foster Dulles, drafted a Charter amendment that disallowed the UN "to intervene in matters which are essentially within the domestic jurisdiction of any states."[8] Five years later, senators from Jim Crow states, fearing the implications for race segregation of the Universal Declaration of Human Rights (UDHR), sought to strip President Eisenhower of his treaty-making power.[9] Eisenhower alternatively pledged not to ratify another human rights treaty and dismissed Eleanor Roosevelt, a key UDHR proponent, from her UN position.[10]

During the Cold War the US government demonized the domestic use of human rights as anti-American or pro-Soviet. American feminists of color, like Josephine Baker and Lena Horne, were prime targets of such tactics, but the women's movement soon pushed back. Leaders like Bella Abzug, Aileen Hernandez, Barbara Jordan, Robin Morgan, the Reverend Dr. Pauli Murray, and Gloria Steinem reasserted human rights as a framework for women's domestic concerns.[11] The National Organization for Women's 1966 founding charter described it as "part of the worldwide revolution of human rights taking place within and beyond our national borders."[12] The 1977 US National Women's Conference in Houston demanded for all women "as a human right a full voice and role for determining the destiny of our world, our nations, our families and our individual lives."[13]

Ronald Reagan's 1980 election unleashed a conservative backlash to the breakdown of the exceptionalism/inequality dynamic wrought by these progressive social movements.[14] The Houston Conference, inspired by the UN's Decade of Women and reflective of American feminism's commitment to both human rights accountability and full equality, proved to be the only national women's meeting of its kind.[15] With the exception of the US anti-apartheid struggle,[16] the worlds of international and domestic activism again diverged. By the time I came of political age in the 1980s, one could either be a human or a civil rights activist, but rarely both. Government, philanthropy, and even civil society institutionalized this global/local split. The US government viewed human rights as *foreign* policy and has yet to establish a formal mechanism to oversee its *domestic* compliance.[17] Human rights funding did not encompass the United States. Human rights NGOs, like Human Rights Watch (HRW), still had no US divisions, and US civil rights and liberties groups, like the National Association for the Advancement of Colored People (NAACP) and the American Civil Liberties Union (ACLU), rarely invoked human rights. Women's groups de-linked international and domestic work.[18]

In this context it is fair to say that the Beijing Conference woke a sleeping giant. With more American participants than any previous world conference,[19] Beijing allowed US feminists to see ourselves once again as a part of a global movement and to connect to one another across the domestic divisions of gender, race, ethnicity, and class that so consistently dissipate our influence. The conference enabled US-based international women's organizations, like the Center for Women's Global Leadership (CWGL), the International Women's Health Coalition (IWHC), and Women's Environment and Development Organization (WEDO), to relink their global work to the US women's movement, and that movement, in turn, reclaimed its internationalist bent.

My own experience is illustrative. I arrived in Beijing in 1995 late in my tenure as the founding director of the Women's Rights Division of HRW.[20] When I returned home, I called for the "internationalization" of the US women's movement[21] and issued one of HRW's earliest US-focused human rights reports on the sexual abuse of women in state prisons.[22] Soon after, I left my job as an "international" human rights advocate and became an independent "local" one, consulting with domestic groups to revive a US human rights movement linked across race, class, ethnicity, gender, sexuality, and nation, and connected to like-minded movements elsewhere.[23]

The Beijing effect: renewed movement to bring human rights home

> When our rights are limited, when our rights are violated, we need a
> domestic human rights program.
>
> Barbara Jordan[24]

Beijing reinforced two fundamental principles within the United States—the interconnections between global and local struggles and the collective power of women across gender, race, class, and ethnicity. Many organizations, including the Advocates for Human Rights, the Border Network for Human Rights, Breakthrough, the Bringing Human Rights Home Lawyer's Network, Global Rights, the Mississippi Workers Center for Human Rights, the Poverty Initiative, SisterSong, and the Vermont Worker's Center re-dedicated themselves to countering both US exceptionalism and domestic inequality.

Newly minted groups like WILD for Human Rights, for example, bypassed federal government opposition to CEDAW and implemented the treaty as local law in San Francisco.[25] This bottom-up approach was soon replicated in other locales[26] like New York City, where advocates sought joint implementation of both CEDAW and the International Convention on the Elimination of All Forms of Racial Discrimination (ICERD).[27] Long-established organizations like HRW and the ACLU developed US and human rights units, respectively.[28] The largest US association of civil rights groups, the Leadership Conference on Civil Rights, changed its name to Leadership Conference on Civil and *Human* Rights. By 2005, it was possible to launch the US Human Rights Fund, through which leading philanthropists and activists supported a re-emerging domestic movement for human rights.[29]

The 2002 founding of the US Human Rights Network (USHRN), the nation's first domestic human rights membership organization, exemplifies the Beijing effect.[30] The network arose out of the leadership of a diverse group of US women, many of them Beijing attendees, who had earlier resolved to recoup the internationalist and intersectional feminist politics of the Houston conference.[31] In the following decade, both the local implementation of human rights and women's collective action across gender, race, ethnicity, class, and other differences increased. Their combined effect was visible, for example, in the growing use of international human rights mechanisms by US activists, facilitated to this day by the USHRN, and by an unprecedented joint complaint by the ACLU's Women's and Human Rights units before the Inter-American Commission on Human Rights, which successfully charged the United States with a failure to protect against domestic violence.[32]

By contrast, formal government action on women's and human rights stalled in this period. The Clinton administration submitted CEDAW to the Senate in 1994, but the late Senator Jesse Helms attacked it as the work of "radical feminists" with an "anti-family agenda."[33] By the time George W. Bush was elected in 2000, CEDAW was still unratified, and his administration, with some exceptions, such as denouncing rights abuses in Zimbabwe and Sudan, became notable for its hostility to both human rights accountability and women's equality. Despite President Bush's contention that "W stands for Women,"[34] he also re-imposed the Global Gag Rule, which prohibits foreign NGOs receiving US funds from using any of their monies for anything abortion-related,[35] and he supported a Federal Refusal Clause,[36] which allows healthcare providers who oppose abortion to prohibit doctors in their employ from providing or making referrals for the service.[37]

The Bush Administration's response to the attacks of 11 September 2001 further intensified the ongoing tug-of-war over human rights accountability and full equality in the United States. In the attack's aftermath, prominent national conservatives like the Reverend Jerry Falwell blamed "anti-American" feminists and gays and lesbians for inciting God's wrath and cast domestic human rights groups as in league with terrorists.[38] The Bush Administration vigorously contested the applicability of human rights norms to its conduct of the "war on terror," including the harsh treatment of non-citizens under US jurisdiction outside of the United States and of immigrants within its own borders.[39] US human rights proponents just as intensely contested this stance.[40] By the time President Obama was elected in 2008, it was necessary for him to restate the US prohibition on torture,[41] and to oppose racial, ethnic, and religious profiling.[42]

The precarious now

> I believe in American exceptionalism with every fiber of my being.
>
> President Barack Obama

President Obama's election signaled a potential sea change in the politics of human rights exceptionalism and domestic inequality in the United States. The new president promptly reversed Bush era detention and interrogation policies,[43] vocally supported the ratification of CEDAW,[44] and pledged to review other key human rights norms.[45] His Secretary of State, Hillary Clinton, created the position of ambassador-at-large for global women's issues[46] and focused the Department's Quadrennial Diplomacy and Development Review on gender equality.[47] One of the President's first domestic policy acts was to sign the Lilly Ledbetter Fair Pay Act of 2009,[48] and soon thereafter he established the White House Council on Women and Girls. He acted quickly to pursue comprehensive health care[49] and immigration policy reform, with a commitment to combat domestic inequality and ensure all people's dignity and rights.

However, hopes for a more thorough shift in the exceptionalism/inequality dynamic in the United States soon dimmed. In part because of these early initiatives to expand rights, President Obama became the target of a harsh backlash. The black conservative Shelby Steele, for example, argued that, "in Mr. Obama, America gained a president with ambivalence, if not some antipathy, toward the singular greatness of the nation he had been elected to lead."[50] The defeated vice-presidential candidate, Sarah Palin, in comments reminiscent of the red-baiting of the 1950s, called the new President "a socialist."[51] Anti-abortion groups denounced his healthcare initiative as "a radical march to socialism and state funded child-killing," and conservatives condemned his immigration reform effort as a tactic "to manage the ethnicity of America and quicken the demise of the white majority."[52] The President's nuanced attempt to reshape the exceptionalism/inequality dynamic culminated in a 2014 speech at West Point where he said, "I believe in American exceptionalism with every fiber of my being," and quickly added "but what makes us exceptional is not our ability to flout international norms and the rule of law; it's our willingness to affirm them through our actions."[53] Conservatives critiqued the President's human rights-respecting formulation of American exceptionalism as "a rebuke to US greatness."[54]

Powerful resistance to human rights accountability and domestic equality continue to stymie American progress on both fronts, as is evident in the country's still uneven implementation of the Beijing Platform for Action (BPFA). An assessment of US women's current status with respect to three BPFA provisions illustrates the problem.

Political participation

Women—and women of color in particular—now play a pivotal role in federal and state elections in the United States.[55] In the 2012 re-election of President Barack Obama, women voters supported Obama over his Republican opponent, Mitt Romney, by a difference of 10 percent and ensured Obama's victory.[56] Notably, a majority of white women (56 percent) voted for Mr. Romney, while majorities of both black women and Latinas chose the President.[57] During the 2014 mid-term elections, gender gaps of 6 to 16 percentage points were evident in all 22 of the US Senate races and among 21 gubernatorial races, 18 saw gender gaps of 5 to 17 percent. In each of these races women were more likely to support the Democratic candidate.[58]

Despite this mounting electoral power, women still fall far short of full representation in political life. The United States now ranks a shocking 72nd worldwide in the percentage of national legislative seats held by women, *down* from 59th in 1998.[59] As of 2013, women comprised only 24 percent of state legislators.[60] For women of color, the level of under-representation astounds. Women of color currently constitute only 5.8 percent of the US Congress, and no black female has graced the Senate since 1999.[61] Voter suppression laws, introduced in 15 largely Republican-controlled states since 2013,[62] have been shown to affect women of color disproportionately.[63] As Shirley Chisholm, the first black woman elected to Congress bemoaned more than 40 years ago, black women's "political mobility ... threatens the doctrines of white supremacy and male superiority so deeply embedded in the American culture."[64] Today, 100 years after US women got the vote, 71 percent of political offices in the United States are held by men, 90 percent of whom are white.[65]

Economic status

This growing, if still vastly unequal, political power parallels women's increasing but still constrained economic participation. Women now represent nearly half of the American workforce.[66] Our participation has increased by 53 percent in the past 50 years, a trend led by black women.[67] In 2012, women represented half of those employed in several sectors including finance, education, and health and hospitality.[68] Four in ten US women now serve as primary breadwinners.[69]

However, despite growing workforce participation, women continue to confront unequal pay rates and gender bias in the workplace, a situation compounded by continued job segregation and racial and other discrimination. White women in full-time work experience on average a 27-cent pay gap compared with white men, a differential which mounts to 39 cents for African-American women and an astonishing 48 cents for Latinas. The United States has one of the largest gender wage gaps among developed nations,[70] even as evidence shows that closing the gap would boost US GDP by as much as 9 percent.[71] Across the board women are sequestered in jobs with lower wages. We hold two-thirds of the jobs at the federal minimum wage, which has not been raised in two decades and excludes tipped workers, who are most often women.[72] Women of color are again doubly disadvantaged: African-American women have an estimated median wealth of $5.00 compared with $42,600 for white women.[73] In the aftermath of the 2008 recession, they faced unemployment rates nearly twice that of whites.[74]

These disparities result in especially punishing circumstances for poor women of every age and race. Twenty-eight percent of black women and 20 percent of white women work in the service industry, where wages and benefits are typically low.[75] The United States remains the only industrialized country that guarantees neither subsidized job-protected leave for parents nor paid sick days.[76] Nor does it effectively ban pregnancy discrimination in the workplace, despite legislation that prohibits it. According to one study, the United States imposes twice the earnings penalties on mothers as exist in other countries with expansive publicly funded childcare.[77] Even the US's highest earning female executives spend 25 hours per week on childcare, while their white male counterparts spend only 10 hours.[78]

Violence Against Women

The Obama administration has been outspoken in its opposition to violence against women. The President actively supported the 2013 reauthorization of the 1994 Violence Against Women Act (VAWA),[79] including its expansion to Native American and immigrant women, and, with bi-partisan support, he recently established a task force to protect students from sexual assault on college campuses.[80]

Despite these positive trends, a 2014 report found that violence against women in the United States approaches epidemic proportions. One in four women has experienced severe physical violence from an intimate partner; one in five has been raped; and one in six has been stalked.[81] The federal Office of Juvenile Offenders recently found that girls are at four times the risk of sexual abuse as boys,[82] and reports of forcible sex offenses on college campuses grew by 50 percent from 2009 to 2012.[83] While violence prevails across economic and social status, black women have recently seen a small rise in intimate partner violence and are significantly more likely than white women to be raped or sexually assaulted by a stranger.[84]

Public condemnation of violence is common, but its remediation remains problematic.[85] A recent study of the official response to violence against women in New Orleans found that "police routinely discouraged sexual assault victims from pursuing prosecution."[86] The Massachusetts Institute of Technology found in 2014 that only 5 percent of students who had experienced unwanted sexual contact reported it to campus officials.[87]

Conclusion

> When there is a supposed conflict between human and national rights, it is safe to go to the side of humanity.
>
> Frederick Douglass, Boston, 1869[88]

Even this brief account of US women's current status with respect to the global standards of the BPA illustrates the degree to which America's professed superiority to other countries in terms of rights masks a continuing pattern of domestic inequality. This exceptionalism/ inequality dynamic in turn reflects the twin legacy of the country's founding self-conception as a "city upon a hill," and its constitutional deference to white, propertied men. The domestic social movements of the twentieth century did much to remedy this divisive legacy, and both US human rights accountability and American women's status improved. Yet, US exceptionalism and systemic inequality across gender, race, ethnicity, and class persist and imperil both America's moral leadership and women's transformative power. Further progress requires the US government and the US women's movement to recognize that human rights exceptionalism and domestic inequality are two sides of the same tarnished coin and to resolve, at once and for all, to dispense with them both.

Notes

1 Tom Watson, "Connected Feminism Shows A Muscular Commitment To Change—And Civil Rights," *Forbes*, 9 October 2014, http://onforb.es/ 1yQAgdb.
2 Hillary Rodham Clinton, "Remarks to the UN 4th World Conference on Women Plenary Session," the UN 4th World Conference on Women, Beijing, China, 5 September 1995.
3 Pauli Murray, *Pauli Murray: The Autobiography of a Black Activist, Feminist, Lawyer, Priest, and Poet* (Knoxville: University of Tennessee Press, 1989), 195.

4 Patricia Hill Collins, *Black Feminist Thought: Knowledge, Consciousness, and the Politics of Empowerment*, second edn (New York: Routledge, 2009), 229.

5 Andrew J. Bacevich, *The Limits of Power: The End of American Exceptionalism* (New York: Holt Paperbacks, 2008); Stephen M. Walt, "The Myth of American Exceptionalism," *Foreign Policy*, 11 October 2011.

6 Sen. James Alexander Reed, "Racial Equality and The League of Nations" (speech in the Senate of the United States, Washington, DC, 26 May 1919).

7 Stettinius, diary, Box 29, File "Stettinius Diary, Week of 8–14 April 1945," *Notter*; Stettinius, diary, Box 29, File "Stettinius Diary, Week of 15–23 April 1945 (Section Ten)," Irene Diggs to Walter White, memo, 6 November 1944, Box 634, File "United Nations: Bretton Woods Conference, 1944–46," *Papers of the NAACP* in Carol Anderson, *Eyes Off the Prize: The United Nations and the African American Struggle for Human Rights, 1944–1955* (Cambridge and New York: Cambridge University Press, 2003), 41.

8 Hamilton Fish Armstrong's handwritten minutes of US Delegates Meeting 5:30, 2 May 1945, Box 84, Folder 23, *Armstrong Papers*; in Anderson, *Eyes Off the Prize*, 49.

9 "Bringing the Constitution Up-To-Date: Address by Senator John W. Bricker before the Annual Convention of the Ohio State Bar Association at Cincinnati, Ohio," 22 April 1953, Box 160, File "2," *Bricker Reports* cited in Anderson, *Eyes Off the Prize*, 223–27.

10 Treaties the United States has ratified include the International Covenant on Civil and Political Rights (ICCPR), the International Convention on the Elimination of all forms of Racial Discrimination (ICERD), and the Convention against Torture and Other Cruel, Inhuman or Degrading Treatment or Punishment (CAT). US Human Rights Network, "Advancing Human Rights: A Status Report on Human Rights in the United States" (New York: US Human Rights Network, 2013), 4.

11 See, e.g., Pauli Murray, *Human Rights U.S.A.: 1948–1966* (Cincinnati, Ohio: Service Board of Missions, Methodist Church, 1967); Barbara Jordan, "Opening Session Speech," National Women's Conference, Houston, Tex., 18–21 November 1977, 4, available at www.texasarchive.org/library/index.php?title=2014_00417.

12 Betty Friedan, *National Organization for Women's Statement of Purpose*, 29 October 1966, Washington, DC, http://now.org/about/history/statement-of-purpose/.

13 United States, National Commission on the Observance of International Women's Year, *The Spirit of Houston: the First National Women's Conference: an Official Report to the President, the Congress and the People of the United States* (Washington, DC: National Commission on the Observance of International Women's Year, 1978), 3.

14 Tamar Jacoby, "The Reagan Turnaround on Human Rights," *Foreign Affairs* (Summer 1986), available at www.foreignaffairs.com/articles/41064/tamar-jacoby/the-reagan-turnaround-on-human-rights.

15 *The Spirit of Houston*, 9–12.

16 Steven V. Roberts, "Senate, 78 to 21, Overrides Reagan's Veto and Imposes Sanctions on South Africa," *New York Times*, 3 October 1986, www.nytimes.com/1986/10/03/politics/03REAG.html.

17 See Catherine Powell, *Human Rights at Home: A Domestic Policy Blueprint for the New Administration,* American Constitution Society for Law and Policy, October 2008, www.ushrnetwork.org/sites/ushrnetwork.org/files/acs_human_rights_at_home.pdf.

18 Dorothy Q. Thomas, "We Are Not the World: U.S. Activism and Human Rights in the Twenty-First Century" in *Feminisms at a Millennium,* ed. Judith A. Howard and Carolyn Allen (Chicago, Ill. and London: The University of Chicago Press, 2000).

19 Nearly 7,000 US citizens traveled to China for Conference, www.gpo.gov/fdsys/pkg/GAOREPORTS-NSIAD-96-79BR/html/GAOREPORTS-NSIAD-96-79BR.htm.

20 Dorothy Q. Thomas, "The Revolution Continues" in *The Unfinished Revolution: Voices from the Global Fight for Women's Rights,* ed. Minky Worden (New York: Seven Stories Press, 2012), 325–32.

21 Dorothy Q. Thomas, "Advancing Rights Protection in the United States: An Internationalized Advocacy Strategy," 9 *Harv. Hum. Rts. J.* 9 (Spring 1996): 15–26.

22 Human Rights Watch, *All Too Familiar: The Sexual Abuse of Women in U.S. State Prisons* (New York, Washington, DC, London and Brussels: Human Rights Watch, 1996).

23 These included the Atlantic Philanthropies, the Ford Foundation, the JEHT Foundation, the Human Rights Unit of the American Civil Liberties Union, the Shaler Adams Foundation, the US Human Rights Fund, the US Human Rights Network, the US Program of Human Rights Watch, and WILD for Human Rights.

24 Jordan, "Opening Session Speech", 4.

25 The US signed CEDAW in 1980; however, the Senate has yet to ratify. "CEDAW Ordinance," City and County of San Francisco Municipal Code Administrative Code, see, e.g., http://sfgov.org/dosw/cedaw-ordinance, and the US Committee 2013 report available at www.state.gov/j/drl/rls/cerd_report/210605.htm.

26 As of July 2005, 47 cities as well as 17 states and 19 counties were in support of CEDAW. *CEDAW in the United States: Why a Treaty for the Rights of Women?,* available at www.wedo.org/wp-content/uploads/cedaw-factsheet.pdf.

27 *American Civil Liberties Union Written Statement in Support of the New York City Human Rights Government Audit Law (GOAL) Int. No. 512,* available at http://goo.gl/nnKYft.

28 The ACLU established its US Human Rights division in 2004. See American Civil Liberties Union, *Human Rights,* www.aclu.org/human-rights. The US Program of Human Rights Watch was developed in 2001. See www.hrw.org/bios/jamie-fellner.

29 US Human Rights Fund, *US Human Rights Fund: Honoring Past, Present & Future Victories,* 30 November 2012 (New York: US Human Rights Fund).

30 See US Human Rights Network, *Something Inside So Strong: A Resource Guide on Human Rights in the United States* (New York: US Human Rights Network, 2004), available at www.ushrnetwork.org/sites/ushrnetwork.org/files/something_inside_so_strong.pdf.

31 Women's Institute for Leadership Development for Human Rights and Shaler Adams Foundation, *Making the Connections: Human Rights in the United States*, a report of the Meeting at Mill Valley, California, 7–10 July 1999 (San Francisco, Calif.: WILD for Human Right and the Shaler Adams Foundation, 2000).

32 "International Commission Finds United States Denied Justice to Domestic Violence Survivor," ACLU Press Release, 17 August 2011, available at www. aclu.org/womens-rights/international-commission-finds-united-states-denied -justice-domestic-violence-survivor.

33 Ellen Chesler, "A Progressive Agenda for Women's Rights" in *What We Stand For: A Program for Progressive Patriotism*, ed. Mark Green (New York: Newmarket Press, 2004), 215–16.

34 Jodi Enda, "Barbara Bush Tells Women What 'W' Stands For," *WeNews*, 31 August 2004, available at http://womensenews.org/story/campaign-trail/ 040831/barbara-bush-tells-women-what-w-stands#.VG4uV4f-pDI.

35 "The Bush Global Gag Rule: Endangering Women's Health, Free Speech and Democracy," Press Release from the Center for Reproductive Rights, 1 July 2003.

36 Barbara Finlay, *George W. Bush and the War on Women: Turning Back the Clock on Progress* (New York: Zed Books, 2006), 75.

37 Lynn M. Paltrow and Jeanne Flavin, "Pregnant, and No Civil Rights," *New York Times*, 8 November 2014, A21.

38 *The 700 Club*, Christian Broadcasting Network, 13 September 2001, cited in John F. Harris, "God Gave U.S. 'What We Deserve,' Falwell Says," *Washington Post*, 14 September 2014.

39 *A Call to Courage: Reclaiming Our Liberties Ten Years After 9/11*, an ACLU report (New York: American Civil Liberties Union, 2011).

40 "Not the Way to Fight Terrorism: Neglecting Human Rights," *International Herald Tribune*, 16 January 2003.

41 Barack Obama, "Ensuring Lawful Interrogations," Executive Order 13491, 22 January 2009, www.whitehouse.gov/the_press_office/EnsuringLawfulInte rrogations.

42 "Attorney General Says Ending Racial Profiling Is Priority For Obama Administration," ACLU Press Release (7 May 2009), available at www. aclu.org/racialjustice/racialprofiling/39542prs20090507.html cited in "ERPA and Racial Profiling," The Leadership Conference, March 2014, www. civilrights.org/criminal-justice/racial-profiling/resouces/erpa.html.

43 *2008 Country Reports on Human Rights Practices*, US Department of State Bureau of Democracy, Human Rights, and Labor report, 25 February 2009, available at www.state.gov/j/drl/rls/hrrpt/2008/frontmatter/118984.htm.

44 "President Obama's Administration Views CEDAW as a Powerful Tool for Making Gender Equality a Reality," Thirtieth Anniversary of the United Nations' Adoption of CEDAW, White House Press Statement, Washington, DC, 18 December 2009.

45 "ACLU Disappointed with Senate's Failure to Ratify Convention on the Rights of Persons with Disabilities," ACLU Press Release, 4 December 2012, available at www.aclu.org/human-rights/aclu-disappointed-senates-failure-ratify-convention-rights-persons-disabilities; see also Human Rights Watch, *United States Ratification of International Human Rights Treaties* (New York and Washington, DC: Human Rights Watch, July 2009) available

at www.hrw.org/sites/default/files/related_material/Treaty%20Ratification%
20Advocacy%20document%20-%20final%20-%20Aug%202009.pdf; Karen
DeYoung, "Obama Administration Endorses Treaty Banning Torture,"
The Washington Post, 12 November 2014, www.washingtonpost.com/
world/national-security/obama-administration-endorses-treaty-banning-tor
ture/2014/11/12/b6131e68-6a8c-11e4-9fb4-a622dae742a2_story.html.

46 See Isobel Coleman, "Clinton Was a Powerful Voice for Women Around
the World," *New York Times*, 12 May 2013, available at www.nytimes.com/
roomfordebate/2013/05/12/judging-hillary-clinton-as-secretary-of-state/clinton-
was-a-powerful-voice-for-women-around-the-world.

47 *Leading Through Civilian Power: The First Quadrennial Diplomacy and
Development Review*, United States Department of State and the United
States Agency for International Development, 2010, available at www.state.
gov/documents/organization/153108.pdf.

48 See Robert Pear, "House Passes 2 Measures on Job Bias," *New York
Times*, 9 January 2009, available at www.nytimes.com/2009/01/10/us/
10rights.html?hp.

49 "President Obama Announces White House Council on Women and Girls,"
The White House Press Release, 11 March 2009, available at www.whitehouse.
gov/the_press_office/President-Obama-Announces-White-House-Council-o
n-Women-and-Girls/.

50 Shelby Steele, "Obama and the Burden of Exceptionalism," *Wall Street
Journal*, 1 September 2011, http://online.wsj.com/articles/SB1000142405311
1904787404576532623176115558.

51 Nick Wing, "Sarah Palin: 'Barack Obama Is A Socialist,' Communism
Could Be Coming," *The Huffington Post*, 4 December 2012, www.huffing
tonpost.com/2012/12/04/sarah-palin-obama-socialist_n_2237163.html.

52 See L. Todd Wood, "Scary: Here's How Obama Plan On Destroying America
As We Know It," *Western Journalism*, 29 July 2014, www.westernjournalism.
com/obama-way-illegal-immigration-racism-will-destroy-america/#loiLufV
KirWUKYqm.99.

53 "Remarks by the President at the United States Military Academy Com-
mencement Ceremony," West Point, NY, 28 May 2014, available at www.
whitehouse.gov/the-press-office/2014/05/28/remarks-president-united-states-m
ilitary-academy-commencement-ceremony.

54 See Pamela Geller, "Obama at West Point: Rebuke to U.S. Greatness,"
World Net Daily, 1 June 2014, available at www.wnd.com/2014/06/obama
-at-west-point-rebuke-to-u-s-greatness/.

55 Deborah L. Rhode, *What Women Want* (New York: Oxford University
Press, 2014), 155.

56 "Women's Votes Decisive in 2012 Presidential Race," Center for American
Women in Politics press release, 7 November 2012, www.cawp.rutgers.edu/
press_room/news/documents/PressRelease_11-07-12-gendergap.pdf.

57 Imani Gandy, "Black Women Are an Electoral Voting Force. Recognize,"
RH Reality Check, 4 March 2014, http://rhrealitycheck.org/article/2014/03/
04/black-women-electoral-voting-force-recognize/.

58 "Women's Votes Decisive in 2012 Presidential Race," Center for American
Women in Politics Press Release; Laura Meckler, "Midterm Elections 2014:
Coalitions Persist, but Turnout Favors GOP," *The Wall Street Journal*,
5 November 2014, http://online.wsj.com/articles/early-exit-polls-show-a-

nation-dissatisfied-1415146566?tesla=y&mg=reno64-wsj&url=http://online.
wsj.com/article/SB11550989027533334316504580257101177495236.html.

59 Interparliamentary Union, *Women in Parliaments World Classification*, updated 15 February 2015, www.ipw.org/wmn-e/classif.htm (accessed 16 April 2015).

60 Representation 2020: A Century from Suffrage to Parity, *State of Women's Representation 2013–2014*, p. 41, http://www.representation2020.com/2013-2014-report.html.

61 *Black Women in the United States, 2014*, a report of the Black Women's Roundtable, March 2014 (Washington, DC: National Coalition on Black Civic Participation, 2014), 60; Gandy, "Black Women Are an Electoral Voting Force. Recognize."

62 American Civil Liberties Union, *The Battle to Protect the Ballot: Voter Suppression Measures Passed Since 2013*, available at www.aclu.org/maps/battle-protect-ballot-voter-suppression-measures-passed-2013.

63 The North Carolina law was overturned in part by the State Appeals Court on 1 October 2014—a decision the state intended to appeal. Richard Fausset, "2 New Limits On Voting Are Rejected By U.S. Court," *New York Times*, 2 October 2014, A18.

64 Shirley Chisholm, "The Black Woman in Contemporary America" (speech given at a conference on black women in America at the University of Missouri, Kansas City, 17 June 1974).

65 Emily Baxter, "The Excessive Political Power of White Men in the United States, In One Chart," *ThinkProgress.org*, 10 October 2014, available at http://thinkprogress.org/justice/2014/10/10/3578399/survey-finds-white-men-have-eight-times-as-much-political-power-as-women-of-color/.

66 US Department of Labor, *Women's Bureau Facts Over Time*, www.dol.gov/wb/stats/facts_over_time.

67 *Black Women in the United States, 2014*, 22.

68 "50 Years Later," infographic created for the 50th Anniversary of the American Women report available at www.dol.gov/wb/pcswinfographic.pdf.

69 See "Clinton: More Women Working Equals Faster Economic Recovery," Georgetown University, 30 October 2014, www.georgetown.edu/news/hillary-clinton-international-council-relaunch.html#_ga=1.222530715.12230937 00.1417575599.

70 Maria Shriver et al., *The Shriver Report: A Women's Nation Pushes Back from the Brink*, ed. Olivia Morgan and Karen Skelton (New York: Palgrave MacMillan, 2014), 76. [hereinafter Shriver Report].

71 World Economic Forum, *The Global Gender Gap Report 2013*, p. 31, available at www3.weforum.org/docs/WEF_GenderGap_Report_2013.pdf.

72 The Restaurant Opportunities Centers United Forward Together, *The Glass Floor: Sexual Harassment in the Restaurant Industry*, 7 October 2014, available at http://rocunited.org/wp-content/uploads/2014/10/REPORT_The-Glass-Floor-Sexual-Harassment-in-the-Restaurant-Industry2.pdf.

73 Sophia Kerby, "How Pay Inequity Hurts Women of Color," Center for American Progress, 9 April 2013.

74 *Black Women in the United States, 2014*, 22.

75 The Leadership Conference Education Fund, *Economic Security for Women and Families: A Conversation Guide* (Washington, DC: The

Leadership Conference Education Fund, 2014), 14, available at www.am ericanwomen.org/body/EconSecurityToolkit_National.pdf.

76 Jazelle Hunt, "Black Women Are Still Penalized for Race and Gender," *The Louisiana Weekly*, 24 February—2 March 2014, *Ethnic NewsWatch* via ProQuest; Family and Medical Leave Act of 1993 as amended, Public Law 103–3 (21 December 2009).

77 Stephanie Coontz, "Progress at Work, But Mothers Still Pay a Price," *New York Times*, 9 June 2013, 5.

78 Claire Cain Miller, "When Women's Goals Hit a Wall of Old Realities," *New York Times*, 30 November 2014, 3.

79 See Lisa N. Sacco, "The Violence Against Women Act: Overview, Legislation, and Federal Funding," Congressional Research Service, prepared for the members and committees of congress, 6 March 2014, http://fas.org/sgp/crs/misc/R42499.pdf, 1.

80 Valerie Jarrett, "A Renewed Call to Action to End Rape and Sexual Assault," *The White House Blog*, 22 January 2014, www.whitehouse.gov/blog/2014/01/22/renewed-call-action-end-rape-and-sexual-assault; "Memorandum—Establishing a White House Task Force to Protect Students from Sexual Assault," Press Release from the Office of the Press Secretary, The White House, 22 January 2014, www.whitehouse.gov/the-press-office/2014/01/22/memorandum-establishing-white-house-task-force-protect-students-sexual-a.

81 Matthew J. Breiding, et al., "Prevalence and Characteristics of Sexual Violence, Stalking, and Intimate Partner Violence Victimization—National Intimate Partner and Sexual Violence Survey, United States, 2011," US Centers for Disease Control and Prevention, Division of Violence Prevention, National Center for Injury Prevention and Control, CDC, 5 September 2014, 63(SS08): 1–18, available at www.cdc.gov/mmwr/preview/mmwrhtml/ss6308a1.htm; stats compiled from Catherine Cloutier, "Report Fnds Women Carry Burden of Sexual, Domestic Violence."

82 Michael T. Baglivio et al., "The Prevalence of Adverse Childhood Experience (ACE) in the Lives of Juvenile Offenders," Office of Juvenile Justice and Delinquency Prevention *Journal of Juvenile Justice*, V. 3, Is. 2 (Spring 2014), 9, available at www.journalofjuvjustice.org/JOJJ0302/JOJJ0302.pdf.

83 Nick Anderson, "Forcible Sex Offense Reports Ddouble at U-Md. and U-Va., Echoing Increase Across U.S.," *The Washington Post*, 5 November 2014, www.washingtonpost.com/local/education/forcible-sex-offense-reports-double-at-u-md-and-u-va-echoing-increase-across-us/2014/11/04/bf7bc38a-6440-11e4-836c-83bc4f26eb67_story.html; Nick Anderson, "Sex Offense Statistics Show U.S. College Reports are Rsing," *The Washington Post*, 1 July 2014, www.washingtonpost.com/local/education/sex-offense-statistics-show-us-college-reports-are-rising/2014/07/01/982ecf32-0137-11e4-b8ff-89afd3-fad6bd_story.html.

84 *Black Women in the United States, 2014*, 51.

85 United Nations, *15 Years of The United Nations Special Rapporteur on Violence Against Women (1994–2009)—A Critical Review*, available at www.ohchr.org/documents/issues/women/15yearreviewofvawmandate.pdf.

86 Campbell Robertson, "New Orleans Police Routinely Ignored Sex Crimes, Report Finds," *New York Times*, 13 November 2014, A 20.

87 Richard Pérez-Peña, "Rare Survey Examines Sex Assault At M.I.T.," *New York Times*, 28 October 2014, A23.
88 Frederick Douglass, "Composite Nation" (speech, Boston, 1869), in Philip S. Foner and Robert James Branham, eds, *Lift Every Voice: African American Oratory, 1787–1900* (Tuscaloosa: The University of Alabama Press, 1998), 497.

14 Turning tides and making a difference in Nepal

A reflection

Renu Adhikari Rajbhandari

I am a physician by training. I became a full-time women's rights activist after working in public hospitals in Nepal for more than 10 years. My journey began in 1991, when I met a young trafficked girl (whom I call Rani) then being held in police custody. I was sent to test her for HIV. Those were the early days of open HIV discussions in Nepal. The experience was transformative.

Rani, a 19-year-old from a very remote village of Nepal returned from India after several years and was brought to me by police officers who rudely asked her to tell me her story. There was a huge difference in how they treated the two of us. Looking at Rani's face, I understood her anger, pain, and apparent contempt for me, the police, and the larger healthcare and criminal justice systems. Reluctantly, the police finally allowed me to talk to her in private.

As soon as we were alone, Rani became very aggressive. "Yes! I was in Bombay, India," she said. "Yes! I was involved in sex work! Yes, I might have HIV, but why should I give my blood to you? You will sell my blood and make money for yourself! What is there for me? What will this get me?"

She began to cry and eventually told me her story.

Rani's mother was a deaf-mute, also mentally challenged. She came from a family of Dalits or "untouchables." Considered a burden on her family, she had been left homeless to fend for herself on the streets, where she was apparently raped and became pregnant. Late in her pregnancy she was sent by people who knew her to her brother's home, the same brother who had earlier kicked her out. Considered "polluted" by the oppressive patriarchal norms of her family because of being pregnant on the street, she was not allowed to re-enter the house but managed to stay in a cowshed, where she delivered a baby girl.

By Rani's telling, no one in her family home except the uncle who had originally thrown her mother out was ever kind—or even spoke to her during her childhood. When Rani turned 12, that uncle convinced her that having a sewing skill would help her find a job so she could care for herself and her mother. He took her on a three-day journey to India.

What happened next is almost indescribable. The uncle left Rani with a woman she had never seen before and disappeared. She had been sold to a brothel in Mumbai, and after a couple of days was forced to take clients. Initially, she resisted and was punished severely— eventually thrown from the brothel's fifth floor window. Rani survived but sustained severe head injuries. During the five months of treatment in a Mumbai hospital, her new "aunt," the brothel owner, came to visit her and bought food and medicine. This was the only shred of humanity Rani experienced. So she went to work for this woman who had shown her kindness and lived as a sex worker in Mumbai for more than five years. She tried to run away a few times, but every time the police would catch her and return her to another brothel, where she experienced more torture and pain.

Finally she was able to escape and somehow reached Kathmandu in Nepal, where we met. After sharing her story, Rani asked me if any of these experiences were her fault. Was it her fault that she had been born to a poor Dalit mother who could not hear or talk and was abused throughout her life? Was it her fault that she had trusted her uncle, or later the brothel owner, the only people who had ever treated her with any love or dignity?

Rani also asked where she should go next. "I am not a criminal, so I will be released," she told me. "But then what? The minute I am out, people will treat me as an object to be exploited." I had no answers. I gave her a few "theoretical" words of counsel, knowing very well they would not help.

I had been funded to do this work by the World Health Organization (WHO) through Nepal's Health Ministry. Our grant was based on the number of HIV positive people we could identify. In a sense Rani was correct in saying that I would sell her blood. My salary was dependent on the grant, and this thought made me very uncomfortable. After testing Rani for HIV, I could not stop crying on the long five-hour journey home. And I remained at home and depressed for a week.

Moved by this experience and with financial help from a small group of friends, I started the Women's Rehabilitation Centre (WOREC) in 1991 to provide support to vulnerable women like Rani. I tried to track her down but never found her. Her tortured journey had turned my life around. As I began working on trafficking, I came to understand that it is always an outcome of many other violations of women's rights. I broadened the scope of my work on violence against women. The work requires commitment, passion, and above all, political will. I began focusing on community organizing, starting with women, but slowly we engaged men as well. We began with a small group of seven women but have now reached more than 1.7 million women. We have also managed to create a national plan of action against trafficking and revise policies to support survivors of trafficking.

One of our major achievements in 1996 was to repatriate 126 Nepalese girls trafficked to Mumbai. After a police raid these girls were set free, and after persistent advocacy efforts, we managed to bring them home and place them in shelters. As a result of this work, we formed the first survivors' organization in the country named "Shakti Samuha." According to the US Department of State, this was the first survivors' organization of this kind in the world.

"Shakti Samuha" continues to provide shelter for survivors of trafficking and has also initiated an anti-trafficking campaign in alliance with survivors from all over the country. We have been recognized by many different international human rights organizations and by the US Department of State, and we recently received the "Magsaysay" Award, which many consider the Nobel Peace Prize of Asia.

WOREC has also formed a group called the "Mahila ko Nimti Mahila Manch" or "Women for Women Forum," which has organized more than 5,000 women entertainers who work in bars, restaurants, massage parlors, and singing clubs—including some sex workers. It has evolved into an established organization working to protect women's rights as workers.

Even as a medical doctor I have also always found it challenging to talk openly about reproductive and sexual health issues in our communities. In my work, I witnessed several deaths caused by unsafe illegal abortion. At one point, I met with a woman who had cut up and inserted a rubber flip flop in her vagina to support her prolapsed uterus. To respond, I developed a training module for local laywomen whom we called "barefoot gynecologists." We established community-based health and counseling centers for women and lobbied intensively to get these spaces recognized and funded by the state. We called attention to the widespread problem of uterine prolapse (often a consequence of multiple or difficult childbirths) and developed a national strategy to address it. With the help of our "barefoot gynecologists" and several other human rights organizations, we also worked to establish a woman's right to safe and legal abortion.

Women in my country work day and night to create change—rescuing trafficked women, resisting violence, serving as "barefoot" gynecologists among poor and rural women—but we are still often not recognized as human rights defenders. We are not always educated or articulate, attributes most often associated with human rights defense.

During the 10 years of violent political conflict in Nepal (from 1996 to 2006), women who resisted violence and demanded women's rights were, on the one hand, branded Maoists (insurgents demanding justice for the most marginalized by the established security forces) or, on the other hand, feared as informers by the Maoists themselves. After 2005, when King Gyanendra Bir Bikram Shah declared war and seized power from the democratically elected government, the situation of human rights defenders became even more precarious, and advocates for women's rights bore the brunt.

To respond to this situation, WOREC organized the National Consultation of Women Human Rights Defenders, and we took an active role in the movement for democracy. I also played an instrumental role in having a UN-sponsored human rights office—a branch of the Office of the High Commissioner of Human Rights (OHCHR) —established in Nepal. OHCHR today plays a very important role in monitoring human right violations and in creating safety mechanisms for human rights defenders, including women working at the community level. With support from the OHCHR and the International Coalition of Women's Human Rights Defenders, we have also built a National Alliance of Women Human Rights Defenders, with chapters now in 75 districts of the country. We have established a rights-based culture.

Through 20 years of activism, I've learned many lessons. First, nothing can be altered without passion, commitment, hard work, and courage. Second, we must build movements to support our work and give it legitimacy and authority. Movements embolden women and give us the courage to continue. Recently, in Nepal we have launched a new movement to demand more action to end violence against women—a National Anti-Rape Campaign. Women from all sectors have joined our weekly protests and also staged a two-week sit-in. Hundreds of survivors joined us. We are demanding that all sexual violence during the political conflicts in our country be documented and that perpetrators be brought to justice. We are also calling for reform of Nepal's rape laws and for a national action plan on peace and security that specifically addresses the problem of sexual violence in conflict.

In 2012, in a global study on policymaking to end violence against women, Mala Htun and Laurel Weldon concluded that the single most important factor in achieving policy and legal change for women's rights is the existence of autonomous feminist movements. This is why I'm especially happy that our organizations in Nepal are affiliated with the Asia Pacific Forum on Women, Law and Development (APWLD).

APWLD represents grassroots movements and helps make our voices heard outside of our own country. It supports feminist participatory action research within grassroots communities and insures that local findings inform policymaking nationally, regionally, and internationally. It also fosters opportunities for collective analysis—for comparing and analyzing country-level data within and across regions.

APWLD operates from the ideological premise that structural causes of women's rights violations lie at the intersections of globalization, militarism, and fundamentalisms—all fused by patriarchy. Together with other social movements in the Asia Pacific region, we are calling for a new economic and political order where inequalities of wealth and power are more equitably distributed and for an overall framework of "development justice" that encompasses necessary realignments in gender relations, in economic and social hierarchies, and in accountability to the people and to the planet we inhabit.

15 My evolution as a young feminist in Lebanon

A reflection

Hayat Mirshad

Feminist activism is nothing new in Lebanon. Lebanese women have been struggling for many years, as have women all over the world. Indeed, facts demolish one of the most widespread myths—that Lebanese women are the most liberated in the Arab world.

Consider the following examples:

- Many in my country still refuse to vote for women who seek elective office because they think we lack the strength and intelligence to stand up for ourselves and others. Our current Parliament has 128 deputies, carefully distributed between Christians and Muslims, but there are only four women—a paltry 3 percent. The first two female ministers in Lebanese history were only appointed in 2004;
- Lebanese women are second-class citizens in another respect. When we marry foreigners we cannot pass on our nationality status to our husbands or our children. In this respect our children are treated as strangers in their mother's homeland and enjoy no rights;
- The Lebanese Penal Code still contains any number of discriminatory provisions including one which exonerates the rapist of any crime if he agrees to marry his victim;
- We have no law that protects women and girls from sexual harassment in the streets, in schools or workplaces. The feminist group Nasawiya has actively lobbied for legislation to protect women from violence, sexual harassment, and all forms of rape, including marital rape. Recently Ghassan Moukheiber, a member of parliament from the Change and Reform bloc, submitted an urgent bill to criminalize sexual harassment and racist abuse, but it has not advanced; and

- Patriarchal and religious norms and practices result in high rates of early marriage, and there are no laws that ban the practice. Family law is still governed by varying mindsets of sectarianism, religious fanaticism, and outdated religious strictures.

After presenting this brief background about women's situation, allow me to introduce myself as a young feminist and human rights activist, researcher, and journalist, struggling for equality, democracy, and peace in my country.

At the age of 15, I stumbled across the writings of the mid-twentieth century Egyptian feminist, Nawal El Saadawi, and a revolution ignited inside me. Saadawi's book *Women and Sex* unveils the injustices experienced by Arab women. Her words reinforced many injustices I had myself witnessed and had a profound impact. I grew passionate about women's rights, undertook further research, and began writing articles of my own. I became increasingly gender-sensitive and started identifying myself as a proud feminist.

A second turning point in my life came with meeting my husband, also a feminist, who pushed me into a life of activism. It is not easy to be a committed feminist in Lebanon, and the importance of having someone supportive on my side cannot be underestimated.

Many women call themselves feminists but do not apply their beliefs and values to their personal lives because traditional practices and family pressures are too strong. Patriarchy is an entrenched and rotten system that did not ask for permission when it first controlled and oppressed us. So we should not ask for permission to revolt against it, but many still do. Lebanese society continues to be heavily influenced by traditional culture and sectarian democracy. The discrimination and oppression my mother, grandmother, and so many of my female friends have endured inspires the work I do today.

Why am I a feminist?

- I am a feminist because society tells us that the rape victim is somehow to blame. If she is not at fault for how she dresses, then it must be because she has been drinking too much. She is condemned for flirting or for liking sex. If she does not say "no," then automatically she must mean "yes." Or perhaps she just did not say "no" loudly enough. No matter the case, the victim is told that the fault lies with her.
- I am a feminist because my best friend was raped at the age of 20 by a drunk bus driver and did not dare to speak up for fear of being blamed.

- I am a feminist because as a woman I am both discriminated against and misrepresented. Men with sexual experience are seen as attractive. Women who claim sexual experience are labeled sluts or whores. My own mother told me that the most precious gift I could give my husband on my wedding night was my virginity.
- I am a feminist because when I take charge of a situation I am labeled bossy, pushy, or demanding, but when my brother or male friends or colleagues take the same action they are called authoritative and heralded for strong leadership skills.
- I am a feminist because after marrying I did not immediately want children and was considered strange and selfish, while my husband was never questioned. Then when I chose to become pregnant, everyone wished I would have a son, and when I delivered my beloved baby boy their wishes turned to "may you get him a brother soon."
- I am a feminist because I was obliged to return to work just two months after giving birth as maternity leave in Lebanon is limited in duration. Still, I was accused of being heartless and am still made to feel guilty every time my son gets sick or just cries. My critics forget that to work is my right and that the economic situation of my family obligates me to handle two jobs, not just one. My husband, on the other hand, is never viewed as heartless and selfish for leaving his son to work.

For these many reasons I decided to stand up for the rights of women—for my own rights. At the age of 18, I became active in various campaigns and initiatives to promote equality and change attitudes that sanction discrimination, oppression, exploitation, and abuse of women and other marginalized groups. Over time I acquired an unshakable belief in and respect for individual difference and freedom—for diversity among people, including women and the LGBT community. I have come to believe that according full citizenship rights and legal equality to all is a necessary obligation of a civil state.

My first activism was through the Collective for Research and Training on Development Action (CRTDA), a non-governmental organization based in Beirut. I worked with CRTDA for four years as a project officer of its Active Citizenship and Gendered Social Entitlements Project (ACGEN), where I contributed to building the capacity of local groups. I organized regular workshops about issues related to human rights and gender, and promoted the concept and practice of women's active citizenship, with women enjoying rights equal to the obligations and responsibilities they fulfill in their communities and families. I mobilized and pushed the boundaries of debate around the constitutionally protected practice of "confessionalism," which entitles religious institutions to representation in civil government and distributes power proportionally between Muslims and Christians.

At CRTDA, I also remain an active volunteer in the Women's Right to Nationality Campaign, where I take part in networking with and mobilizing civil society and women's organizations to expand awareness through discussion groups, demonstrations, petitions, and public awareness campaigns at universities and elsewhere about women's rights to nationality and inclusive citizenship.

My ultimate contentment derives from the leadership training I hold for women and their families with the support of the US-based Women's Learning Partnership (WLP) started by Mahnaz Afkhami. During this training, women often share moving stories about the challenges their families face in accessing education, health care, social security, and the like.

During my years with CRTDA, I have also worked as an editor at Lebanon's Knowledge and Development Gateway, a project established by the World Bank, which also advances understanding of the relationship between gender empowerment and social and economic development. One research project I managed addressed the failure of civil law in Lebanon to cover inheritance, which is governed by religious laws that vary by sect and discriminate against women. As a result, many couples hand over their wealth and real estate to their children early on with provisions that they can access them until they die.

Most recently, I have led a number of campaigns urging parliament to adopt a law to protect women from domestic violence. I organized a large public protest in July 2013 following the death of Roula Yaacoub, a 31-year-old woman, who was taken to the hospital after midnight by neighbors who found her bruised and unconscious. She had confided privately that her husband was abusive, but like so many other victims had been too frightened to speak out publicly. We discovered that 24 women had been killed in cases of domestic violence between 2010 and 2013 in Lebanon, and the media reported seven additional cases of domestic violence between January and March 2014. But members of parliament and religious leaders remained silent.

No more! I am currently leading an online advocacy campaign about domestic violence. Finally, on 1 April 2014 the Parliament approved a law that protects women against domestic violence, but with critical amendments—so it is not a total victory, just a partial achievement after all this struggle.

The draft law to protect women from domestic violence was first submitted to parliament by women's rights NGOs in 2010. A legislative

subcommittee began studying it a year later and finalized its amendments in August 2012. The amendments altered the title of the text,
which now refers to violence against the family, as opposed to women
specifically. A key clause to make marital rape illegal was removed by
the committee, the reason being that marriage by its definition implies
sexual consent between husband and wife.

During these years of activism, I have found that the media's representation of women is also most harmful. Lebanese media is not very interested
in civil society causes and typically denigrates women, especially in advertising. I soon found myself searching for a platform to discuss and raise
awareness on a range of women's issues that extend beyond the fashion,
astrology, and cooking content that is commonly covered by the press.

So, with a group of young women and human rights activists, I co-
founded Fe-Male, a non-profit, non-sectarian organization that works
under the umbrella of Human Rights Charter to ensure women's
rights as an integral part of human rights, to raise awareness through
mass and social media, to empower and eliminate stereotyping and
objectification of women, and to change discriminatory laws.

Fe-Male's most prominent initiative is the first feminist radio program in Lebanon and the Middle East, *Sharika wa Laken* ("A Partner,
but Not Yet an Equal"), which aims to raise awareness of women's
rights in Lebanese society by airing interviews with pioneering figures
campaigning for gender equality. I anchor and produce the show
purely on a volunteer basis.

Over more than two years, we have built a large audience, promoted
the work of many women's rights groups and NGOs, and received lots
of positive feedback. The episodes are also broadcast online through
the Voice of People's website. In addition, we launched a social media
campaign on Facebook and Twitter. The program's Facebook page is
very interactive and has already gathered more than 6,500 fans. Here,
let me share with you two inspiring stories from my program.

First, one day, while riding with an old taxi driver on my way back
home, I discovered by chance that he was listening to our program and
is a fan of it. Second, about the same time a listener to our program
called to report that a domestic worker in her neighborhood was a victim
of violence. The call came after we had broadcast eight episodes about
domestic workers rights with the support of the International Labour
Organization. We were able to then follow up and help the victim
escape to a safe shelter. Both these stories demonstrate the trust our
audience has in us.

In addition, Fe-Male has launched various online awareness-raising
campaigns; the latest called "Not by Commodification Your Product

Sells." This campaign aims to demonstrate how advertisements that commodify and sexualize women lead to gender violence.

I'm now also a project coordinator for the "Women's Response to the Arab Spring" project, which is a regional project funded by the EU and implemented by Oxfam Novib in partnership with five Arab non-governmental organizations in Lebanon, Egypt, the occupied Palestinian territory, Morocco, and Tunisia. The overall objective of this project is to contribute to strengthening democratic practices and respect for human rights through the promotion of equitable political participation for men and women.

At the same time, I'm volunteering to manage the media work of various feminist organizations—helping to sensitize and train them on misrepresentation of women. Recently, in June 2014, *The Daily Star*, the leading English language newspaper in the Middle East, wrote a feature about me as part of a series of weekly articles interviewing pioneering Lebanese women. They described me as a young feminist leader who has been championing women's causes over the last few years.

One final thought. I bring my very young son to demonstrations, hoping to show him a different way of thinking. How a boy is raised obviously influences the way he sees gender roles. In patriarchies, men are often raised to see themselves as the sole protectors of the household. Any sign of vulnerability is a sign of weakness. Girls, by contrast, learn to view themselves as a broken wing. As my own personal act of rebellion I'm trying to show my boy a father who cooks and cleans the house and a mother who has a career, so he can make choices when he is an adult.

My activism will of course not stop here, but will continue until my last breath. Who knows, maybe I'll be able one day to actualize my big dream of founding a Feminist Party in Lebanon!

I will remain a proud post-feminist in the post-patriarchy and never give up struggling until a rotten system is smashed. I predict a long and difficult path, but I still have hope that change will happen. I will never stop fighting for it. So long as we all carry that flame inside us, hope does not die.

Change can be possible only with persistence and solidarity among all feminists and marginalized individuals worldwide. Women's rights and women's issues cannot be dissociated from an understanding and practice of inclusive democracy. Indeed, there is no democracy without equality and vice versa. When the powers that be support or simply ignore extremist practices, occupation, injustice, armed conflict, dictators, invasion, and the use of violence, they act directly in support of gender inequality. There is no place for double standards in a real democracy.

Part III
Achieving economic justice

16 Gender equality and economic growth
A win-win policy agenda?

Naila Kabeer

The persisting preoccupation of policymakers with economic growth, combined with their growing interest in gender equality, has surprisingly given rise to very few macroeconometric studies exploring the relationship between the two—studies that might establish a potential "win-win" policy agenda. In a recent paper Luisa Natali and I synthesized the findings.[1] We conclude that evidence showing that gender equality makes a positive contribution to economic growth is fairly robust and holds across different country contexts and periods of time. Evidence for the reverse relationship—that economic growth contributes to gender equality—is far less consistent and generally confined to high-income countries.

One possible reason for this asymmetry is that the two sets of studies do not always use the same measures of gender equality. Growth models have a long history within mainstream economics and tend to confine themselves to a narrow range of largely economistic variables in their estimation procedures. Their measures of gender equality tend to be restricted to education, labor force participation, and wages.

Gender equality models, on the other hand, are relatively new and less restricted in their choice of variables. Here we find a wider range of measures: education, labor market participation, and wages, but also health (mortality and life expectancy), rights (e.g. rights within marriage and equal pay legislation), and political participation (percentage of women in parliament). So the different findings reported for the two sets of relationships might simply reflect the fact that they use different measures of gender equality. We cannot know in advance what the result might be if both used the same set of variables.

A second, more interesting reason may be that the two sets of relationships operate through different causal pathways. A major limitation of macroeconometric studies is their reliance on highly aggregated data, generally at cross-country level. It is rarely possible to distill the causal pathways through which gender equality might impact on economic growth or growth might impact on gender equality. More detailed, lower-level analysis is necessary to understand what these pathways might be.

This paper has a twofold objective. It will review micro-level studies that can help to illuminate possible causal pathways underlying both sets of relationships, with the focus on developing countries. And it will draw on feminist institutional theory to interpret the findings to move beyond the individual rational choice theory that underpins mainstream economic analysis[2] and take account of the structural nature of the gender inequalities under consideration.

Gender, structure, and agency: a feminist economic perspective

Like mainstream neo-classical economists, feminist economists recognize that individuals make choices subject to constraints. But while the former focus on individual constraints on choice, such as income or education, feminist economists are also interested in limits on choice imposed by the structural distribution of rules, norms, assets, and identities among different groups in a society—what Nancy Folbre first called "the structures of constraint."[3] While these take different forms in different contexts, I have found it analytically useful to develop a stylized categorization of these constraints from a gender perspective, drawing on Ann Whitehead's distinction between social relationships that are "intrinsically" gendered and those that are "bearers of gender."[4]

The first set of constraints refers to the customary norms, beliefs, and values that characterize the "intrinsically gendered" relationships of family and kinship. These spell out dominant models of masculinity and femininity in different societies, allocating men and women, boys and girls, to different roles and responsibilities on the basis of their presumed aptitudes and dispositions, with female attitudes and dispositions generally assigned a lower value.

The gendered division of labor between productive and reproductive work observed in different regions of the world partly reflects this set of constraints. The primary breadwinning responsibilities assigned to men in many cultures helps to explain their generally higher labor force participation rates. Women's labor force participation, on the other hand, varies considerably across regions. Almost all societies ascribe primary responsibility for unpaid reproductive work to female family members but vary considerably in expectations of their contributions to productive activity.

In some contexts, women are expected to share in breadwinning responsibilities and may have their own farms and enterprises to do so.

In others, they are not only expected to confine themselves to unpaid domestic work, including housework and childcare, but there may be strong cultural restrictions on their mobility in the public domain. These restrictions, giving rise to lifelong female dependency and a strong culture of son preference, contribute to the much lower rates of female labor force participation found in the Middle East and North Africa (MENA) region and South Asia than elsewhere.

The norms, values, and practices associated with the "private" domain of family and kinship are reinforced in most societies by the "imposed" gender constraints encountered in the "public" domains of states and markets. Despite the purported gender-neutrality of these institutions, they become "bearers of gender" when they reflect, reproduce, and exacerbate preconceived notions about masculinity and femininity as routine aspects of their rules, procedures, and practices.

Gender-related constraints, both intrinsic and imposed, underpin many of the gender inequalities documented in international statistics. They may operate invisibly and routinely through institutionalized bias, overtly through the discriminatory actions of powerful individuals and groups, or silently under cover of family, custom, and religion. They may also operate through feedback mechanisms where responses to existing inequalities serve to perpetuate inequality.

One other point is relevant to this analysis, although it will not be dealt with in detail in this chapter.[5] Gender is not the only form of inequality in a society. Many of the disadvantages faced by women from marginalized households in their struggle to make a living are shared by men from such households, but gender generally (though not always) intensifies class and other forms of disadvantage. Thus many of the gender inequalities discussed in this chapter tend to be much larger at the lower end of the income distribution and among socially marginalized groups.

The impact of gender equality on economic growth: exploring the causal pathways

My review with Luisa Natali uncovers strong evidence to support the positive contribution of gender equality to economic growth. Stephan Klasen suggests two causal pathways through which this impact might operate.[6] The family-mediated pathway revolves around the assumption that, given their association with reproductive responsibilities, women are more likely than men to translate resources at their disposal into investments in children's human capital, thereby increasing the productivity of the next generation of workers. A second market-mediated pathway is based on the assumption that innate talents and abilities are randomly distributed between men and women, so that equalizing the gender distribution of resources and opportunities will maximize the productivity of the human resources available to an economy. We explore the micro-level evidence for each of these pathways in turn.

Gender equality and the "human capital" effect

Micro-level evidence for the family-mediated pathway is fairly conclusive: numerous studies support the hypothesis that women's access to a range of valued resources, including wages, cash transfers, credit, and productive assets is associated with increased investments in family welfare, including children's health and education.[7] The impact of male access is generally smaller or insignificant. While mainstream economic models of household bargaining would interpret these findings in terms of the enhancement of women's ability to allocate household resources in closer alignment with their own preferences, the systematic nature of the findings suggests a structural element to the formation of these apparently individual preferences. It is not "women" per se who feature in these studies, but women in specific familial relations, most often mothers, sometimes grandmothers. While parents might be assumed to have special feelings for their children, the systematic association between mother's resources and children's welfare highlights the widespread significance of social constructions of motherhood in terms of special responsibility for children, one aspect of the structures of constraint noted earlier.

At the same time, and the two interpretations are not mutually exclusive, the association may also reflect the fact that, where these structural constraints cut off women more than men from resources and relationships beyond the household, their social identities and self-interests are bound up to a greater extent with the welfare and interests of their family. One reason for questioning any essentialist notion of maternal altruism as an explanation for maternal behavior is that these investments may be gender-biased rather than equity-oriented. For instance, in regions characterized by strong norms of son preference, women's own preferences, their status within the household and their security in old age all revolve around producing sons, ensuring their survival and winning their loyalty. In such contexts women's access to education has been found to reduce overall child mortality while raising mortality rates among higher birth order daughters.[8]

There are exceptions, of course, to this positive relation between women's access to resources and children's welfare. Poorer women who take up agricultural wage labor must often keep older daughters back from school to share in their domestic responsibilities, or take their children to work with them in fields and roadsides—with adverse consequences for the children's welfare. By and large, however, the results are sufficiently consistent for Doepke and Tertil to conclude in their review of this literature: "... the fact that a variety of studies using different data sources and empirical methodologies arrive at essentially the same conclusions strongly suggests that these findings are robust features of the data."[9]

Gender equality and "economic efficiency" effect

The micro-level evidence in support of the market-mediated pathway between gender equality and economic growth is far less persuasive. The problem is not simply that women across the world are less likely than men to be involved in the kind of market-oriented activities that are included in measurement of the Gross National Product and hence in the measurement of growth. It is also that the market-oriented activities in which women *do* engage generally generate lower returns than those associated with men. Consequently, merely increasing women's activity rates relative to men will not lead to a higher increase in income at either household or national levels. It will also be necessary to improve women's productive capacity relative to men. This requires us to better understand the factors that give rise to these gender disparities in returns.

One category of explanation has focused on *gender differentials in individual endowments*. Studies have made it clear that gender disparities in returns to labor reflect multiple, often mutually reinforcing endowment deficits. For instance, research into gender wage gaps highlights inequalities in education, skills, work experience, and occupational status.[10] Research into gender differentials in agricultural productivity highlights inequalities in education, landholdings, security of land tenure, use of inputs, visits by agricultural extension officers, and relevance of extension advice.[11] Research into gender gaps in enterprise earnings highlights gender differentials in education, size of enterprise, access to start-up capital, age of firm, and line of business.[12]

A second category of explanation adds gender differentials in *returns to these endowments* to the analysis. Here studies find that while education generally increases labor force participation rates and earnings for both men and women, returns to education are often higher for men than women for any given level of education. Returns to female education have been rising relative to male in recent years in many countries, but the gender gap in earnings persists.[13]

A third category of explanation suggests that gender disparities in earnings reflect the gender-segregated nature of occupational structure across the world. In other words, while lower returns to female endowments sometimes reflect direct discrimination, (i.e. lower returns within the same occupations), they more often reflect the fact that men and women are located in different tasks, crops, activities, occupations, and sectors, which are, in turn, characterized by different levels of productivity and rates of return.[14] Women are more likely than men to be found in "atypical" forms of work—part-time, seasonal, casual, and irregular employment, generally in the informal economy.[15]

As the World Bank points out, two types of explanations are generally put forward for this marked and pervasive stratification of the opportunity structure: firstly, gender discrimination in the labor market, and, secondly, the voluntary selection by men and women into different sectors and occupations in response to differences in their domestic responsibilities.[16] Insights from feminist literature require us to qualify both explanations.

First of all, discrimination goes deeper than allowed for in the economic literature.[17] Economists generally decompose gender gaps in earnings into two components—one can be explained by gender differentials in individual endowments, and a second by a residual component which they describe as "discrimination." In reality, many differentials in individual endowments are themselves the product of gender discrimination. Most women do not choose to educate themselves less than men—the decision was made by their parents. Nor do they choose to own less or poorer quality land, to be visited by fewer extension agents or to exclude themselves from formal credit channels or on-the-job training opportunities. Some of these differences are generated by the structures of constraint discussed earlier;[18] others reflect feedback mechanisms; and still others may be the product of active discrimination.

Secondly, it is not always clear that women's primary responsibility for housework and childcare is "voluntary." Some may welcome their socially assigned responsibilities; others may simply accept them as a "given" features of their lives. But recent growth in many regions of the world in female heads of households, a "flight from marriage" and dramatic declines in fertility to below net replacement rates suggest that when a real choice becomes possible, compliance with these roles cannot be taken for granted.[19]

To sum up, therefore, gender disparities in market returns to labor appear to be pervasive and persistent. There are no simple explanations for why this should be the case, nor are the explanations likely to be the same everywhere. But what they do suggest is that any efficiency argument for gender equality has to be based on a *structural* understanding of gender inequality and thus on a coordinated and multi-dimensional approach to tackling it. It cannot be tackled through piecemeal approaches, which focus on one or other constraint.

The impact of economic growth on gender equality: exploring the causal pathways

As noted earlier, our review of the macroeconometric literature found weak and inconsistent support for the hypothesis that economic growth contributes to gender equality. Standard economic theories would predict otherwise. Unsubstantiated claims about the "the trickle-down" or "rising tide" effects of economic growth offer generalized explanations why this might be the case. The literature also suggests additional gender-specific explanations. A market-mediated explanation says that competitive market forces in growing economies should increase the costs of gender-discrimination to employers.[20] A family-mediated explanation argues that benefits of growth should ease scarcity-related constraints, which otherwise force households to discriminate against less productive or valued members.[21]

These pathways, however, depend on the capacity of growth strategies to generate competitive markets and benefit poorer households. Furthermore, the forces that create scarcity and wealth in a society are not necessarily the same forces that create and perpetuate gendered structures of constraint. There are no *a priori* reasons why economic growth will translate into gender inequality.

Economic growth and gender equality in market opportunities

The explanation for the uneven impact of economic growth on gender inequality in market opportunities can be unpacked into a number of different components. First of all, it is important to note that the dominance of the neo-liberal agenda in international policy circles of late has led to a major shift away from the import-substituting, state-led industrialization that marked the post-Second World War era toward export-oriented growth strategies based on the liberalization of markets, trade, and capital flows.

The pace of this export-led growth has not been uniform across the world. In fact, it has been associated with declines in per capita growth rates in most low- and middle-income countries until the mid-1990s, particularly in Sub Saharan Africa and Latin America, until the mid-1990s, with some recovery thereafter.[22] The exceptions to this generalization are

India and China, which have reported strong and steady growth since the 1980s.

Secondly, export-led growth has reduced the global gender gap in labor force participation. While this reflects the higher female (relative to male) elasticity of employment for export-oriented growth in many contexts, it also evidences stagnant or declining male participation rates in a number of countries, a less desirable mechanism for closing gender inequalities.[23]

In addition, the gender-specific elasticity of export-oriented growth varies considerably by *type* of export, giving rise in variations in the gender distribution of employment gains and losses by region and sector.[24] Women have predominated in waged employment generated by the export of labor-intensive manufacturing, such as garments and textiles, while men have predominated in wage opportunities generated by capital-intensive extractive industries. Growth in traditional agricultural exports has largely benefited male cultivators because women are less likely to be engaged in the independent farming of commercial crops—although they may be major providers of unpaid family labor. As far as non-traditional export agriculture is concerned, women have largely benefited as wage laborers rather than independent cultivators. Indeed, women farmers receive a tiny fraction of contracts associated with out-grower schemes. As Catherine Dolan points out, companies need to secure access to land and labor for a guaranteed supply of primary produce: women do not generally have statutory rights over land, nor do they exercise the authority over family labor of dominant male family members.[25]

Cutbacks in the state's role in the economy, central to the neo-liberal agenda for market-led growth, provide a further reason why economic growth has not translated more systematically into progress on gender equality. Although men enjoyed favored access to public sector employment in most countries of the world, the public sector was, and generally remains, among the better paid and more gender equitable forms of employment available to women.[26] However, women lost out disproportionately in public sector retrenchments that accompanied economic liberalization across the world. How they have fared subsequently has varied considerably, reflecting differences in the gendered structures of opportunity and constraint in different contexts. This is evident from a recent report comparing Egypt, Ghana, and Bangladesh.[27]

In Egypt, which had a larger public sector with a higher percentage of female employees than the other two countries, women have lost out in the process of privatization because restrictions on their geographical mobility make it difficult to travel far in search of work and because of the discriminatory attitudes they encounter in the private formal sector. In Bangladesh, women have always been a minority in public sector employment, but they have benefited from (semi-)formal wage labor in the expanding export garment industry. However, this represents a very small percentage of female employment; much of the increase in female labor force participation in recent years has been in unpaid family labor. In Ghana, women made important inroads into public sector employment but lost these jobs in disproportionate numbers during the structural adjustment years. They have not benefited from the sectors prioritized for export promotion. Men dominate wage employment in the oil and timber industries and are primary cultivators of cocoa, the main agricultural export. However, a long-standing tradition of female entrepreneurship has allowed large numbers of women to take up off-farm enterprise where their earnings are higher than in most other sectors of the economy.

While female elasticity of employment with respect to export-oriented growth helps explain growing gender parity in labor force participation rates, variations in patterns of export orientation account for the unevenness of impacts on other labor market inequalities. As a result, there has been a very gradual reduction in the horizontal segregation of occupational structure by gender and almost no change in its vertical segregation since the 1980s.[28] There been some decline in the gender pay gap but primarily in higher income countries.[29] Furthermore, as a 2007 International Labour Organization (ILO) report reminds us, the decline in the gender wage gap cannot always be seen as positive, as it may reflect a decline in male wages rather than a rise in female ones.[30] There is also evidence that earlier gains by women in export-led manufacturing may be eroding over time as countries upgrade their technologies and move up the global value chain.[31]

Economic growth and gender equality in well-being and agency

We also find weak evidence in the macroeconometric literature to support the hypothesis that economic growth has contributed to gender equality in capabilities or rights. However, one finding that stands out in a number of studies we reviewed is that women's access to education and employment does appear to be an important driver of change in other measures of their well-being and agency, including composite measures of gender equality. This macro-level finding receives some support from the micro-level literature. While we have already noted the positive association between women's access to valued resources, such as employment, education, and children's well-being, such an association generally reflects conformity with expected behavior on the part of women. By contrast, if such access translates into changes in women's own well-being and capacity for agency, it has the potential to challenge the gendered structures of constraint.

Micro-level studies generally support the positive impact of women's education on aspects of their well-being and agency. The impact of women's labor force participation is less straightforward because it appears to be conditioned by the form it takes. In general, paid work that takes women outside the home and offers reasonably regular earnings is likely to have the most positive impacts.[32]

For instance, the comparative study of Egypt, Ghana, and Bangladesh cited earlier finds that in all three contexts, women's participation in formal paid employment proves consistently positive for a range of empowerment indicators—sense of agency, role in household decision-making about health care and asset management, position in the community, and the like. In Ghana and Bangladesh, women's participation in off-farm employment or work outside the home also has been positive, but less consistently so.

However, formal sector jobs for the women in these three countries fall mainly in the public sector, which is on the decline as it is elsewhere. Instead, market-generated jobs at the larger-scale end of global value chains are emerging as some of the better jobs available to women, although few reproduce the benefits provided by the public sector.[33] Still, not all women wageworkers in global value chains are directly contracted by multi-nationals, and pay and working conditions decline in direct relationship to their distance from lead firms. The empowerment potential of work subcontracted out to small sweatshops or home-based workers is far less obvious.

In addition, studies point to certain aspects of gender inequality in intra-household relations that have proved resistant to changes in family economic circumstances and in the wider economy—or have changed in perverse and unexpected ways. They remind us of the point made earlier: the forces that perpetuate gender inequality are not necessarily the same as those that drive economic growth.

The first of these inequalities relates to the gender division of unpaid labor within the home. As we have seen, this is one of the key factors explaining women's disadvantaged position in the occupational hierarchy. Standard economic theory predicts that increasing returns to women's work in the market-place should lead to some reallocation in the division of labor in unpaid work within the home. In reality, their unpaid responsibilities are either reallocated to other female family members, perhaps the eldest daughter, or else simply result in a longer working day. The same normative structures that associate femininity with caring roles also appear to define masculinity in terms of its distance from these roles. This resilience in traditional divisions of unpaid work generally means that economically active women wind up with a longer working day.

This pattern holds true to a varying degree across the world, but variations appear to reflect the impacts of public policies and of local cultural norms, rather than rates of growth. For instance, recent estimates by the World Bank find women devoting 50 percent more time to housework and childcare than men in Cambodia and Sweden, but three times more in Italy and six times more in Iraq.[34]

A second aspect of intra-household inequality that appears to resist change is domestic violence. The experience of domestic violence is universal, but its incidence varies considerably across contexts, once again reflecting local cultural norms defining masculinity and femininity, along with variations in public policies that mean to tackle the problem. While it might be expected that improving women's access to material resources strengthens their bargaining power within intimate relationships, the findings are very mixed.

Rachel Jewkes offers one possible—and plausible—explanation.[35] She suggests that a key trigger for intimate partner violence across different contexts is transgression of gender norms and the failure to fulfill cultural expectations of gender roles. What constitutes such transgression is likely to vary by setting, thus leading to cross-national variation in behaviors that pose the risk of violence. Where men's role as family breadwinner and dominant decision-maker is deeply entrenched in societal norms, improvements in women's economic status and bargaining power through work, credit, or property often threaten male self-worth, triggering a violent response.

A final area where gender inequalities within the household not only proved resistant to growth, but have been affected perversely by it, relates to the phenomenon of "missing women" associated with the culture of son preference. This refers to a deficit of women in the overall population of a country, reflecting forms of gender discrimination severe enough to lead to excess levels of female mortality. While this phenomenon has declined in some places, the decline does not appear to correlate with economic growth.

Indeed, in India and China, despite experiencing the fastest rates of growth in recent decades, "missing women" have given way to "missing daughters." Abnormally high ratios of males to females in the younger age groups reflect a persistence of excess female mortality among children and the growing practice of female-selective abortion made possible by the dissemination of new ultrasound technologies. It is beyond the scope of this chapter to discuss the factors that explain this new phenomenon, but it reminds us once again that local structures of patriarchal constraint will mediate in ways that confound easy predictions about the impact of growth on gender equality.

Conclusion

I speculate at the start of this chapter that one reason for asymmetry in the two-way relationship between economic growth and gender equality is differences in the causal pathways involved. The micro-level analysis presented here offers some support for this conjecture. It suggests that the positive contribution of gender equality to economic growth has largely operated through what we have described as the "family-mediated" pathway. This rests on the culturally sanctioned support for women's care responsibilities that prevail in many different contexts, one element of the structures of patriarchal constraint. The empirical evidence on market-mediated pathways is much weaker because of the deep-seated barriers that curtail women's productivity in the economy relative to men. To reap the gains from gender equality in the market-place will require radical public action to transform these underlying structural constraints.

Turning to the reverse relationship: the fact that the impact of economic growth on gender equality is mediated by local-level patriarchal structures rules out the likelihood that it will be uniform for men and women across the world. However, current patterns of growth across the world, characterized as they are by the global mobility of capital, the restricted mobility of labor and the reduced capacity of the state to create a level playing field, do not bode well for the working poor. Moreover, the inequalities in bargaining power between capital and labor inherent in these patterns are further exacerbated in the case of women workers by the unequal terms on which they enter the market-place and their confinement to limited segments of the labor market. It is clear that market-led growth will not be adequate to address these structural inequalities. Once again we return to the need for radical public action to dismantle them.

Gender advocates understandably make "win-win" arguments or "the business case" for gender equality, which rests on evidence of its positive impact on economic growth, to persuade policymakers to tackle discrimination. Our analysis suggests that these impacts are substantially mediated by conformity to socially ascribed gender roles, especially around unpaid care responsibilities. Such conformity undermines the ability of women to contribute in other ways to economic growth or to benefit on more equal terms from its gains.

This therefore leads us to question the desirability of a vision of economic progress that benefits from the unpaid labor of women but fails to recognize, let alone, reward it. I suggest that gender equality will have to be argued for as a matter of social justice, a good in its own right, regardless of "the business case." As such, it may require measures that do not necessarily contribute to economic growth in the short term—indeed may be detrimental to it—but will make for a fairer and more sustainable road to development in the long run.

Notes

1 Naila Kabeer and Luisa Natali, "Gender Equality and Economic Growth: is There a Win-win?," Working Paper No. 417, 2013 (Brighton: IDS, 2014).

2 See my blog on the Feminist Economics website for a brief critique of the rational choice approach. Naila Kabeer, "Esther Duflo on 'Women's Empowerment and Economic Development': A Must Read for Feminist Economists?," *Feminist Economics Posts* (blog), *International Association for Feminist Economics*, 19 September 2013, http://feministeconomicsposts. iaffe.org/2013/12/19/esther-duflo-on-womens-empowerment-and-economic-development-a-must-read-for-feminist-economists/.

3 Nancy Folbre, *Who Takes Care of the Kids? Gender and the Structures of Constraint* (London: Routledge, 1994).

4 Ann Whitehead, "Some Preliminary Notes on the Continuing Subordination of Women," *IDS Bulletin* 10, no. 3 (1979): 10–13.

5 Naila Kabeer, *Can the MDGs Provide a Pathway to Social Justice? The Challenge of Intersecting Inequalities* (Brighton: Institute of Development Studies/MDG Achievement Fund, 2010).

6 Stephen Klasen, "Does Gender Inequality Reduce Growth and Development? Evidence from Cross-country Regressions," *Sonderforschungsbereich* 386, Paper 212 (2000), http://epub.ub.uni-muenchen.de/1602/1/paper_212. pdf.

7 See, for instance, Mathhias Doepke and Michèle Tertilt, "Does Female Empowerment Promote Economic Development?," Policy Research Working Paper 5714 (Washington, DC: World Bank, 2011).

8 Monica Das Gupta, "Selective Discrimination against Female Children in Rural Punjab, India," *Population and Development Review* 13, no. 1 (1987): 77–100.

9 Doepke and Tertilt, "Female Empowerment," 19.

10 Doris Weichselbaumer and Rudolf Winter-Ebmer, "A Meta-analysis of the International Gender Wage Gap," Working Paper No. 0311, Department of Economics, Johannes Kepler University of Linz, 2003.

11 A. R. Quisumbing, "Gender Differentials in Agricultural Productivity: A Review of the Empirical Evidence" FCND Discussion Paper No. 5, (Washington, DC: IFPRI, 1995).

12 Mary Hallward-Driemeier, "Enterprising Women. Expanding Opportunities in Africa" (Washington, DC: World Bank, 2011).

13 Dorrit Posel and Daniela Casale, "Gender, Education and Access to Labour Markets" (paper prepared for UN Women Expert Group Meeting, New York, 3–5 November 2014).

14 World Bank, *World Development Report: Gender Equality and Development* (Washington, DC: World Bank, 2012).

15 Martha A. Chen, Joanne Vanek, Francie Lund, James Heintz with Renana Jhabvala and Chris Bonner, *Progress of the World's Women 2005: Women, work and poverty* (New York: UNIFEM, 2005).

16 World Bank, *World Development Report*, 2012.

17 Deborah Figart "Gender as More than a Dummy Variable: Feminist Approaches to Discrimination," *Review of Social Economy* LXIII no. 3 (2005): 509–536.

18 For instance, in a review of data from 141 countries in the world, the World Bank found widespread evidence of legally sanctioned inequalities between men and women which differentiated their resource endowments and capacity for responding to available opportunities. See World Bank, *World Development Report*, 2012.

19 Naila Kabeer, "The Rise of the Female Breadwinner: Reconfigurations of Marriage, Motherhood and Masculinity in the Global Economy," in *New Frontiers in Feminist Political Economy*, ed. Shireen Rai and Georgina Waylen (London: Routledge, 2013), 62–84.

20 Gary Becker, *The Economics of Discrimination* (Chicago, Ill.: University of Chicago Press, 1971).

21 Esther Duflo, "Women Empowerment and Economic Development," *Journal of Economic Literature* 50, no. 4 (2012): 1051–1079.

22 James Heintz, "Globalisation, Globalization, Economic Policy and Employment: Poverty and Gender Implications," Employment Policy Unit Working Paper 2006/3 (Geneva, Switzerland: ILO, 2006).

23 Heintz, "Globalisation, Globalization"; See also, Guy Standing, "Global Feminization Through Flexible Labor: A Theme Revisited," *World Development* 27, no. 3 (1999): 583–602.

24 Stephanie Seguino and Elissa Braunstein, "The Impact of Economic Policy and Structural Change on Gender Employment Inequality in Latin America," MPRA Paper 43261, University Library of Munich, Germany, 2012.

25 Catherine Dolan, "The Good Wife's Struggle Over Resources in the Kenyan Horticultural Sector," *Journal of Development Studies* 37, no. 3 (2001): 39–70.

26 Chen et al., *Progress of the World's Women*, 2005.

27 Naila Kabeer, with Ragui Assaad, Akosua Darkwah, Simeen Mahmud, Hania Sholkamy, Sakiba Tasneem and Dzodzi Tsikata, *Paid Work, Women's Empowerment and Inclusive Growth: Transforming the Structures of Constraint* (New York: UN Women, 2013).

28 Richard Anker, Helina Melkas, and Ailsa Korten, "Gender Based Occupational Segregation in the 1990s," International Labour Organisation Working Paper 16 (Geneva, Switzerland: ILO, 2003).

29 Remco Oostendorp, "Globalization and the Gender Wage Gap," *World Bank Economic Review* 23, no. 1 (2009): 141–161.

30 International Labour Organization, *Equality at work. Tackling the challenges* (Geneva, Switzerland: ILO, 2007).

31 Sheba Tejani, "The Gender Dimension of Special Economic Zones" in *Special Economic Zones. Progress, emerging challenges and future directions*, ed. Thomas Farole and Gokhan Akinci (Washington, DC: World Bank, 2011): 247–283.

32 Naila Kabeer, *Paid Work, Women's Empowerment and Gender Justice. Critical Pathways of Social Change* (Brighton: Institute of Development Studies, 2008).

33 Naila Kabeer, *Paid Work, Women's Empowerment and Gender Jjustice. Critical Pathways of Social Change* (Brighton: Institute of Development Studies, 2008); Miet Maertens and Johann F.M. Swinnen, "Gender and Modern Supply Chains," LICOS Discussion Paper 231 (Leuven, Belgium: LICOS Centre for Institutions and Economic Performance, 2008).

34 World Bank, *World Development Report*, 2012.

35 Rachel Jewkes, "Intimate Partner Violence. Causes and Prevention," *The Lancet* 359, no.1 (2003): 1423–1429.

17 Revaluing caregiving

Recent victories for domestic workers' rights

Nisha Varia

> We got [the Domestic Workers Convention] because we worked for it. We gathered our strength and urged others to get involved.... . There is still much to do—to get the laws improve, and put [them] into practice. But we made history. Now it is time for our government to learn from others—where they already have work contracts, working hours, pay and so on.
>
> Sayuti, Tunas Mulia Domestic Workers' Trade Union, Indonesia[1]

Growing movements for domestic workers' rights—at local, national, and international levels—are exposing and challenging the devaluation of caregiving work.

Domestic work includes cleaning homes to make them comfortable, cooking meals, and providing care, attention, and support to children, the elderly, and the disabled. Many households consider these services essential as they struggle to reconcile domestic responsibilities with employment outside the home. The demand for domestic help has increased in many countries as more women—often the traditional providers of caregiving—enter the formal workforce, as countries with growing elderly populations seek to keep them at home, and as public policies and policies and workplace structures remain slow to provide flexible work arrangements.[2]

The International Labour Organization (ILO) conservatively estimates that there are at least 53 million domestic workers worldwide.[3] While these numbers do not include those below the legal working age, typically 15 or 16, the ILO also estimates that some 11.5 million young people under the age of 18 are employed as domestics.[4]

Documentation by domestic worker organizations, human rights groups, UN agencies, and the media have highlighted a wide array of abuses. A combination of factors including poor legal protection, isolation in private homes, discriminatory attitudes, and restrictive immigration policies contribute to long working hours with little or no pay, inadequate rest, workplace confinement, verbal, physical, and sexual abuse—and little hope of any redress. The ILO identifies domestic work as one of the most common sectors for forced labor and trafficking.

Long among the ranks of the most marginalized and exploited, domestic workers, however, now constitute a growing force in labor movements globally. During the past ten years, the strength and sophistication of their organizing has grown dramatically, and they are successfully demanding recognition and respect. Numerous campaigns at the national level sparked legal advances in at least 30 countries between 2011 and 2014, and advocacy across international borders led to the 2011 ILO Domestic Workers Convention, a new international labor treaty demanding the same rights for domestic workers as other workers are granted.

These include basic but long denied labor protections, such as a minimum wage and a day off each week; specific protections tailored to the unique characteristics of domestic work, such as remuneration for standby time when domestic workers are on call but not working; collective bargaining agreements; and policies to address work-life balance, including protection for sick leave, maternity leave, disability, and retirement.

In October 2013, domestic workers from around the world gathered in Uruguay to found the first global union of domestic workers. Despite a steady string of successes, this women worker-led movement has struggled to gain attention and resources long focused instead on campaigns that frame exploited workers as modern-day slaves who must be rescued. This chapter is intended to frame a new and more hopeful perspective on these developments.

The devaluation of caregiving and abuses against domestic workers

Domestic workers nurture families and homes—what many people consider the most intimate and important parts of their lives. Yet this work has long been undervalued. Historically, few governments have accorded domestic work the protection provided elsewhere or have failed to regulate the sector entirely, leaving workers at the whim of unaccountable employers. These exclusions reinforce discriminatory social norms that assign a low status to work typically performed by women and girls, especially if they are poor women of color and migrants. Domestic work is typically denigrated as an unskilled and undesirable form of labor, and in many instances is seen as "help" rather than "work."

In a recent survey of labor laws around the world, the ILO found that only ten percent of domestic workers are covered by general labor laws granted to other workers.[5] Almost 30 percent are completely excluded from even the most basic protections, such as minimum wage, maximum hours, and a day or more off.[6] Most fall in between these extremes and enjoy minimal but not comprehensive protections. Regional disparities are great, with countries in Latin America and Europe offering relatively stronger protection than Asia and the Middle East.

This weak regulation has far-reaching impact because of the large number of women employed in the domestic sector. The ILO estimates that one out of every four female wage earners in Latin America and the Caribbean is a domestic worker—almost one in three in the Middle East.[7] The poor recognition they are given also contrasts sharply with their contributions to national economies. For example, domestic workers comprise a significant proportion of migrants who send billions of dollars annually in remittances to their families in countries such as the Philippines and Indonesia.[8]

Even where domestic work is properly regulated, enforcement remains a huge challenge. Governments and employers have been slow to treat homes as workplaces subject to labor regulation and inspection. Domestic workers are typically isolated and may not have a chance to interact or exchange information with other workers. They may be prohibited from joining or forming workers' associations and are often unaware of their rights or how to claim them. For example, only half of domestic workers are participating in national security schemes in Uruguay, which is considered a global leader in domestic work legislation.[9] One study found that less than ten percent of domestic workers in Medellín, Colombia were receiving overtime pay despite recent legal reforms there.[10]

Domestic worker organizations, human rights groups, academics, governments, and UN agencies have all extensively documented high levels of abuse and exploitation.[11] The most common abuses include long working hours without rest or overtime pay, lack of days off, and restrictions on freedom of movement. Live-in domestic workers who reside in their employer's home are especially isolated, may end up being "on call" at all hours, and have their movements restricted. Domestic workers often report low wages that are a fraction of the prevailing minimum wage and are delayed or not paid at all.[12]

Human Rights Watch (HRW) investigations on domestic work in countries as diverse as Guinea, Indonesia, Jordan, Saudi Arabia, Singapore, the UK, and the US have documented verbal, psychological, physical, and sexual abuse.[13] These include threats, insults, beatings, burns from boiling water or hot irons, sexual harassment, and rape.[14] In some cases domestic workers lose their lives through murder, suicide, or work-related accidents.[15] Domestic work is a high-risk sector for forced labor, trafficking, and slavery-like conditions.[16]

Migrants and children are at heightened risk of abuse. Children may be separated from their families and have less ability to assert their rights with their employers. Domestic work can impede children's education, and heavy workloads take additional tolls on their health.[17] Migrant domestic workers may be subject to deceptive and coercive recruitment practices, excessive recruitment fees that put them deeply in debt, and confiscation of passports. Restrictive immigration policies may contribute to trapping them in exploitative situations for fear of arrest and deportation.[18] The *kafala* (sponsorship) system used in many Middle Eastern countries requires migrant domestic workers to live with their employers and receive their permission to change jobs, often fostering situations of forced labor, including trafficking.

Domestic workers confront many barriers to reporting and redressing abuse, including their lack of mobility, inadequate information about their rights, gaps in legal protections, and ignorance or discriminatory attitudes from state authorities. Employers may accuse, or threaten to accuse, domestic workers with spurious allegations of theft to pressure them to drop their complaints. The length, complexity, cost, and uncertain outcomes of legal proceedings deter most injured parties from pursuing justice.[19]

The ILO domestic workers convention

There has been a groundswell of attention to exploitation in domestic work. The number of domestic worker organizations began growing in the 1990s and 2000s, particularly in Latin America.[20] They began campaigning for recognition and stronger legal protections, achieving some notable successes including a 2006 law regulating domestic work in Uruguay, a 2007 collective bargaining agreement in Italy, and a 2008 reform extending labor laws to domestic workers in Jordan.[21] These pockets of activity drove greater attention to gaps in regulation and mistreatment of domestic workers around the world.

International human rights and migrants' organizations, including Anti-Slavery International, Human Rights Watch (HRW), the Labor Solidarity Center, and Migrant Forum Asia, also focused on domestic workers. For example, HRW investigated and published several reports on serious abuses against domestic workers in countries such as Saudi Arabia and Lebanon, where local labor movements were prohibited or biased against migrants. UN agencies such as the ILO and the United Nations Women's Fund (UNIFEM) carried out research and assistance programs on domestic work in many countries, and increasingly viewed the sector as a priority area for pursuing a decent work agenda and women's labor rights.

In 2006, domestic workers from around the world and allied activists met in Amsterdam and decided to push for a new ILO treaty to establish the first global labor standards on domestic work.[22] They formed alliances with global trade unions, especially the International Union of Food, Agricultural, Hotel, Restaurant, Catering, Tobacco and Allied Workers' Associations (IUF), and the International Trade Union Confederation (ITUC). These new relationships helped challenge and shift historical patterns of trade unions that had previously shown little interest in organizing or prioritizing domestic workers.

By 2009, the International Domestic Workers Network (IDWN), a global network of membership-based domestic worker organizations, was launched with the support of IUF and Women in Informal Employment: Globalizing and Organizing (WIEGO).

The constellation of these newly organized domestic workers' groups, with strong support from global trade unions and other civil society organizations, and deeply committed advocates within the ILO and key governments, led to the initiation of a three-year ILO standard setting process on domestic work.[23] This included preparation of an in-depth report on laws and practices on domestic work around the world[24] that built the case for international labor standards; a questionnaire to ILO members on what the content of such standards should include; and two rounds of negotiations in June 2010 and June 2011 to finalize the exact wording of the provisions and to vote on whether it should be a legally binding treaty or non-binding set of guidance.

Many governments were skeptical about the practicality of regulating work in private households and called for tailored approaches to diverse national contexts instead of global standards. Employers worried about increased regulation that might bring burdensome and unrealistic compliance requirements.

The process of the negotiations helped dissipate doubts. The ILO's unique tripartite structure allows representatives of labor, business, and government to sit and negotiate in the same room and to all have a vote in the final outcome. The process led participants to become sensitized about the extent and gravity of abuse against domestic workers and to learn about models of regulation and enforcement in countries as diverse as Brazil, France, South Africa, and Uruguay. The presence of domestic workers representing themselves at the negotiations was powerful—domestic workers from South Africa, Jamaica, the US, and Brazil participated in their national labor delegations, and Anti-Slavery International sponsored a delegation of child domestic workers.

Ultimately, several factors contributed to strong standards and overwhelming support for the Domestic Workers Convention, including domestic workers' organizing; alliances among domestic workers, trade unions, and civil society; national-level advocacy that bolstered government champions of domestic workers' rights; engagement with all stakeholders, including employers; and a growing body of research.[25]

The convention stipulates that governments provide domestic workers the same labor protections as other workers, including in regulating working hours, minimum wage coverage, rest periods, and social protection. The convention provides protection from violence and harassment and sets out guidance on employment contracts.[26] The convention also includes specific protections to address the heightened risks and specific needs of children and migrants.[27] The convention is accompanied by more detailed guidance in ILO Recommendation 201.[28]

National level reforms[29]

The adoption of the ILO Domestic Workers Convention—spurred by the strong mobilization of domestic workers and their allies and coupled with participatory and awareness-raising negotiations—provided a transformational moment for the domestic workers' movement. The fight to realize rights and dignity for domestic workers is now among the most vibrant, innovative and quickly growing social justice movements. There has been a proliferation of domestic workers' associations, trade union activity, civil society activism, research, policy initiatives, and donor funding.[30]

The IDWN held its founding congress in October 2013 and became a global trade union—the International Domestic Workers' Federation (IDWF). The ITUC coordinated a "12 by 12" campaign to lobby for 12 ratifications of the Domestic Workers Convention by the end of 2012, catalyzing its national affiliates to organize domestic workers, mount numerous public actions, and fight for local reforms.[31] National groups have employed creative strategies and tactics to challenge social attitudes, including viral videos, celebrity spokespersons, and alliances with employers.

As of November 2014, 16 countries had ratified the Domestic Workers Convention, with others fairly advanced in their national ratification processes.[32] At least 30 countries improved legal protections for domestic workers between 2011 and 2014. These range from comprehensive laws covering all aspects of domestic work to reforms on discrete issues, such as raising the minimum wage for domestic workers or ratification of the Domestic Workers Convention:

- Argentina adopted a new domestic work law in March 2013, providing for maximum working hours of 48 hours per week, a weekly rest period, overtime pay, annual vacation days, sick leave, and maternity protections.[33] Article 15 of the law provides additional protections for live-in domestic workers and those under age 18.[34]
- Brazil adopted a constitutional amendment in March 2013 that entitles its estimated 6.5 million domestic workers to overtime pay, unemployment insurance, pensions, a maximum 8-hour work day and 44-hour work week.[35]
- In December 2012, a court in Kenya ruled that verbal contracts between domestic workers and their employers confer rights and are enforceable. The landmark ruling places domestic workers under the protection of the employment law, extending to them the national minimum wage and social security benefits.[36]
- The Philippines enacted the Domestic Workers Act in January 2013, requiring contracts and extending an improved minimum wage, social security, and public health insurance to an estimated 1.9 million domestic workers in the country. The new law also prohibits employment agencies and employers from charging recruitment fees and makes private employment agencies liable, along with employers, for payment of wages and provision of benefits.[37]
- In Spain a legally binding Royal Decree issued in November 2011 sets out requirements for a minimum wage, weekly and annual leave, maternity leave, and compensation for stand-by time when employees are not working but required to be on call.[38] In August 2011, Spain incorporated social security for domestic workers into its General Social Security Scheme. The government reduced the administrative charges payable by employers to facilitate greater compliance with the requirements.[39]

Other countries have not adopted comprehensive laws but have tackled specific aspects of domestic workers' labor rights or adopted incremental reforms. For example, some have increased domestic workers' minimum wage, including Zambia, Tanzania, and Italy.[40] In India, the government extended the Rashtriya Swasthya Bima Yojana (RSBY) health insurance scheme to domestic workers in May 2012, including hospitalization expenses.[41] India also included domestic workers in a 2013 law prohibiting sexual harassment in the workplace that sets out complaints mechanisms and obligates employers to provide a safe working environment.[42]

In September 2013, the US extended minimum wage and overtime protection to an estimated two million home care workers providing in-home services to the elderly and to people with disabilities. Almost all of these workers are employed by home care agencies rather than directly by the households to which they provide services.[43] The change took effect on 1 January 2015, although workers employed directly by households receiving services, and engaged primarily in providing companionship, are still excluded from these protections.[44]

Other countries have improved some protections for domestic workers but have failed to remedy the broader exclusion of domestic workers from key protections of their national labor laws. These include Thailand, which imposed a minimum age of 15 on domestic work; Singapore, which capped migrant domestic workers' recruitment fees; and Bahrain, which regulated annual leave and labor dispute mediations.[45]

Conclusion

Despite the impressive successes of this worker-led movement, many challenges remain. Millions of domestic workers worldwide continue to labor in precarious conditions where their work is devalued. They still experience a range of labor rights violations, abuse, and often insurmountable barriers to redress. Domestic workers may face challenges in organizing, such as sustained prohibitions on forming or joining trade unions in Bangladesh, Thailand, and the US.[46]

Progress has been deeply uneven, with tremendous strides in labor organizing, legal reform, and enforcement in Latin America, and only the beginnings of more public awareness and attempts at partial reforms in the Middle East. The clearest successes have included key legal reforms and a demonstrable increase in domestic worker organizing. Still, far more work is needed to raise awareness about these changes and to ensure that they are enforced.

The struggle for domestic worker rights and dignity can claim a growing list of victories and a long list of challenges. The same factors that have contributed to positive outcomes may be critical ingredients to future successes: the mobilization and leadership of domestic workers themselves; strategic alliances with groups ranging from trade unions to employers groups; research and awareness-raising; and accountability mechanisms to ensure that legal reforms are implemented on the ground.

228   *Nisha Varia*

Notes

1 Celia Mather, "'Yes, We Did It!' How the World's Domestic Workers Won Their International Rights and Recognition," WIEGO, 2013, 70, http://wiego.org/sites/wiego.org/files/resources/files/Mather_Yes%20we%20d id%20it!_2013.pdf.

2 International Labor Office, *Domestic Workers across the World: Global and Regional Statistics and the Extent of Legal Protection*, 2013, www.ilo.org/wcm sp5/groups/public/—dgreports/—dcomm/—publ/documents/publication/wc ms_173363.pdf.

3 Ibid., 19.

4 International Labour Office, International Programme on the Elimination of Child Labour (IPEC), *Marking progress against child labour—Global estimates and trends 2000–2012, 2013*, www.ilo.org/wcmsp5/groups/public/ —ed_norm/—ipec/documents/publication/wcms_221513.pdf. While child labor in other sectors has declined, the ILO estimates that child domestic labor increased by nine percent between 2008 and 2012.

5 ILO, *Domestic Workers across the World*, 50. For a detailed discussion of legal protections for domestic workers under national and international laws, see also ILO, *Decent Work for Domestic Workers, Report IV(1)*, 2013, www. ilo.org/wcmsp5/groups/public/@ed_norm/@relconf/documents/meetingdocu ment/wcms_143337.pdf.

6 Ibid.

7 ILO, *Domestic Workers across the World*, 19–21.

8 World Bank, *Remittance Data Inflows October 2014*, http://econ.worldbank. org/WBSITE/EXTERNAL/EXTDEC/EXTDECPROSPECTS/0,,contentMD K:22759429~pagePK:64165401~piPK:64165026~theSitePK:476883,00.html.

9 Mary R. Goldsmith, "Collective Bargaining and Domestic Workers in Uruguay," WIEGO, 2013: 3, http://wiego.org/sites/wiego.org/files/resources/ files/Goldsmith-Collective-Bargaining-Uruguay-ISBN.pdf.

10 Escuela Nacional Sindical, "Barriendo la Invisibilidad de las Trabajadoras Domesticas Afrocolombianas en Medelin," http://ens.org.co/apc-aa-files/ 45bdec76fa6b8848acf029430d10bb5a/Informe_ejecutivo.pdf.

11 For example, see Anti-Slavery International, *Domestic Work and Slavery*, http://www.antislavery.org/english/slavery_today/domestic_work_and_slaver y/default.aspx; Human Rights Watch, *Domestic Workers*, www.hrw.org/top ic/womens-rights/domestic-workers; ILO, *Making Decent Work a Reality for Domestic Workers Worldwide*, www.ilo.org/global/topics/domestic-wor kers/lang–en/index.htm. See also *Report of the Special Rapporteur on Contemporary Forms of Slavery, Including its Causes and Consequences, Gulnara Shahinian: The Manifestations and Causes of Domestic Servitude*, (A/ HRC/15/20), 18 June 2010.

12 Ibid.

13 Human Rights Watch (HRW), "Bottom of the Ladder: Exploitation and Abuse of Girl Domestic Workers in Guinea" 2007; HRW, "Hidden in the Home," 2000; HRW, "Hidden Away: Abuses against Migrant Domestic Workers in the UK," 2014; HRW, "Domestic Plight: How Jordanian Laws, Officials, Employers, and Recruiters Fail Abused Migrant Domestic Workers," 2011; HRW, "'As If I Am Not Human': Abuses against Asian Domestic Workers in Saudi Arabia," 2008; HRW, "Swept Under the Rug:

Abuses against Domestic Workers Around the World," 2006; HRW, "Maid to Order: Ending Abuses Against Migrant Domestic Workers in Singapore," 2005; and HRW, "Help Wanted: Abuses against Female Migrant Domestic Workers in Indonesia and Malaysia," 2004.

14 HRW, "Slow Reform," 20–21.

15 HRW found that in Lebanon one domestic worker died on average per week from suicide or botched escape attempts from open windows. HRW, *Lebanon: Migrant Domestic Workers Dying Every Week*, 27 August 2008, www.hrw.org/news/2008/08/24/lebanon-migrant-domestic-workers-dying-every-week.

16 *Report of the Special Rapporteur on Contemporary Forms of Slavery* (A/HRC/15/20), 18 June 2010.

17 International Labour Office and IPEC, *Ending Child Labour in Domestic Work and Protecting Young Workers from Abusive Working Conditions*, 2013, www.ilo.org/ipec/Informationresources/WCMS_207656/lang–en/index.htm.

18 HRW, "Walls at Every Turn: Abuse of Migrant Domestic Workers through Kuwait's Sponsorship System," 2010.

19 Caritas and ILO, "Access to Justice for Migrant Domestic Workers in Lebanon," 2014.

20 Celia Mather, "'Yes, We Did It!' How the World's Domestic Workers Won Their International Rights and Recognition," Women in Informal Employment: Globalizing and Organizing (WIEGO), 2013, http://wiego.org/sites/wiego.org/files/resources/files/Mather_Yes%20we%20did%20it!_2013.pdf; Jo Becker, "Organizing for Decent Work for Domestic Workers: The ILO Convention," in *Campaigning for Justice: Human Rights Advocacy in Practice* (Stanford, Calif.: Stanford University Press, 2013).

21 Mary R. Goldsmith, "Collective Bargaining and Domestic Workers in Uruguay," WIEGO, 2012, www.socioeco.org/bdf_fiche-document-3284_en.html; ILO, "Domestic Workers Negotiate New Collective Agreements in Uruguay and Italy," 2 May 2013, www.ilo.org/travail/areasofwork/domestic-workers/WCMS_212212/lang–en/index.htm; Regulation No. 90 of 25 August 2009 on Domestic Workers, Cooks, Gardeners, and Their Like, *Hashemite Kingdom of Jordan Official Gazette* no. 4989, 1 October 2009.

22 International Restructuring Education Network Europe (IRENE) and the International Union of Food, Agricultural, Hotel, Restaurant, Catering, Tobacco and Allied Workers' Associations (IUF), "Respect and Rights: Protection for Domestic/Household Workers!" report from the Protection for Domestic Workers Conference, FNV Trade Union Headquarters, Amsterdam, Netherlands, 8–10 November 2006.

23 For a more detailed history of the constellation of activists and organizations that came together to found the IDWN and the genesis of the ILO Domestic Workers Convention, see Mather, "'Yes, We Did It!'"(2013) and Becker, "Organizing for Decent Work for Domestic Workers," (2013). As discussed later in this chapter, the IDWN became a federation of domestic workers' organizations and unions and renamed itself the International Domestic Workers' Federation (IDWF) in October 2013.

24 ILO, "Decent Work for Domestic Workers, Report no. IV(1)," 2013.

25 Jo Becker, "Organizing for Decent Work for Domestic Workers: The ILO Convention," in *Campaigning for Justice: Human Rights Advocacy in Practice*, Jo Becker (Stanford, Calif.: Stanford University Press, 2013): 51–54.

26 ILO Convention No. 189 concerning Decent Work for Domestic Workers (Domestic Workers Convention), adopted 16 June 2011, entered into force 3 September 2013.

27 Ibid.

28 ILO Recommendation No. 201 concerning Decent Work for Domestic Workers (Domestic Workers Recommendation), adopted at the 100th ILC Session in Geneva, 16 June 2011.

29 Much of the following section is reproduced or adapted from HRW, IDWN, and ITUC, "Claiming Rights: Domestic Workers' Movements and Global Advances for Labor Reform," 2013. HRW, IDWN, ITUC, "Claiming Rights," 2013. IDWF, www.idwfed.org/en. ITUC, "12 by 12 Campaign," www.ituc-csi.org/domestic-workers-12-by-12. Barnard Center for Research on Women, "Justice in the Home: Domestic Work Past, Present, and Future," Conference at the Diana Center, New York, 16–17 October 2014, http://bcrw.barnard.edu/event/justice-in-the-home-domestic-work-pa st-present-and-future/.

30 HRW, IDWN, ITUC, "Claiming Rights," 2013. IDWF, www.idwfed.org/ en. ITUC, "12 by 12 campaign," www.ituc-csi.org/domestic-wor kers-12-by-12. Barnard Center for Research on Women, "Justice in the Home: Domestic Work Past, Present, and Future," Conference at the Diana Center, New York, 16–17 October 2014, http://bcrw.barnard.edu/ event/justice-in-the-home-domestic-work-past-present-and-future/.

31 "12 by 12." Campaign partners include IDWN, the International Union of Food, Agricultural, Hotel, Restaurant, Catering, Tobacco and Allied Workers' Associations (IUF), Public Services International (PSI), the European Trade Union Confederation (ETUC), HRW, Solidar, Amnesty International, Migrant Forum Asia, World Solidarity, Anti-Slavery International, Caritas, FOS and the Global March against Child Labour, www. ituc-csi.org/domestic-workers-12-by-12.

32 These include Argentina, Bolivia, Colombia, Costa Rica, Ecuador, Germany, Guyana, Italy, Ireland, Mauritius, Nicaragua, Paraguay, the Philippines, South Africa, and Uruguay. Countries that are far along in their national ratification processes include the Dominican Republic and Switzerland. See ILO, *Ratifications of C189*, www.ilo.org/dyn/normlex/en/f?p=NORMLEXPUB: 11300:0::NO::P11300_INSTRUMENT_ID:2551460

33 Law 26.844, 2013 of 13 March 2013, Régimen Especial de Contrato de Trabajo para el Personal de Casas Particulares, 3 April 2013, www.trabajo. gov.ar/downloads/domestico/ley_26844.pdf.

34 Ibid., Arts. 15 and Chapter II.

35 Law no. 72 of April 2013, in Constituição da República Federativa do Brasil, Emenda Constitucional, http://presrepublica.jusbrasil.com.br/legisla cao/1034514/emenda-constitucional-72-13. ILO News, "Victory for Domestic Workers in Brazil," *Equal Times*, 3 April 2013, /www.equaltimes. org/victory-for-domestic-workers-in-brazil#.VQx9sI6sVvo.

36 Robai Musinzi v Safdar Mohamed Khan [2012] eKLR, Industrial Court of Kenya, Cause 267 of 2012. Solidarity Center, *Kenya: Court Rules*

Employment Law Covers Domestic Workers, 6 May 2013, www.solidarityce nter.org/kenya-court-rules-employment-law-covers-domestic-workers/.

37 Ibid., sections 13 and 36.

38 Real Decreto 1620/2011 of 14 November 2011, por el que se regula la relación laboral de carácter especial del servicio del hogar familiar, In BOE núm. 277, of 17 November 2011, 119046–119057. ILO, "Spain Approves New Regulations for Domestic Employees," in *Developments in Law and Practice 2012* (Geneva, Switzerland: ILO, 2012), www.ilo.org/wcmsp5/group s/public/@ed_protect/@protrav/@travail/documents/publication/wcms_173686. pdf.

39 Ibid.

40 Statutory Instrument No. 3 of 7 January 2011 under the Zambia Minimum Wages and Conditions of Employment (Domestic Workers) Order in Laws, Volume 14, Cap. 276. Government Notice No. 196 of Labor Institutions Wage Order, 28 June 2013, in Supplement No. 24. Verbale di accordo per il rinnovo del contratto collettivo nazionale di lavoro nel settore domestic of 9 April 2013 in Roma, Corso Trieste 10. ILO, *Domestic Workers Negotiate New Collective Agreements in Uruguay and Italy*, 2 May 2013, www.ilo.org/ travail/areasofwork/domestic-workers/WCMS_212212/lang–en/index.htm.

41 Rashtriya Swasthya Bima Yojana (RSBY), *Guidelines for Extension of RSBY to Domestic Workers*, http://rsby.gov.in/docs/RSBY%20Guidelines% 20for%20Domestic%20Workers%2026.6.11.pdf.

42 Sexual Harassment of Women at Workplace (Prevention, Prohibition and Redressal) Act 2013 (No. 14 of 2013) of 22 April 2013, in Registered No. DL-(N)04/0007/2003–13.

43 United States Department of Labor, "Application of the Fair Labor Standards Act to Domestic Service," 2013, www.dol.gov/whd/homecare/final_ rule.pdf. US Department of Labor, Wage and Hour Division, "Information on the Final Rule: Application of the Fair Labor Standards Act to Domestic Service," 2013, www.dol.gov/whd/homecare/finalrule.htm.

44 US Department of Labor, Wage and Hour Division, "Minimum Wage, Overtime Protections Extended to Direct Care Workers by US Labor Department," 17 September 2013, www.dol.gov/whd/media/press/whdp ressVB3.asp?pressdoc=national/20130917.xml.

45 Ministerial Regulation No. 14 (B.E. 2555) under the Labour Protection Act B.E. 2541 (1998) of November 2012, in Government Gazette, Volume 129, Part 105 Kor of 9th. ILO, "Thailand: New Ministerial Regulation Offers Better Protection of Domestic Worker's Rights," in *Developments in Law and Practice 2012* (Geneva, Switzerland: ILO, 2012). Ministry of Manpower (MOM), "Changes to the Employment Agency Regulatory Framework," 9 February 2011, www.mom.gov.sg/Documents/foreign-manpower/ Employment%20Agencies/Guide%20for%20employment%20agencies%20o n%20new%20regulatory%20framework.pdf. MOM, "Weekly Rest Days for Foreign Domestic Workers," 5 March 2012, www.mom.gov.sg/newsroom/ Pages/PressReleasesDetail.aspx?listid=411%20. Domestic workers are covered by 46 out of 197 articles in Bahrain's new law. See Article 2 of the Bahrain Labor Law for the Private Sector, No. 36 of 2012, in Official Gazette No. 3063, 2 August 2012. See also HRW, IDWN and ITUC, "Claiming Rights," 2013 for more examples.

46 Bangladesh Labour Act, 2006 (XLII of 2006). Thailand Labour Protection Act of 1998, in Government Gazette. ILO, *Domestic Workers in Thailand: Their Situation, Challenges and the Way Forward*, January 2010 www.ilo.org/wcmsp5/groups/public/—asia/—ro-bangkok/documents/publication/wcms_120274.pdf. United States National Labor Relations Act, 1935, 29 U.S.C. §§ 151–169.

18 Women, employment, fertility—and other women

Wendy Chavkin

Feminists have long observed that the bifurcation of labor between employment and home is central to women's disadvantage in both spheres. Today, this takes specific forms. Profound social, demographic, and economic changes during the past half-century have altered how most people in the developed world lead their private lives. Women now participate widely in paid employment. Single parenthood and divorce have escalated.[1] Women have fewer children at significantly later ages and often postpone childbearing until work and wages are established. This, in turn, has had significant consequences for population dynamics, marked in most places by declines in birth rates.

In the context of a globalized world characterized by rapid movements of capital, people, information, and new medical technologies, these developments have also fuelled a disaggregation of the biologic and caregiving components of motherhood, and spurred transnational movements of people: poor women from the developing world migrate to perform childcare work in wealthy countries, and traffic moves in both directions as women relinquish or obtain babies through adoption and seek assisted reproductive technologies.

This chapter asserts that such dramatic changes in basic human arrangements deserve greater scrutiny and should serve as impetus for the development of improved public policies that support these new realities and redress some of their untoward consequences. It further maintains that this policy formulation must deal with sex-based biological difference, if gender equity is our goal. We need to better incorporate insights from second-wave feminism about the relationship between women's disadvantage in the workplace and their responsibilities for reproduction and domestic life. Then we can understand the decline in birth rates as a result (at least in part) of the continued inadequacy of governmental provision to support women at work and at home.

Better understanding fertility decline

But first we need to understand fertility decline as one of a cluster of demographic developments that transpired over the course of the twentieth century, with the pace and global sweep of change having accelerated dramatically during the last few decades. These changes include reduced childbearing and improvements in maternal and infant mortality, on the one hand, along with longer lifespans on the other. They have occurred all over the developed and, more recently, the developing world, least in Sub Saharan Africa. In the developed world the shifts have been so dramatic that most European and "Asian tiger" countries now have fertility rates well below the replacement level of 2.1 births per woman.[2]

Together with extended longevity, declining birth rates have led to an "aging of the population," with a shrinking working-age cohort available to support both children and older, retired people.[3] Such significant shifts in population age structure give rise to broad macroeconomic and political concerns, as the size and productivity of a country's labor force has obvious consequences for its economy and for the tax base available to support social programs. Age shifts also have consequences for disease patterns and healthcare provision, with chronic diseases and long-term care needs predominating.[4] These many factors, in turn, have profound implications for pension and health systems and could aggravate competition for resources between the old and the young.

Why have these changes occurred? While theorists differ regarding the contributions of specific factors, in general they agree that fertility decline is associated with all the demographic changes outlined, as well as with urbanization, female education and employment, increased "individualism," and technological advances in contraception.[5]

Certainly, female employment has increased dramatically over the past decades, including the employment of married women and mothers of young children. Some posit that when educational and employment opportunities are significantly reduced by motherhood, or the task of juggling work and home responsibilities is very burdensome, women sharply reduce the number of children they have.[6] Some states provide benefits geared to accommodate the double burden of women workers and implicitly accept the gendered division of responsibility for childrearing and domestic life. As female responsibility for social as well as biological reproductive work has been associated with occupational segregation and a gender wage gap virtually everywhere, however, women remain disadvantaged in the workplace and have responded by having very few children.

Others offer an "equality" or gender sameness model that does not acknowledge social or biological reproductive responsibilities and thus leaves working women staggering under the double burden—to which they have again responded by delaying marriage and not having children. Only the Scandinavian countries have adequately addressed gendered responsibilities for domestic life and its workplace consequences, with a series of incentives and mandates to increase paternal participation in childrearing.

Yet, through empirical observation of patterns of birth rates, family and work arrangements, and public supports, such mainstream players as the European Union (EU), the Organisation for Economic Co-operation and Development (OECD), and the United Nations (UN) have accepted feminist insights about the need to address social reproduction and gender relations simultaneously by supporting work-family reconciliation policies that enable women and men to participate both in paid employment and in childrearing responsibilities.[7] These "work-family reconciliation" efforts include such measures as financial compensation for the costs associated with childrearing (cash grants, tax credits, subsidized childcare, access to housing, loans) and work conditions that enable employees to perform their domestic responsibilities (maternity and paternity leave, flexible work hours, subsidized childcare, tax structure that values "second" lesser income).[8] Such policies are, of course, predicated on a generous welfare state, one that provides some social reproductive functions, such as subsidized childcare or eldercare.

Taking globalization into account

The rise of "globalization" and the ascendency of transnational corporations and economic institutions such as the International Monetary Fund (IMF), World Bank, World Trade Organization (WTO), etc. has resulted in a growing interconnectedness of production and communication around the world and reduced barriers to trade. This, in turn, has allowed for increased movement of people for trade and work—and has exerted pressure toward contraction of the welfare state. These developments have also brought supranational actors into national social policy formulation, pressing individual nation states to cut taxes, regulations, and public expenditure, and to increase job insecurity.

All of this has also led to increased migration of women from the developing world seeking work as nannies, an ever-available pool of babies for adoption, and the recruitment of women to sell their gametes and bodies as egg "donors" and surrogates. These same push factors at an institutional level have fueled a burgeoning business in both legal and black markets for assisted reproductive technologies (ARTs) and for the brokerage of nanny and adoption services.[9]

Pressure on wages and state provisioning in the developed world, in tandem with the forces previously described, align to create reciprocal "pull" factors. Women in the developed world face the predicament of needing their salaries, inadequate work-family supports, and the reduced fertility resulting from delayed childbearing. Some women attempt to resolve this dilemma by seeking cheaper and unregulated ARTs and associated body parts (surrogates and gametes), adoptable babies, and caregivers for these babies.

Factoring in the realities of female biology

Moreover, even the most generous of work-family benefits are predicated on employment. Therefore, there are built-in structural incentives to delay childbearing until salary level and job status are well established. This discordance between employment trajectories and the female reproductive biological clock disadvantages women both economically and biologically. The implicit assumption that the male worker is the norm goes deep. It extends beyond the question of social responsibilities and assumes male reproductive biological patterns as well because the hard facts are that the ability to become pregnant and carry to term begins to decline for women by their late twenties and drops very sharply after the late thirties.[10] The secular trend to delay childbirth thus leaves women a narrow window of biological opportunity for childbearing. Many are then demanding recourse to adoption and to ARTs.

International adoption became a significant phenomenon after the Korean War. The United States remains the number one recipient of adoptees, followed by some European countries. Comparative rankings of countries sending the most babies abroad vary—currently Ethiopia is the leading provider for the West—but the major reasons countries send babies abroad for adoption do not vary, and these include conflict, poverty, stigma of unmarried childbearing, and discrimination against girls—in sum, some version of tragedy or oppression.[11] Intercountry adoption has generated a host of concerns about legality, coercion, developmental consequences for children, the meaning accorded to race, to genetics, and to nurturance, and the nation state's power to regulate, protect, and define membership or citizenship. Individual countries have forbidden adoption from specified countries, decrying coercive or discriminatory practices, but other countries then rise to the top as sending nations, and a vast underground thrives as well. Efforts to use international treaties and covenants to achieve harmonization across borders have thus far had limited efficacy.

Other women confronted by age-related declining fertility have turned to ARTs, a term that comprises a variety of measures, ranging from the simpler interventions like artificial insemination or ovarian stimulation, to ones where sperm and egg meet in the laboratory—in vitro fertilization being the most common and well known of this group. Success rates for the IVF-associated group of procedures are still low (overall, roughly 30 to 50 percent of IVF cycles lead to a live birth and success diminishes with maternal age).

The complications we know about for the babies born of such procedures include increased rates of preterm delivery, low birth weight, perinatal death, certain specific rare birth defects, and increased rates of twin and higher order multiple pregnancies (triplets, quadruplets).[12] Follow-up studies indicate neurological and cognitive deficits in long-term survivors of very low birth weight multiple births, and we also know that women who carry multiple gestation pregnancies are at risk for worrisome pregnancy complications. We know about certain short-term risks for women undergoing the hormonal stimulation required to make ova and uteri ready for these procedures, but we know far less about the long-term consequences for women's health, as this has not been well studied.[13] Success for ARTs also declines with increasing maternal age,[14] which has led to a sharp rise in the use of ova from younger women or "egg donation." This appears to be a widespread thriving global business.

Pregnancy puts women at risk—more than half a million women die annually of pregnancy-related complications in the developing world.[15] Women serving as surrogates—particularly in the developing world—must therefore be understood to face significant risks to their health. As women age and have had a longer time to acquire age-related health problems like hypertension or diabetes, the complications of pregnancy climb. Pregnancy complications for women and fetuses also increase significantly when a woman carries twins or triplets. Women in the developed world undergoing ARTs at later ages are thus facing increased chances of pregnancy-associated health problems for themselves and their fetuses. This is certainly also true for those serving as surrogates in the Global North or South. For example, Indian surrogates are contractually compelled to use the eggs of others and undergo IVF. They often have too many embryos transferred on the incorrect assumption that this increases the likelihood of success, and then, if those embryos all "take" are made to undergo selective reduction of some of them. Throughout these procedures, they are made to live in special monitored sites and then to have Caesarean sections as a matter of course, in a country where pregnancy-associated death rates are still high.

Whether babies arrive via adoption or ARTs, the working mothers of the developed world still face the pressures of work and family that led them to delay childbearing in the first place. Unless they live in Scandinavia or the few other countries that provide high-quality affordable childcare, many resolve this dilemma by turning to other poorer women for childcare and other domestic tasks.[16] As the twenty-first century dawns, women constitute approximately half of all migrants in the Global North and South. And more than half of these migrant women are domestic workers—in Europe, the United States, the Gulf States or the affluent countries of Asia. The billions of dollars sent home as remittances by these women—and migrant men—are the largest source of financial flows to their countries of origin after direct foreign investment.[17] Inter-country adoptees are often also sources of remittances for their birth families.[18]

These economic push/pull factors and state protections line up in accord with the familiar North–South global divisions of resources and power. While poor and disenfranchised women are most vulnerable to the economically coercive and exploitative aspects of these circumstances, women in the highly developed world are also affected. Thus we see that progress towards gender equity in both employment and domestic responsibilities for women from the developed world relies, in part, on economic and gendered inequities confronting other groups of women. This interaction perpetuates gender-associated limitations for both, although neither equally, nor similarly.[19]

Declining fertility poses such a significant problem for the economic and social order of highly developed nations that some have entertained structural—and political—adaptation. Both the EU and the OECD have formally stated that work-family reconciliation is a goal in itself, as it should improve the quality of life, increase the labor supply and national income, provide families with more secure income, lead to better child development outcomes, enable families to have the desired number of children (and thus increase fertility), and promote gender equity.[20] However, as benefits are predicated on employment, pressure to defer childbearing persists. Alternatively, work-family benefits could be provided to all and thus enable women and men to have children and state support while they undertake training, education, and early career.

From a human rights and reproductive rights perspective, a society should provide a quality of life sufficient for its members to feel it possible to have children. The OECD formulation indicates acceptance of the Cairo-Beijing model of respect for individual decision-making and repudiation of coercion, as well as endorsement of the necessity of services and income to enable people to rear children.

Conclusion

Feminist insights of the past 30 years about the centrality of gender inequity and social reproductive responsibility have been vividly confirmed by widespread declines in fertility. This dramatic development provides an opportunity to deepen our understanding of the relationships among employment, social reproduction, gender, biology, the state, and global interactions. Concern about fertility levels has led certain mainstream political players to support work–family reconciliation efforts as well as the promotion of paternal involvement in childrearing.

Let us parlay this concern into policies that enable women and men to choose both employment and children without financial hardship, biological risk, or exploitation of those in harsher circumstances. These demographic developments and political concerns offer the opportunity to advance strategies to redefine gender roles and norms related to social reproduction and work.

Notes

1 Colleen M. Fox, "Changing Japanese Employment Patterns and Women's Participation: Anticipating the Implications of Employment Trends," *Manoa Journal* 3 (1995): 1–5. Ann Orloff, "Gender in the Welfare State," *Annual Review of Sociology*, 22 (1996): 51–78. Peter McDonald, "The 'Toolbox' of Public Policies to Impact on Fertility: A Global View" (paper presented at the Annual Seminar 2000 of the European Observatory on Family Matters, Low Fertility, Families, and Public Policies, Seville, Spain, 15–16 September 2000), https://digitalcollections.anu.edu.au/bitstream/1885/41446/3/sevilleMcD1.pdf.
2 Clarence Lochhead, "The Trend Toward Delayed First Childbirth: Health and Social Implications," *Isuma* 1 (2000): 41–44; Rodolfo A. Bulatao and John B. Casterline, eds, *Global Fertility Transition* (New York: Population Council, 2001).

3 Clarence Lochhead, "The Trend Toward Delayed First Childbirth: Health and Social Implications," *Isuma* 1 (2000): 41–44; Rodolfo A. Bulatao and John B. Casterline, eds, *Global Fertility Transition* (New York: Population Council, 2001).

4 United Nations, *Replacement Migration: Is it a Solution to Declining and Aging Populations?* (New York: UN Population Division, Department of Economic and Social Affairs, 2000). Herbert Brücker, *Can International Migration Solve the Problems of European Labour Markets?* (Geneva, Switzerland: United Nations Economic Commission for Europe, Economic Analysis Division: 2002).

5 Constance Sorrentino, "The Changing Family in International Perspective," *Monthly Labor Review* 113 (1990): 41–58. Karen Oppenheim Mason and An-Magritt Jensen, eds, *Gender and Family Change in Industrialized Countries* (New York: Oxford University Press, 1995).

6 Constance Sorrentino, "The Changing Family in International Perspective," *Monthly Labor Review* 113 (1990): 41–58; Karen Oppenheim Mason and An-Magritt Jensen, eds, *Gender and Family Change in Industrialized Countries* (New York: Oxford University Press, 1995); Jean-Claude Chesnais, "Fertility, Family, and Social Policy," *Population and Development Review* 22 (1996): 729–39; Peter McDonald, "The 'Toolbox' of Public Policies to Impact on Fertility: A Global View" (paper presented at the Annual Seminar 2000 of the European Observatory on Family Matters, Low Fertility, Families, and Public Policies, Seville, Spain, 15–16 September 2000), https://digitalcollections.anu.edu.au/bitstream/1885/41446/3/sevilleMcD1.pdf; Francis G. Castles, "The World Turned Upside Down: Below Replacement Fertility, Changing Preferences and Family-friendly Public Policy in 21 OECD Countries," *Journal of European Social Policy* 13 (2003): 209–27.

7 Organisation for Economic Co-operation and Development, "Balancing Work and Family Life: Helping Parents into Paid Employment," in *OECD – Employment Outlook* (Paris, France: OECD, 2001). Organisation for Economic Co-operation and Development, *Babies and Bosses – Reconciling Work and Family Life (Vol. 4): Canada, Finland, Sweden and the United Kingdom* (Paris, France: OECD, 2005).

8 David Cheal, Frances Woolley, and Meg Luxton, *How Families Cope and Why Policymakers Need to Know* (Ottawa: Canadian Policy Research Networks Inc., 1998); Clarence Lochhead, "The Trend Toward Delayed First Childbirth: Health and Social Implications," *Isuma* 1 (2000): 41–44; Rodolfo A. Bulatao and John B. Casterline, eds, *Global Fertility Transition* (Population Council, 2001); Guy Laroque and Bernard Salanie, "Fertility and Financial Incentives in France," *CESifo Economic Studies* 50, no. 3 (2004): 432–450. Organisation for Economic Co-operation and Development, *Babies and Bosses – Reconciling Work and Family Life (Vol. 4): Canada, Finland, Sweden and the United Kingdom* (Paris, France: OECD, 2005).

9 Debora L. Spar, *The Baby Business: How Money, Science, and Politics Drive the Commerce of Conception* (Boston, Mass.: Harvard Business School Press, 2006).

10 Odile Frank, P. Grace Bianchi, and Aldo Campana, "The End of Fertility: Age, Fecundity and Fecundability in Women," *Journal of Biosocial Science* 26 (1994): 349–68; David V. Dunson, Bernardo Colombo, and Donna D.

Baird, "Changes with Age in the Level and Duration of Fertility in the Menstrual Cycle," *Human Reproduction* 17 (2002): 1399–1403.

11 Peter Selman, "Intercountry Adoption as Globalized Motherhood" in *Globalization of Motherhood: Deconstructions and Reconstructions of Biology and care*, ed. Wendy Chavkin and Jane Maree Maher (London and New York: Routledge, 2010). Barbara Yngvesson, "Transnational Adoption and the Transnationalization of Motherhood: Rethinking Abandonment, Adoption and Return, Motherhood" in *Globalization of Motherhood: Deconstructions and reconstructions of biology and care*, ed. Wendy Chavkin and Jane Maree Maher (London and New York: Routledge, 2010).

12 Mark Evans, Linda Littmann, Lori St. Louis, Laurie LeBlanc, Jeanne Addis, Mark Paul Johnson, and Kamran S. Moghissi, "Evolving Patterns of Iatrogenic Multifetal Pregnancy Generation: Implications for the Aggressiveness of Infertility Treatments," *American Journal of Obstetrics and Gynecology* 172 (1995): 1750–5. Norbert Gleicher, Denise M. Oleske, Ilan Tur-Kaspa, Andrea Vidali, and Vishvanath Karande, "Reducing the Risk of High-Order Multiple Pregnancy after Ovarian Stimulation with Gonadotropins," *New England Journal of Medicine* 343 (2000): 2–7.

13 Mark Evans, Linda Littmann, Lori St. Louis, Laurie LeBlanc, Jeanne Addis, Mark Paul Johnson and Kamran S. Moghissi, "Evolving Patterns of Iatrogenic Multifetal Pregnancy Generation: Implications for the Aggressiveness of Infertility Treatments," *American Journal of Obstetrics and Gynecology* 172 (1995): 1750–5; Norbert Gleicher, Denise M. Oleske, Ilan Tur-Kaspa, Andrea Vidali and Vishvanath Karande, "Reducing the Risk of High-Order Multiple Pregnancy after Ovarian Stimulation with Gonadotropins," *New England Journal of Medicine* 343 (2000): 2–7.

14 Victoria C. Wright, Laura A. Schieve, Meredith A. Reynolds, and Gary Jeng, "Assisted Reproductive Technology Surveillance – United States, 2000" *MMWR Surveill Summ* 52 (2003): 1–16.

15 World Health Organization, *Maternal Mortality in 2005: Estimates Developed by WHO, UNICEF, UNFPA and the World Bank*, World Health Organization, 2007, http://apps.who.int/iris/bitstream/10665/43807/1/978924 1596213_eng.pdf?ua=1.

16 Sonya Michel and Ito Peng, "All in the Family? Migration, Nationhood and Care Regimes in Asia and North America," *Journal of European Social Policy* 22 (2012): 406; Joan C. Tronto, "The Nanny Question in Feminism," *Hypatia* 17 (2002): 34–51.

17 Manuel Abrantes, "What about the Numbers? A Quantitative Contribution to the Study of Domestic Services in Europe: Women's Labour Force Participation: Gendered Patterns and Trends," *International Labour Review* 153 (2014): 223–243; Herbert Brucker, *Can International Migration Solve the Problems of European Labour Markets?* (Geneva, Switzerland: UN Economic Commission for Europe, Economic Analysis Division, 2002).

18 Barbara Yngvesson, "Transnational Adoption and the Transnationalization of Motherhood: Rethinking Abandonment, Adoption and Return, Motherhood" in *Globalization of Motherhood: Deconstructions and reconstructions of biology and care*, ed. Wendy Chavkin and Jane Maree Maher (London and New York: Routledge, 2010).

19 Wendy Chavkin, "Biology and Destiny: Women, Work, Birthrates, and Assisted Reproductive Technologies," in *Global Empowerment of Women:*

Responses to Globalization, Politicized Religion and Gender Violence, ed. Carolyn Elliott (New York: Routledge, 2008).

20 Organisation for Economic Co-operation and Development, "Balancing Work and Family Life: Helping Parents into Paid Employment," in *OECD – Employment Outlook* (Paris, France: OECD, 2001); Organisation for Economic Co-operation and Development, *Babies and Bosses – Reconciling Work and Family Life (Vol. 4): Canada, Finland, Sweden and the United Kingdom* (Paris, France: OECD, 2005).

19 The MENA's woman problem

Progress and challenges in women's economic participation

Isobel Coleman and Aala Abdelgadir

Across the Arab world, women have made substantial gains in recent decades. Despite conservative cultural norms and strong religious influences that seek to constrain women's role in society, Arab women have nevertheless attained greater legal rights, increased political inclusion, and broader social freedom. While progress varies considerably from country to country, the most consistent gains for women across the region have been in education. Many countries have closed their gender gaps in primary and secondary education, and a reverse gender gap has emerged at the tertiary level. In at least eight Middle East and North Africa (MENA) countries, women now outnumber men at the university level—in some cases by a significant number.[1] Fully 60 percent or more of higher education graduates in Tunisia and Algeria are women.[2] Arab women are also well represented in the science, technology, engineering, and math (STEM) fields, making up a majority of science graduates in the region overall.[3]

These impressive educational achievements, however, have yet to translate into commensurate economic gains. The MENA region still has the lowest female workforce participation rate of any region in the world, by a wide margin. At 21 percent, the female workforce participation rate in the MENA was a full 11 percentage points lower in 2012 than in South Asia, the next lowest region with a rate of 32 percent. Sub-Saharan Africa, in contrast, has a 64 percent female workforce participation rate.[4]

The lag in women's workforce participation poses a significant challenge to MENA economies. Governments across the region are making considerable investments in female education, yet are not reaping the benefit of women's economic potential. A recent European Union-funded report estimates that if female labor force participation over the period from 2015 to 2030 increased by five percent over projected rates, the region's gross domestic product (GDP) would increase by 1.3 percent, approximately $525 billion, cumulatively during this period.[5] In some countries, the lost opportunity of women's economic exclusion is substantial. According to a study by Booz & Co., Egypt could increase its GDP by more than a third if it raised its female labor force participation rate to match that of men.[6]

Over time, it is likely that the advances Arab women have made in education and health care as well as legal, political, and social rights will result in broader economic gains. But that process will continue to be sluggish unless restrictive social and cultural norms, discriminatory legal and regulatory frameworks, and exclusionary economic policies are specifically addressed. In the meantime, the region will experience slower growth from the lost economic opportunity of its female human capital.

Closing the gender gaps

As recently as 1980, the MENA region had abysmally poor human development indicators for women. The average number of years of schooling for females (ages 15 to 19) was only 3.5; less than a third of women over the age of 15 were literate; the maternal mortality rate was notably high; and female political participation was among the lowest of any region.[7]

However, in the last several decades, MENA countries have made significant investments in advancing the status of women, and female indicators across the board have improved dramatically. Female life expectancy rose from 54 years in 1970 to 74 years in 2010.[8] Fertility rates also fell from 6.6 children per woman in 1970 to 2.8 in 2010.[9] Maternal mortality fell by 59 percent from 1990 to 2008—the largest rate of decline in the world—and is now well below the global average.[10] Girls' primary school enrollment rose from 49 percent in 1975 to 85 percent in 2010.[11] While boys continue to have a slight edge in access to primary education in some Arab countries, girls' primary and secondary school enrollment overall is almost at parity, and the gap between female and male literacy rates is steadily narrowing.

Gaining legal ground

Legal reforms, although uneven across Arab countries, have also helped to improve the status of women and to expand their participation in social, political, civic, and economic life in many countries. While the constitutions of most MENA countries include provisions that stipulate equal rights for all citizens, personal status laws—the all-important codes that govern family matters such as marriage, divorce, custody, and inheritance—are generally exempt from those provisions. Nevertheless, there have been important reforms even in matters of personal status. Numerous countries have expanded women's divorce, custody, and inheritance rights, and raised the legal age for marriage. Morocco's rewriting of its family code in 2004 was a landmark reform that put women on a more equal legal footing with their husbands, granting them joint responsibility over their marriage and family. The primary changes to the family code included raising the age of marriage, restricting polygamy, granting women the right to initiate a divorce, improving inheritance rights for women, and giving women the opportunity to retain custody of children.[12] Other countries have also tackled aspects of family law. Jordan, for example, amended laws to enable women to pass citizenship to children born of non-citizen fathers in certain circumstances, such as when fatherhood is unsubstantiated or fathers are unknown or stateless.[13]

Legal reforms have also enhanced women's autonomy and freedom of movement—gains that expand women's access to economic opportunities. Guardianship laws, which place women in the legal care of husbands and fathers and require them to obtain permission to do a range of activities, including to work, travel, marry, or access health care, were previously pervasive across the region, imposing constraints on women's economic, political, and social opportunities. The restrictiveness of these laws historically varied from country to country, with Saudi Arabia maintaining the most stringent guardianship framework, but many countries have loosened their restrictions in recent decades. In 2000, a Supreme Court case in Egypt established that women no longer need a man's permission to travel.[14] In subsequent years, other countries, including Jordan, Kuwait, Qatar, and Bahrain, allowed women to obtain passports and travel freely.[15] Such reforms have great potential for enhancing women's welfare, giving them access to economic opportunities previously unavailable.

In the aftermath of the Arab uprisings, women's rights quickly emerged as one of the most contentious political issues in the region. The increased influence of Islamists raised concerns of backsliding on women's legal gains, but so far that has not been the case. Tunisia, long the most progressive country for women in the MENA region, adopted a new constitution that reaffirms and even expands women's rights, and also commits the state to achieving gender parity in elected councils. This is in large part a result of strong and persistent mobilization of women's groups. In Egypt, civil society organizations pushed to ensure women's inclusion in the transition, but embattled activists struggled in an environment historically more hostile to women's rights than

Tunisia. In several high-profile cases, activists had to contend with politically motivated sexual violence, among other challenges. Only four women participated in the 85-member assembly that drafted a new constitution under the Islamist-led Morsi government in 2012, and the resulting document included only ambiguous commitments to women's rights.[16] But a revised constitution, ratified after a military coup deposed Morsi, includes new language committing the state to achieve equality between men and women and to combat gender-based violence.[17] In Yemen, a perennial laggard on women's rights, law-makers included women in the post-Arab uprising National Dialogue process to an unprecedented degree and also introduced legislation to establish a minimum age of marriage.[18] Although these countries' contexts differ, a common theme across all is that determined activism has prevented regression in the face of political conservatism and downright hostility to women's rights.

Addressing political marginalization

Although women's political footprint varies from country to country, the region as a whole has suffered from notably low numbers of women in politics. Governments around the region, however, have been taking steps to ease women's entry into the political realm. Saudi Arabia, the world's hold-out on women's suffrage, capitulated in the fall of 2011 when King Abdullah granted women the right to vote and run in municipal elections, a right they will be able to exercise in the next election cycle set for 2015.[19] The Saudi government also decided to reserve 20 percent of the seats in its Shura Council for women, a senior consultative body that advises the king.[20] Numerous countries, including Algeria, Egypt, Iraq, Jordan, Libya, Morocco, Tunisia, and Sudan, are also using political quotas to boost the relatively low number of women in government at the federal or sub-national levels, either reserving parliamentary seats for women or mandating that parties field a certain percentage of female candidates.[21] In Tunisia, which required political parties to use a zippered list system alternating male and female candidates on party ballots, women now hold nearly a third of the seats in parliament.[22] Whether such quotas will lead to more women-friendly policies and legislation over the longer term remains to be seen, but they are certainly boosting numbers of women in office. Since 2003, the percent of women in MENA parliaments has increased from 6 percent to 17.8 percent in 2013.[23]

Political appointment has also been a popular mechanism for enhancing women's political participation. In 1990, eight MENA countries had only one or two women in ministerial positions, whereas by 2011, cabinets featured between two and six female ministers in most countries.[24] The Gulf Cooperation Council countries (GCC), in particular, are partial to women's political appointments. Five GCC countries have named women to ministerial positions and all have featured women on representative bodies.[25]

While female political participation as a whole has improved across the region, women are still heavily underrepresented in governments and legislatures. Indeed, the MENA region ranks lower than any other in terms of female political empowerment, as measured by the World Economic Forum's *2013 Global Gender Gap Report*.[26]

Lack of economic participation limiting growth

Many Arab countries have expanded women's legal and political rights and increased their access to education and health care, but significant gender gaps persist. One of the most glaring lags is in workforce participation rates. Despite substantial gains in education, women's labor force participation has remained flat over the past few decades, rising from 21 percent in 1990 to only 23 percent in 2012.[27] Within this regional average, large variations exist. The small Gulf states of Qatar, the United Arab Emirates, and Kuwait boast the highest rates of female workforce participation, at 51 percent, 47 percent, and 43 percent, respectively. Outside of the Gulf, Sudan and Libya report the highest female participation rates with 31 percent and 30 percent, respectively. The middle-performing countries cluster around 23 percent and include Egypt, Tunisia, Morocco, and Lebanon, while the stragglers, including Syria, Jordan, Iraq, and Algeria, score around 15 percent.[28] At the current rate of change, the World Bank estimates that the MENA region would require another 150 years to converge with the world's average female workforce participation rate of 51 percent.[29]

In addition, female unemployment rates are consistently higher than male unemployment rates across the region.[30] This stagnation in female economic participation has persisted despite healthy rates of economic growth in several large economies, such as Egypt.[31] Between 2000 and 2008, Egypt's economy grew at a rate of roughly 5 percent per year, but labor force participation rates for women did not increase commensurately.[32] Similarly, Saudi Arabia, the Arab world's largest economy, has also seen strong growth in recent decades, with GDP growth averaging 6.25 percent per year between 2008 and 2012, yet women remain underrepresented in Saudi's economy.[33]

As various experts have shown, underutilizing women's talents is costly for the MENA region, and increasing the number of women in the workforce could significantly increase economic output. A World Bank study suggests that per capita GDP growth rates in the 1990s could have been more than a third higher (2.6 percent instead of 1.9 percent) had female participation rates been at expected levels, given the region's female education, fertility, and age profile.[34] A report from the International Labour Organization (ILO) estimates that if MENA countries reduced the gender gap in workforce participation rates by 20 percentage points (from 50.6 to 30.6 percentage points) from 2012 to 2017, the region's GDP could be $415 billion larger.[35] This would be a significant gain to the region's economy, which had a GDP of $4.3 trillion in 2012.[36]

Barriers to progress

A number of studies have explored the key factors constraining women's economic participation in the Middle East. Overall, researchers have not identified a single barrier, but rather a set of related factors that limit women's employment. These include legal, social, and economic structures that affect the preferences, abilities, and opportunities of women to participate in the economy.

Legal barriers

Legal and regulatory barriers can constrain women's economic opportunities in a number of ways. Restrictive labor laws are the most obvious means of limiting women's economic participation. Indeed, countries that regulate women's work hours or industry sector, not surprisingly, have on average significantly lower female labor force participation rates.[37] A Freedom House study conducted on women's rights across MENA countries found that almost every state has laws that prohibit women from working in certain industries perceived as dangerous, hazardous, or harmful to women's reputation and from working at night.[38]

Other legal provisions could also be having an adverse effect on women's employment opportunities across the region. A World Bank study speculates that generous paid maternity leave, while well intentioned, could be contributing to employers' reluctance to hire women, especially in those countries where employers are responsible for paying the full cost of maternity benefits.[39] Jordan, in an effort to lessen the burden on companies of hiring women, has in recent years moved to publicly financed maternity leave, a trend that the ILO encourages to reduce discrimination against women in the workforce.[40]

Another factor depressing female employment could be that women receive retirement benefits at a younger age than men, encouraging an earlier departure from the workforce.[41] An earnings gap between women and men also makes work less attractive to women.[42] Not only do studies show that salaries are lower for women than for men at the same professional level, but women also have less access to non-wage benefits.[43] Throughout the region, provisions such as social security, housing allowances, subsidies, and parental benefits are frequently allocated only to men who are seen as the heads of household. For example, in Lebanon the salaries of married working women are taxed as if they are unmarried, while married men or male heads of households receive tax breaks.[44] In Jordan, married male civil servants are granted a family allowance, whereas married female civil servants are not, unless they are widowed or married to a person with a disability.[45]

Cultural barriers

Cultural attitudes also play a significant role in shaping the work environment for women and contribute to their low numbers in the Arab workforce. Across the region perceptions of women's rights, status, role, and responsibilities are generally traditional. Indeed, data from a recent World Values Survey (WVS) show that Arab countries express more traditional gender norms than the global average.[46] First, region-wide conventions place a higher value on women's domestic role as homemaker relative to the world average. As reported through the WVS, 74 percent of men and 67 percent of women in the Middle East agreed that "being a housewife is as fulfilling as working for pay," whereas among respondents from the rest of the world, 60 percent of men and 61 percent of women agreed.[47] Additionally, men are widely seen as primary breadwinners. Indeed, about two-thirds of Arab survey respondents agreed that when unemployment is high, scarce jobs should go to men instead of women, compared with one-third of respondents from the rest of the world.[48] There is also a belief that women are less capable than their male counterparts. In fact, 75 percent of male and 53 percent of female Arab WVS respondents agreed with the statement, "Men make better business executives than women," compared with 43 percent of male and 31 percent of female respondents from the rest of the world.[49]

One result of the strong cultural emphasis on women's domestic roles is that married women are far less likely to work than single women across the region. After marriage, it is not uncommon for women to exit the workforce. In Egypt, for example, a World Bank report details that there is a 22 percent chance that a woman will quit a public sector job after she marries, and the likelihood climbs to 54 percent in the private sector.[50] The difference in economic participation rates between single and married women ranges from about 10 percentage points in Egypt to 17 percentage points in Morocco.[51] Because there is widespread assumption that women will prioritize domestic responsibilities after marriage, female employment prospects diminish. Private sector employers cite a number of reasons for preferring male over female employees, chief among them is the belief that women are likely to quit after marriage. Additionally, men are thought to be able to accommodate overtime, whereas married women are believed to have limited flexibility because of household responsibilities.[52] Women's own professional aspirations are affected by domestic responsibilities. By and large, women prefer public sector employment because it is associated with fewer hours, more flexible schedules, and good benefits, particularly maternity leave, and is thus more compatible with women's domestic responsibilities.

Traditional gender norms not only limit wage and salaried employment opportunities, but also affect women's self-employment chances. Gender attitudes limit support for female entrepreneurs, tolerance for entrepreneurial endeavors, and formal investment in female-owned or -run businesses. Without sufficient support for business and entrepreneurial activity, Arab women face additional challenges in an already tough business environment. Indeed, the data reflect this discrimination, as working women are only half as likely to be self-employed as men.[53]

In part, women's low access to financial assets and property stems from unequal inheritance laws derived from an Islamic tradition that allocates girls half of the inheritance of their brothers. With fewer assets, women's business prospects decrease. As a result, they are unable to meet banks' standard lending criteria of a strong credit history and the existence of collateral, and are less likely to receive formal loans.[54] Indeed, in countries where property ownership and inheritance rights differ by gender, fewer women can access loans than in countries with gender neutral property laws.[55]

Unequal inheritance laws interact with weak privacy laws and conservative lending practices in the Middle East to handicap women entrepreneurs and businesses. Banks' risk assessments, which do not account for the specific circumstances of female business owners and entrepreneurs, disproportionately affect women-owned enterprises as female entrepreneurs and business owners often have less business experience and may lack sufficient training to prepare adequate business plans.

Without adequate financing or access to other productive inputs, women's enterprises have little chance of growing and developing, and, indeed, women own less than 15 percent of formal SMEs in the Middle East.[56]

Nascent government efforts to address women's economic lag

State governments across the Middle East have started to focus efforts on supporting women-owned enterprises and female entrepreneurship as a means of increasing female economic participation. Government policies have targeted women's lack of funding, underdeveloped support services, and societal stigma.

Entrepreneurship promotion has become popular throughout the region. Kuwait's UNDP-sponsored "Economic Empowerment of Kuwait Women" initiative, for example, aims to promote female entrepreneurship and change perceptions of female business ownership. In a similar vein, the United Arab Emirates established the Emirates Women Award in 2003 to celebrate businesswomen as a way to promote and normalize women's leadership in business. Even Saudi Arabia has taken steps to encourage women-owned businesses. The government has created a special Women's Higher Technical Institute to offer entrepreneurship training programs, established the Prince Sultan bin Abdul Aziz Fund to Support Women's Small Enterprises, and granted women the right to hold commercial licenses in 2005.[57] These, among other initiatives, are explicitly designed to boost female self-employment and create the conditions for job growth.

Another strategy has been to equip women with economically attractive skills. For example, Jordan has made significant investments in information and communication technology (ICT), establishing over 100 knowledge stations around the country to train Jordanians to use ICT.[58] These policies have been an enabler for greater female entrepreneurship and have benefited women's employment. Today, women make up about one-third of Jordan's ICT workforce.[59] According to the European Training Foundation, women in this industry are largely employed as professionals, with some rising to top managerial positions.[60]

Conclusion

With women representing an increasing share of the MENA region's educated workforce, the urgency of expanding their economic possibilities grows by the day. The concern that creating more job opportunities for women will come at the expense of men ignores research showing that adding women to the workforce stimulates economic activity and creates more jobs for both men and women. Indeed, countries with higher levels of female workforce participation tend to have lower levels of overall unemployment.[61]

Governments across the region, recognizing the link between female employment and economic growth, are finally getting serious about improving the labor environment for women. The increased focus of MENA governments on female entrepreneurship and business ownership has increased opportunities for women, but it is too early to tell how broad-reaching these reforms are. Yet, as the International Finance Corporation (IFC) estimates that as many as half of women-owned SMEs in the Middle East are either constrained in their access to finance or are without access to any financing, improving the chances of women in entrepreneurship and business requires addressing financial constraints.[62]

Governments have made important strides in reforming laws across the region to facilitate women's increased economic participation, yet implementing laws can be harder than passing them. As many of the barriers facing women are social in nature, change requires adjustments in attitudes from both men and women. That takes time.

But change is happening—and in some countries more rapidly than others. The opening of new retail sectors to women in Saudi Arabia is part of a seismic shift, one that has already led to a nearly 10-fold increase in female private sector employment in just five years.[63] In other countries, improvements in women's family rights, new equality laws, continued education attainment, and declining fertility will continue to expand the pool of talented women desiring to work outside the home. The future of the MENA economies depends on their ability to recognize that opportunity and continue to break down the barriers facing women who want to apply their talents as entrepreneurs and in the workplace.

Notes

1 Data for 2011 from UNESCO Institute for Statistics. More than half of graduates from higher educational institutions in Algeria, Lebanon, Oman, Palestine, Qatar, Sudan, Saudi Arabia, and the United Arab Emirates are women. The indicator used is "the percentage of students in tertiary education who are female."

2 Data for 2011 from UNESCO Institute for Statistics. The percentage of female graduates in tertiary education (ISCED 5 and 6) is the number of females graduating from ISCED 5 and 6 expressed as a percentage of the total number of ISCED 5 and 6 tertiary graduates (male and female).

3 UNESCO *Institute for Statistics Global Education Digest 2010: Comparing Education Statistics Across the World*, www.uis.unesco.org/Library/Docum ents/GED_2010_EN.pdf.

4 Data for 2012 from World Bank Databank. Indicator used is "labor force participation rate, female (% of female ages 15+) modeled ILO estimate."

5 Stella Tsani, Leonidas Paroussos, Costas Fragiadakis, Ioannis Charalambidis, and Pantelis Capros, "Female Labor Force Participation and Economic Development in Southern Mediterranean Countries: What Scenarios for 2030?" *MEDPRO Technical Report No. 19*, December 2012. The dollar amount is in 2007 US dollar value. www.medpro-foresight.eu/system/files/MEDPRO%20TR%20No%2019%20WP7%20Tsani_0.pdf.

6 DeAnne Aguirre, Leila Hoteit, Christine Rupp, and Karim Sabbagh, "Empowering the Third Billion. Women and the World of Work in 2012," (San Francisco, Calif.: Booz & Company, 2012); Katrin Elborgh-Woytek, Monique Newaik, Kalpana Kochhar, Stefania Fabrizio, Kangni Kpodar, Philippe Wingender, Benedict Clements, and Gerd Schwartz, "Women, Work, and the Economy: Macroeconomic Gains from Gender Equity," International Monetary Fund, September 2013, www.imf.org/external/pubs/ft/sdn/2013/sdn1310.pdf.

7 World Bank, *Opening Doors: Gender Equality and Development in the Middle East and North Africa* (2013) https://openknowledge.worldbank.org/bitstream/handle/10986/12552/751810PUB0EPI00206010Opening0doors.pdf?sequence=1; Farrukh Iqbal, *Sustaining Gains in Poverty Reduction and Human Development in the Middle East and North Africa*, World Bank, April 2006, http://elibrary.worldbank.org/doi/pdf/10.1596/978-0-8213-6527-4; Margaret C. Hogan, Kyle Foreman, Mohsen Naghavi, Stephanie Y. Ahn, Mengru Wang, Susanna M. Makela, Alan D. Lopez, Rafael Lozano, and Christopher J. L. Murray, "Maternal Mortality for 181 Countries, 1980–2008: A Systematic Analysis of Progress Towards Millennium Development Goal 5," *The Lancet* 375, no. 97726 (2010): 1609–1623; Political participation earliest data from 1990, when Middle East had lowest proportion of seats held by women in national parliament. Data from World Bank Databank, http://databank.worldbank.org/data/home.aspx.

8 Data from World Bank Databank. Indicator is "life expectancy at birth, female (years)." Rounded up from 53.9 years in 1970 and 73.8 years in 2010, http://databank.worldbank.org/data/home.aspx.

9 Data from World Bank Databank. Indicator is "fertility rate, total (births per woman)."

10 Margaret C. Hogan, "Maternal mortality for 181 countries, 1980–2008: A Systematic Analysis of Progress Towards Millennium Development Goal 5," *The Lancet*.

11 Data from UNESCO Institute for Statistics. Indicator is "net enrollment rate, primary, female (%)."

12 Fatima Harrak, "The History and Significance of the New Moroccan Family Code," *Institute for the Study of Islamic Thought in Africa Working Paper Series*, no. 09–002 (March 2009).

13 UN High Commissioner for Refugees, *Background Note on Gender Equality, Nationality Laws and Statelessness 2014*, 7 March 2014. www.unhcr.org/4f5886306.html.

14 Mulki Al-Sharmani, *Recent Reforms in Personal Laws and Women's Empowerment: Family Courts in Egypt* (Cairo: American University in Cairo Social Research Center, 2007). http://s3-eu-west-1.amazonaws.com/pa

thwaysofempowerment-org-staging/downloads/family_courts_in_egypt_ori ginalf3794be8244c7d3be8d2f3efade96d7d.pdf.

15 Julia Breslin and Toby Jones, "Qatar"; Haya al-Mughni, "Kuwait"; Rana Hus-seini, "Jordan"; and Dunya A. Abdullah Ahmed, "Bahrain" in *Women's Rights in the Middle East and North Africa*, eds Sanja Kelly and Julia Breslin (New York: Freedom House; Lanham, Md.: Rowman & Littlefield, 2010), https://freedomhouse.org/report/women039s-rights-middle-east-and-north-a frica/womens-rights-middle-east-and-north-africa-2010#.VInoNzHF_zg.

16 Abdel-Rahman Hussein, "Egyptian Assembly Passes Draft Constitution Despite Protests," *The Guardian*, 30 November 2012, www.theguardian. com/world/2012/nov/30/egypt-constitution-morsi.

17 Amr Moussa, "Blueprint for a new Egypt," *New York Times*, 8 January 2014. www.nytimes.com/2014/01/09/opinion/blueprint-for-a-new-egypt.html.

18 Human Rights Watch, "Yemen: End Child Marriage," 27 April 2014. www.hrw.org/news/2014/04/27/yemen-end-child-marriage.

19 Neil MacFarquhar, "Saudi Monarch Grants Women Right to Vote," *New York Times*, 25 September 2011.

20 Sara Hamdan, "Women Appointed to Saudi Council for First Time," *New York Times*, 16 January 2013.

21 Data from the Quota Project, *Global Database of Quotas for Women*, www. quotaproject.org/uid/search.cfm#.

22 Inter-Parliamentary Union Database, www.ipu.org/parline-e/reports/2392_A .htm.

23 Drude Dahlerup Zeina Hilal, Nana Kalandadze, and Rumbidzai Kanda-wasvika-Nhundu, *Atlas of Electoral Gender Quotas*, International Institute for Democracy and Electoral Assistance, 2013. www.idea.int/publications/ atlas-of-electoral-gender-quotas/loader.cfm?csModule=security/getfile&page ID=63855.

24 Rowaida Al Maaitah, Hadeel Al Maaitah, Hmoud Olaimat, and Muntaha Ghareibeh, "Arab Women and Political Development," *Journal of International Women's Studies* 12, no. 3 (2011), http://vc.bridgew.edu/cgi/view-content.cgi?article=1110&context=jiws.

25 May Al Dabbagh and Lana Nusseibeh, "Women in Parliament and Politics in the UAE: A Study of the First Federal National Council Elections," Dubai School of Government, February 2009.

26 World Economic Forum, *Global Gender Gap Report 2013*.

27 Data from World Bank Databank. The indicator used is "female labor force participation rate."

28 Data for 2012 from World Bank Databank. The indicator used is "female labor force participation rate," and the data are sourced from the ILO. The ILO's Key Indicators of the Labour Market Database defines the female labor force participation rate as: "the proportion of the [female] population ages 15 and older that is economically active; all people who supply labor for the production of goods and services during a specified period." This figure captures the proportion of the working-age female population who are actively employed or unemployed but looking for work. For more information on the definition, consult ILO's Key Indicators of the Labour Market at http://kilm.ilo.org/2011/download/kilm01EN.pdf.

29 World Bank, *Capabilities, Opportunities, and Participation: Gender Equality and Development in the Middle East and North Africa Region*, (2011).

http://siteresources.worldbank.org/INTMENA/Resources/World_Developm
ent_Report_2012_Gender_Equality_Development_Overview_MENA.pdf.

30 OECD, *Empowering Women-led SMEs: Economic Development in the New
Arab World*, Draft Paper, MENA-OECD Investment Programme, May 2012,
Paris. www.oecd.org/mena/investment/Empowering%20women-led%20SMEs.
pdf; Unemployment as defined by ILO is: a person without work, currently
available for work, and actively seeking work in a recent period; those not
seeking work because they are discouraged, discriminated against, etc. are
referred to as "hidden unemployed" or "discouraged workers" and are not
included in the unemployed statistics. This definition can be found in the ILO's
"Key Indicators of the Labour Market," December 2013. www.ilo.org/
empelm/what/WCMS_114240/lang–en/index.htm.

31 World Bank, *Opening Doors: Gender Equality and Development in the
Middle East and North Africa*, https://openknowledge.worldbank.org/bit
stream/handle/10986/12552/751810PUB0EPI002060130Opening0doors.pdf
?sequence=1.

32 UN, *World Economic Situation and Prospects 2010* (2012), www.un.org/en/
development/desa/policy/wesp/wesp_archive/2010annex.pdf.

33 International Monetary Fund, *Saudi Arabia: Staff Report for the 2013
Article IV Consultation*, 24 June 2013, www.imf.org/external/pubs/ft/scr/
2013/cr13229.pdf.

34 Predicted values signify the number of women expected to be participating
in the labor market given the country's levels of female education, fertility,
and age profile. These values represent the potential for women's participation. The World Bank report compares these values with the actual participation rates reported. World Bank, *Gender and Development in the
Middle East and North Africa: Women in the Public Sphere*, (2004), www-
wds.worldbank.org/servlet/WDSContentServer/WDSP/IB/2004/03/09/00009
0341_20040309152953/Rendered/PDF/281150PAPER0Gender010Develop
ment0in0MNA.pdf.

35 International Labor Organization, *Global Employment Trends for Women*
(December 2012), www.ilo.org/wcmsp5/groups/public/—dgreports/—dcomm/
documents/publication/wcms_195447.pdf.

36 IMF World Economic Outlook 2013 Database. GDP based on PPP
valuation of country GDP in current international dollar.

37 World Bank, *World Development Report 2012: Gender Equality and
Development*, (2011): 200.

38 Sanja Kelly, "Hard-Won Progress and a Long Road Ahead: Women's Rights
in the Middle East and North Africa," in *Women's Rights in the Middle East
and North Africa*, ed. Sanja Kelly and Julia Breslin (New York: Freedom House;
Lanham, Md.: Rowman & Littlefield, 2010).

39 World Bank, *Removing Barriers to Economic Inclusion: Measuring Gender
Parity in 141 Economies*, (2011), http://wbl.worldbank.org/~/media/FPDKM/
WBL/Documents/Reports/2012/Women-Business-and-the-Law-2012.pdf.

40 Stefanie Brodmann, Irene Jillson, and Nahla Hassan, "Social Insurance
Reform in Jordan: Awareness and Perceptions of Employment Opportunities
for Women," *Social Protection & Labor Discussion Paper*, No. 1402 (June
2014) https://openknowledge.worldbank.org/bitstream/handle/10986/19994/
891870NWP0P132085273B00PUBLCI001402.pdf?sequence=1; Laura Addati,
Namoi Cassirer, and Katherine Gilchrist, *Maternity and Paternity at*

Work: Law and Practice across the World, ILO, 13 May 2014, www.ilo. org/wcmsp5/groups/public/—dgreports/—dcomm/—publ/documents/public ation/wcms_242615.pdf.

41 World Bank, *Gender and Development in the Middle East and North Africa: Women in the Public Sphere* (2014).

42 USAID, *Jordan: Gender Analysis and Assessment* (2012); Amirah El-Haddad, "Female Wages in the Egyptian Textiles and Clothing Industry: Low Pay or Discrimination?," *Economic Research Forum Working Paper Series*, 2011; World Bank, *Opening Doors: Gender Equality and Development in the Middle East and North Africa*, 2013, https://openknowledge.worldba nk.org/bitstream/handle/10986/12552/751810PUB0EPI002060130Opening0 doors.pdf?sequence=1.

43 World Bank, *Opening Doors: Gender Equality and Development in the Middle East and North Africa*.

44 M.C. Khalif, "Lebanon" in *Women's Rights in the Middle East and North Africa: Progress Amid Resistance*, ed. Sanja Kelly and J. Breslin (New York: Freedom House; Lanham, Md.: Rowman & Littlefield, 2010).

45 UNDP, *Gender Equality and Women's Empowerment in Public Adminis-tration: Jordan Case Study*, 2012. www.undp.org/content/dam/undp/library/ Democratic%20Governance/Women-s%20Empowerment/JordanFinal%20- %20HiRes.pdf.

46 World Value Surveys 2010 to 2014 Data. Specifically used questions V139, V53, V51, V47, V48, and V45. www.worldvaluessurvey.org/WVSDocument ationWV6.jsp.

47 Author calculations based on the 2010–2014 World Value Survey Data.

48 Author calculations based on the 2010–2014 WVS Data. Specifically, question V45, "When jobs are scarce, men have more right to a job than women."

49 Author calculations based on 2010–2014 WVS Data. Specifically, question V45, "When jobs are scarce, men have more right to a job than women."

50 World Bank, *World Development Report 2012: Gender Equality and Development*.

51 World Bank, *Opening Doors: Gender Equality and Development in the Middle East and North Africa*.

52 Matthew Groh, Nandini Krishnan, David McKenzie, and Tara Vishwa-nath, "Soft Skills or Hard Cash: The Impact of Training and Wage Subsidy Programs on Female Youth Employment in Jordan," *Policy Research Working Paper*, July 2012. http://elibrary.worldbank.org/doi/pdf/10.1596/ 1813-9450-6141.

53 OECD, *Competitiveness and Private Sector Development Women in Busi-ness: Policies to Support Women's Entrepreneurship Development in the MENA Region: Policies*, 8 October 2012. www.oecd.org/mena/investment/ Empowering%20women-led%20SMEs.pdf.

54 MENA-OECD Investment Programme, "Exploring Bank Financing for Women Entrepreneurs in the MENA Region: A Preliminary Analysis of Survey Data on Financing Practices of MENA Banks," Working Draft for Discussion at OECD-MENA Women's Business Forum, December 2013. http:// www.oecd.org/mena/investment/Bank%20Finance.pdf; Anna Stupnytska, Kathryn Koch, Amy MacBeath, Sandra Lawson, and Kathy Matsui, *Giving Credit Where It Is Due: How Closing the Credit Gap for Women-owned*

SMEs can Drive Global Growth, Goldman Sachs, February 2014. www.goldma nsachs.com/our-thinking/investing-in-women/gmi-report-pdf.pdf.

55 Nayda Almodovar-Reteguis, Khrystyna Kushnir, and Thibault Meilland, *Mapping the Legal Gender Gap in Using Property and Building Credit*, World Bank, January 2013. http://wbl.worldbank.org/~/media/FPDKM/ WBL/Documents/Notes/Legal-Gender-Gap-in-Using-Property-and-Building-Credit.pdf.

56 Anna Stupnytska, Kathryn Koch, Amy MacBeath, Sandra Lawson, and Kathy Matsui, *Giving Credit Where It Is Due: How Closing the Credit Gap for Women-owned SMEs can Drive Global Growth.*

57 OECD, *Implementation of the 2007 Declaration on Fostering Women's Entrepreneurship in the MENA Region*, MENA-OECD Investment Programme Draft Stocktaking Report, November 2009. www.oecd.org/mena/ investment/44092636.pdf; WEF "Accelerating Entrepreneurship in the Arab World," in collaboration with Booz & Co., October 2011. www3.weforum. org/docs/WEF_YGL_AcceleratingEntrepreneurshipArabWorld_Report_2011. pdf; Eleanor Abdella Doumato, "Saudi Arabia," *Women's Rights in the Middle East and North Africa: Progress Amid Resistance*, ed. Sanja Kelly and J. Breslin (New York: Freedom House; Lanham, Md.: Rowman & Littlefield, 2010).

58 World Bank, *The Economic Advancement of Women in Jordan: A Country Gender Assessment*, May 2005. http://siteresources.worldbank.org/ INTMNAREGTOPGENDER/Resources/JordanCGA2005.pdf

59 UN Women, *Jordanian Women in the ICT Space,* March 2014. http://jorda n.unwomen.org/~/media/field%20office%20jordan/attachments/publications/ 2014/ict-study-updatedtxt-4.pdf.

60 Outi Karkkainen, ed., "Women and Work in Jordan: Tourism and ICT Sectors: A Case Study," *European Training Foundation*, 2011. www.etf.europa. eu/webatt.nsf/0/BE3D52C73C5D0031C12578CC0056B2DA/$file/Women%20 and%20work%20in%20Jordan%20-%202011_EN.pdf.

61 World Bank, *Gender and Development in the Middle East and North Africa.*

62 IFC, *Strengthening Access to Finance for Women-Owned SMEs in Developing Countries*, October 2011 www.ifc.org/wps/wcm/connect/a4774a004a3f66539f0f 9f8969adcc27/G20_Women_Report.pdf?MOD=AJPERES.

63 Data originally from Saudi Arabian Monetary Agency. See Economics Intelligence Unit, "Female Labour Force Participation Surges," 19 June 2014. www.eiu.com/index.asp?layout=displayIssueArticle&issue_id=421930 626&article_id=1941929978.

20 Public policy innovations to help American men and women succeed as providers and caregivers

Ellen Bravo

More women in the United States want and need paid employment. More men want and need to participate in caregiving. Yet as a result of outmoded workplace practices and inadequate public policies, success in one area can jeopardize success in the other, with harmful impacts on women and families but also on public health and the economy.

Consider the following examples:

Shelby Ramirez works as a hotel security guard in Denver, Colorado. When her father and daughter each had surgery within days of each other, Shelby took unpaid time from work to care for them. For doing what a good daughter and mother does, Shelby nearly wound up homeless and had to pawn the one thing of value she owned, a ring given to her by her father many years earlier.[1]

Rhiannon Broschat lives in Chicago, Illinois and supports herself and her child by working as a cashier while going to college.[2] On a day this winter when the Chicago Public Schools closed because it was too cold to be safe for children to go to schools, Rhiannon had no one to care for her special needs son. For safeguarding her child as a good mother does, Rhiannon was accused of "abusing" the attendance policy and was "separated" from her job. What this means is that Rhiannon was fired from a very profitable company for refusing to leave her son home alone.

Lawrence Griffin is employed at a grocery chain in Milwaukee that lists sick days as one of the benefits workers may access after six months of probation—as long as they ask for the time in advance. That works for planned medical procedures but not for colds and flu. So Lawrence works through his own ailments. But each time an asthma attack puts his son in the hospital, Lawrence takes time to be with him. His supervisor demands to know why, given that the boy's mother is available. "Because he's my son," Griffin replies. For being a responsible dad, this father of three was disciplined each time.[3]

When Christina Corvin was pregnant with her son, she worked at a major pizza-delivery chain. The job did not provide health insurance, maternity leave, or sick days. Christina wound up needing an emergency C-section and grappling with postpartum depression, which meant she needed a lot of help to care for the baby when she brought him home. She lost her job, but her husband Tyler had to return to work after a week because the couple couldn't afford to lose any more pay.[4]

As these stories illustrate, the United States faces a grave dilemma: the very thing that makes us good parents or good children to our parents often jeopardizes our ability to make ends meet and compounds income and gender inequality. Many employers already offer the policies we seek, but millions of workers are operating in outdated workplaces designed for men with wives at home full-time.

Two policies—paid sick days and family and medical leave insurance—are common sense solutions that are gaining traction across the country. A growing body of evidence supports expansion of these policies in cities and states, as well as nationally.

Changed demographics

In his 2014 State of the Union Address, President Obama said, "It's time to do away with workplace policies that belong in a Mad Men episode."[5] He was referring to a time when the workforce looked very different than it does today.

The conversation is no longer whether or not American women should work outside the home—by desire and by necessity, they do. Women are now the sole or primary breadwinners for 40 percent of the nation's families, compared with less than 11 percent in 1960.[6] In 2010, nearly three-quarters of children had both parents or their only parent working, close to twice as many as in the "Mad Men" 1960s, and a 13 percent increase since the mid-1980s when the Family and Medical Leave Act 1993, America's existing federal program mandating unpaid leave, was first drafted.[7] Today, a woman's income loss during maternity leave or even a few days with a sick child has significant economic consequences for her family.[8]

And change is occurring not just among women. A recent ad council survey found that 86 percent of men say they want to be more involved with their families than their fathers were.[9]

The number of caregivers is also growing as the population ages. By 2030, the number of Americans over 65 will be 70 million—double today's 35 million.[10] Nearly two-thirds of Americans under the age of 60 expect to be responsible for the care of an aging relative within the next 10 years, and by 2020 about 40 percent of the workforce will be caring for older parents.[11]

Current public policy is insufficient: family leave

Consider the tale of two sisters, both employed in similar jobs. One has a child in Vermont; the other gives birth less than a hundred miles away. The first sister gets no paid time off whatsoever. The other receives 50 weeks of paid leave at 55 percent pay.

The second sister did not win the boss lottery. She lives in Canada, where employees participate in an employment insurance program that guarantees up to 50 weeks for a combination of maternity and parental leave (up to 35 weeks for a parent who does not give birth). The program is financed by small contributions from employers and employees—employers pay slightly more than half.

Imagine the difference in the well-being of the two women—one scrambling to return to work in a matter of weeks, having to cut short breastfeeding and search for expensive infant care. Her husband takes a few vacation days. The second sister breastfeeds for the entire year. Of the 50 weeks, her husband takes 10 and feels like a parent rather than a spare part. The new baby does not trigger bankruptcy or debt. The Canadian employers manage just fine. There has been no exodus to the United States. Those who benefit most are the infants, who are more likely to have doctor visits and immunizations when parents have paid leave.[12]

The Vermont sister is not atypical. Only 12 percent of private sector employees in the United States enjoy paid family leave from an employer.[13] Forty-eight percent of family caregivers who have to take time off to care for a family member lose income during that time.[14] That lack of pay can have a disastrous impact on a family's economic security. Studies show that 7 percent of people who file for bankruptcy cite the birth of a child as the cause.[15] A significant number of bankruptcies also happen after a worker misses two or more weeks of work because of illness.[16]

The United States does have a public policy dealing with leave. Twenty-two years ago, Congress passed the Family and Medical Leave Act (FMLA) with bipartisan support. The FMLA provides up to 12 weeks unpaid time for the occasional longer-term leave people need to care for a new baby or for a serious personal or family illness. It applies to those who work in a firm of 50 or more, have been on the job at least a year and work at least 25 hours a week on average for the same employer. FMLA was a great first step for families—but as President

Bill Clinton pointed out on the law's twentieth anniversary, "laws are not meant to be monuments. They must change with the times." The FMLA leaves out more than 40 percent of the workforce.[17] Furthermore, many of those who are covered are unable to take the time they need because it is unpaid. In 2012, two-and-a-half times as many people as in 2000 needed leave and were eligible but did not take it, mostly because they could not afford it. Many others went back to work too early, without fully recovering.[18]

The need for protection during routine illness

The FMLA also does not address routine illness or preventive care. While an employee covered by FMLA may take leave to care for her father if he has a heart attack, she can be fired for taking Dad to the doctor to get his cholesterol down and prevent a heart attack in the first place.

Connie Ogletree in Atlanta, Georgia is a good example of the problem. When she woke up one morning with her left breast in extreme pain, Connie noticed a huge lump, which was later diagnosed as a cyst that had become abscessed. Her options were to forfeit wages because of no paid time off or go into work in pain. She chose the latter.[19]

Connie is not alone. Before the recent spate of wins, more than 41 million workers in the United States comprising nearly 40 percent of the workforce, do not earn paid sick days.[20] Millions more are not allowed to use the time they earn to care for a sick family member. The number of those with access to sick days is much lower for low-wage workers, and particularly those in closest contact to the public, such as those who work in food preparation and service, and those in personal care.[21]

Access to paid sick days is a jobs issue. Nearly one quarter of adults in the US report that they have been fired or threatened with job loss for taking time off to recover from illness or care for a sick loved one.[22] Even losing a few days' pay can be devastating. For low-income families, going just 3.5 days without wages is equivalent to losing a month's groceries.[23]

The lack of public policy affects public health as well as incomes. The US Center for Disease Control (CDC) found that more than 2.5 million cases of foodborne illness each year are caused by sick restaurant workers contaminating food while they are at work.[24] During the H1N1 epidemic, seven million people caught the virus from co-workers who came to the job while sick.[25]

Health conditions go undiagnosed because workers without paid sick days are less likely to get basic health and cancer screening.[26]

More than one in four parents of a child with asthma (28 percent) have missed a child's medical appointments because he or she could not get time off work.[27] Injuries on the job are also more common when workers go to the job ill.[28]

The human cost of sick days is also borne by businesses and society. "Presenteeism," (the cost of employees' lower productivity when working sick) adds up to $160 billion annually—considerably more than the cost of absenteeism.[29] The lack of paid sick days affects healthcare costs as well. The United States spends $1.1 billion in unnecessary emergency department costs because people cannot take time off to see a doctor during business hours and either go straight to ERs or wait until conditions worsen, and an ER becomes necessary.[30]

How the United States compares with the rest of the world

Many corporate leaders work hard to be included on lists of the best places to work, like the companies in the magazine *Working Mother*. But, as Delta Emerson of *Ryan Accounting* put it at a recent White House Forum on Working Fathers, the very short list of countries without paid leave "is one list we don't want to be on." Of 185 countries and territories surveyed by the International Labour Organization (ILO), the United States stands alone with Papua New Guinea in failing to guarantee paid maternity leave.[31] Seventy of those countries also guarantee some paid time for fathers.

This very long list of those who *do* ensure paid leave include not just Canada but other economic rivals of the United States. Germany and Japan, for example, each offer 14 weeks of paid maternity leave; France offers 16 weeks. Many African countries—Angola, Guinea, Senegal to name a few—offer 14 weeks at full pay.

The United States is also the only wealthy country that does not provide paid sick leave for a worker undergoing a 50-day cancer treatment.[32] And we are one of only three of the 22 richest countries that do not provide paid sick days for a worker missing five days of work because of the flu.[33]

Impact on women's equality

Any policy that impacts job tenure and pay has consequences for the wage gap and women's overall inequality. As women still bear the disproportionate responsibility for caregiving, and many need time to recover from giving birth, the caregiving penalty is a major contributor to women's inequality, lower mobility, and lower chances for advancement. It also accounts in part for their higher percentage among the poor.

Anne Lott in Minneapolis is a good example. Anne once had a well-paying factory job, but she did not have sick time to care for her kids. On six occasions Anne had to stay with one or another sick child over the course of one year—and for that she was fired. Anne and her kids had to double up with her mother to survive. For years she found lower-paying jobs, also without paid sick days. Now in her 50s, Anne is starting over as a personal care attendant, working six days a week to try to get back on her feet.[34]

As was the case for Anne Lott, job loss because of caregiving can lead to a spiral of insecure jobs, a "spotty" work record, debt, bad credit, and assumptions of bad work ethic—all of which make it harder to get a good job and reverse the slide.

Pay loss related to caregiving also impacts women's status and opportunities. Conservatives argue that women would get equal pay with men if they did not take breaks. Having a baby may be a joy—but it is not a break. Studies show that women who experience an interruption in employment do experience a decrease in wages—a reflection of the notion that they have taken a "break" and lowered their value by "not working."[35] Those who spend a few years away from the workplace to raise young children often find their next starting pay, and a lifetime of raises based on that pay, take a substantial hit as a result.

Public policy solutions

Many employers see paid sick days and paid parental leave as a smart way to attract and retain talented employees. But history has shown the need for public policy to guarantee at least minimum protections to everyone. When the FMLA was passed, for example, at least two-thirds of covered employers had to change one or more aspect of their policy to comply with the law.[36] Typically that meant covering men and adoptive parents as well as pregnant women, and including care for a seriously ill child, spouse, or parent as well as for oneself.

What is needed today? We need to expand the FMLA to cover those currently excluded.[37] We also need public policies like the Healthy Families Act (H.R.932/S.497) that address short-term, routine illness and the preventive care that people need every year. The Healthy Families Act introduced in 2014, would allow workers to earn paid sick days they can use to care for their own illness or that of a loved one, or to deal with the aftermath of sexual or domestic violence.[38]

In addition, we need a policy like the FAMILY Act, introduced by Senator Kristen Gillibrand in the Senate and Representative Rosa DeLauro in the House, to establish a family and medical leave insurance fund to address the occasional longer-term leave workers need to care for a new baby or a serious personal or family illness.[39] By pooling small contributions from employees and employers, this fund would enable those needing leave to have some vital income during an already challenging time. In order to win these national standards, however, we need to support more policy wins on the state and local level.

Cities and states are leading the way

My children and I were part of helping to win unpaid Family and Medical Leave in Wisconsin in 1988. That win, along with similar ones in many other states, paved the way for the national FMLA bill, 1993. The state victory helped disprove predictions of job loss and business closings. Family leave, in fact, strengthens families and businesses by helping people keep their jobs and their health insurance. It lowers turnover costs and boosts productivity and morale.

Now states and municipalities are developing models for both family and medical leave insurance and paid sick days. And a growing body of evidence documents the benefits both for women and their families and for business-owners and for the economy.

In 1995 a commission sponsored by the US Department of Labor (DOL) unanimously recommended that states "consider voluntarily establishing or expanding existing temporary disability insurance programs to provide wage replacement for periods of family and medical leave."[40] Research conducted for that commission found that nearly one in 10 (9 percent) of leave-takers had to rely on public assistance to support themselves while on leave, a figure which increased in the most recent survey (9.8 percent).[41] This number grew to more than one in five (20.9 percent) for those earning $20,000 or less.[42]

In 2002, California became the first state to attempt to make family leave affordable. Implemented in 2004, the new law expands the state's existing temporary disability insurance program—just as the federal DOL commission had recommended—to help ensure that working families have income to rely on during family leave. Those needing family leave may take up to six weeks at 55 percent of their pay with a cap of $533 a week as of 2013.[43] New Jersey followed in 2009. Benefits there are typically two-thirds of the last eight weeks of pay, up to $584 a week for up to six weeks.[44]

In 2013, Rhode Island became the third state to pass such a measure. Together these three states have guaranteed access to family leave insurance programs to more than 17 million people. Other states are on their way, with Washington having passed, and hoping to have funding to implement, its program in 2015. In New York legislators are moving a bill forward, and in Vermont and Connecticut, study commissions are laying the groundwork for legislation. Colorado also has a bill pending, and a number of other states are considering similar action.

Economists, business-owners, and workers alike have confirmed the success of these programs. A recent Rutgers study shows that New Jersey's family leave insurance (FLI) program has saved businesses money by improving employee retention, decreasing turnover costs, and improving productivity.[45] Despite "the sky is falling" claims about the potential costs of FLI for business, research from *Unfinished Business*, a book on the success of California's program, shows employers reporting a neutral or positive effect on employee productivity, profitability and turnover. Most employers coordinate their own benefits with the state's paid family leave program.[46] Workers who use paid family or medical leave are more likely to return to the same employer, reducing turnover costs that can range from nearly $5,400 to more than $18,000.[47]

Most employees who used California's paid family leave program also report that leave has a positive effect on their ability to care for a child or ill family member (82.3 percent); allows them to initiate breastfeeding (91.3 percent); has a positive effect on their ability to arrange child care (62.5 percent); and had a positive effect on an ill family member's health (86.5 percent).[48]

In New Jersey women who take paid leave after a child's birth are more likely to be employed the following year than women who do not take leave and report increased wages. Parents who take leave report lower levels of public assistance (about 40 percent less) in the year following their child's birth, when compared with those without paid leave.[49]

Another benefit of family and medical leave insurance is that it increases the male role in caregiving by making it possible for fathers to be involved without the family taking a big financial hit.[50] In California, for example, fathers' leave-taking to bond with a new child rose 12 percent from 2011 to 2012.

Paid family leave also promotes children's well-being. Ensuring that new parents can take time to care for a newborn gives babies their best start in life. Four-fifths of respondents who took paid leave reported that they were better able to care for a new baby.[51] New mothers who take paid leave are more likely to take the minimum doctor-recommended six to eight weeks to recover from birth.[52] Newborns whose mothers take 12 weeks of leave are more likely to be breastfed, receive regular check-ups, and get critical immunizations. An examination of more than two decades of data from 16 European countries shows that paid parental leave policies are also associated with lower rates of infant and child mortality.[53]

And paid family leave promotes the well-being and independence of seniors by enabling families to care for aging parents and by allowing seniors to age in their own homes instead of in state subsidized facilities. This also saves taxpayer money.[54] When cared for by family members, patients in the hospital recover from illness and injury faster, leading to shorter hospital stays, improved health outcomes and decreased health costs.[55]

Businesses support family and medical leave programs, and replacement income provided by Family and Medical Leave Insurance (FMLI) also goes right back into the local economy, as workers spend it to help cover the basics. According to Herb Greenberg, founder and CEO of Caliper, a human resources consulting firm in New Jersey,

> Family Leave Insurance ... has been a huge positive for Caliper. When you think about the cost of individuals leaving, the cost of seeking new employees, the cost of maybe hiring the wrong person, training them, etc., and you compare that to the pennies that Family Leave costs you—there is just no comparison in terms of the pure balance sheet.[56]

A recent survey also found that six in ten small business-owners in New York support a family and medical leave program with shared contributions from employers and employees.[57]

These policies are modest—even meager—compared with the rest of the world. New Jersey's, for example, is structured to give a person taking such leave at most two-thirds of his or her pay for six weeks. In California, workers can draw 55 percent of regular income for six weeks. In Rhode Island, the percentage is about the same, but only for four weeks. Canada far outpasses us. So does Germany, where in addition to 100 percent of pay for 14 weeks, mothers of new babies can receive 65 percent for an additional 12 to 14 months.

Paid sick days

Because of the momentum behind city or state-based paid sick days policies, more than nine and a half million Americans previously uncovered now have that protection. Millions more can now care for an ill family member, and all who earn the time can do so without being disciplined. A growing body of research affirms that these policies help strengthen families while having a positive or neutral effect on business profitability, productivity, performance, and morale.

San Francisco was the first city with the law, followed by wins in Washington, DC, then Seattle and Connecticut. In 2013 alone, paid sick days measures were passed in Portland, New York City, and Jersey City, and were expanded to tipped workers in DC. In 2014, two states and nine cities passed paid sick days and New York City expanded its new law. More wins are likely in 2015. The combined impact on the US economy, families, and businesses is worth noting.

First, economists say job retention policies like paid sick days help reduce unemployment and strengthen the economy,[58] and the local economies where paid sick days policies have been implemented are doing well. For instance, more than two in three businesses in San Francisco support their city's paid sick days law, and six in seven employers report no negative impact on profitability.[59] The city experienced better job growth than in five surrounding counties without earned sick time.[60] PriceWaterhouseCoopers ranked San Francisco as one of the top cities in the world to do business. Even the chief lobbyist against the bill in San Francisco came around and told *Businessweek* it's "the best public policy for the least cost."[61]

Since Connecticut enacted the first statewide paid sick days law, the Department of Labor reports that employment has grown in the states' leisure and hospitality,[62] and education and health services[63] sectors. A recent study by Eileen Appelbaum and Ruth Milkman shows that more than three-quarters of Connecticut employers support the law.[64] The study also finds that the law has minimal effects on the conduct of business. Typically employers cover absent workers by assigning their work to other employees, a solution which has little effect on costs. Since the implementation of the paid sick days law, Connecticut employers have seen decreases in the spread of illnesses and increases in morale, among many more effects.[65]

Administrators of the programs also confirm that they are not a burden on business. Donna Levitt, Division Manager, San Francisco Office of Labor Standards Enforcement, told Connecticut legislators in 2011, "Since [the PSLO took effect in February of 2007,] we have heard relatively few complaints or problems with respect to implementation. ... I am not aware of any employer in San Francisco who has reduced staff or made any other significant change in their business as a result of the sick leave ordinance."[66]

Earned sick days strengthen families. The Healthy Families Act—and local and state bills—make it easier for workers to be good employees and good parents, and let children lead healthier lives, be more successful in school, and better prepared for the future. Seniors also benefit when adult children can afford to take them to the doctor or care for them during an illness. Today, as a hospital administrator in Atlanta testified, hospital hallways are often lined with seniors whose adult children cannot leave work to pick them up after a medical test or minor procedure.

When their parents are able to care for them at home, sick children get better sooner and reduce the risk of spreading the illness to their classmates,[67] and parents with paid sick days are less likely to send a sick child to school.

Sick days also let parents keep their children healthy by getting them to doctor visits for detection, treatment, and vaccinations. Earned sick days protect public health and make our country a safer, healthier place to live.

Small businesses support earned sick days because it is good for their bottom line. The real experiences of small businesses show that earned sick days result in reduced turnover, which saves businesses money. Jim Houser, owner of Houser Automotive Clinic in Portland, Oregon, says that because employees know "we care about their health and well-being, they're loyal to us in return."[68] The average tenure for his employees is 18 years, yielding enormous savings in recruitment and training costs. "Any business person can calculate what that means for overall savings," says Houser.

Paid sick days boost businesses and the economy overall by keeping money in people's pockets. Freddy Castiblanco, owner of Terraza 7 Train Café in Queens, recognizes that other employers' workers are his customers. "If we protect the salaries, if we give job stability, we are going to protect the purchasing power of potential customers," he says. "If you give me tax cuts, I won't be able to generate any more jobs. What really creates jobs in my community is customers."[69]

Conclusion

Recently Melissa Broome, one of the leaders of Maryland's Working Matters Coalition, which is working to win a statewide paid sick days standard, spent a week at Johns Hopkins Hospital with her four-year-old son, Owen. Both Melissa and her husband have paid sick days that allowed them to be at his side so they could, as Melissa put it, hold his hand and whisper in his ear every time he was poked and prodded. Fortunately, Owen will be fine. But Melissa said it broke her heart to see how many children were alone during the day.

When they took Owen for a walk through the halls in a red wagon, he did not ask why so many of the children were bald or hooked up to machines. But he did ask, "Where are that boy's mommy and daddy? ... He shouldn't be all by himself."[70]

It may be very difficult to cure the diseases that afflict these children. But it is not difficult to institute policies so that their parents can hold their hands and whisper in their ears.

We need new minimum workplace standards that allow both women and men to be providers and caregivers—to the benefit of their families and the United States as a whole.

Notes

1 Shelby Ramirez, "Shelby's Story: Why We Need Paid Family Leave," YouTube video, 4:23, posted by "Family Values @ Work," 21 April 2014, www.youtube.com/watch?v=Ofpe3PZXRgM&feature=youtu.be.
2 Rihannon Broschar, "Rhiannnon's Story: A Chicago Mother's Call for Paid Sick Days," YouTube video, 4:33, posted by "Family Values @ Work," 12 May 2014, www.youtube.com/watch?v=lEB1kGP_ghg.
3 Gregory Stanford, "When Work and Illness Collide," *Milwaukee Journal Sentinel*, 14 October 2007.
4 Family Values @ Work, "Voices from the Front Lines," June 2014, http://familyvaluesatwork.org/media-center/voices-front-lines.
5 Barack Obama, State of the Union Address, January 28, 2014, The White House, www.whitehouse.gov/the-press-office/2014/01/28/president-barack-obamas-state-union-address.
6 Wendy Wang et al., "Breadwinner Moms," Pew Research Social and Demographic Trends, 29 May 2013, www.pewsocialtrends.org/2013/05/29/breadwinner-moms/.
7 Linda Houser and Thomas P. Vartanian, "Pay Matters: The Positive Economic Impacts of Paid Family Leave for Families, Businesses and the Public," Rutgers Center for Women and Work, January 2012, http://smlr.rutgers.edu/paymatters-cwwreport-january2012.
8 Heather Boushey, "The New Breadwinners," H. Boushey and A. O'Leary, eds, In *The Shriver Report: A Woman's Nation Changes Everything*, Maria

Shriver and The Center for American Progress, 9 October 2009, http://shri
verreport.org/special-report/a-womans-nation-changes-everything/.

9 Jay Newton-Small, "White House Tries to Get Working Dads Some Time Off,"
Time, 9 June 2014, http://time.com/2850144/white-house-working-dads/.

10 Administration on Aging, U.S Department of Health and Human Services,
"A Profile of Older Americans," Saadia Greenberg, 2011, www.aoa.gov/
Aging_Statistics/Profile/2011/docs/2011profile.pdf.

11 Robert Lerman and Stefanie R. Schmidt, "An Overview of Economic,
Social and Demographic Trends Affecting the US Labor Market," The
Urban Institute, August 1999, www.dol.gov/oasam/programs/history/herma
n/reports/futurework/conference/trends/trends.pdf.

12 Sheila B. Kamerman, "Parental Leave Policies: The Impact on Child Well-
Being," *International Review of Leave Policies and Related Research*, ed.
Peter Moss and Margaret O'Brien (London: Department of Trade and
Industry, 2006), 16–21

13 Bureau of Labor Statistics. "Table 32. Leave benefits: Access, Private
Industry Workers, National Compensation Survey, March 2013,"
Employee Benefits Survey, www.bls.gov/ncs/ebs/benefits/2013/ownership/p
rivate/table21a.htm.

14 Kerstin Aumann et al., "The Elder Care Study: Everyday Realities and
Wishes for Change," Families and Work Institute, 2008, http://familiesa
ndwork.org/site/research/reports/elder_care.pdf.

15 The David and Lucile Packard Foundation, Caring for Infants and Tod-
dlers, *The Future of Children* 11, no. 1 (2001) http://futureofchildren.org/
futureofchildren/publications/docs/11_01_FullJournal.pdf.

16 Heather Boushey and Sarah Jane Glynn, "The Effects of Paid Family and
Medical Leave on Employment Stability and Economic Security," Center
for American Progress, April 2012, http://cdn.americanprogress.org/wp-con
tent/uploads/issues/2012/04/pdf/BousheyEmploymentLeave1.pdf.

17 Jacob Klerman et al., "Family and Medical Leave in 2012: Technical
Report," Abt Associates, Inc., 7 September 2012, Updated 18 April 2014,
www.dol.gov/asp/evaluation/fmla/FMLA-2012-Technical-Report.pdf.

18 Jacob Klerman et al., "Family and Medical Leave in 2012: Technical
Report," Abt Associates, Inc., 7 September 2012, Updated 18 April 2014,
www.dol.gov/asp/evaluation/fmla/FMLA-2012-Technical-Report.pdf.

19 Family Values @ Work, "Voices from the Front Lines."

20 Claudia Williams and Barbara Gault, "Paid Sick Days Access in the
United States: Differences by Race/Ethnicity, Occupation, Earnings, and
Work Schedule," Institute for Women's Policy Research, March 2014,
www.iwpr.org/publications/pubs/paid-sick-days-access-in-the-united-states-
differences-by-race-ethnicity-occupation-earnings-and-work-schedule.

21 Claudia Williams and Barbara Gault, "Paid Sick Days Access in the
United States: Differences by Race/Ethnicity, Occupation, Earnings, and
Work Schedule," Institute for Women's Policy Research, March 2014,
www.iwpr.org/publications/pubs/paid-sick-days-access-in-the-united-states-
differences-by-race-ethnicity-occupation-earnings-and-work-schedule.

22 Tom W. Smith and Jibum Kim, "Paid Sick Days: Attitudes and Experiences," National Opinion Research Center at the University of Chicago,
prepared for the Public Welfare Foundation, June 2010, www.nationalpa

rtnership.org/research-library/work-family/psd/paid-sick-days-attitudes-and-experiences.pdf.

23 Elise Gould et al., "The Need for Paid Sick Days," Economic Policy Institute, 29 June 2011, www.epi.org/publication/the_need_for_paid_sick_days/.

24 John A. Painter et al., "Attribution of Foodborne Illnesses, Hospitalizations, and Deaths to Food Commodities by using Outbreak Data, United States, 1998–2008." *Emerging Infectious Diseases Journal* 19, no. 3 (2013), Centers for Disease Control, wwwnc.cdc.gov/eid/article/19/3/11-1866_article.

25 Robert Drago and Kevin Miller, "Sick at Work: Infected Employees in the Workplace During the H1N1 Pandemic," Institute for Women's Policy Research, February 2010, www.iwpr.org/publications/pubs/sick-at-work-infected-employees-in-the-workplace-during-the-h1n1-pandemic/at_download/file.

26 LA Peipins, A. Soman et al., "The Lack of Paid Sick Leave as a Barrier to Cancer Screening and Medical Care-seeking: Results from the National Health Interview Survey." *BMC Public Health* 12 (2012), 520.

27 LA Smith et al., "Employment Barriers Among Welfare Recipients and Applicants with Chronically Ill Children," *American Journal of Public Health* 92, no. 9 (2002), www.ncbi.nlm.nih.gov/pubmed/12197972.

28 Abay Asfaw et al., "Paid Sick Leave and Nonfatal Occupational Injuries," *American Journal of Public Health* 102, no.9 (2012), e59-e64 http://njtimetocare.com/sites/default/files/14_American%20Journal%20of%20Public%20Health-%20Paid%20Sick%20Leave%20and%20Nonfatal%20Occupational%20Injuries.pdf.

29 Kalorama Information, "The Market for Wellness Programs and Their Impact on Pharmaceutical, Diagnostic and Device Product Markets," 1 October 2009, www.kaloramainformation.com/Wellness-Programs-Impact-2384194/.

30 Kevin Miller et al., "Paid Sick Days and Health: Cost Savings from Reduced Emergency Department Visits," Institute for Women's Policy Research, November 2011, www.iwpr.org/publications/pubs/paid-sick-days-and-health-cost-savings-from-reduced-emergency-department-visits.

31 United Nations Labor Organization, "Maternity and Paternity at Work: Laws and Practices across the World," Geneva: International Labour Office, 2014, www.ilo.org/wcmsp5/groups/——dgreports/——dicomm/——publ/documents/publications/wcms_242615.pdf.

32 Jody Heymann et al., "Contagion Nation: A Comparison of Paid Sick Day Policies in 22 Countries," Center for Economic and Policy Research, May 2009, www.cepr.net/documents/publications/paid-sick-days-2009-05.pdf.

33 Jody Heymann, et al., "Contagion Nation: A Comparison of Paid Sick Day Policies in 22 Countries," Center for Economic and Policy Research, May 2009, www.cepr.net/documents/publications/paid-sick-days-2009-05.pdf.

34 Family Values @ Work, "Voices from the Front Lines."

35 Shelly Lundberg and Elaina Rose, "Parenthood and the Earnings of Married Men and Women," University of Washington, June 1998, https://csde.washington.edu/downloads/98-9.pdf.

36 US Department of Labor, "A Workable Balance: Report to Congress on Family and Medical Leave Policies," 1996, 66, https://archive.org/stream/workablebalancer00unit#page/66/mode/2up.

37 Eileen Appelbaum and Helene Jorgensen, "Expanding Family and Medical Leave to Small Firms," Center for Economic and Policy Research, www.cepr.net/documents/fmla-small-firms-2014-04.pdf.

38 H.R. 1286 – Health Families Act, 113th Congress (2013–2014), Introduced on 20 March 2013 by Rep. Rosa DeLauro [D-CT-3].

39 The Family and Medical Insurance Leave Act (FAMILY) Act (S.1810/H.R.3712), Sponsored by Rep. Rosa DeLauro (D-Conn.) and Sen. Kristen Gillibrand (D-N.Y.).

40 US Department of Labor, "A Workable Balance: Report to Congress on Family and Medical Leave Policies,"198.

41 Jacob Klerman et al., "Family and Medical Leave in 2012: Technical Report."

42 Jacob Klerman et al., "Family and Medical Leave in 2012: Technical Report."

43 See Senate Bill No. 770, Chapter 350, An act to amend Section 3300 of, and to amend, repeal, and add Sections 2708, 3301, 3302, and 3303 of, the Unemployment Insurance Code, relating to unemployment insurance, and making an appropriation therefore (Legislative Councils Digest, 24 September 2013).

44 See New Jersey Temporary Disability Benefits Law 43: 21 (November 2011).

45 Linda Houser and Thomas P. Vartanian, "Pay Matters: The Positive Economic Impacts of Paid Family Leave for Families, Businesses and the Public."

46 Eileen Applebaum and Ruth Milkman, "Leaves That Pay: Employer and Worker Experiences with Paid Family Leave in California," Center for Economic and Policy Research, January 2011, www.cepr.net/publications/reports/leaves-that-pay.

47 Eileen Applebaum and Ruth Milkman, "Leaves That Pay: Employer and Worker Experiences with Paid Family Leave in California," Center for Economic and Policy Research, January 2011, www.cepr.net/publications/reports/leaves-that-pay.

48 Eileen Applebaum and Ruth Milkman, "Leaves That Pay: Employer and Worker Experiences with Paid Family Leave in California," Center for Economic and Policy Research, January 2011, www.cepr.net/publications/reports/leaves-that-pay.

49 Linda Houser and Thomas P. Vartanian, "Pay Matters: The Positive Economic Impacts of Paid Family Leave for Families, Businesses and the Public."

50 Eileen Applebaum and Ruth Milkman, "Leaves That Pay: Employer and Worker Experiences with Paid Family Leave in California."

51 Eileen Applebaum and Ruth Milkman, "Leaves That Pay: Employer and Worker Experiences with Paid Family Leave in California," Center for Economic and Policy Research, January 2011, www.cepr.net/publications/reports/leaves-that-pay.

52 Deanna S. Gomby and Dow-Jane Pei, "Newborn Family Leave: Effects on Children, Parents, and Business," The David and Lucile Packard

Foundation, 2009, www.packard.org/wp-content/uploads/2011/06/NFLA_fullreport_final.pdf.

53 Christopher J. Ruhm, "Parent Leave and Child Health," *Journal of Health Economics* 19, no. 6 (2000), 931–60.

54 Institute of Medicine of the National Academies, "Report Brief: Retooling for an Aging America: Building the Health Care Workforce," April 2008, www.iom.edu/~/media/Files/Report%20Files/2008/Retooling-for-an-Aging-America-Building-the-Health-Care-Workforce/ReportBriefRetoolingforanAgingAmericaBuildingtheHealthCareWorkforce.pdf.

55 MRH Taylor and P. O'Connor, "Resident Parents and Shorter Hospital Stay," *Archives of Disease in Childhood*, National Children's Hospital and Department of Paediatrics, Trinity College, Dublin,1989, http://adc.bmj.com/content/64/2/274.full.pdf+html.

56 Family Values @ Work, "From the Story Bank: Dr. Herb Greenberg's Story," http://familyvaluesatwork.org/story/dr-herb-greenbergs.

57 Small Business Majority, "New York Small Businesses Support Publicly Administered Family and Medical Leave Insurance Pools," 16 December 2013, www.smallbusinessmajority.org/small-business-research/family-medical-leave/121213-NY-FML-report.php.

58 Eileen Appelbaum and Lonnie Golden, "Sick Days for Healthy Recovery," *Philadelphia Business Journal*, 29 April 2011, http://www.bizjournals.com/philadelphia/print-edition/2011/04/29/sick-days-for-healthy-recovery.html?page=all.

59 Robert Drago and Vicky Lovell, "San Francisco's Paid Sick Leave Ordinance: Outcomes for Employers and Employees," Institute for Women's Policy Research. Retrieved 18 May 2014 from www.iwpr.org/publications/pubs/San-Fran-PSD.

60 John Petro, "Paid Sick Leave Does Not Harm Business Growth or Job Growth," Drum Major Institute for Public Policy, March 2010, www.nationalpartnership.org/research-library/work-family/psd/paid-sick-leave-does-not-harm.pdf.

61 James Warren, "Cough If You Need Sick Leave," *Businessweek*, 3 June 2010, www.businessweek.com/magazine/content/10_24/b4182033783036.htm.

62 Connecticut Department of Labor, "Industry Sectors Employment (CES)-State of Connecticut," Office of Research, 20 October 2014, www1.ctdol.state.ct.us/lmi/SecEmp.asp#map8.

63 Connecticut Department of Labor, "Industry Sectors Employment (CES)-State of Connecticut," Office of Research, 20 October 2014, www1.ctdol.state.ct.us/lmi/SecEmp.asp#map8.

64 Teresa Kroeger, "Is Paid Sick Leave Good for Business?" Center for Economic and Policy Research, 6 January 2014, www.cepr.net/index.php/blogs/cepr-blog/is-paid-sick-leave-good-for-business.

65 Eileen Appelbaum and Ruth Milkman, "Good for Business? The Case of Paid Sick Leave in Connecticut," Center for Economic and Policy Research, (presentation, Labor and Employment Relations Association, 3 January 2014) accessible from www.cepr.net/index.php/blogs/cepr-blog/is-paid-sick-leave-good-for-business.

66 Donna Levitt, Labor Standards Enforcement Officer, San Francisco, to Labor and Public Employees Committee, Connecticut, 28 February 2011,

http://cga.ct.gov/2011/LABdata/Tmy/2011SB-00913-R000301-Donna%20Levit t-City%20of%20San%20Francisco-TMY.PDF.

67 Jody Heymann, "We Can Afford to Give Parents a Break," *Washington Post*, 14 May 2006, www.washingtonpost.com/wp-dyn/content/article/2006/ 05/12/AR2006051201817.html.

68 Family Values @ Work and Main Street Alliance, "How Your Business Can Benefit from Paid Sick Days," 2011, from http://familyvaluesatwork. org/wp-content/uploads/2011/10/Business-Outreach-Trifold-Brochure.pdf.

69 Apurva Mehrotra and Nancy Rankin, "Latino Workers Can't Afford to Get Sick," Community Service Society, March 2013, http://b.3cdn.net/ nycss/8edff06bac4f0ab330_4dm6b625v.pdf.

70 Melissa Broome, "Choosing Between Your Child and Your Job," *Baltimore Sun*, 16 May 2014 http://articles.baltimoresun.com/2014-05-16/news/bs-ed-family-leave-20140517_1_johns-hopkins-children-owen-day-care#.U3jS9jnS 6PI.email.

21 On organizing for economic justice in Bangladesh

A reflection

Kalpona Akter

Some would find it surprising that in our predominately Muslim country we have such a large population of working women. Young women are, of course, the heart of the garment industry in Bangladesh. Roughly four million out of the five million of my country's garment workers are women. This industry reflects 75 percent of Bangladesh's exports and has tremendous national and international power. The majority of these women are age 20 to 25, and they are getting an education in economic freedom that requires recognition and a response.

The garment industry in my country has received a lot of international media attention in the past two years. The industry is characterized by poverty wages and by a series of factory fires and building collapses. The worst was the Rana Plaza building collapse on 24 April 2013, in which at least 1,138 workers were killed and 2,000 others injured, many permanently, with their limbs amputated on site to free them from the rubble. Major international brands including Primark, Wal-Mart, Benetton, JC Penny, Joe Fresh, and Children's Place sourced from Rana Plaza. In spite of the massive influence of the garment industry nationally and internationally, garment workers continue to fight for their dignity every day. Dignity here means the right to a decent wage, a collective voice, and safety in their workplace, as well as economic agency and decision-making power in their communities.

I became a garment worker when I was 12 years old. When I was working in factories, I became increasingly aware of the injustices that my co-workers and I faced. I sewed clothing for multi-national corporations and made less than ten dollars a month for 450 hours of work. It was wage theft. We were completely cheated out of promised overtime wages. I stood up with my colleagues at age 14. We went on strike, and we won. But then some strike organizers were fired. I quickly learned that there are laws intended to protect us, and I started organizing my co-workers. I want to thank the Solidarity Center of the AFL-CIO for teaching me how to form a union. I became union president at age 15. Seeking legal support allowed me to be an advocate for change in my workplace and community.

Management harassed me all the time and then at age 16, I was fired and blacklisted. At this point, I could have chosen another job, or I could have even gone to school. Looking back, I believe I could have asked for help from someone to finish my primary, secondary, and university education, but I did not choose that. I wanted to stand up and make change. At 16, I went to work for a union. As a full-time union organizer, I was better able to understand and challenge the powerful politics shaping the industry. In 2000, I co-founded the Bangladesh Center for Worker Solidarity (BCWS). Since the beginning, working together with local trade union federations, BCWS has provided workers' legal support and organized campaigns based on communities' needs. The reason that I formed BCWS was because I wanted to help other young women like me so that they could learn about their rights in the workplace and so that they could gain the courage and skills to organize for change in their workplaces and for broader social change as well.

We have been particularly involved in the fight for the raise in minimum wages and safer workplaces. Since the fire at That's It Sports Wear in 2010 and later Tazreen Fashions and the collapse of Rana Plaza, BCWS has worked hard to highlight the global/local relationship of the industry by demanding that global buyers take responsibility for the working conditions of their contracted factories. Together with national and international allies, including global unions and the International Labour Organization, BCWS has called on major retailers to pay full compensation to the victims of the disasters and for companies to sign the Accord on Fire and Building Safety in Bangladesh. The accord is a binding agreement between labor unions and brands and retailers to make factories safer in our country so that we do not experience a horrific collapse like Rana Plaza ever again. The accord marks the first time brands have accepted legal responsibility for workers' safety in contractor factories. So far, almost 200 multinational corporations have signed. This is one step towards responding to these women workers' demands for dignity.

Even in its short history, my country has made outstanding improvements in maternal mortality rates, rates of missing daughters, education for young girls, and female employment. Some point to the political roles woman hold nationally, but this does not tell the reality of women's empowerment in my country. Although there are reserved seats for women in parliament, it is clear that those women do not have a loud voice. Even the fact that our prime minister and opposition leader are both female has not strengthened the voices of women in Bangladesh as much as it may seem. These are women who inherited their political power from men in their families. So dynasty is there, and as they did not achieve it for themselves, it does not change the deep social barriers that prevent women from challenging gender norms within their families and communities. Many women are still unable to decide when and to whom they marry—when and how many children to have—when and how to travel alone without fear of being assaulted. This is why it is important that a movement to empower women is a progressive movement that has women's rights, human rights, and labor rights at its heart, and is not a movement only about numbers in representative positions.

There is still a deep distrust of the legal system that prevents women from knowing their rights and seeking help. Of the 300 members of parliament, over 10 percent are factory-owners, so to some extent, our legislator is our factory owner in Bangladesh. I have experienced this in my own life. In 2010, falsified criminal charges were brought against me and two of my co-workers. I was imprisoned for 30 days in harsh conditions until there was enough political pressure for my release on bail. I continued to face those charges for three years until they were finally dismissed for lack of evidence. It is because of the corrupt legal system and collusion between factory owners and politicians that I faced completely baseless charges for so long. Women are prevented access to rights and legal protections because of this distrust, lack of knowledge of their rights, and social barriers that restrict mobility.

Employment for women has begun to challenge these gender norms in my country. For instance, we know women who, before beginning work, would not approach a police officer out of fear of not knowing what to say or the consequences of doing so. Now, we see women having a voice in their community, voting according to their own decisions and voicing their concern when they see something wrong.[1] While many women continue to work in informal sectors like domestic work, construction, and agriculture, there are an increasing number of women working in telecommunications, banks, and hospitals as well. Because of its size and accessibility, the garment industry in particular has helped create the large women's workforce we have in Bangladesh today. Employment has demanded that women play an active role in industry, challenging dated notions of women's voice and agency. Employment has helped women understand that there is a world bigger than their communities, even bigger than their country, which has inspired thoughts of social change.

Still, working hours, wages, and workplace safety vary among these professions. Sexual harassment and gendered expectations within communities are shared among all working women. In Bangladesh a woman's economic freedom is not only limited by her meager salary but also by these realities that limit her decision-making power within her family and community. It is not enough for her to simply earn a wage, but it's the power to bargain for how much, and to be able to choose what she does with that wage that we strive to achieve. It is for this reason that to be a labor organizer, one must also be a community organizer. BCWS among others not only fights for a living wage but also to educate community members on their legal rights so that they can be agents of change. It is clear to us that gaining ownership of one's workplace encourages greater contributions to the community as a whole.

As women become more aware of their rights and gain agency in their workplace, we've begun to see increased community involvement. The majority of workers holding leadership positions in garment unions are women. That leadership, along with the unity among union members, also strengthens community involvement. It is important that as women become leaders in unions, they always prioritize the voices of the most oppressed and the young working women in all that they do. The potential for social change is most obvious among garment workers whose houses often surround their factory.

Tania is a factory worker who has worked in the garment factory for the last 10 years. She had experienced long shifts, verbal abuse, harassment, and intimidations. One day she came to our center looking for help. She learned labor laws and her rights, and she stood up. She taught her co-workers these laws as well. Under her leadership they started organizing a union at her factory and were able to get the union registered. Later, after much back and forth, they have achieved a collective agreement with the factory management. Now they have a voice in the workplace. Through Tania's leadership they were able to stop sweatshop conditions and harassment at their workplace. Since then Tania is not only the leader of her factory union, she is also a community leader working to organize other factory workers in her industrial belt.

Living in close quarters with one's colleagues further encourages active workers to be better able to contribute to their communities. That is why our fight for workers' rights extends beyond the factory gate. We must continue to fight for a living wage and a safer workplace while simultaneously mobilizing communities to challenge restrictive gender and labor relations outside of the workplace.

But when workers speak out, all too often they face repression. The fate of my friend and colleague Aminul Islam stands as a reminder of what we risk when we fight for change. In April 2012, he disappeared. His body was found by the side of the road. He had been brutally tortured to death. All signs pointed to retaliation by our government's security forces for Aminul's work to help workers exercise their legally guaranteed right to form unions. Imagine having the courage to speak out and organize in a situation like this.

That is exactly what increasing numbers of young women in the garment industry are doing. And when enough of them speak out, we are able to stop the repression, get laid-off union organizers rehired, and secure signed union neutrality agreements between unions and factory-owners. However, often we need international pressure and support. For example, when we demanded a transparent, independent investigation into the murder of Aminul Islam no-one listened to us. Secretary Hillary Clinton traveled to Bangladesh to speak out publicly in the media and to our government, and only then did they at least start listening to our demands. After the brutal retaliation against worker organizers and tragedies such as the collapse of Rana Plaza, there was an outpouring of powerful international support. The US government took a bold move in July 2013 by suspending the generalized system of preferences (GSP) trade benefits it had given our country. With that, the US government sent a strong message to the government of Bangladesh that workers' rights to freedom of association must be respected and unions must be allowed to register and collectively bargain.

The government of Bangladesh can no longer ignore the issues within the garment industry. Within the .past year, about 160 factory-level garment worker unions have been registered. This is compared with only one or two unions successfully registering in the prior couple of years. Additionally, nearly 200 sourcing brands have been encouraged by consumers and governments to sign the Accord on Fire and Building Safety in Bangladesh. However, we must look closely behind these numbers at the daily reality for the workers who struggle to form unions. In case after case workers report intimidation, harassment, and sometimes even mugging and beating. In one case, a union organizer was severely beaten and then thugs permanently removed all the belongings from his family's home, every single household item and piece of food, even the lightbulbs. As I write this, four union organizers are being held in prison on falsified charges. The need for vocal support and solidarity is urgent.

There is a role for so many different stakeholders in this work to reform the global supply chain so that it respects women's rights, human rights, and workers' rights, and can ultimately help achieve the poverty alleviation and development goals that companies claim they support. As consumers, every one of us has a responsibility to the working conditions of women workers and to those who advocate for change around the world. Through facing disaster, Bangladesh's labor activists are beginning to see change in the industry, and we continue to call on the international community whose purchasing power has real tangible effects on the lives of millions of workers around the world. The international community must continue to hold brands responsible for the working conditions in the contracted factories throughout the world. There is still a lot of work to be done.

- Businesses must be accountable across the supply chain from the factory workers, to the workers in the dye houses, textile and yarn mills, and cotton fields whose labor is vital to the garment industry. The industry is rife with labor abuses; for example in Uzbekistan the government forces over a million people to pick cotton each year under one of the largest state-sponsored forms of forced labor.[2]

- Foreign governments must hold our government accountable for our commitments under the International Labour Organization trade agreements and treaties. Government officials can speak out vocally in individual cases, like Secretary Clinton did in the case of Aminul Islam. Governments can use their economic power through exercising labor rights and human rights clauses in trade agreements. Governments can also join together to urge brands based in their countries to pay full and fair compensation to the Rana Plaza victims through the process facilitated by the ILO. Governments could also cease imports of cotton from Uzbekistan, until the Uzbek government ends its system of forced labor cotton production. Citizens must pressure their governments to take such direct actions.

- Investors can tell corporations in which they invest that they expect them to comply with human rights, women's rights, and labor rights. At the moment, we ask that investors require apparel companies in which they invest to join the legally binding Accord on Fire and Building Safety in Bangladesh.

- Donor organizations can move away from development projects that fund voluntary and ineffective company-controlled social compliance programs, and instead support worker-led initiatives. The Alliance for Bangladesh Worker Safety is a non-binding document initiated by Gap, Wal-Mart, VF Corporation, and other

North American retailers. The Alliance agreement fully neglects the worker's voice. These corporations are not taking any responsibilities towards repair and renovation after their inspections; neither are they sharing the findings of these inspections with workers or unions. The accord supported by BCWS includes workers who are not hand-picked by management during inspection. It also includes bringing back the findings and correction action plan to the workers. The accord includes a transparent process with reports that are made public, while the alliance agreement is not sufficient in these areas.

• Consumers have an important role to play in bringing our voices and demands to the attention of the multi-national corporations whose clothing we sew. They can publicly show their support for better working conditions and agree to pay a few dimes more if they know that workers are receiving a living wage. They can engage in protests at storefronts and join social movements that put pressure on companies to reform and governments to be held accountable. Institutional consumers, like schools that buy student uniforms and t-shirts and governments that buy public employee uniforms, can require that the companies they do business with are transparent with their apparel and cotton supply chains and respect workers' rights.

How do we know the change that is needed and what to call for? It is important that groups pushing for change have a close collaboration with workers' organizations and truly listen to them for guidance, vision, and shared strategy. For the workers themselves are learning firsthand what economic freedom can be. Coordination between worker organizations in different countries is important, and we must continue to build on this knowledge. If we organize factory by factory, or if we only organize within Bangladesh, we do not get as far. That is why we bring the stories of young women workers to international audiences and why we coordinate closely with non-governmental advocacy organizations in Europe and North America where most of the goods that we make are sold. I am not here to make you feel hopeless about working conditions or the lives of garment workers. Even though we face a huge struggle in the garment industry in my country, I have seen so much change already in the situation of women that it gives me the hope that I need to keep fighting. As I have said, four million young women workers are working in this industry. They have just learned what economic freedom is. At the end of the day, we totally need these jobs and we want these jobs with dignity.

Notes

1 Jeni Klugman, Lucia Hanmer, Sarah Twigg, Tazeen Hasan, Jennifer McCleary-Sills, and Julieth Santamaria, *Voice and Agency: Empowering Women and Girls for Shared Prosperity* (Washington, DC: World Bank Group, 2012), 5.
2 International Labor Rights Forum, *Uzbekistan's Cotton Industry Relies on State-orchestrated Forced Labor of Children and Adults*, www.laborrights. org/industries/cotton.

Part IV

Educating girls and eliminating child marriage

22 Be the change

A reflection

Malala Yousafzai

Several weeks before she was awarded the Nobel Peace Prize, the now world-renowned Pakistani defender of girls' education and human rights, Malala Yousafzai, recorded a personal video message for the Women and Girls Rising Conference in New York City. Recovered from a nearly fatal assassination attempt by local Taliban fundamentalists, she currently attends school in London.

I am 17, I have to get back to my education, do my homework, so for that reason I could not be with you in person. I am really sorry for that.

My message is very simple: If you want change, then you must be the change.

When I was growing up in Pakistan's Swat Valley, the quality of education for girls was totally inferior. I saw no future for myself.

Once girls reached a certain age, we were not allowed to go alone outside the house. We were not allowed to be independent and to have an identity of our own. We were supposed to be daughters, sisters, wives, and mothers only. We were never to be known as human beings, in our own right. And this is what I could not tolerate. I could not accept my lot. So I said I would speak up for my rights!

I decided that raising my voice was very important, if I wanted to see change in my community and in the larger society. And I've proved that to the world, that yes, my voice is powerful. I can bring change through speaking. And so can you.

There are so many problems all over the world. In Syria children are suffering from the civil war. Many are now refugees in Jordan, Lebanon, and Turkey. I went to Jordan recently and saw so many children, especially girls, who want to go back to their own homes and get back to school. They want to see their dreams come true, but they don't even have an opportunity to get a quality education.

On my seventeenth birthday this year, I met children in Nigeria, including girls who had escaped from abduction by Boko Haram. It was sad to realize that even as millions of people are highlighting this tragedy on social media, no-one is really helping the girls left behind.

All of us have a duty right now to contribute to the change that we want to bring. This then is my message right now to every woman and girl, to every man and boy.

If you seek change—if you seek justice and peace—equality and unity—in our world, then you must contribute from all sides. And everything starts with more education. Join me in this big campaign of seeing every child go to school. We can achieve it. We just need to work hard and stand together.

23 Raising the global ambition for girls' education

Rebecca Winthrop and Eileen McGivney

Over the past 20 years, the world has witnessed a striking amount of progress in girls' education. In 1990, just under half of girls in low-income countries were enrolled in primary school. By 2011 that figure had climbed to nearly 80 percent. In some countries today the prospects are even better for girls than boys. But while these gains are important and rightly celebrated, many challenges remain. There are still hotspots—countries where millions of girls are missing from primary and secondary school, at risk of forced early marriage and of threats to their safety in school. And many girls who do enter and safely complete school learn little there as a result of the poor-quality of education, and then struggle to transition into higher levels of education or into jobs. Reaching the most marginalized girls who have the triple handicap of being female, poor, and living in remote rural settings continues to be an especially vexing problem.

In this chapter, we take stock of impressive successes and set out continuing challenges—what we call the "second generation" of girls' education issues. Our analysis includes data on enrollment of girls in Sub Saharan Africa, and South and West Asia who still face many barriers to education; a look at the most hostile areas where schools are under attack and where girls face sexual harassment in their classrooms; and a survey of learning and labor market outcomes for girls who do attend or complete school in developing countries.

There is a clear rationale for prioritizing girls' education as a fundamental human right and as an instrument for advancing health, economic, social, and overall development outcomes. Educating girls helps improve health: if every mother in the world had a primary education, deaths during childbirth would fall by 66 percent according to UNESCO.[1] The economic benefits are clear: failing to educate girls to the same level as boys has resulted in an estimated loss of nearly $1 billion in potential economic growth.[2] And because women make up a large share of the world's farmers, improvements in girls' education also leads to increased agricultural output and productivity.[3]

According to the 2012 World Development Report on Gender Equality and Development, progress in girls' education has come in areas where lifting one barrier was sufficient to create change— either by increasing wages and labor market opportunity for educated girls, removing institutional constraints, or increasing household incomes.[4] Further gains, however, may require more localized and complex solutions that address multiple barriers to access, learning, and safety.

Taking stock of progress

For more than two decades, girls' education has been recognized as a global priority and incorporated into development targets, which has rallied governments, NGOs, foundations, and international organizations. The 1995 Fourth World Conference on Women in Beijing included education and training for women in its platform for action, calling for equal access to education and vocational training, eradication of illiteracy, non-discriminatory education, sufficient resources, and promotion of lifelong learning.[5] The Millennium Development Goals (MDGs) include universal access to and gender parity in primary education, and catalyzed all UN member states.[6] The Education for All (EFA) movement convened in 2000 in Dakar, Senegal and committed to end gender disparity in education by 2005 and achieve parity by 2015.[7] Along the way, countless other organizations and initiatives have taken a strong interest in the matter.

Global progress in parity

Global policy priorities in girls' education largely focus on equal access to primary education, which has indeed become a success story. Since 1990, the number of girls in low-income countries enrolling in primary school has increased two-and-a-half times, from 23.6 million to nearly 63 million in 2012. This has translated into a large increase in the girl-boy ratio in low-income countries, from 82 to 95 girls per 100 boys in primary school. For low- and lower middle-income countries combined, the number of girls enrolled reached over 200 million girls in 2012, an almost 80 percent increase, and, globally, two-thirds of countries have near-equal numbers of boys and girls enrolled at the primary level.[8]

A regional and localized focus

Although girls' education has been prioritized as a universal concern, there are major differences in progress among regions and populations. Some of the biggest gains have been in regions struggling the most. In 1990, in South and West Asia, there were only 74 girls enrolled in primary school for every 100 boys, but by 2012 the region had achieved equal numbers of enrollment. Similarly, Sub Saharan Africa, which had the lowest levels of girls' schooling in 1990, has experienced marked improvement, with the girl-boy ratio increasing from 83 to 92 girls per 100 boys in primary school.[9]

Additionally, the focus on getting girls into school has helped close gender gaps in relation to other factors such as wealth and location of residence. The fact that family income and urban or rural locality are now the most likely indicators of school enrollment is a big victory for girls' education. The World Inequality Database on Education (WIDE) shows that in India, for example, in 1992, 38 percent of girls and 25 percent of boys of primary school age were not in school. In 2005, that gap had narrowed to 24 percent of girls and 22 percent of boys. However, the gap between the richest and poorest children's attendance is even starker—37 percent of children from the poorest 20 percent of families versus just 11 percent of the richest 20 percent are out of school.[10]

And in many areas, girls actually outpace boys, especially at higher levels of education. In one-third of countries, there are now more girls than boys enrolled in secondary school.[11] Also, girls often do better once in school, with boys making up 75 percent of grade-repeaters in primary school. Globally, more women are currently enrolled in higher education than men.[12]

Remaining challenges

These overall advances, however, do not mean girls are ahead in every country or that gender disparities do not remain in many places. Girls outpace boys in very few low-income countries, with an average of 80 girls per 100 boys in upper secondary school, and a meager 70 percent of girls who finish primary school then transitioning on into secondary school.[13] Women in Sub Saharan Africa also remain behind men in enrollment in higher education.[14] Additionally, the fact that gender gaps play a smaller role than other economic and geographical factors does not mean all gender gaps have vanished. In fact, being a girl exacerbates the effect that family income and location have on access to education, making poor, rural girls a population with three handicaps. As the 2012 World Development Report argues, much of the progress over the last two decades has come in areas where it was sufficient to remove one of these barriers, but many girls still face multiple, intertwined obstacles.[15]

As many of the MDG and EFA targets goals to improve girls' education are close to being reached, it is important to re-focus girls' education initiatives on issues of access safety, quality, and the assurance of a successful transition beyond school. Primary school access is certainly an important step toward gender equality, but the intense efforts around gender parity in enrollment have left other critical issues behind.

The missing millions

Although overall access to education has improved, there are still over 30 million girls of primary school age who are not in school, and another 34 million missing from lower-secondary school.[16] Many of these girls live in "hotspots," like Nigeria and Pakistan, where, respectively, 5.5 million and 3 million girls of primary age are not enrolled in school. In Sub Saharan Africa and South and West Asia, gender parity indices have improved greatly, but regional averages mask significant variation among countries. The latest data on Somalia (2007) show that there are still only 55 girls enrolled in primary school for every 100 boys, 70 in Chad, 71 in the Central African Republic, and 67 in Afghanistan.[17] Girls in these countries are missing from the education system, and should not be forgotten because of progress elsewhere.

Being a girl exacerbates the extreme disadvantages of all countries with continued high levels of rural poverty. In Sub Saharan Africa, at current enrollment rates, it will take until the year 2086 for all of the poorest girls to attend primary school, a full 65 years behind the richest boys. Poor girls will not achieve universal lower-secondary schooling until 2111—compared with 2042 for the richest boys. And while income levels affect boys' enrollment as well, poor boys in Africa are still expected to reach universal lower-secondary education more than 20 years ahead of poor girls.[18]

Furthermore, success in expanding primary school access has not necessarily translated into increased enrollment at the secondary level. Many of the benefits of educating girls come when they complete secondary school, which improves their independence and labor market participation rates. Yet only 70 percent of girls in low-income countries complete primary school and transition into secondary schools,[19] translating into a 41 percent gross enrollment rate. Boys in these countries are not ahead by huge gains, but gross enrollment is 5 percent higher for boys in secondary school, translating into an 88-to-100 girl-boy ratio.[20]

An important factor explaining the persistence of education gaps for girls is early marriage. In Niger, 75 percent of girls marry before the age of 18.[21] No surprise then that only 12 percent of girls of lower-secondary school age, and 57 percent of primary-age, are enrolled in school.[22] Poverty is also a factor. Globally, poor girls marry before age 18 at rates almost twice those in higher income households.[23] A critical question is whether pressure to marry early pulls girls out of the education system, or if lack of educational opportunities and low-quality education push girls into marriage. While, typically, early marriage is seen as a barrier to getting girls into school, recent research has called this assumption into question and shown that in fact girls leave school because the quality of schooling is so low and then marry because they do not have any other options.[24] Studies from Indonesia, Sri Lanka, and Thailand have shown a correlation between increases in girls' education and lower incidence of early marriage.[25]

Safety

Even girls able to access school may face serious threats to their safety on their way and once inside. The 2012 shooting of Malala Yousafzai in Pakistan and the 2014 kidnapping of over 200 Chibok schoolgirls in northern Nigeria highlight the peril that confronts many girls whose education is under attack. Elsewhere, girls and young women regularly encounter sexual harassment and violence making their schooling environments unsafe.

The Global Coalition to Protect Education from Attack (GCPEA) reports that since 2009, schools in 30 countries have come under direct attack or been used for military purposes in armed conflict. It cites attacks specific to girls in 14 countries.[26] These vary from incidents specifically orchestrated to disrupt schooling and damage school infrastructure to those targeting individuals through abduction, rape, or harassment. In Afghanistan and Pakistan, recent attacks have included threats to girls, parents, and teachers with gas and acid. In Pakistan, the outright ban on female education by the Taliban forced 900 schools in the Swat Valley to close or stop enrolling female students. Although the military regained control and re-opened the schools, a year later many girls were still too afraid to return to school.[27]

Further threats to girls include abductions in Somalia similar to the Nigerian case, with kidnappings and forced marriage to Al-Shabaab fighters, or else murders on the spot. These instances invariably cause panic, as in Somalia where 12 girls were abducted and 150 more dropped out of school out of fear. GCPEA also reports that in conflict settings schoolgirls routinely become victims of sexual violence, often from military officials and police. Recent incidents are cited from Colombia, the Democratic Republic of Congo, India, and Libya.[28]

Sexual harassment and assault in schools, unrelated to larger outbreaks of violence, are also tragically common, with teachers coercing students.[29] A study in Kenya found that 8 percent of secondary school girls reported pressure from school staff to engage in sex. In South Africa one-third of girls raped before age 15 reported a teacher as the perpetrator.[30] Twenty percent of teachers in a Malawi survey said that they were aware of sexual relationships between teachers and students.[31] The Mandela Foundation in South Africa reported that violence, harassment, and abuse were serious issues for girls traveling to and from school, and once inside, with peers and teachers as perpetrators.[32]

Quality learning

Quality of schooling and improved learning outcomes remain a critical challenge facing boys and girls. We know that 250 million children, many of whom have been in school for four years, do not have basic reading and math skills.[33] The EFA Global Monitoring Report (GMR) reports that, even as enrollments increase, low levels of literacy and numeracy among children who have spent time in school signals great inefficiencies and is evidence of a "learning crisis" in developing countries.[34] Again, the disparities between regions are huge. Ninety-six percent of children in North America and Western Europe stay in school until grade four and learn basic reading skills, but only one-third of students in South and West Asia, and 40 percent in Sub Saharan Africa do so.[35] In a study of 74 countries, Malawi demonstrated the lowest learning levels, with just 8 percent of students achieving basic math skills, and only 5 percent both meeting basic standards and finishing four years of school.[36] Moreover, a lack of regular, comparable assessments makes it hard to gauge exactly how far behind these students are, and a critical shortage of technical expertise prevents low-income countries from measuring learning outcomes effectively.[37]

The GMR points out that marginalized groups suffer the most. Income level correlates directly with learning outcomes. For example, in El Salvador only 42 percent of poor children finish fourth grade and achieve basic skills, compared with 84 percent of rich children. Here again, gender exacerbates the challenges. In Benin, only 6 percent of poor girls achieve basic numeracy skills compared with 60 percent of rich boys.[38]

In some countries, girls outpace boys in learning,[39] but there is also evidence that girls' learning is more strongly affected by activities outside the classroom. This may leave some girls more vulnerable to conditions outside the classroom, but it could also provide a path to improve learning outcomes, where they are through informal education.[40]

Transitions to life beyond secondary school

Finally, the issue of transitioning into a productive life beyond secondary education, through employment or higher education is crucial. Women who are educated and work are more productive, gain greater control over family income and decision-making, and invest more in their families. One World Bank study estimates that women and girls who earn income reinvest 90 percent of it in their families, promoting better health and future productivity.[41]

However, increased educational attainment for girls is still failing to translate into productive workforce participation in many countries. In Jordan, for example, labor force participation among women in 2012 remains at a meager 15 percent, compared with 66 percent for men, even as equal numbers of girls and boys enroll in primary and secondary schools.[42] Globally, women are also more likely than men to be employed in "vulnerable" jobs, often informal, unpaid, and without benefits and security. In developing countries, 65 percent of employed women fall into these categories, according to a 2013 World Bank Study.[43] The reasons for disparities between women's educational achievement and employment are complex, and are also rooted in cultural expectations. Achieving gender parity is only a partial response and localized solutions addressing dynamics outside the education system are key. Still, it is important to ask how schools can better address gender stereotypes and help increase the number of women finding stable formal employment.

In much of the world today, more women than men are enrolled in colleges and universities, although as a percentage of total population, enrollment levels remain low.[44] Major exceptions are Sub Saharan Africa and South and West Asia—also hotspots for low levels of girls in primary schools. Only 61 women for every 100 men seek high education in Sub Saharan Africa—81 for every 100 men in South and West Asia.[45] Tertiary education correlates strongly with enhanced sense of self and empowerment, increased economic and public participation, and lower levels of domestic violence.[46]

Conclusion

While admirable progress has been made in primary school enrollments for girls in most places in the world, clear challenges remain
before millions of girls have access to safe schooling of high quality.
We have laid out a framework of second-generation challenges facing
girls today: hotspot regions where girls still cannot access primary
education; extremely disadvantaged poor and rural girls who lag
behind; unsafe environments that threaten millions of schoolgirls; low-
quality learning opportunities; and compromised opportunities to
transition to higher education and secure jobs. Moving forward will
require more localized solutions that vary widely in different contexts.
Fortunately, there are successful small-scale interventions addressing
these challenges at the local and country level from which we can
learn.[47] Our challenge is to bring them to scale.

Notes

1 UNESCO, *Education Transforms Lives* (Paris: UNESCO Publishing,
   2013).
2 Plan International, *Paying the Price: The Economic Cost of Failing to
   Educate Girls* (Woking: Plan International, 2008).
3 IFPRI, *Women: Still the Key to Food and Nutrition Security* (Washington,
   DC: The International Food Policy Research Institute, 2005).
4 The World Bank, *World Development Report 2012: Gender Equality and
   Development* (Washington, DC: The World Bank, 2011).
5 UN Women, *Strategic Objective B: Education and Training of Women,
   Fourth World Conference on Women, Beijing, China*, 1995, www.un.org/
   womenwatch/daw/beijing/platform/educa.htm.
6 United Nations, *The Millennium Development Goals Report 2014* (New
   York: United Nations, 2014).
7 UNESCO, *The Dakar Framework for Action Education for All: Meeting
   Collective Comments* (Paris: UNESCO, 2000).
8 UNESCO Institute of Statistics, *UIS.Stat Data Centre* (Montreal:
   UNESCO Institute of Statistics, 2014).
9 UNESCO Institute of Statistics, *UIS.Stat Data Centre*.
10 *World Inequality Database on Education*, www.education-inequalities.org/.
11 UNESCO, *Atlas of Education and Gender Equality* (Paris: UNESCO Publishing, 2012).
12 UNESCO, *Atlas of Education and Gender Equality*; The World Bank,
   World Development Report 2012: Gender Equality and Development
   (Washington, DC: The World Bank, 2012).
13 UNESCO Institute of Statistics, *UIS.Stat Data Centre*; UNESCO, *Education for All Global Monitoring Report 2013/14* (Paris: UNESCO Publishing, 2014).
14 The World Bank, *Engendering Development through Gender Equality in
   Rights, Resources, and Voice*.

15 The World Bank, *Engendering Development through Gender Equality in Rights, Resources, and Voice.*

16 UNESCO, *Education for All Global Monitoring Report 2013/14.*

17 UNESCO Institute of Statistics, *UIS.Stat Data Centre.*

18 UNESCO, *Education for All Global Monitoring Report 2013/14.*

19 UNESCO, *Education for All Global Monitoring Report 2013/14.*

20 UNESCO, *Education for All Global Monitoring Report 2013/14.*

21 UNICEF, *State of the World's Children Statistics: Child Protection* (New York: UNICEF, 2013).

22 UNESCO, *Education for All Global Monitoring Report 2013/14.*

23 ICRW, *Child Marriage and Poverty Factsheet* (Washington, DC: The International Center for Research on Women, 2006).

24 Gordon Brown. *Out of Wedlock, Into School: Combating Child Marriage through Education* (London: The Office of Gordon and Sarah Brown, 2012).

25 ICRW, *Child Marriage and Education Factsheet* (Washington, DC: The International Center for Research on Women, 2006).

26 GCPEA, *Education Under Attack 2014* (New York: Global Campaign to Protect Education for Attack, 2014).

27 GCPEA, *Education Under Attack 2014.*

28 GCPEA, *Education Under Attack 2014.*

29 Shireen Jejeebhoy and Sarah Bott, *Non-consensual Sexual Experience of Young People: a Review of the Evidence from Developing Countries* (New Delhi: Population Council, 2003).

30 Jejeebhoy and Bott, *Non-consensual Sexual Experience of Young People: a Review of the Evidence from Developing Countries.*

31 UNESCO, *Education for All Global Monitoring Report 2013/14.*

32 Nelson Mandela Foundation, *Emerging Voices: A Report on Education in South African Rural Communities* (Cape Town: Human Sciences Research Council Press, 2005).

33 UNESCO, *Education for All Global Monitoring Report 2013/14.*

34 UNESCO, *Education for All Global Monitoring Report 2013/14.*

35 UNESCO, *Education for All Global Monitoring Report 2013/14.*

36 Nadir Altinok, *A New International Database on the Distribution of Student Achievement* (Paris: UNESCO, 2011).

37 Learning Metrics Task Force, *Toward Universal Learning: Implementing Assessment to Improve Learning* (Montreal and Washington, DC: UNESCO Institute of Statistics and Center for Universal Education at the Brookings Institution, 2014).

38 UNESCO, *Education for All Global Monitoring Report 2013/14.*

39 Liesbet Steer, Hafez Ghanem, and Maysa Jalbout. *Arab Youth: Missing Educational Foundations for a Productive Life?* (Washington, DC: Brookings Institution Press, 2014).

40 Unterhalter, et al., *Interventions to Enhance Girls' Education and Gender Equality* (London: Department for International Development, 2014).

41 The World Bank, *Engendering Development through Gender Equality in Rights, Resources, and Voice* (Washington, DC: The World Bank, 2001).

42 *World Inequality Database on Education*, www.education-inequalities.org/.

43 The World Bank. *Atlas of Global Development: A Visual Guide to the World's Greatest Challenges* (Washington, DC: The World Bank, 2013).

44 The World Bank, *World Development Report 2012: Gender Equality and Development.*
45 UNESCO Institute of Statistics, *UIS. Stat Data Centre.*
46 Unterhalter et al., *Interventions to Enhance Girls' Education and Gender Equality.*
47 Unterhalter et al., *Interventions to Enhance Girls' Education and Gender Equality.*

24 Girls' education as a peace and security issue

US policy toward Afghanistan

Catherine Powell and Hannah Chartoff

Educating girls is critical first and foremost to help them realize their fullest potential. Yet in international affairs, such issues are often brushed aside in favor of matters of war and peace that receive the most attention and resources. For decades, however, research has demonstrated that girls' education is also a proven method for growing economies, reducing extremism, and creating stability.[1] Increasing US investment in education abroad—particularly girls' education—would thus be a more sustainable, humane, cost-effective way to reduce threats to national security interests than pouring billions of dollars into military interventions after full-scale conflicts erupt. Using Afghanistan as a case study, this chapter argues for reorienting US foreign policy to prioritize girls' education as a dimension of a more broadly defined national security policy.

As the United States winds down its military involvement in Afghanistan and shifts attention to new threats, policymakers ought to consider the changing face of security in the twenty-first century and rethink the efficacy of expensive military interventions. Rather than invest billions of dollars to fight terrorists and extremists *after* they have a firm toe hold in strategically important sites—as in Afghanistan, Iraq, Syria, and Nigeria—why not invest more in creating stable, prosperous societies *before* conflicts broaden?

Prioritizing girls' education may be the most effective strategy available to realize this goal and therein expand conventional notions of peace and security so they embrace human security,[2] economic security, and inclusive security.[3] In 2008, Barack Obama campaigned on a promise to create a global education fund[4] as a positive step toward reorienting US security priorities and employing "smart power."[5] Instead, US Agency for International Development (USAID) investment in education in Afghanistan actually dipped during his presidency,[6] in part because of congressionally imposed funding cuts.

This call for reorienting US national security policy away from traditional military responses is not new. But unlike the call for "books not bombs" from the 1960s, we envision a smarter policy, one not constrained by the silos of hard and soft power. We situate this call in the context of global women, peace, and security efforts, stemming from UN Security Council Resolution (SCR) 1325 (2000), which affirms "the important role of women in the prevention and resolution of conflicts, peace negotiations, peace-building, peacekeeping, humanitarian response and in post-conflict reconstruction."[7] In urging a gender perspective, Resolution 1325 "calls on all parties to conflict to take special measures to protect women and girls from gender-based violence, particularly rape and other forms of sexual abuse, in situations of armed conflict."[8] It also requires special attention to the needs of women and girls during repatriation and resettlement, rehabilitation, and reintegration—including girls' education. Numerous countries, including the United States, have adopted National Action Plans (NAPs) to implement 1325. Both the US NAP[9] and the UN Secretary General's report on 1325[10] identify girls' education specifically as an area for investment and development to improve women's rights and agency. As we celebrate the 15-year anniversary of SCR 1325—as well as the anniversaries of the 1995 Beijing Fourth UN Conference on Women and the 2000 Millennium Development Goals—it is important to reexamine girls' education as a security issue, in addition to being a critical equality and development matter.

The drawdown of US troops from Afghanistan after more than a decade of war provides another compelling reason to do so. As President Obama noted, "Now, even as our troops come home, the international community will continue to support Afghans as they build their country for years to come. But our relationship will not be defined by war—it will be shaped by our financial and development assistance, as well as our diplomatic support."[11] This support is crucial: the Taliban is resurgent in Afghanistan, undermining both Afghan and US security interests. Afghan women and girls continue to live in insecurity, which restricts their participation in social and economic life. The tremendous advances they have made in access to education and other sectors remain fragile.[12] Fortunately, Afghanistan is developing its own NAP, and Afghans elected a new pro-women's rights-leaning president, Ashraf Ghani, in 2014—both promising developments for women and girls, which the US should support as it draws down its military presence.

SCR 1325 rests on the theory that including women in peace and security issues is necessary not only as a matter of principle, but also for preventing the recurrence of conflict and developing more sustainable peace.[13] Bringing a gender lens to peace and security efforts—and deepening investment in girls' education as part of this—helps societies become more prosperous and correlates with greater moderation and less conflict. As the Brookings Institution's Rebecca Winthrop has noted, the very factors that can be minimized through girls' education—an oversized youth population, mass poverty, and limited economic opportunity— are among those mostly likely to foster extremism.[14] As hard-fought military gains in Afghanistan risk slipping back into extremist control, the United States must seize the moment and reassess what it is doing to bolster conflict prevention through girls' education and other steps to create inclusive human security.

The benefits of educating girls

Research reveals that beyond its moral dimension, increased investment in girls' education pays dividends for prosperity and stability. As an investment in human capital, spending on girls' education actually yields a greater return than spending on boys' education.[15] This is not necessarily an argument for favoring one over the other, but for gender parity. Benefits include the positive correlation between girls' education and increased female workforce participation, economic productivity, and earnings, as well as improved maternal and child health, higher economic growth, greater poverty reduction, and other economic and social benefits.[16]

Furthermore, educated women and girls pay their income and education forward into their communities, families, and children. When girls and women earn money, they are likely to reinvest 90 percent of it into their families.[17] Moreover, girls with higher levels of education marry later, have smaller families, and experience reduced incidences of HIV/AIDS,[18] minimizing the potential of poverty for their children. A child whose mother can read is 50 percent more likely to survive past the age of five, and each extra year of a mother's schooling reduces the probability of an infant dying by 5 percent to 10 percent.[19] Thus, educating mothers is an essential investment in the next generation, with economic and social benefits that have cumulative consequences for the community's well-being and stability.

The exclusion of girls from Afghan schools under the Taliban—and the attacks on Afghan girls, girls' schools, and female teachers during this period—are indicative of dangers girls face from extremists and terrorists elsewhere—such as Boko Haram's abduction of schoolgirls in Chibok, Nigeria, and the attack on Malala Yousafzai in Swat, Pakistan. Under such circumstances, a cycle is created: poverty, a youth bulge, and massive youth unemployment create fertile ground for extremism; instability and the presence of extremists further limit girls' educational opportunities; out-of-school girls cannot contribute to economic growth and are more likely to marry early and have more children; as those children mature, many will remain impoverished, unemployed, and susceptible to recruitment by extremists. Investing in girls' education upfront can break this cycle, creating stability and shrinking the opportunity for extremists to put down roots.

Afghanistan under the Taliban

Nowhere is there a more poignant story of girls' education being sacrificed to extremism than in Afghanistan under Taliban rule. The Taliban came to power in 1996, and in an edict a year later called for a nationwide ban on public education for all women and girls. Afghan women then tried to work around the law, setting up hundreds of schools in private homes, but in 1998, the regime stipulated that privately funded education be limited to girls under eight and restricted to teachings of the Quran. At the same time, Taliban sympathizers shut down 100 of these private schools in Kabul, seeking to make an example of any attempts at resistance. During the five years of Taliban rule, women's literacy rates fell to among the lowest in the world, at 13 percent in cities and three to four percent in rural areas.[20]

Over this period, the United States and other international actors did little to challenge these harsh policies. Two UN Security Council resolutions issued in 1998, Resolution 1193[21] and Resolution 1214,[22] called for the end of discrimination against women and girls in Afghanistan amid a laundry list of condemnations and demands, but neither specifically referenced education. By the time the Taliban were forced from power in 2001, only 900,000 Afghan boys were enrolled in public school and virtually no girls.

Only after the catastrophic terror attacks of 11 September 2001, did US government officials fully appreciate the degree to which the Taliban's tolerance of the terror group al-Qaeda went hand in hand with extremist views toward governance, including the harsh deprivation of human rights, especially women's rights. A November 2001 State Department report, *The Taliban's War against Women*, enumerates the abuses inflicted on women and describes the result as the loss of a "tremendous asset" to Afghan society. The report notes that "restricting women's access to work is an attack on women today; eliminating women's access to education is an assault on women tomorrow."[23] In the same month, then-First Lady Laura Bush took over her husband's weekly radio address and directly linked US intervention to these matters, saying "the fight against terrorism is also a fight for the rights and dignity of women."[24] The September 11 attacks were the primary reason for the US invasion of Afghanistan, but addressing the repressive rule of the Taliban—particularly against women—became a prominent justification in the policy debate that helped to secure strong, broad support.

Women and girls have made dramatic strides in Afghanistan since 2001. Currently, there are over ten million children in school, over three million of whom are girls. From 2002 to 2011, primary school enrollment rates for girls increased from less than 40 to more than 80 percent, and secondary school enrollment rates rose from five to over 34 percent. Moreover, Afghans have experienced fundamental shifts in attitudes toward girls' education: more than 80 percent now believe that women should be educated, compared with less than 60 percent in 2006.[25]

Yet there is more work to be done: over half of all Afghan girls still do not attend school, and persistent Taliban attacks continue to threaten existing gains. The Afghan education system's infrastructure and capacity are in need of improvement—and these weaknesses disproportionately affect girls.[26] A 2010 UNICEF report notes that nearly half of state schools still lacked safe sanitation facilities.[27] And a 2010 report of the Afghan Ministry of Education found that 49 percent of all schools did not occupy their own buildings, and 68 percent of schools lacked a protective, surrounding wall.[28] These circumstances present challenges to cultural values of modesty and may result in girls dropping out of school.

In recent years, Taliban insurgents and sympathizers continue to attack girls seeking education as a means to strike out at the state and counter its influence. Numerous attacks on girls, girls' schools, and female teachers were reported from 2005 to 2008. According to the Civil-Military Fusion Centre, 49 percent of girls' schools in Paktika, 69 percent in Zabul, and 59 percent in Helmand were burned or attacked between 2006 and 2009.[29] A World Bank-funded CARE report shows that 85 percent of schools stay closed for one to three months following an attack; and in five of eight provinces studied, female attendance is more likely to be affected than male attendance.[30] Opposition to the targeting of schools—including an Afghan co-sponsored resolution by the UN Human Rights Council—has helped reduce the number of these attacks, but they remain a persistent threat.[31]

The correlation between Afghan girls' access to education and other gains

Still, dramatic improvements in girls' access to education and in women's rights generally since 2001 correlate with considerable economic growth and the reemergence of democratic institutions in Afghanistan. Although it is too soon to draw *causal* links between girls' education and other gains, a relationship between the two is consistent with findings elsewhere in World Bank and other studies. More broadly, Afghan women have also made strides in political participation, with women holding three cabinet seats in the new government. In the April 2014 election, the female voter participation rate was 36 percent,[32] and almost 300 women candidates ran for provincial council seats.[33] Access to basic health services has improved—as has the training of women as midwives—resulting in reduced maternal mortality rates from 1,600 per 100,000 births in 2001 to 327 deaths in 2013.[34]

Afghanistan's progress—albeit uneven—marks the turnaround of a rogue state that posed a significant threat to US interests. But these gains are tenuous. Following a disputed election, Ashraf Ghani's young presidency and his cooperation in signing a bilateral security agreement (BSA) with the United States—after months of stalemate under former President Hamid Karzai—have paved the way for a smoother security transition. The BSA provides for the continued presence of US and international troops in an advisory capacity, as full responsibility for the nation's security is transferred back to the Afghan government, and is intended to ensure security and safety on the ground, especially for Afghan women, in the coming months and years.

Yet President Ghani was careful to couple the agreement with promises to maintain Afghan sovereignty in the transition period, signaling his recognition that much of Afghanistan's recent improvement is inflated by sustained international presence and donor aid. The country will still face the challenge of development when US and other international assistance diminishes. Afghanistan provides an example of successful US investment in girls' education and in the training of women as key actors in post-conflict stabilization and reconstruction.[35] However, USAID's funding for Afghan education has recently decreased, and a newly launched USAID initiative to support Afghan women, the Promote program, does not target education as a priority sector.[36]

Conclusion

Using Afghanistan as an example, we have argued that investing in girls abroad—especially girls' education in potential conflict zones—should be considered a strategic priority for the United States. Why does this remain a hard sell for foreign policymakers?

First, as Cynthia Enloe notes, experts who focus on women are often seen as arguing for "minority issues" that inherently do not embrace the "big picture."[37] Yet, while women, like minorities, often lack political power, as half the global population women are certainly not a numerical minority, and their circumstances—as the situation in Afghanistan illustrates—have profound consequences for the big picture. Second, women's issues are often construed as personal or private in nature, in contrast with what are perceived to be the more significant public matters of security. But again, as demonstrated above, improving the status of women and girls correlates with broader economic and social factors—such as poverty and youth unemployment—that underlie extremism.

Echoing President Obama's campaign promise to create a global education fund, US Secretary of Education Arne Duncan has voiced support for investing in education abroad, writing in *Foreign Affairs*: "Education has immeasurable power to promote growth and stability around the world. Educating girls and integrating them into the labor force is especially critical to breaking the cycle of poverty."[38] The Education for All Act, introduced in the House of Representatives in 2011 and 2013, would have increased US education aid abroad to $3 billion per year but was never passed.[39]

With the current pivot of attention from Afghanistan to the Islamic State in Iraq and Syria (ISIL), resources will likely shift as well.[40] Fortunately, however, the Obama Administration recently launched the Let Girls Learn initiative, which will expand the Peace Corp to support community-based programs that work to eliminate barriers adolescent girls face in education. For Afghanistan to become a prosperous, stable country, the United States and its partners need to provide long-term development support, particularly for girls' education. Having invested US lives and treasure there, the United States should not reduce assistance for educational opportunities that pave the way for a prosperous and stable country.

Finally, however, we want to acknowledge that while reframing girls' education as a security issue may facilitate greater support, there may be downsides as well. As feminism has infiltrated international law, women's issues have moved from the margins to become more integral to peace and security discussions. While this chapter celebrates this trend—and the move toward more gender-inclusive approaches to security—we also recognize inherent risks.

Framing girls' education as a security matter utilizes an instrumentalist approach that may have normative and practical implications.[41] One risk is that it may obscure the central goal of improving girls' education for the sake of girls—strengthening their dignity, opportunities for growth, and their right to realize their highest potential—as opposed to the broader goal of peace and security. A second risk is that a security framework may be used to support militarizing feminism in ways that lend momentum to the use of force.

To the first concern, we respond that while the primary justification for supporting girls' education remains for the sake of girls themselves, broader and more strategic claims are necessary from the standpoints of institutional and democratic accountability[42] and as additional levers to mobilize resources in a more substantial, meaningful and sustainable way. Addressing the second concern, we argue for a security framework that emphasizes conflict prevention and smarter, more effective ways of supporting sustainable post-conflict reconstruction to create lasting peace. In contrast, militarized feminism argues for using military force to address women's rights concerns. For several years, calls for the United States to use military force have been linked to women's rights violations. As mentioned above, the Bush Administration linked its 2001 invasion of Afghanistan to the Taliban's violation of Afghan women's rights, although its primary justification was to fight terrorist threats. This militarization of women's rights shadows the rise of humanitarian intervention as a tool of statecraft.[43]

However, militarizing women's rights suffers from a number of drawbacks. First, it adds momentum to the march toward war, when, in many cases, other tools should be more seriously considered. Second, militarizing women's rights tends to obscure the role of local women's rights movements, casting the women who constitute these movements as victims whom only the West can rescue.[44] Third, it often ends up reinforcing negative images of Muslim[45] and other men of color, recreating the "savior-victim-savage" dynamic,[46] in which an "enlightened" West imposes its positive "Western values" on others.[47]

By contrast, the SCR 1325 framework emphasizes the importance of preventing conflicts and creating a sustainable peace that prevents the recurrence of conflict. It has also been implemented in ways that elevate local knowledge and the role of local women's rights organizations and movements. While many observers associate the ongoing viability and visibility of Resolution 1325 efforts with Hillary Clinton—and other Western diplomats who paved the way for subsequent resolutions building on it—it was Netumbo Nandi-Ndaitwah, then-Minister of Women's Affairs in Namibia, who initiated the resolution.[48] Women from Rwanda and other parts of the global South have also been leaders in the move to implement Resolution 1325,[49] disrupting the view that women's human rights and the use of a security framework to advance women's rights are merely "Western" concepts.

Investing in girls' education and taking other steps to *prevent* conflict and failed states will reduce the need to use force or intervene in conflicts. Furthermore, by incorporating questions of women's and girls' rights into post-conflict rebuilding discussions, greater stability and more sustainable peace can be achieved in the future.

Notes

1 World Bank, *Gender Equality and Development*, World Development Report 2012, 2011, http://siteresources.worldbank.org/INTWDR2012/Resources/7778105-1299699968583/7786210-1315936222006/Complete-Report.pdf.

2 The 1994 UN Human Development Report shifted the focus from the security of a state to "human security," defined as "protection from the threat of disease, hunger, unemployment, crime, social conflict, political repression and environmental hazards." See United Nations Development Program (UNDP), *Human Development Report 1994*, http://hdr.undp.org/sites/default/files/reports/255/hdr_1994_en_complete_nostats.pdf.

3 Swanee Hunt and Cristina Posa, "Women Waging Peace," *Foreign Policy* 124 (2001): 38–47.

4 David Gartner, "A Global Fund for Education: Achieving Education for All," Brookings Institution, 2009, www.brookings.edu/research/papers/2009/08/education-gartner.

5 For definitions of smart power, a term that evolved in the mid-2000s, see Suzanne Nossel, "Smart Power," *Foreign Affairs* 83, no. 2 (2004) and Richard Armitage and Joseph Nye, Jr., "Final Report of the CSIS Commission on Smart Power," Center for Strategic and International Studies, 2007.

6 Catherine Powell, "Women and Girls in the Afghanistan Transition," Council on Foreign Relations, 2014, 15.

7 Office of the Special Advisor on Gender Issues and Advancement of Women, United Nations, "Landmark Resolution on Women, Peace and Security," www.un.org/womenwatch/osagi/wps/ (stressing "the importance of their equal participation and full involvement in all efforts for the maintenance and promotion of peace and security").

8 Ibid.

9 The White House, "United States National Action Plan on Women, Peace, and Security," 2011, 8 (noting "successful conflict prevention efforts must rest on key investments in women's economic empowerment, education, and health").

10 *Report of the Secretary General on Women, Peace, and Security* (Security Council document S/2002/1154), 16 October 2002 (identifying girls' education specifically as part of necessary social reconstruct efforts following armed conflict).

11 Barack Obama, "Statement by the President on Afghanistan," White House, 27 May 2014, www.whitehouse.gov/photos-and-video/video/2014/05/27/president-obama-makes-statement-afghanistan#transcript.

12 Catherine Powell, "Women and Girls in the Afghanistan Transition," Council on Foreign Relations, 2014, www.cfr.org/women/women-girls-afghanistan-transition/p33152 (discussing the fragile gains Afghan women and girls have made).

13 See, e.g., Valerie Hudson et al., *Sex and World Peace* (New York: Columbia University Press, 2012) (demonstrating that gender equality is one of the best predictors of a state's peacefulness, over other indicators including wealth and democracy); Theresa de Langis, "Across Conflict Lines: Women Mediating for Peace," The Institute for Inclusive Security, 2011. See also Alice Nderitu and Jacqueline O'Neill, "Getting to the Point of Inclusion: Seven Myths Standing in the Way of Women Waging Peace," The Institute for Inclusive Security, 2013, 6 (quoting General Lazaro Sumbeiywo, chief mediator in the Sudan negotiations, who noted, "A peace agreement without women participating at the highest level is a recipe for short-term, not long-term, solutions").

14 Kevin Watkins and Rebecca Winthrop, "What Focusing on Drones and Detention Misses," Brookings Institution, 20 April 2012; UN Women, *Women's Participation in Peace Negotiations: Connections between Presence and Influence*, October 2012, 4 (noting the relationship between social exclusion and intrastate conflict).

15 George Psacaropoulos and Harry Anthony Patrinos, "Returns to Investment in Education: A Further Update," *Education Economics* 12, no. 2 (August 2004): 111–34, 116. See also UN Girls' Education Initiative, "All Girls Achieving and Learning," 2013.

16 Mercy Tembon and Lucia Fort, eds, "Girls' Education in the 21st Century," Washington, DC: World Bank, 2008.

17 UN Girls' Education Initiative, "Investing in Girls Is the Right and Smart Thing to Do," www.ungei.org/resources/files/Infographic_Girls_Right_Smart_Full(1).jpg.

18 UN Girls' Education Initiative, "All Girls Achieving and Learning," 2013.

19 UN Girls' Education Initiative, "Investing in Girls Is the Right and Smart Thing to Do," 2014.

20 Public Broadcasting Service, "A Woman Among Warlords," *Wide Angle*, 11 September 2007, www.pbs.org/wnet/wideangle/episodes/a-woman-among-warlords/womens-rights-in-the-taliban-and-post-taliban-eras/66/.

21 Security Council Resolution 1193, 28 August 1998.

22 Security Council Resolution 1214, 8 December 1998.

23 Bureau of Democracy, Human Rights and Labor, "The Taliban's War against Women," US Department of State, 17 November 2011, www.state.gov/j/drl/rls/6185.htm.

24 Laura Bush, "Don't Abandon Afghan Women," *Washington Post*, 18 May 2012.

25 Catherine Powell, "Women and Girls in the Afghanistan Transition," Council on Foreign Relations, 2014 (discussing the fragile gains Afghan women and girls have made).

26 Word Bank, "Women's Role in Afghanistan's Future: Taking Stock of Achievements and Continued Challenges," 14 April 2014.

27 UNICEF, Regional Office in South Asia, *WASH for School Children in South Asia*, 2010, 10.

28 Islamic Republic of Afghanistan Ministry of Education, Directorate General of Planning and Evaluation, Directorate of EMIS, "Education Summary Report, Year 1388 (2009–2010)," http://moe.gov.af/Content/files/079_1388%20English%20Report.pdf.

29 Stefanie Nijssen, "The Peace Process and Afghanistan's Women," Civil-Military Fusion Centre, April 2012, 6.

30 Marit Glad, "Knowledge on Fire: Attacks on Education in Afghanistan," CARE International, September 2009, 39–41.

31 United Nations Human Rights Council, "Resolution Adopted by the Human Rights Council Addressing Attacks on School Children in Afghanistan," 23 June 2010 (A/HRC/14/15).

32 Margherita Stancati, "Women Playing an Unusually Public Role in Afghan Elections," *Wall Street Journal*, 2 April 2014.

33 Euan McKirdy, "Women could make the difference as Afghanistan turns out to vote," CNN.com, 9 April 2014.

34 James Dobbins, "Getting Beyond 2014 in Afghanistan," Statement delivered at a United States Institute of Peace Conference, Washington DC, 28 February 2014.

35 USAID, *Afghanistan: Education*, www.usaid.gov/afghanistan/education; Catherine Powell, "Women and Girls in the Afghanistan Transition," Council on Foreign Relations, June 2014, 5 (discussing USAID's investment in training women as midwives).

36 USAID, *Promote*, www.usaid.gov/afghanistan/promote.

37 Cynthia Enloe, *Bananas, Beaches, and Bases: Making Feminist Sense of International Politics, Second Edition* (Berkeley, Calif.: University of California Press, 2014).

38 Arne Duncan, "Back to School: Enhancing U.S. Education and Competitiveness," *Foreign Affairs* 89, no. 6 (November/December 2010).

39 H.R. 2780: Education for All Act (introduced 22 July 2013).

40 As one humanitarian worker observed by analogy, "We saw a drop in humanitarian assistance in Iraq and Kosovo after the international military forces withdrew." "Afghanistan: Military drawdown could hit aid flows," *IRIN*, 14 May 2014.

41 See also Catherine Powell, "Gender Indicators as Global Governance: This is Not Your Father's World Bank," forthcoming chapter in *Big Data, Big Challenges in Evidence-Based Policy Making*, ed. Kumar Jayasuriya (St Paul, Minn.: West Academic Press, 2014) (cautioning that the shift toward using instrumentalist arguments to advance women's rights in global governance has normative and practical implications for feminist goals).

42 Because donors, such as USAID, are held accountable to taxpayers and other stakeholders (beyond those who care about girls' education solely for the sake of girls), projects that are funded must often demonstrate that they meet a broad set of goals with which these stakeholders agree. Ibid.

43 Karen Engle, "'Calling in the Troops': The Uneasy Relationship among Women's Rights, Human Rights, and Humanitarian Intervention," *Harvard Human Rights Journal* 20 (Spring 2007): 189.
44 Catherine Powell, "Lifting Our Veil of Ignorance: Culture, Constitutionalism, and Women's Human Rights in Post-September 11 America," *Hastings Law Journal* 57 (2005): 331, 346, 375–377.
45 Aziza Ahmed, "When Men Are Harmed: Feminism, Queer Theory, and Torture at Abu Ghraib," *UCLA Journal of Islamic and Near Eastern Law* 11 (2012): 1.
46 Makau Matua, "Savages, Victims, and Saviors: The Metaphor of Human Rights," *Harvard International Law Journal* 42, no. 1 (Winter 2001): 201.
47 Antony Angie, *Imperialism, Sovereignty, and the Making of International Law* (Cambridge, Mass.: Cambridge University Press, 2007).
48 Nandi-Ndaitwah introduced the resolution when Namibia chaired the Security Council. Barbara Miller et al., "Women in Peace and Security through United Nations Security Resolution1325: Literature Review, Content Analysis of National Action Plans, and Implementation," George Washington University Institute of Global and International Studies, May 2014: 7.
49 Swanee Hunt, "The Rise of Rwanda's Women: Rebuilding and Reuniting a Nation," *Foreign Affairs* 93, no. 3 May/June 2014.

25 Financing girls' education

A reflection

Carol Bellamy

In a world without a lot of good news these days, there is one accomplishment in which we can take pride. With the principle of gender parity in schooling enshrined in the Millennium Development Goals (MDGs) of 2000, and since embedded in national education plans, the vast majority of girls around the world now complete primary school. While the greatest improvements have been seen in South Asia, some countries in Sub Saharan Africa have also made impressive progress from a low starting point. Ethiopia, in particular, has emerged as a global leader, increasing the number of children enrolled in primary education fivefold between 1994 and 2012, and introducing a special policy focus on girls' education.[1]

Still, according to the 2014 Education for All Global Monitoring Report, 15 percent of all countries will still not have achieved gender parity in primary schools by 201—and 7 percent will be very far from it; three-quarters of them in Sub Saharan Africa.[2] And girls still account for more than half—53 percent—of the children out of primary school worldwide.

The new Sustainable Development Goals (SDGs), currently being drafted at the UN, present a vision of development for the next 15 years that places an even greater emphasis on equity, justice and inclusiveness than the MDGs provided. The education targets shift focus from absolute numbers of children in primary school to the equitable inclusion of all children in education through to secondary school—by the year 2030.[3]

These are laudable goals but difficult ones to achieve. So it is time for a reality check on the necessary innovation and scale in programming and finance that will be needed. The children we are now targeting are the very hardest to reach, and the costs of their inclusion are going to be higher than average. With respect to girls, we also need a new mindset—one that looks beyond education itself to larger strategies addressing gender discrimination that will generate transformative social change.

Why finance based on "business as usual" won't work

Those still left behind by wider progress on education are, overwhelmingly, the most marginalized girls—the poorest and most exploited—those caught up in conflict, or living in rural areas, or those with disabilities. Very often, disadvantage breeds disadvantage, with girls who are out of school more vulnerable to trafficking and other forms of exploitation, from commercial sex work to hazardous child labor.

These are also girls who face rigid social norms and expectations around gender. As they grow up, the pressures imposed by cultural norms grow as well. For too many, puberty is seen as a signal for marriage and childbirth and marks the beginning of their subordination to husbands, instead of just to mothers and fathers.[4] In times of severe crisis, as in Syria today, child marriage often escalates. Among Syrian refugees living in Jordan, for example, the rate of child marriages has grown from 18 per cent of total marriages in 2012 to a shocking 32 percent in the first quarter of 2014, compared with a pre-war average within Syria of 13 percent of marriages.[5]

Even for those who do not marry young, the school environment may undermine their learning and accelerate their dropout rates. Poor quality schools often do not provide safe, supportive, and welcoming environments, and, all too often, the discrimination girls experience elsewhere is reflected in the classroom, with the expectations of teachers and students skewed by traditional perceptions of gender and by a chronic lack of female teachers to provide much-needed role models.

If their schools are far from home, girls face the risk of assault en route. If their schools are under-resourced, they will most likely lack private latrines and washing facilities—a particular issue for adolescents who are menstruating, which has been cited in studies as a factor in why girls abandon their education.[6] Few of these girls have access to alternative family or community structures that provide a route back into schooling, job training, or skills development.

As a result, "business as usual" approaches to expand the number of school places will not suffice. The challenges that keep girls out of school, prevent them from thriving there, and cause them to drop out do not begin and end within the boundaries of the school itself. What we need is a combination of three distinct investments within the education sector, along with wider social and economic reforms that address the conditions of families living in extreme poverty.

Investment within the education sector

Our ambition must be to ensure that even the most disadvantaged girl has access to a school close to home that respects her safety and privacy, gives her a good-quality education, and, above all, values her presence. It is difficult, if not impossible, to put a precise dollar figure on what is needed in terms of global finance. But we do know what works and, therefore, where available resources should be targeted.

Invest in schools close to home

In Afghanistan, for example, the introduction of village-based schools in Ghor Province in the north of the country, with support from Catholic Relief Services, has increased enrollment and resulted in better test scores for all students. Girls have benefitted disproportionately and the gender gap was eliminated completely within the first year of this initiative.[7]

Invest in girl-friendly schools

In Burkina Faso, gender-friendly schools called BRIGHT schools, built in deprived and under-served rural areas, have boosted the enrollment of all children aged 5 to 12 by 20 percent, with girls—once again—benefitting disproportionately. These schools provide a mix of interventions including separate latrines for boys and girls, canteens, take-home rations, and textbooks, as well as local advocacy and mobilization.[8]

Invest in more female teachers

Scholarships targeted to women will help close the gender gap among teachers and, in turn, provide needed role models for girl students. In South Sudan, women make up about 65 percent of the post-conflict population, yet less than 10 percent of all teachers are women. A recent program has directed financial and material incentives to over 4,500 girls, so they can complete secondary school and enter teacher training programs.[9]

Returning to Afghanistan, an estimated four million children remain out of school—60 percent of them girls. The Global Partnership for Education (GPE), which I was privileged to chair for a number of years, is working with the government to mobilize communities and to provide funds and flexible approaches to get girls into school. One-third of GPE's program implementation grant for Afghanistan is allocated to increasing the number of female teachers in the country's most remote districts.[10]

And in Yemen, GPE and other partners have worked with the Ministry for Education to train and deploy more than 1,500 female teachers. At the same time, GPE partners launched a girls' education campaign using local media and traditional community and religious leaders, and also eliminated school fees, so that poor families could afford to send their daughters to school. As a result, girls' enrollment increased by 23 percent in the targeted schools between 2006 and 2012.[11]

Investment in wider social reforms

As the Yemen example demonstrates, the value of investment within the school system can be strengthened by investment in wider social reforms to remove obstacles to their schooling, including poverty and discriminatory norms.

Invest in anti-poverty measures

Families living in poverty face tough choices about where and how to spend meager resources. For some, the cost of education is just too high, especially for daughters. Anti-poverty measures incentivize girls' education by eliminating dependence on child labor. Cash transfers to households, granted on the condition that children attend school, have been shown to work. In Bangladesh, the Female Secondary School Stipend Program has shown progress on girls' school enrollment and on delaying marriage.

Invest in national efforts to counter gender discrimination

Investment is essential to encourage governments and communities to enforce laws mandating compulsory education and a minimum age for legal marriage. Media and information campaigns modify age-old beliefs around gender and make the case for girls' education. One example is the "Hey Girls, Let's Go to School" campaign in Turkey, a partnership between public institutions, civil-society organizations, and volunteers, that has resulted in the enrollment of an estimated 350,000 additional children.[12]

Parents need reassurance that educating their girls will have real benefits. A study in India, for example, found that providing villagers with precise information about the availability of jobs for girls with a secondary education resulted in higher numbers of teenage girls remaining in school, delaying marriage and looking for paid work.[13]

Investment to target the girls hardest-to-reach

Investment in the hardest-to-reach should better target children lagging behind by geography and other demographic characteristics.

Invest in educational support for pregnant girls and young mothers

Pregnant girls and young mothers need special support to remain in school, including childcare and counseling. Policy alone is not enough here: multi-sectoral approaches that include sexual and reproductive health, child protection, and economic support are all needed alongside narrower education policies on this issue—and, of course, all require donor support.

Invest in non-formal education

Non-formal education is often seen as "second best," but for some girls it is the only option. Non-formal education also often generates innovative approaches to teach girls basic skills and, quite often, provide a route back into formal schooling.

Invest alongside new partners

I am encouraged by growing examples of successful collaboration with the private sector, given its vast resources and reach. One prime example is the Girls Education Challenge (GEC), funded by Britain's Department for International Development (DFID), which aims to help some of the world's poorest and most marginalized girls in 17 countries access education. The GEC funds strategic partnerships with businesses, exploring innovative ways to improve learning opportunities for girls in remote and marginalized communities.

For example, Discovery Communications, home of the multiple platforms of the Discovery channels, is investing £12.3 million in girls' education in Ghana, Kenya, and Nigeria, which DFID will match. The program will also establish 1,000 Learning Centers in schools, providing advanced technology and exciting video programming, along with media training for 8,000 teachers to improve the classroom experience. This initiative will also collaborate with girls and gender experts to develop nationally broadcast television talk shows, where issues of gender are woven into the public dialogue. It will also train and support communities to develop their own action plans to address gender marginalization by supporting clubs for girls in and out of school, which encourage them to become more educated in order to succeed.[14]

Here I want to flag collaborations forged successfully by the Global Partnership for Education. GPE recognizes that education is everybody's business. While GPE's key partners are always governments, and they remain firmly in the driver's seat, the partnership also works with donors, international organizations, civil-society, private sector corporations, and many others to deliver good-quality and inclusive education. In my view, the five principles that guide GPE's approach to aid effectiveness provide a useful checklist for others to follow.

- First is country ownership: GPE partner countries design, implement, and monitor their own education plans, and they must provide some measure of local, domestic finance.
- Second is alignment: GPE funding is aligned to the public financial management and procurement systems of our partner countries. In other words, it works with the grain of the country concerned.
- Third is harmonization: GPE partners are encouraged to coordinate their work and ensure that their external funding is, once again, aligned to the country systems.
- Fourth is managing for results: GPE encourages its partners to track progress in the implementation of their education plans.
- Finally, mutual accountability. Every partner in a country's education sector is accountable for its actions.[15]

Conclusion

Why go through all this trouble? Why commit resources desperately needed elsewhere to the education of girls? Why try so hard to get our investments and policies right?

The moral case is overwhelming: education is a fundamental human right that helps to forge more equitable societies. It is also a pathway to wider economic and social objectives grounded in basic morality. It helps to break cycles of poverty and poor health, with adolescent girls in school less likely to marry early and against their will, less likely to die in childbirth, less vulnerable to disease, including HIV and AIDS. Educated girls are more likely to acquire the information and skills that lead to increased earnings.[16] They are also more likely to have healthy babies of their own and to send their own children onto school. It has been estimated that half of the reductions in maternal and infant mortality over the past four decades can be attributed to the expansion of girls' education, especially when they finish primary school and complete at least lower secondary school.[17] As the current chair of the board of End Child Prostitution, Child Pornography and Trafficking of Children for Sexual Purposes (ECPAT), an international alliance, I'm also well aware of just how vital education is to protect girls against appalling exploitation and just how vulnerable girls with no education are to the perpetrators of such abuse.

While the moral case for investment should be enough to persuade any policymaker, it is also important to spell out the macroeconomic bottom line. Countries with greater gender parity in primary and secondary education are more likely to have higher economic growth. Drawing on World Bank research and data and UNESCO education statistics, one recent study estimates that the economic cost to 65 developing countries of failing to educate girls to the same standard as boys is a staggering $92 billion each year, just under the combined $103 billion annual aid budget of OECD countries in 2007. India alone misses out on potential economic growth worth about $33 billion per year. Other major losers include Turkey ($20 billion) and Russia ($9.8 billion).[18]

Why then so much entrenched resistance, why so many hurdles? While the moral and economic arguments are clear for greater investment in girls' education, and more efficient allocation of limited resources, we must acknowledge in conclusion, the "elephant in the room": politics. Gender equity is intensely political. So are poverty reduction, equitable economic growth, and peace and security, of course. All work in development and human rights is inherently political, but I'm not aware of the same pressure to justify investment in these areas, as we are always asked to do for girls' education.

And, as we know, educating girls can bring transformative social changes in the structures of families, communities, and entire societies. So, of course, the work is likely to meet with resistance from those who fear such change, no matter how compelling the larger arguments in its favor. Those of us working in this field need to be aware that even the most carefully targeted and well-resourced initiative is likely to run into road-blocks. Those of us drawing up the plans for girls' education, hunting down the resources, and spending the money need more than sound organizational, budgeting, and management skills. We also need a sound political radar to ensure that our efforts work with, rather than against, the grain of local realities.

Notes

1 Abeyot Nega, *Improving Education Quality, Equity and Access in Ethiopia: Findings from the Young Lives School Component. Ethiopia Policy Brief 1. Addis Ababa: Young Lives in Ethiopia* (Addis Ababa: UK Aid and the Ministry of Foreign Affairs, Netherlands, 2012), www.younglives.org.uk/files/policy-papers/yl-ethiopia-pb1-education.
2 UNESCO, *Teaching and Learning: Achieving Quality for All* (Paris: UNESCO, 2014).
3 United Nations. *Outcome Document—Open Working Group on Sustainable Development Goals* (New York: United Nations, 2014), http://sustainabledevelopment.un.org/focussdgs.html.
4 Equality Now, *Protecting the Girl Child. Using the Law to End Child, Early and Forced Marriage and Related Human Rights Violations* (New York: Equality Now, 2014).
5 UNICEF Jordan, *A Study on Early Marriage in Jordan 2014* (Amman: UNICEF Jordan, 2014), http://childrenofsyria.info/wp-content/uploads/2014/07/UNICEFJordan_EarlyMarriageStudy2014.pdf.
6 Marni Sommer, "Where the Education System and Women's Bodies Collide: The Social and Health Impact of Girls' Experiences of Menstruation and Schooling in Tanzania," *Journal of Adolescence* 33, no. 4 (2010): 521–29.
7 Dana Burde and Leigh L. Linden, *The Effect of Village-based Schools: Evidence from a Randomized Controlled Trial in Afghanistan*, Working Paper Series No.18039 (Cambridge, Mass.: National Bureau of Economic Research, 2010).
8 Harounan Kazianga, Dan Levy, Leigh L. Linden, and Matt Sloan, *The Effects Of Girl-Friendly Schools: Evidence From The Bright School Construction Program In Burkina Faso*, Research Working Paper No. 18115 (Cambridge, Mass.: National Bureau of Economic Research, 2012).
9 UNESCO, *Teaching and Learning: Achieving Qquality for All* (Paris: UNESCO, 2014).
10 Launched in 2002 with a secretariat at the World Bank in Washington, DC, GPE is the only multi-lateral partnership dedicated to education. Designed to support national education plans with technical assistance—to coordinate and galvanize aid and improve its effectiveness—GPE currently works in 59 developing countries, with fragile states and girls' education among its areas of focus. GPE estimates that it has helped nearly 22 million children attend school, 10 million of them girls. Former Prime Minister of Australia, Julia Guillard recently replaced Carol Bellamy as chair. Alice Albright is CEO. (GPE, 2014) GPE (2014a) Aid effectiveness web-page, www.globalpartnership.org/focus-areas/aid-effectiveness.
11 GPE, *Factsheet: Girls' Education* (Washington, DC: Global Partnership for Education, 2014), www.globalpartnership.org/content/girls-education.
12 UNICEF and UIS, *Turkey Country Study, Global Initiative on Out-of-School Children* (Ankara: UNICEF and the UNESCO Institute for Statistics (UIS), 2012), www.uis.unesco.org/Education/Documents/turkey-oosci-report-2012-en.pdf.
13 Robert, T. Jensen, *Economic Opportunities and Gender Differences in Human Capital: Experimental Evidence for India*, NBER Working Paper

No. 16021 (Cambridge, Mass.: National Bureau of Economic Research, 2010).

14 UK Government, *Girls Education Challenge (GEC)*, www.gov.uk/girls-education-challenge.

15 GPE, *Aid effectiveness*, www.globalpartnership.org/focus-areas/aid-effectiveness.

16 UNESCO, *Gender and Education for All, The Leap to Equality*, EFA Global Monitoring Report (Paris: UNESCO, 2013).

17 Emmanuela Gakidou, Krycia Cowling, Rafael Lozano, and Christopher J. L. Murray, "Increased Educational Attainment and its Effect on Child Mortality in 175 Countries between 1970 and 2009: A Systematic Analysis," *The Lancet* 376, no. 9745 (2010): 959–974.

18 Plan, *Paying the Price: The Economic Cost of Failing to Educate Girls* (Woking: Plan Ltd, 2008), http://plan-international.org/files/global/publications/education/girls_education_economics.pdf.

26 A short history of the long and continuing struggle to eliminate child marriage

An African case study

Judith Bruce and Annabel Erulkar

Every year, some 14 million girls around the world marry by the age of 18—that is, as children. Today, following decades of hard work by researchers and advocates, the phenomenon is firmly embedded in the rhetoric of global public policy for what it plainly is—a fundamental human rights abuse.

In 2000, the US State Department first sent cables to country desk officers seeking assessments of the magnitude of forced and "early" marriage. Evidence of interest from the foreign policy establishment was signaled more recently with the publication by the Council on Foreign Relations in 2014 of *Child Brides: Global Consequences.*[1] The Elders, a group of prominent global leaders, also founded *Girls Not Brides*, a formal advocacy organization on the subject. And child marriage was a core subject of the recent Girls' Summit[2] in Britain, and prominent in the Girls' Declaration.[3]

Still, even as the phenomenon is highlighted far and wide, the poorest girls in the poorest communities are not receiving the resources they need to avoid becoming victims of forced sex, inside and outside of marriage. Child marriage not only violates their human rights and endangers their health, but often anchors them and subsequent generations in poverty. Eliminating child marriage ought to be central to all human rights, economic development, and poverty alleviation initiatives. What can we do to move from well-meaning dialogue to concrete actions that make a difference?

This chapter will review the long road it has taken to get as far as we have come, but first, the headlines. Here are the actions we strongly recommend, if we hope to make real progress:

- We must prioritize investments in the 113 locations in 27 countries where more than 15 percent of the girls are still married under age 15. These levels occur in every part of the developing world, and reach as high as 58 percent in Zinder, Niger. Marriages under 18 are ill-advised, but those forced on girls under age 15 are unambiguously "child" marriages and provide the bedrock of poor health, poverty, and lifelong subjugation of females. Such investment is also warranted by the availability of a strong, well-documented field experience in Ethiopia (described below), which demonstrates the feasibility of preventing the youngest child marriages and effectively engaging those already married into "married girls clubs" in poor rural communities.[4]

- It is thus time for bi-lateral, multi-lateral, and larger institutional donors to make specific commitments to eliminate child marriage by divvying up the "hot spots." Virtually all the places with high levels under 15 are in "program" countries of bi-laterals, which have made public commitments to end child marriage.

- We must tighten our policy focus and program investments on girls in late childhood into early adolescence, the window from ages ten to 14.[5] Policy and "norm" change will require the strong underpinning of ground targeted, evidenced-based investments. The returns on high visibility advocacy are diminishing, and there is a risk public statements will take precedence over—or be substituted for—public spending. Even where good laws are in place, there is very little will or incentive to implement them. Individual cases may be heard, but there is rarely justice for girls.[6] Recent research on the impact of early sexual abuse (inside and outside of marriage) underscores the catastrophic consequences individually and inter-generationally. Our programmatic emphasis therefore must be on prevention in young populations.

- We must frame child marriage as more than a cultural practice and underscore its economic determinants and consequences. Marrying girls as children, as a response to poverty, seasonal scarcities, and emergency circumstances,[7] is part of an economic strategy and needs to be understood as such.

- Ultimately, if we are to serve girls, we must see them, disaggregate their experiences, and craft age- and gender-specific programs.

- Adolescent girls—especially the poorest girls in the poorest communities—most at risk of child marriage are currently embedded in (but not served by) many other policies—youth, women, indigenous people, children's policies. Further puberty, a vital agespan for girls (age 10–14),[8] has virtually no explicit, gender-differentiated policies associated with it.

This chapter is organized chronologically to reflect an historical sequence of events and learning. A great deal of intellectual and policy work had to precede the on-the-ground investment in Ethiopia by the Population Council, which is the basis of this case study. The ways in which we gained donor attention are important to explain, including the resistances we encountered, some form of which will likely be met in every new intervention. It is thus worth sharing our experience— how we selected and presented quantitative and qualitative data; how we constructed successful arguments for gatekeepers and stakeholders; how we uncovered and addressed the strong emotional attachment to marriage as a "safe place."

We begin by summarizing what we learned from early "campaigns" against child marriage in the United States and international forums. We then present a description of our work in Ethiopia, which arguably provides the best examples so far of scalable programs that have actually moved up the age of marriage and fostered delayed child-bearing among married girls.

Developing constituencies for a campaign and investments to end child marriage

Making adolescent girls and child marriage visible within other policy categories

From the UN conferences in Mexico City in 1975, to Nairobi, Copenhagen, and Beijing, the international community over two decades turned its attention to discrimination against women and began to call attention to the particular needs of adolescent girls. At that time, and still today, girls lived in the shadow of other categories such as "women," "youth," "children," and "marginalized indigenous communities." Girls were/are the population most affected by child marriage and the exclusive victims of genital mutilation (usually practiced in childhood in preparation for a "decent" marriage). With adolescent girls accounting for half of all first births in the developing world, they were/are principal victims of maternal mortality, which disproportionately kills the youngest first-time mothers.[9] They were/are the most at risk of HIV/AIDS, although the age and gender impacts of the epidemic were not firmly established until after 2000. In order to bring attention to child marriage, girls had to become core subjects, not hidden under other policy "headers" or buried in other categories.

Adolescent girls were/are often treated as a subset of women (junior women, or, as the phrase often went, the second half of "women and girls"). From an analytic point of view, it is important to understand that women are the survivors of girlhood, and some girls never make it. Seeing and understanding women's lives does not automatically mean seeing and understanding girls.

Conventionally, the public policy agenda defines "youth" as ages 15 to 30 (sometimes as high as 35), which excludes puberty, the most sensitive point in a girl's life and an age at which most of the worst abuses are perpetrated. Today, these youth programs continue to absorb substantial resources, often raised in the name of girls, but with no clear plan to prioritize or reach them. Indeed, youth programs continue to attract older youths, often in their twenties, along with disproportionately male and socially favored populations, such as those unmarried, in school, and native-born.[10] Youth movements often serve as platforms for young male political engagement, and youth clubs expand the male youth space—often at the expense of younger females who enjoy little or "no space" of their own.[11]

"Youth" programs are crowd-pleasing but ignore the gendered differentials that begin at birth and intensify in the run-up to puberty. "Child-friendly spaces" are still what places for girls are called in emergency or refugee settings, for example, and these rarely provide the peer support or dedicated programming young adolescent girls need.[12]

Crucially, the policy architecture has a serious gap between childhood and early adolescence. No country we know of has specific policies for 10- to 14-year-olds apart from school attendance (with one exception, Rwanda, which is implementing the first 12-Plus program).[13] For girls especially, there are no meaningful benchmarks apart from going to school. In too many places, it remains completely possible that a girl will not be "seen" by a healthcare professional after her immunizations, ending around the age of three, and the next prioritized connecting point—a prescribed number of prenatal appointments, which typically occur no later than age 18, when she and half of her peers are pregnant.[14]

Indigenous struggles and the politics of marginal populations are typically dominated by male leadership, with rare exceptions such as Rigoberta Menchu in Guatemala. Although females are present, male agendas get attention, so much so that in resolving conflicts, impunity is often granted for crimes against females. Sexual enslavement of girls including so-called marriages, as we are seeing most recently in the actions of Boko Haram in Northern Nigeria, are key strategies of subjugation but are rarely dealt with.

And finally, though unintentionally we are not always well served by the emergence of a policy emphasis on "gender," which suggests that what happens to males and females is somehow equivalent, rather than explicitly recognizing that the young female is far more likely to experience extreme human rights abuses than the young male. This false equivalency is exposed if you ask boys if they would like to be a girl. They would not, and they can detail why. Without focusing on the gender-differentiated experiences, especially of the youngest adolescents, most countries not only miss child marriage, they also miss girls.

Data presentation to see the youngest girls at risk in the run up to child marriage

Data displays and analyses in the past also often obfuscated the full abuse of child marriage. Typically, child marriage figures were shown at the national level and recognized as prevalent among those aged 15 to 19. This presentation concealed the wide sub-national variations in practice, and therein provided cover for the assertion that child marriage is a "cultural practice." With sub-national data, one is able to see often-dramatic variations in practice that belie the assertion that child marriage is an intractable "tradition." National prevalence data obscure the largest populations of girls left behind. "Hot spot" data, by contrast, show where resources should be directed. Mapping child marriage is essential to determining where investment is most needed.

National prevalence data also offer a human rights abuse "average," rather than revealing by what age and how many girls have been affected. Presenting data by using life table methods, by contrast, discloses exactly what proportions of girls are married by specific ages, such as 15 or 18. They often result in higher, more striking percentages overall and give a more accurate picture of affected girls. For example, when we first began work in West Africa, the prevalence of child marriage among girls aged 15 to 19 in Burkina Faso was identified at just about 34 percent. However, the proportion of girls actually married by age 18 was 62 percent. A more recent analysis of Niger shows that whereas 59 percent of girls 15–19 were married, 75 percent were married by age 18 and an astonishing 36 percent by age 15, which means the disinvestment in girls starts very early. Thus, programs need to reach girls in late childhood.

Providing data on both the proportion married by age 15 and by age 18 is essential to persuade skeptical policymakers because—despite the Convention on the Rights of the Child and other human rights instruments—many still do not believe that childhood and its protections extend to age 18. According to the World Policy Analysis Center, even 10 years ago when this issue was most contentious, the legal age of marriage (with or without parental consent) in most countries exceeded 15. Presenting data not only by sub-national region but also disaggregated by age citing the proportions of girls married under age

15 and under age 18, allows policymakers to select either age or both as problematic.

Life table data also enable more strategic program decisions about the timing of meaningful interventions. If a girl is married at 15, "something happens" before then. Preventive actions must get ahead of the curve, perhaps as early as age 10. It is very rare, for example, that girls "drop out of school" to get married—the reality is that they are "dropped" out of school or never there from the start. Their marriages cannot be constructed as chosen because of their age. They marry in the absence of other accepted social identities or economic alternatives or process of representation through which to protest marriages. This is important to remember, because even as literal, sanctified child marriage may fade, the sexual exploitation of girls will endure without continued vigilance.

Shifting the language

Beginning some 15 to 20 years ago, the UN, the US Agency for International Development (USAID) and the US State Department began to sponsor meetings about "early marriage and harmful traditional practice." The authors had the experience of presenting at many of these sessions. There was frequent discomfort with and outright political objection to the phrase "child marriage." Underpinning explicitly political considerations was/is a psychological and cultural bias to see marriage as an inevitable outcome for girls, but also as a good outcome and "a safe place." The labeling battle was crucial. "Early marriage" and "early pregnancy" are terms that portray girls as simply precocious and making a positive "adult" transition. Other common terms out of academic sociology such as "transitions to adulthood"— intentionally insipid—suggest a far more positive and leisurely transition than girls actually experience. "Early marriage" is also an easier concept than "child marriage" for some to digest, because it obscures the disquieting image of millions of girls denied their childhood, and, in preparation for marriage, often deprived of their autonomy and even of parts of their body through female genital mutilation.

A pivotal moment came in 2002 at a very high-level United Nations Children Fund/United Nations Population Fund-sponsored panel, and during an explicit conversation with program organizers. My (Bruce) presentation entitled "Child Marriage: the Largest Regularly Occurring Human Rights Abuse in the World" was refused until it was presented with a slightly different title, an edited slide titled "Early/Child Marriage." The term "child marriage" gained increasing acceptance in the years following, but took root only after the 2008 US elections brought new leadership to Washington.

While there has been significant progress in moving from "early" to "child" marriage, we still are left with the problem of the word "marriage" itself. In the 1990s and early in the 2000s, the family values lobby used the word "marriage" to sanitize everything around it. During the administration of US President George W. Bush, much admired for his investments to fight HIV/AIDS in Africa through the President's Emergency Plan for AIDS Relief (PEPFAR), "child marriage" was sensitive, because policymakers were beholden to fundamentalists who were indiscriminately pro-marriage. The problem was/is not only political.[15] Demographers also have attachments to marriage as an analytic category. Marriage is therefore often treated as a far more specific and stable condition than it actually is. Whereas a category like "child" is very exact in definition (under the age of 18 and subject to specific protections), marriage is variable across contexts, often unstable, and also suggests a voluntary choice. Yet by legal definition, child marriages (especially those under 15) cannot be considered consensual. Many girls do not know the person, who is often far older, to whom they are married. The term "marriage" is used to cover a range of arrangements that are culturally supported, economically anchored, and assure unimpeded access to young female bodies with impunity.

Ethiopia as a case study of policy transformation and on-the-ground investment

Seeing girls as married children

When we began work on child marriage in Sub Saharan Africa more than a decade ago, we continued to confront skepticism from policymakers and public health professionals. Once married, girls were considered to have assumed the status of adult women, and it was assumed that they had the same access to services. In 2000, Ethiopia's Revised Family Code outlawed marriage below age 18. Many in the capital, Addis Ababa, considered child marriage a cultural practice confined to a few rural areas and were unaware of the magnitude of the problem. Further, they would portray the practice as a positive bond between families. Local gatekeepers commonly denied the human cost to individual girls, asserting that while engaged "young," most were not forced into co-residence or sexual relations with their husbands until they were ready, assertions not supported by Population Council research among girls themselves.[16] We also confronted resistance to the plausibility that economic considerations may drive the practice, not simply a desire by families to protect their daughters. We had to point out that many practices harm girls in the guise of "protection," such as removing them from school to save their reputations, cutting their genitals to safeguard eligibility for marriage, or marrying them as ostensible protection from HIV infection.[17]

These embedded values needed to be challenged by quantitative and qualitative data. An initial mapping exercise established the extent of child marriage and its geographic variation, and assisted in garnering support for work in the Amhara region. Life table data, disaggregated by sub-national regions in colorful maps at a joint meeting of Ethiopian and European parliamentarians, started a productive conversation. They visualized considerable variation in marriage rates and provided evidence that marriage is not a bedrock national tradition. At the time, rates in Ethiopia were 22 percent nationally, but twice that rate in the Amhara region, where nearly 50 percent of all girls were married by their 15th birthday. Despite preferences for other regions on different grounds, the sheer number of girls at risk in Amhara—the second largest region in Ethiopia—defined where we needed to work.

The instability and unseen risks of marriage

The HIV epidemic in Ethiopia was, at the outset, affecting slightly more females than males. Our work there thus immediately initiated a contentious discussion of the contribution of child marriage to the HIV epidemic, with family values-oriented policymakers resisting the idea that child marriage may elevate HIV risk. We believed, to the contrary, that child marriage transits girls into an unsafe zone of frequent and unprotected sexual activity, economic dependence on men, and power imbalances that translate into high levels of marital dissolution—all factors raising their risk of infection over time. Multi-country studies provided strong cross-sectional data suggesting that married populations aged 25 to 29 indeed show higher HIV prevalence than sexually active unmarried females at comparable ages.[18]

These studies, in turn, suggest three different strategies to reduce HIV risk: male circumcision, condom use, and the elimination of "early" marriage.[8] There were constituencies for the first two, but many saw marriage as immutable and/or protective. In the Ethiopian setting, we arguedthe case against child marriage in the context of an HIV epidemic using data analysis showing that as girls under 18 are rarely sexually active before marriage they are therefore better protected from HIV by remaining unmarried.

Another unconventional and consequential insight from our research is that the marriages into which the girls are forced are rarely stable. When we began our work, Demographic and Health Surveys (DHS) data indicated that about 8 percent of girls in Amhara were married and divorced by age 20. In our baseline sample, the number reached 12 percent. In the HIV context, the consequences of divorce are especially risky, as many child brides flee their circumstances and may have few choices apart from transactional sex to sustain themselves and their children.

Given this threat and others, we commissioned projections across Africa of the proportion of adolescent girls who would become single mothers with dependent children at some point in their reproductive years. For Ethiopia, the number is well over 50 percent—a mid-level for the continent where figures rise to a startling 92 percent in the case of Liberia.[19] In the Ethiopian case, single motherhood is more typically the result of divorce or widowhood than of having a child out of wedlock. Moreover, girls in polygamous unions, informally abandoned, or with a non-supportive husband, are not included in this count, which is thus a low estimate. By age 30, 30 percent of Ethiopia's adolescent girls will already be single mothers, with chances much greater for those who are married and bear children in their adolescence. Child marriage in Amhara thus lays a powerful foundation for poverty and single motherhood.[20]

Encouraging commitment to ending child marriage

Data-based arguments and quantitative projections were powerful tools, but often unspoken resistance required additional argumentation. We experimented with different ways of conveying the realities of girls' lives using their own voices and overcoming social distances, policy, and language barriers in the process. To guarantee authenticity and avoid filtering these voices through an outsider's perspective, we provided quotes from young married girls in original Amharic and had them read out by female interviewers who had gone into the field. This methodology contrasted with many other qualitative studies. We did not employ focus groups, which we find distorting and inappropriate for the youngest girls. We did not just visit girls for one interview, but carried out private discussions over three visits, which gave them time to become more comfortable and more candid. The interviews were tape-recorded, transcribed, and translated into English.

Despite all this, many among the relatively elite Ethiopians working in international NGOs were not ready for the message. Many reacted to the trauma conveyed by the voices of the girls we interviewed with the claim that we had misunderstood local cultures and traditions, as well as the good intentions of parents and in-laws. There was a tendency to deny the human costs of the practice. By contrast, there was more receptivity and understanding at the sub-national level. Government and civil society officials living closer to the conditions of poverty and ill health that sustain child marriage were ready to act.

Major steps in crafting the Berhane Hewan program strategy and crafting a sustainable delivery system

In preparing for the intervention and indeed in designing it, engagement with parents and other duty-bearers was essential, while maintaining the critical understanding that girls themselves were our core clients. We engaged with the community to gain trusted access and crafted multi-level program content for community leaders, households, and also especially influential males. While not ignoring this context, we nonetheless focused on unmediated engagement with girls, believing firmly that no-one can "stand in" for them.

As one example, the public health community insisted that, whereas girls may be engaged or betrothed during childhood, their sexual relationships started much later, and only when they were "ready." As mentioned briefly, our baseline research tested the assertion that early marriage does not necessarily condone immediate sexual relationships. Our data found that of the high percentage of girls married as children two thirds of them reported that they had sex before menses and for a vast majority, the initiation was forced. This quote is typical:

> I hate early marriage. I was married at an early age, and my in-laws forced me to sleep with my husband. He made me suffer all night. After that, whenever it starts to get dark, I get worried, thinking it will be like that. This is what I hate the most.
> Amhara girl, age 11, married at age 5, first sex at age 9[21]

Still, our findings were disputed, with many in the policy community continuing to doubt the validity of the girls' testimony. It took two years following this formative research to secure funding for a program to delay the age at marriage and support married girls. Many donors and even some among our own saw this as an impossible task and preferred "trickle down" social change to a bold ground-level intervention.

Another unexpected challenge was the construction of marriage norms as cultural. We recognize child marriage as a market-influenced decision, not just a matter of tradition and social standing. Interviews with families made that clear. Our program "Berhane Hewan" included the provision of economic incentives (including a goat and support of school supplies) in exchange for benchmarked levels of schooling and delay of marriage. Donors who feared that such exchanges would be interpreted as offensive, finally relented. Still, this aspect of the program was the least understood and most criticized, but possibly the most effective.

Another dimension of our "market" theory of child marriage was to re-price girls as a "class." This required that we define a necessary "tipping point"—a minimum proportion of eligible girls in a given community that would make continued schooling and delayed marriage a norm and not an exception. It was important that girls with more education and new skills found a place in their community during and after the intervention. Engaging the majority of eligible girls and households in our program created an enabling environment, as did new, accessible, community-sponsored structures, where young women of different ages—married and unmarried—could safely meet (up to four times a week for the unmarried girls aged 12 to 15). These ranged from modestly renovated small buildings to simple mats placed under a tree. We also recruited a local cadre of slightly older female mentors to support them—young women, widely known and respected in their communities, who could act on behalf of girls as surrogate social workers. Building their capacity has meant that, there is an interest group to sustain the effort to end child marriage after project funds come to an end.

Our aim was not just to launch a program but to build a movement by engaging communities in taking concrete actions, enlisting a "tipping point" of households and girls, and building a cadre of local women leaders to anchor them. Our work links philosophically to Brazilian educator and philosopher Paulo Freire's idea of giving voice and place, combined with hard economics. Girls at risk of child marriage live alongside others already married. Believing that our female mentors could guide multiple activities, we also established clubs for married girls (of which over 70 percent are currently contracepting). Within the demographic of girls at risk of child marriage, aged eight to 15, we distinguished two important subgroups: those who had the opportunity to attend a local school, and those who had no nearby schooling options but for whom a regularly available girls' space with social, economic, and some cognitive content could be provided. These spaces were designed to increase social capital and set up the connections young girls need to help build their lives and defend against pressures for forced marriage.

We also observed a link between the conditions of girls in Amhara villages and nearby cities. Many of them flee to escape child marriage, or following divorce, to the regional capital, Bahir Dar. So we established a twin program there, "Biruh Tesfa," for girls aged eight to 20, focusing on those living apart from parents, often in "domestic service." Their situation, once investigated, often revealed dire conditions of virtual slavery, including the exchange of sex for gifts or money.

Conclusion

Much has been written about the "Berhane Hewan" program in Ethiopia, which happily is now considered a benchmark intervention. To summarize some of the results:

- At the end line, girls aged 10 to 14 in pilot sites were one-tenth as likely to be married as girls in the control sites.
- They were three times more likely to be in school (after controlling for other factors in the analysis, such as age and levels of poverty).
- Married girls were more than three times as likely to use family planning and delay a first childbirth.[22,23]

The program demonstrated that it is possible to engage with traditional communities to build social, economic, and health assets for extremely isolated girls, and to raise the age of marriage in a short time period. Moreover, we were able to achieve an authentic understanding of all the ways in which child marriage links to poverty. We are now extending our initial, ongoing experiment to test different forms and combinations of economic incentives. We are also moving this approach elsewhere in Ethiopia, Tanzania, and Burkina Faso.[24]

Individuals, families, and communities in all three countries face tremendous frustration. They know "something is wrong." They are beginning to question child marriage, but they feel powerless to change it and they do not want to feel judged. It is necessary to authenticate their desire for a better life without authenticating the practice of child marriage. These programs are now subject to evaluations using the most rigorous research methods. There is enough information now to craft a specific investment plan for the 113 sub-national "hot spots" in the developing world, where 15 percent or more of girls are married under age 15. We have been privileged to work as partners in Ethiopia on an evidence-based program that has improved lives and shaped opportunities for girls and their families in one community, and also serves as a powerful tool for advocacy elsewhere. We hope that our experience supports many others in making this journey.

Acknowledgements

Rachel Friedman for her assistance in editing.
Dana Smiles for her assistance in production.
We are indebted to Jen Redner for providing an overview of Washington-based efforts to end child marriage from her vantage point as an active member of the Coalition for Adolescent Girls and as Co-Chair of Girls not Brides.

Notes

1 Gayle Lemmon and Lynn ElHarake, *Child Brides, Global Consequences* (New York: Council on Foreign Relations, 2014).

2 Department of International Development, "Girl Summit 2014: A Future Free from FGM and Child and Forced Marriage," conference, Walworth Academy, London, UK, 22 July 2014.

3 The Girl Effect, "The Girl Declaration," http://www.girleffect.org/2015-beyond/the-declaration.

4 Annabel Erulkar and Eunice Muthengi, "Evaluation of *Berhane Hewan*: A Program to Delay Child Marriage in Rural Ethiopia," *International Perspectives on Sexual and Reproductive Health* 35, no. 1 (2009): 6–14.

5 Erica Chong, Kelly Hallman, and Martha Brady, *Investing When it Counts* (New York: Population Council, 2006). Currently being updated for publication in 2015.

6 Equality Now Adolescent Girls' Legal Defense Fund, "Learning from Cases of Girls' Rights," Equality Now, 2012, www.equalitynow.org/sites/default/files/Learning_From_Cases_of_Girls_Rights.pdf.

7 As of this writing, there are widespread reports that girls are being sold as brides by refugee families in Syria.

8 Erica Chong, Kelly Hallman, and Martha Brady, "Investing When it Counts: Generating the Evidence Base for Policies and Programmes for Very Young Adolescents," UNFPA and Population Council, 2006, www.popcouncil.org/uploads/pdfs/InvestingWhenItCounts.pdf.

9 Judith Bruce and John Bongaarts, "The New Population Challenge," in *A Pivotal Moment: Population, Justice, and the Environmental Challenge*, ed., Laurie Mazur (Washington, DC: Island Press, 2009).

10 There are nine coverage exercises to date. Annabel Erulkar, Tekle Ab Mekbib, Negussie Simie, and Tsehai Gulema, "Differential Use of Adolescent Reproductive Health Programs in Addis Ababa, Ethiopia," *Journal of Adolescent Health 38*, no. 3 (2006): 253–60. Judith Bruce, "The Girls Left Behind: Out of the Box and Out of Reach," (paper presented at Gender Dimensions of HIV & Adolescent Programming, Addis Ababa, Ethiopia, 11 April 2007).

11 Kelly K. Hallman, Nora J. Kenworthy, Judith Diers, Nick Swan, and Bashi Devnarain, "The Shrinking World of Girls at Puberty: Violence and Gender-divergent Access to the Public Sphere among Adolescents in South Africa," *Global Public Health: An International Journal for Research, Policy and Practice* 10 (2014): 1–17.

12 Girls in Emergencies Collaborative is a group formed after a major meeting in December 2013 on child marriage.

13 Judith Bruce, "A Modest Proposal: The 12-year-old Check-in," in *Start with a Girl: A New Agenda for Global Health*, eds, Miriam Temin and Ruth Levine (Washington, DC: Center for Global Development, 2009).

14 Judith Bruce, "A Modest Proposal: The 12-year-old Check-in," in *Start with a Girl: A New Agenda for Global Health*, eds, Miriam Temin and Ruth Levine (Washington, DC: Center for Global Development, 2009).

15 There is a new era of concern for these girls and their HIV risks. Daniela Ligiero, Jennifer Kates, Judith Bruce, Peter Donaldson, Annabel Eruklar, Wafaa El-Sadr, and Heileleul Siyoum, "Turning the Tide for Girls and Young Women: How to Achieve an AIDS-Free Future," Expert Panel, Kaiser Family Foundation, Washington, DC, 8 October 2014.

16 Annabel Erulkar, Tekle Ab Mekbib, Negussie Simie, and Tsehai Gulema, *The Experience of Adolescence in Rural Amhara Region Ethiopia* (New York: Population Council, 2004).

17 Judith Bruce, "Preface," in *Girl Safety Toolkit: A Resource for Practitioners* (London: Girlhub, 2013).

18 At the Council, we had a whole seminar on these subjects and the data from the Rakai study were shared, which indicated that girls who are in and out of marriage at young ages, by 20 had an elevated risk of HIV in comparison with unmarried sexually active girls of the same age. Ron Gray, Fred Nalugoda, David Serwadda, and Maria Wawer, "Marriage and HIV Risk: Data from Rakai, Uganda" (paper presented at Exploring the Risks of HIV/AIDS Within the Context of Marriage, Population Council, New York, November 2004).

19 Shelley Clark and Dana Hamplovà, "Single Motherhood and Child Mortality in Sub-Saharan Africa: A Life Course Perspective," *Demography* 50, no. 5 (2013): 1521–1549.

20 Shelley Clark and Dana Hamplovà, "Single Motherhood and Child Mortality in Sub-Saharan Africa: A Life Course Perspective," *Demography* 50, no. 5 (2013): 1521–1549.

21 Annabel Erulkar, Tekle Ab Mekbib, Negussie Simie, and Tsehai Gulema, *The Experience of Adolescence in Rural Amhara Region Ethiopia* (New York: Population Council, 2004).

22 Annabel Erulkar and Eunice Muthengi, "Evaluation of *Berhane Hewan*: A Program to Delay Child Marriage in Rural Ethiopia," *International Perspectives on Sexual and Reproductive Health* 35, no. 1 (2009): 6–14.

23 Eunice Muthengi and Annabel Erulkar, *Building Programs to Address Child Marriage: The Berhane Hewan Experience in Ethiopia*, Population Council, 2011.

24 Annabel Erulkar, "Building Evidence on Effective Programs to Delay Marriage and Support Married Girls in Africa," Population Council, 2014, www.popcouncil.org/uploads/pdfs/2014PGY_EvidenceBaseDelayedMarria ge_Africa.pdf.

27 Child marriage in India

Involving men and boys in cultural and behavioral changes

Ravi Verma

A close examination of the trends and patterns of child marriage in India reveals that deeply entrenched patriarchal norms, together with the low social and economic value of girls compared with boys, are at the root of this widespread harmful practice. These factors are aggravated in the context of poverty and marginalization, but continue to exert their influences even with rising income and educational opportunities for girls and women. Widespread, child marriage in India has declined modestly nationwide over the last 15 years with an increase of only 0.4 years in the mean age at marriage, from 16.7 years to 17.1 years.[1] The urban-rural differential over the same period also remains substantial, with rural girls marrying younger than 18 at nearly twice the rate of urban girls.

It is a matter of concern that despite improved socio-economic conditions, increased education among girls, and various programs and legislative initiatives,[2] these rates continue to remain high in many parts of the country. Close to 48 percent of all women aged 20–24 years had been married by the age of 18 in 2005–06, with some states like Jharkhand and Bihar still showing current rates of 63 and 69 percent of girls, respectively.[3] Within these states and others like Uttar Pradesh, West Bengal, Orissa, and Rajasthan, 16 districts show more than 75 percent—in some cases 85–86 percent—of girls married before 18. How widespread the practice remains can be gauged from these data sets: in 192 out of 604 districts in India, between 50 and 75 percent of girls are married off before they are 18, and in 286 districts, between 20 and 50 percent of girls are married off.[4]

Child marriage is a human rights violation and has numerous and serious educational, health, and developmental consequences for girls.[5] The data clearly show that girls married at an early age have much larger age differences with their spouses than those married later,[6] and this in turn, has serious implications for women's equality and balances of power.

A recent review of programs by the International Center for Research on Women (ICRW)[7] suggests that while there are several programs with the potential to prevent child marriages in India, very few of them are rigorously evaluated. Moreover, most programs tend to impact child marriage practices indirectly.[8] They generally employ different strategies, either stand-alone or various combinations, to enhance the worth of a girl child. These strategies range from building life skills among adolescent girls, to retaining them in schools through conditional cash transfer schemes and/or engaging with parents and communities to change the norms around marriage. Whether these programs also address the root causes of child marriage embedded in unequal gender norms, or make other efforts to enhance the societal value of girl children, is not well understood or documented. This chapter will summarize and evaluate ICRW's research and assess its implications.

Why engage with men and boys to address child marriage?

The World Bank Group[9] has recognized that a high prevalence of child marriage is driven by social norms and expectations and by gendered discrimination that devalues women and girls and their right to make choices for themselves. Unequal gender norms impacting child marriage in India are characterized by strong son-preference and the perceived need to control women's/girls' sexuality. A recent population-based study of over 9,000 men and 5,000 women from seven Indian states with unfavorable sex-ratios[10] found that a higher proportion of men compared with women prefer sons over daughters, and men with a rigid sense of masculinity[11] have stronger son-preference[12] than those with gender-equitable attitudes.

The association between masculine attitudes and son preference is universal across all the seven Indian states where sex-ratios are highly unfavorable to girls, and the number of girls born is declining. These are also the states with pockets of very high child marriage rates.

Fewer men with rigid masculine ideas (55 percent) compared with men with equitable ones (65 percent) support the idea that girls should marry when they want and that girls can choose their own partners for marriage (45 percent versus 57 percent).

What needs to be recognized, however, is that norms around masculinities that connote power, hierarchy and entitlement are neither static, nor maintained and perpetuated, by men only. Connell[13] postulates the concept of multiple masculinities that are dynamic and constantly shaped by institutions, expectations, and practices within the society. Women—mothers, sisters, mother-in-laws, and sister-in-laws—also reinforce and justify the power hierarchy within families, usually in favor of men, and they may justify the dominant position of men in decision-making, or even in wife-beating.[14]

Inequitable gender norms in India also tie girls' sexuality—especially their virginity—to family and community honors, and controlling female sexuality impacts other aspects of girls' lives. For example, marriage around the time a girl reaches puberty—"coming of age" as known in India—is seen as a social mechanism to ensure that her sexuality is controlled within the institution of marriage and that she does not begin sexual activities as per her choice and exploration. A qualitative study of the causes and consequences of child marriages in India by ICRW and Plan International[15] shows that parents consider it their responsibility to marry off their daughters, and to protect their chastity until they are married. Early marriage ensures an "honorable" discharge from this duty. The safety and security of young girls worries parents, who believe that an unmarried girl is especially vulnerable to sexual exploitation and abuse. Marriage is seen as a preventive measure to protect young girls from potential danger. Sexual violence and harassment of girls are important triggers for child marriage, particularly in situations of poverty and marginalization, and important justifications for parents to marry girls off at an early age, even to a much older man. "You must marry the daughter at a 'right age' before anything goes wrong (*Gadbad na ho jaye*). She has to after all go to another house and it is a matter of honor (*izzat*) if she goes unblemished (*bedaag*)," says one mother of a daughter married as a child. "They (girls) have to anyway look after the in-laws, house, and take care of others (*Ghar Kaam karna hai*)—then why wait. As soon as you find a match (*Jodi*) you must marry them," says a father of an unmarried, under-18 girl. "You can domesticate (*gharelu banana*) a girl easily only if she is young or else she develops her own mind," says a key community leader in the rural areas of Rajasthan, India. Early marriage also ensures that a girl is seamlessly transitioned into her primary reproductive role as early as possible, which is, in turn, prescribed and supported by unequal gender and masculine norms.

Parents, however, are increasingly coming to recognize the value of education, even as they continue to support early marriages for daughters and believe in traditional roles for women as home-makers. "Some" level of education is deemed necessary for girls to become a better home-maker. As one father puts it, "If she is somewhat educated, (*Thodi-bahut padhi likhi*) it will help the family, and also she will look after the children well." On the other hand, young girls once educated do not want to marry early and seek instead to explore higher studies and a career. Similarly, many boys in the ICRW/Plan study recognize these increasing opportunities and the aspirations of girls, and some support their desires for higher studies and a career, although they remain unclear about "giving up" their control over them. They still define the primary responsibility of women as home-makers, serving the needs of their families.

It is imperative to engage with these men and boys, including fathers and other male members of families and communities, to alter the norms surrounding marriage and relationships and to build on changing aspirations and opportunities. Engagement with men and boys should help create safe spaces for girls and help girls to advance, delay age of marriage, and lead a life without fear and harassment within domestic and public spaces. Such engagement may also help men and boys eliminate violence in their families and sustain more equitable and respectful relationships.

Increasingly, with deeper understanding of how masculine norms are learned, manifested, and experienced by both men and women, it is evident that engagement with men and boys is an important and inevitable strategy for preventing child marriage and mitigating its negative impacts. Through these interventions it is also becoming clear that engaging men and boys necessitates our working with and seeking the support of institutions that surround families and inculcate values, including schools and other community-based institutions.

Principles of engaging with men and boys and ICRW experience

ICRW studies, drawing from Connell's conceptualization of masculinities, recognize that unequal gender norms are harmful not only to women, but also to men and boys. So too, there is no "one" fixed form of masculinity but, instead, multiple masculinities that are dynamic and changing. Perhaps most notably, men and boys are challenging traditional norms in their own ways. ICRW programs engage with them as important allies to create new norms or alter harmful ones. It is important to start early and work within institutional frameworks or structures that shape and formulate ideas about manhood and relationships. Places like schools and sports facilities are where exclusive, dominant, and aggressive forms of masculinities are played out, reinforced, and rewarded.

What follows are brief findings by ICRW and our partners from three innovative learning models engaging men and boys and girls.

Learning Model I: Parivartan: (meaning Transformation)

The *Parivartan* program uses sports as a platform for encouraging positive male role models to challenge inequitable gender norms and transform communities into safe environments for both girls and boys.[16] Sport is predominantly a "masculine" institution with explicit manifestations of power, control, and entitlement. Coaches embody power, define hierarchies and inequalities, and are looked up to as role models. It is critical to confront and question masculinity norms and practices within sports.

ICRW and our partners implemented a multi-level intervention for over two years with cricket coaches, athletes, their families, and communities in the slum communities of Mumbai. Interventions were carried out for two groups of athletes: one group was in schools and the other had dropped out of the schools. Select school-based coaches and community-based mentors were identified to raise awareness about abusive and disrespectful behavior, promote gender-equitable and non-violent attitudes, and develop skills among male athletes from both schools and communities separately, who were encouraged to speak up and intervene when witnessing harmful behaviors toward women and girls. Our expectation was that this would help transform traditional masculine norms that condone disrespect and even abuse.

The intervention components included workshops for coaches and mentors (12 days each, every four months), weekly sessions of mentors with their athletes, on-the-job training of athletes using the principle of "teachable moments," and also public education campaigns within the larger school and community, which reached about 10,000 boys and girls. The weekly sessions of coaches, mentors, and athletes included a card-based curriculum on respect, fair-play, aggression, and abusive language. This also addressed violence, including sexual violence and harassment, intention to intervene, and bystander intervention.[17]

Both the school-based and the community-based sports programs were evaluated using a quasi-experimental design in which intervention participants were compared with comparable control groups drawn from schools and communities.[18] The quantitative results show that participants from both schools and communities became more supportive of gender-equitable norms overall than non-participants from the respective control groups. There was a perceptible decline in the number of boys agreeing with the following statements: "A wife should always obey her husband," "Violence against girls is perpetrated by strangers," and "If a girl says no, it means yes." The trained athletes were significantly less supportive of physical abuse of girls. There was a decline in their agreement with all the statements about when girls deserve to be beaten, although strong agreement continued for women's "help with household chores." On self-reported behaviors, the most profound change was "stopping the use of abusive language," whereas for the boys in the community it was "have begun helping with household chores." Both school and community athletes reported greater intentions to positively intervene in response to hypothetical scenarios of abuse against girls. Female relatives and partners also noted improvements in the men's attitudes and behavior in areas of communication with family members, sharing of household responsibilities, day-to-day views about women and girls, aggressive behavior, and expressions of emotions and sexual intimacy.

The following statement from one coach describes the kind of changes noticed during the sessions: "With each session, I can vouch there was a change in the cognition of these boys. Once you go in the depths of a discussion-making it light, yet serious at the same time— you will see there is a change in their thinking level. And this you will see has also resulted in a change in their attitude level." Despite positive shifts in attitude, areas of concern remained. For example, coaches and mentors wrestled with questions about women and girls' mobility. They identified various security and safety considerations for justifying male domination. During informal discussions, coaches and mentors still blamed girls for inviting "troubles," if they wore "provocative" dresses and went outside alone.

Learning Model II: Gender Equity Movement in Schools (GEMS)

Schools are important because they influence and shape thought processes, attitudes, and behaviors. They are stable institutions that can create lasting impact and alter gender stereotypes.

ICRW and our partners implemented an extra-curricular program in the public schools of Mumbai to reach younger adolescents in schools.[19] GEMS programs employ a gender-transformative approach to examine, question, and change rigid gender norms and imbalances of power as a means of achieving gender equity objectives. GEMS programs engage with schools to teach children to recognize, anticipate, and challenge these norms as they play out in their daily lives. The goal is to prevent or reduce consequent violence.

GEMS was implemented and validated in 45 municipal schools reaching out to 8,000 boys and girls in grades VI and VII, aged 12 to 14 years over two academic years, 2009–2011. The first-year sessions focused on concept building around gender, body, and violence, and the second year specifically addressed skills building around gender, relationships, emotion, communication, and conflict resolution. First-year sessions separated boys and girls, while the second year brought them back together.

Evaluation results for the GEMS programs demonstrate that the first round of the intervention yielded a positive shift in attitudes toward gender equality. Children who participated in two rounds of the interventions, moreover, sustained their support for gender equality more than those who only attended one. There was a significant positive trend among students exposed to comprehensive gender programming that girls should delay marriage beyond the legal age of 18 years. "A girl should study further. But if her parents will force her, she will not be able to do anything. She will have to marry. If that girl is 20 or 21 years old, then it's ok to think about marriage, but if she is 15 or 16 years old, parents should not think about marriage," said one girl from GEMS school."A girl should study. She has the right to study. It is illegal to get her married before the age of 18 and no-one should be married off at a young age. One should get married after the age of 18 or 20," said a boy from GEMS school.

Boys and girls from schools exposed to comprehensive programs reported greater changes in their own behavior than boys and girls from comparison schools. After the second round of the intervention, more children from GEMS schools claimed they would take action in response to sexual harassment. Overall, students from GEMS schools are more likely to score higher on measurements of gender equality, to support a higher age at marriage (age 21 or older) and higher education for girls, and to oppose partner violence.

The GEMS experience provides evidence of a useful and feasible methodology for discussions around gender equality within schools. The findings suggest that methodologies involving students in self-reflection have the potential to make positive differences in attitudes and behaviors.

Learning Model III: Parivartan for girls

ICRW is engaged in current research to assess the feasibility of a community-based sports program for girls, designed to create a safe and enabling environment for girls to participate in sports. The program aims to address existing constraints that restrict presence and mobility in public spaces. The programmatic innovation is in triggering change by providing girls a chance to play a "masculine" sport called *Kabaddi*. It involves multi-stakeholder engagement including adolescent girls, 12 to 16 years old, living in a slum community in Mumbai, peer mentors aged 18 to 24, and parents, especially fathers, and other community members. It is expected that by participating in sports, girls will increase their confidence and self-esteem, learn negotiation skills and teamwork, and have the confidence to claim their own space. These competencies are expected to transfer into their individual lives and ultimately into continued education and delayed marriage.

Conclusion

There is clearly a need to mainstream gender-transformative approaches to address structural factors that drive masculinities and inequalities that harm the lives of girls and women. The International Men and Gender Equality Survey[20] reveals that more than 80 percent of Indian men have witnessed an incident of physical violence by a man against a woman at home during their childhood (before age 18), and, of these, 90 percent have themselves experienced physical violence in the home. Two-thirds report having been physically violent against another child or youth.

Subsequent studies also show that childhood experiences matter, as substantial numbers of men who experienced or witnessed violence growing up demonstrate greater need to control others and use violence in multiple ways against women. This affirms the need to work with men and boys when they are still young, and to involve families and communities in interventions that sustain altered norms. Longitudinal interventions within an institutional framework are critical to ensure that boys begin to question gender inequalities as they grow up. Programs must treat men as partners, and part of the solution. Many men report confused ideas about gender relations, while others already view women and girls as equals, and we must engage both groups systematically.

ICRW research indicates that there is great potential to work with boys and men. The interventions described in this chapter, however, raise several questions and also point to challenges in designing sustainable, gender-inclusive, and effective child marriage interventions.

The implementation of GEMS and Parivartan required significant commitment from the educational authorities, including school-teachers, principals, and coaches, and from the families of the children who participated. This raises questions about how best to bring these programs to scale and secure necessary commitments and resources. GEMS has been scaled-up from 45 to 350 schools of Mumbai city and

80 schools of two rural districts of Jharkhand state in India. GEMS has also been adapted and scaled-up in the Da Nang province of Vietnam. Key learning from these various scaling-up exercises suggests that programs must be adapted to the local cultural contexts and that careful preparation is required to ensure the delivery of the gender modules with utmost integrity and high-quality skills. In many settings investments may be needed to create a cadre of local gender trainers who will sustain programs in the long run. In other settings, opportunities should be explored to engage with external agencies to deliver the gender modules.

A second challenge is to sustain the positive changes observed in the two programs. This will take more than men with improved attitudes. It will also require more comprehensive programming for girls, including programs that enhance accessibility and quality of education overall, promote life-skills training, including reproductive and sexual health education and services, and provide economic empowerment and skills. Girls need equal opportunity in education and employment, as well as access to safe public spaces. For these purposes, an enabling legal and policy environment must be created. Innovation and scale are needed, a tall order indeed but not an impossible one. Programs of this nature, once considered unattainable in the developed world, are now becoming standard.

Notes

1 International Institute for Population Sciences (IIPS), *National Family Health Survey (NFHS-1), 1992–93* (Mumbai, India: 1995); International Institute for Population Sciences (IIPS) and Macro International, *National Family Health Survey (NFHS-3), 2005–06* (Mumbai, India: 2007).
2 The Prohibition of Child Marriage Act (2006).
3 International Institute for Population Sciences (IIPS), *District Level Household and Facility Survey 2007–08 (DLHS-3)* (Mumbai, India: 2010).
4 International Center for Research on Women (ICRW), *District Level Study of Child Marriages in India: Analysis, Program Review and Next Steps* (New Delhi, India: ICRW, 2014).
5 Shireen Jejeebhoy and Sarah Bott, *Non-consensual Sexual Experiences of Young People: A Review of the Evidence from Developing Countries, Regional Working Paper*, South And South East Asia 16, (New Delhi, India: Population Council, 2003); Saranga Jain and Kathleen Kurz, *New Insights on Preventing Child Marriage: A Global Analysis of Factors and Programs* (Washington, DC: ICRW 2007); Anju Malhotra, Ann Warner, Alison McGonagle, and Susan Lee-Rife, *Solutions to End Child marriage: What the Evidence Shows* (Washington, DC: ICRW, 2011); Sanyukta Mathur, Margaret Greene, and Anju Malhotra, *Too Young to Wed: The Lives, Rights, and Health of Young Married Girls* (Washington, DC: ICRW

2003); UNICEF, *Early Marriage: Child Spouses*, Innocenti Research Centre (Florence: UNICEF, 2001); UNICEF, *The State of the World's Children; Adolescence-An Age of Opportunity* (New York: UNICEF, 2011).

6 International Institute for Population Sciences (IIPS) and Macro International, *National Family Health Survey (NFHS-3), 2005–06* (Mumbai, India: 2007).

7 International Center for Research on Women (ICRW), *Too Young to Wed: Education and Action Toward Ending Child Marriage, Brief on Child Marriage and Domestic Violence* (Washington, DC: ICRW, 2006); ICRW, *Delaying Marriage for Girls in India: A Formative Research to Design Interventions for Changing Norms* (New Delhi, India: ICRW, 2010); Sreela Das Gupta, Sushmita Mukherjee, Sampurna Singh, Rohini Pande, and Sharmishtha Basu, *Knot Ready, Lessons from India on Delaying Marriage for Girls* (Washington, DC: ICRW, 2008); Anju Malhotra, Ann Warner, Alison McGonagle, and Susan Lee-Rife, *Solutions to End Child marriage: What the Evidence Shows* (Washington, DC: ICRW, 2011).

8 Some of the well-known programs to enhance the value of a girl child include: Apni Beti Apna Dhan (our daughter our wealth)—a conditional cash transfer scheme implemented in the mid-1990s in Haryana, which entitled a girl approximately Rs. 25,000 (a little less than $500) when she reached age 18 unmarried, pledged to her at the time of birth. Many Indian states followed with different variations of the conditional cash transfer schemes. Bal Vivah Virodh Abhiyan (Child Marriage Protest Program) (2005) is another nationwide awareness-raising program against child marriage; the Kasturba Gandhi Balika Vidyalaya (KGBV) (2007) program as part of a Universal Education Campaign has set up residential schools at upper primary level for girls belonging predominantly to socially and economically marginalized communities.

9 World Bank Group, *Preventing Child Marriage: Lessons from World Bank Group Gender Impact Evaluations* (Washington, DC: The World Bank, 2014).

10 International Center for Research on Women (ICRW) and UNFPA, *Masculinities, Preference for Sons and Intimate Partner Violence in India: Preliminary Findings* (New Delhi, India, 2013).

11 Masculinity was measured using men's level of support for gender equality (e.g. sharing of housework, responsibility for contraception) and control of wife's actions (e.g. who she spends time with, whether she makes household decisions); using these indicators four typologies of men were identified: favorable attitudes toward gender equality and weak support for controlling behavior (Equitable); favorable attitudes toward gender equality but strong support for controlling behavior; unfavorable attitudes toward gender equality but weak support for controlling behavior; and unfavorable attitudes toward gender equality and strong support for controlling behaviors (Rigid).

12 Son-preference in the study was created as an index from a series of attitudinal statements, for example having a son was important for carrying on the family name, sons were needed for old-age care, having a son made them more of a real man, whether not having a son was enough reason to divorce a wife or partner.

13 R.W. Connell, *Masculinities* (Cambridge: Polity Press, 2005); Raewyn Connell and James Messerschmidt, "Hegemonic Masculinity: Rethinking the Concept; Gender Society," *Gender & Society* 19 (December 2005): 829–859.

14 International Institute for Population Sciences (IIPS), *National Family Health Surveys (NFHS-2,) 1998–1999* (Mumbai, India, 2000); International Institute for Population Sciences (IIPS) and Macro International, *National Family Health Survey (NFHS-3), 2005–06* (Mumbai, India, 2007).
15 International Center for Research on Women (ICRW) and Plan International, *Asia Child Marriage Initiative: Summary of Research Findings in Bangladesh, India and Nepal* (New Delhi, India: ICRW, 2013).
16 Madhumita Das, Sancheeta Ghosh, Ravi Verma, Brian O'Connor, Sara Fewer, Maria Catrina Virata, and Elizabeth Miller, "Gender Attitudes and Violence among Urban Adolescent Boys in India," *International Journal of Adolescence and Youth* 19 (January 2014): 99–112.
17 Ibid.
18 Elizabeth Miller, Madhumita Das, Daniel J. Tancredi, Heather L. McCauley, Maria Catrina D. Virata, Jasmine Nettiksimmons, Brian O'Connor, Sancheeta Ghosh, and Ravi Verma, "Evaluation of a Gender-Based Violence Prevention Program for Student Athletes in Mumbai, India," *Journal of Interpersonal Violence* 29 (March 2014): 758–78.
19 Nandita Bhatla, Pranita Achyut, Ravi Verma, Shubhda Maitra, and Sujata Khandekar, "Gender-based Violence and Sexual and Reproductive Health and Rights: Looking at the Health Sector Response in the Asia-Pacific Region," *Arrows for Change* 17 (December 2011).
20 International Center for Research on Women (ICRW) and Instituto Promundo, *Evolving Men: Initial Results from the International Men and Gender Equality Survey (IMAGES)* (Washington, DC: ICRW, 2011).

28 Working with adolescent girls in Egypt
A reflection

Hala Youssef

At the time this chapter was first prepared, I was leading Egypt's National Population Council (NPC), a public entity where I oversaw the development and launch of a number of participatory national strategies, including a renewed effort to combat child marriage. In November 2014, the current government and NPC leadership launched a new national population strategy, which includes the Preventing Early Marriage initiative described herein. The strategy is consistent with global principles articulated in the Program of Action adopted by the UN International Conference on Population and Development (ICPD) in Cairo, in 1994, the UN Millennium Development Goals, and its proposed Sustainable Development Goals (SDGs), while also upholding Egypt's national laws and religious and cultural values. I have since assumed a new position as Egyptian Minister of State for Population and am pleased to reflect on the significance of our ongoing governmental effort to improve the future for women and girls.

Recognizing challenges that remain

The ICPD provided a framework for Egyptians to examine our country's population challenges and improve people's lives. It codified a landmark international consensus affirming that individual human rights and dignity, including the sexual and reproductive health and rights of women and girls, are necessary preconditions for sustainable development. And it called for a wide range of investments by governments to realize those rights by improving girls' education and providing comprehensive health care, including the provision of voluntary family planning services.

Since 1994, Egypt has seen substantial changes in the family planning field. With improved services now reaching from the cities to almost every village in the country, national contraceptive prevalence rates (CPR) increased slowly from 47.9 percent to 60.3 percent in the 13 years from 1995 to 2000, although geographic and socio-economic disparities remain.[1] Achievements have been made in education as well. Primary school enrollment of girls is now nearly universal, youth illiteracy is being eradicated, and growing numbers of young women complete secondary school and attend university.[2]

Egypt has also recognized that rapid population growth remains a major challenge to the country's sustainable development. According to our Central Agency for Statistics (CAPMAS), despite expanded services, the total population reached 86 million early in 2014, with more than 40 percent under the age of 29. Moreover, a quarter of the population lives below the poverty line, a number that increases to 40 percent in rural Upper Egypt. Rights protections, especially for vulnerable groups such as young girls and women, inevitably suffer in such circumstances, especially when poverty combines with conservative religious values and puts pressure on families to marry off their daughters at a young age.

Recent political unrest also temporarily impeded progress. The post-January 25th revolution Islamic regime, although transient, halted programs to end the practice of female genital mutilation (FGM) and slowed down efforts to educate youth about sexual and reproductive health (SRH). As a consequence of all these factors, early marriage has been increasing in certain communities, and fertility rates are again rising.

In the process of preparing for the post-2015 Sustainable Development Goals, Egypt recently reassessed its progress across many sectors and uncovered a lack of coordination between vertically organized programs in family planning, health, education, and other services, along with a marked deficiency in the monitoring and evaluation of strategies, programs, and institutional capacity overall. To address these deficiencies, the NPC has adopted a new multi-sector approach to the protection of youth, with the rights of girls and young women as a focus. NPC is now utilizing well-designed, participatory strategies to ensure that girls and young women are educated and receive the services they need to prevent child marriage and decrease population growth.

The Egyptian Demographic and Health Survey (EDHS) for 2008 shows that 17 percent of women aged 20 to 24 years old report having married before the age of 18. Further research uncovered even higher numbers in Upper Egypt's rural and Frontiers' governorates—Qena, Fayoum and Giza[3]—and that targeting those geographic areas is a necessary policy strategy.[4]

Strategizing to end child marriage

NPC received funds from the Ford Foundation and technical support from Pathfinder International to take the lead in developing a national population and development strategy to end child marriage. Our aim was to engage all stakeholders in protecting and promoting rights and opportunities for girls to these ends.

We first conducted a review of all relevant and available studies of similar interventions and compiled our findings into an informative report, which was broadly distributed as a source for evidence-based policymaking. The report emphasizes the complexity of the problem and how deeply it is affected by cultural beliefs, economic circumstances, and continuing lack of access to high-quality education. Education is defined broadly to address formal schooling but also to encompass learning through cultural activities, media, families, peers, and religious leaders.

Egyptian law currently sets the legal age of marriage at 18, but societal and economic challenges persist and loopholes permit informal, religious-based, or customary marriages to continue. For example, families seeking "Sotrah"—that is, to protect a girl's reputation in case a wealthy groom is available, or out of fear that she will delay or never be married,[5] or because of a desire to comply with traditions particularly in tribal areas—may get around the law.

NPC began an inclusive participatory process with governmental agencies, non-governmental and private sector organizations. Our Prevention of Child Marriage (PCM) strategy goal is to reduce the prevalence of child marriage by 50 percent between 2014 and 2019. If achieved, we will not only spare individual girls the harmful lifetime consequences of early marriage, but will also help slow national population growth. Building on the experience and challenges identified in Egypt, the strategy is focusing on geographic areas, or so-called hot spots, where the phenomenon is prominent and/or increasing.

The new PCM strategy employs a rights-based approach, which recognizes that boys and girls enjoy religious protections as well as civil rights under the Egyptian constitution. It took 14 successive workshops attended by more than 120 experts, representing 64 governmental and non-governmental bodies, to prepare. The workshops identified four sectors with challenges to confront: education, health, economics and finance, and lastly, social and cultural challenges, encompassing religious, and media outreach.

Focus groups in six governorates with higher child marriage rates tested community acceptance of the strategy. The strategy also engaged religious leaders. Both the Islamic Research Forum and the Egyptian Church made declarations against early marriage.

The national strategy's objectives are to: (a) support girls who have already married to minimize the negative impacts on the girls, their children, and society; (b) complete and update legislation to reflect the current constitution and enforce existing child protection laws, and close the legal loopholes that allow families to marry off their underage daughters; (c) address social and economic factors that encourage early marriage; (d) empower, educate, and prepare young girls to address family and societal pressures; and (e) mobilize officials, communities, and families to advocate for the prevention of child marriage. Implementing partners include the ministries of health and population, planning, education, and social solidarity, along with Egypt's national councils on women, childhood, and motherhood. NPC created a new governmental entity to coordinate activities among these partners and others in the governmental, non-governmental, and research sectors.

Strengthening educational infrastructure and improving the accessibility of preparatory and secondary schools in rural areas has been identified as critical to preparing girls for jobs, so the plan also calls for a routine review of the education system and its outcomes. Because low economic status is another crucial factor in child marriage, the strategy also advises a government-led expansion of small-scale industries, and the provision of technical and financial support to girls and families who seek and find work, by increasing pensions and conditional cash transfers (CCT) and linking youth to health and education subsidy programs. The strategy notes the importance of increased public and private investment in innovative labor opportunities in underprivileged areas to fight unemployment. Finally, community awareness campaigns are planned to include messaging from religious leaders about the harmful effects of early marriage, along with positive messaging targeting boys and girls about gender equity.

Finally, the strategy contemplates complex data analysis with use of quantitative and qualitative indicators, which are being developed by various research institutions. For example, the strategy seeks to measure the numbers of youth reached by awareness campaigns, the percentage of girls who enroll or drop out of school and the percentages of married girls receiving adequate reproductive health services and prenatal care. NCP will also measure the percentage of single mothers who receive pensions, among other indicators intended to evaluate their effectiveness. Utilizing EDHS, success will ultimately be determined over the five-year span of the plan, however, by improvements in such outcomes as an increase in the average age of first marriage among girls and boys, a decrease in the percentage of married girls under the age of 18, and a decrease in the percentage of married women younger than 20 years old giving birth. Key to ensuring adequate implementation will be integration of the strategy within established systems and the NCP's ability to secure necessary financial resources. Public, corporate, and NGO sector partnership is critical.

Conclusion: the way forward

In Egypt, the youth population is outpacing the economy and straining the capacities of social institutions. In a country with a poverty level of 25 percent and expectations of increased life expectancy, the quality of life of future generations is of great concern. Unless Egypt invests in the sexual and reproductive health and rights of young people and ends harmful practices such as early marriage, the future is uncertain.

With the development of the PCM strategy, the current government of Egypt has made these goals a national priority. Additionally, NPC is currently in the process of developing a more effective national strategy to ensure universal accessibility of sexual and reproductive health programs that empower families to more effectively plan the number and spacing of their children. Making higher quality services universal would help to lift women and youth out of poverty and bring myriad benefits to society.

The PCM strategy process is an example of a useful government intervention to address a serious problem. By targeting areas with higher rates of early marriage, vetting the proposed activities at the community level, and building sound mechanisms for monitoring the implementation and success of the program, Egypt has shown leadership in addressing a deeply harmful practice.

Notes

1 Fatma El-Zanaty and Ann Way, *Egypt Demographic and Health Survey 2008* (The Egyptian Ministry of Health, El-Zanaty and Associates and Macro International, 2009).

2 Asmaa Elbadawy, "Education in Egypt: Improvements in Attainment, Problems With Quality and Inequality," *Economic Research Forum* no. 854 (Giza, Egypt, 2014), www.erf.org.eg/CMS/uploads/pdf/854.pdf.

3 Heba El Kalaawy, *Child marriage in Rural Upper Egypt, Reasons, Consequences and Prospects for Change*, Draft Report, Population Council, 2013.

4 uhMamdoWahba and Elham Fateem, *The study of Reproductive Health; Information, attitudes and Practices of Bedouin Youth* (Egyptian Family Health Society, Ford Foundation, 2012).

5 M. Adly, N. Fawzy, and N. El Toukhi, et al., *Child Marriage in Egypt, Field Research* (El Nadim Center for Rehabilitation of Victims of Violence, 2013).

Part V

Taking on the new challenge of climate justice

29 Gender equality, human rights and climate justice

Reflections and a call to action

Noelene Nabulivou[1]

I reflect here on global warming and other ecological realities, and call for a strategic feminist response to this unprecedented global context. Climate change immediately threatens the entire planet and especially its most vulnerable populations living in the Global South. It is not a naturally occurring phenomenon but a problem accelerated by individual behaviors, societal, development, and business practices, which can and must be altered. Meaningful change will require bold and progressive strategies for sustainable development—strategies that also incorporate a central and transparent concern for human rights, gender equality, and social justice. Only through such a comprehensive approach can we hope to achieve what I and others are now calling climate justice.

My thinking is inspired and informed by the work of national and regional feminist groups and coalitions including the Pacific Feminist SRHR Coalition (PFSC), Pacific Partnerships to Strengthen Gender Climate Change and Sustainable Development (PPGCCSD) and the Gender, Economic and Ecological Justice Initiative (GEEJ). I also value and build on 30 years of work by Southern feminist networks such as Development Alternatives for Women of the New Era (DAWN), as well as global feminist advocates including Resurj, the International Women's Health Coalition (IWHC), and, more recently, the Women's Major Group (WMG) on Sustainable Development.

Acknowledging the scale of the ecological challenge

In the fifth Intergovernmental Panel on Climate Change (IPCC) report, the scientific community sounds a clarion call about the urgency of global warming, climate change, and environmental degradation. Over 2,000 IPCC scientists confirm that changes in precipitation and weather patterns now severely threaten agricultural production and the world's food supply. They marshal evidence to demonstrate that we are experiencing severe sudden onset disasters, such as cyclones, tsunamis, and tidal surges, as well as the steady onset of riverbank erosion, drought, salinity ingress, ocean acidification, and an overall increase in ocean surface temperature.[2]

The effects are already visible.[3] The 2013 International Program on the State of the Ocean (IPSO) calls urgently for a halt to ocean degradation. It warns that the cumulative impact of ocean warming from higher temperatures in the atmosphere, together with a loss of oxygen caused by coastal nutrient run-off, will destroy the protective shield the seas have long provided, as rising sea levels also threaten coastal populations.[4]

Glaciers also continue to shrink worldwide. As permafrost warms, the thawing of ice and snow in high-altitudes affects run-off and water resources downstream, placing the freshwater resources of over one billion people at risk.[5] Many terrestrial, freshwater, and marine species have shifted geographic ranges, seasonal activities, and migration patterns, affecting their numbers and interactions. Over 150 to 200 species are facing extinction daily.[6]

On issues of food security, the IPCC5 report also observes that climate change is reducing wheat and maize yields in many regions. The report, drawing from studies covering a wide range of regions and crops, shows that negative impacts of climate change on crop yields are already commonplace.[7]

The World Health Organization (WHO) also warns that "between 2030 and 2050, climate change is expected to cause approximately 250,000 additional deaths per year, from malnutrition, malaria, diarrhea and heat stress."[8] A recent study in the UK showed that heat-related deaths are expected to rise precipitously by 2050.[9] In many countries, local changes in temperature and rainfall have already altered the distribution of such water-borne illnesses and diseases as malaria, dengue, and Ebola.[10]

The situation of global ecological damage has become ever more urgent as transnational corporations run out of soil-based reserves of oil, gas, water, and minerals, and move on to exploit those below water or rock. Along with fracking of shale rock, new and often untested science and geo-engineering technologies are being used to explore seas, lakes, and rivers for oil, gas, and mineral deposits, despite strong and growing opposition from many indigenous and local communities, as well as from frontline civil society.[11]

So too, this global extractive enterprise is often supported by unfair monetary, financial, and trade rules, unsustainable production and consumption patterns, and prevailing systems of political decision-making and resource distribution that worsen economic and social inequalities.[12] In this context of intertwined ecological, social, and economic challenges, we need more than "sustainable development," we need urgent systemic repair.

Recognizing the adverse impacts on women and girls

Even prior to the landmark United Nations Earth Summit in Rio in 1992, many feminist thinkers and advocates around the world began to frame global struggles for social justice and sustainable development as encompassing "diverse territories and geographies including the body, land, ocean and waterways, communities, states and epistemological grounds."[13] Reiterated at Rio+20 in Brazil, southern feminists recognized these terrains as, "fraught with the resurgent forces of patriarchy, finance capitalism, neo-conservatism, consumerism, militarism and extractivism."[14]

Nonetheless, many key constituencies of women still see environment and climate change as issues not "central" to their agenda. This remains true even as so many women and girls face unfair and unequal burdens in sustaining the economic and social well-being of their communities.

As the result of norms around gendered divisions of labor and decision-making, for example, rural women tend to work in informal employment that is more dependent on natural resources; they do most of the agricultural work and are generally the household members responsible for collecting water and fuel. Along with men in their families who often travel long distances to work in mines and other polluting industries, these women are exposed disproportionately to environmental contaminants and harm.[15] Women and girls also face the threat of violence when they need to travel long distances for water. In Nigeria, for example, a link has been demonstrated between reduced access to clean water as a result of oil extraction and a rising incidence of sexual violence.[16]

At the same time "mancamps" employing often unmonitored security forces, established to protect private and public assets, may implicitly license sexual assault on nearby women and girls.[17] In India, women and adolescent girls working in or near the mines of Rajasthan are experiencing a greater than average incidence of physical and sexual abuse, as well as other negative health outcomes and heightened levels of poverty.[18]

Additional adverse health outcomes also result from environmental degradation, many of them related to sexual and reproductive health.

Water contaminated by industrial pollutants and lack of sanitation remains a large cause of maternal and child morbidity and mortality. For example, the Niger Delta in Nigeria, a heavily industrialized region, is also experiencing rising levels of HIV and other sexually transmitted disease, along with adverse impacts on pregnant women from oil flares and other consequences of drilling.[19] Pregnant Nigerian women living near oil fields experience miscarriage at 2.5 times the rate of others farther away.[20] Studies also link birth defects to chemicals routinely used in industry and agriculture.[21]

↳ IRAQ BIRTH DEFECTS LUNCH LECTURE

Advocating for a complex systems approach to change

Many feminist advocates had hoped that the Sustainable Development Goals (SDGs), currently under negotiation at the UN, would monitor and measure these issues—but confidence in the process is equivocal in these final months of negotiations toward the post-2015 development agenda. Reference to gender in the proposed language on environment is still relatively weak and employs words like "promote," "encourage," or "pay special attention" to the needs of women and girls, but is not establishing actual targets or real accountability.

In addition, women's participation in solving these problems is overlooked. There is little consideration of the specific impacts of environmental damage on women, nor recognition of a potential role for women in mitigating these impacts. An explicit reference to gender is left out, even as the document acknowledges that indigenous peoples, including farmers, fishers, and other tradespeople must be conscripted to bring meaningful reform.   BRING WOMEN INTO CONVO/MITIGATION

Feminist advocates have put forth an alternative "complex systems" approach to gender justice, human rights, and sustainable development—one acknowledging that social, economic, financial, and ecological systems function within a single sphere. In this analysis, climate change, global warming, and environmental degradation are viewed as "drivers of inequalities" and therein as central to all transformative feminist approaches to universal human rights, gender equality, and social justice, and not as so-called externalities.

While the ongoing SDG negotiations on our concerns continue, we are beginning to see some success in other domains. First, we have forged an agreement among a global coalition of women's human rights defenders on a broad set of issues and are currently working together in multiple venues, including the post-2015 development agenda negotiations, the UNFCCC, and elsewhere. Together, we are attempting to protect climate justice, sustainable development principles, and environmental issues, along with a wide range of gender justice and human rights concerns.

In national and regional work, coalitions of feminists are insisting that there be no regress on universal human rights and gender equality commitments long accepted by the United Nations on ending sexual- and gender-based violence, and advancing sexual and reproductive health and rights (SRHR). We are working to ensure that these critical measures are understood as core issues across all development platforms that address poverty and inequalities. We are also asking for more rigorous regulation of transnational private sector interests and for a fairer global system in trade and monetary policies. The outspoken voices of women advocates are calling for a stronger focus on the means of implementation (MOI) of all development policies, including established levels of overseas development aid, the just distribution of technology, intellectual property, and many other such matters.

Second, feminists are also clearer on development "soft points"– meaning instances in which states may negotiate and trade away long agreed human rights commitments to secure other concessions. Gender equality and human rights claims are too often used as bargaining chips, as we have observed recently in many negotiating spaces, such as the 20th anniversary meetings around Rio and Cairo. This is an ongoing concern for those of us still working on Beijing+20, on the SDGs, and on climate negotiations. Some governments from the South, for example, have been willing to secure progressive socio-economic policies and regulatory measures to address climate change by agreeing to roll back agreements on women's rights and human rights. Conversely, some governments from the North present women's human rights and gender equality as a condition of economic and political reforms in the South while simultaneously resisting necessary changes in economic, social, and security paradigms and practices of their own that may harm women and men in the South.

Third, we see no point in defending multi-lateral language and national policy on either human rights or climate justice without paying attention to overall development policies. Feminist groups are increasingly questioning established parameters of "development" and "human rights," and propose instead the more complex alternatives I have already described. The WMG on Sustainable Development[22] is very clear, for example, that post-2015 development agendas must challenge existing models. And we are buoyed by stronger calls from progressive social movements and civil society overall for "system change, not climate change."[23]

This advocacy has had the greatest impact so far in regional and sub-regional forums including the preparatory meeting for UN climate negotiations held in Venezuela in November, 2014, where ministers from 40 countries did appear responsive to our concerns.[24] Earlier, an inaugural meeting of Pacific governments and diverse civil society groups in Fiji in June, 2014 actually produced outcome documents that incorporate language drafted in collaboration with civil society calling for a coherent regional approach to challenges in social, economic, and ecological sustainability.[25]

Fourth, feminist groups, together with larger social movements, are demanding greater oversight and accountability from governments and the UN on the degree to which business and financial institutions dominate state responses to climate change and other challenges. According to Nicole Bidegain Ponte and Corina Rodríguez Enríquez of DAWN, proposals on private and corporate accountability are still weak overall. But that is not deterring advocates, who continue to call for a binding multi-lateral code of conduct for transnational corporations, one that monitors compliance with human rights obligations and environmental standards. We find multi-lateral advancements in this area, for example through a recent UN Human Rights Council resolution entitled, "Elaboration of an International Legally Binding Instrument on Transnational Corporations and other Business Enterprises with respect to Human Rights."[26]

At the global level, in anticipation of the final year of the post-2015 development agenda process and UNFCCC climate summit scheduled for Paris in 2015, feminist groups must ensure better and more rigorous regulation of corporations. The SDGs are instead promoting an increasingly central role for the corporate sector as a driver of development without adequate provisions for regulation and accountability.[27] Despite intensive civil society lobbying, recent drafts of the SDGs contain no language on the responsibility of business to protect and advance human rights and no regulatory framework for their governance.[28] The potential hazards of such common business practices as environmental contamination, tax evasion, or suppression of labor rights are nowhere acknowledged.[29]

Conclusion

A complex systems approach to environmental challenges requires new paradigms that integrate gender, climate change, and sustainable development. We also need stronger progressive alliances that acknowledge current intra- and inter-state inequalities and changing global geo-politics, but also assist to transcend geographies and disciplines. The stressed and chaotic state of our ecosystems—the uneven progress of sexual and gender justice and human rights—the inadequate and inequitable development paths proposed to date—urgently demand a more compelling response, and feminists have an obligation and opportunity to provide it.

Notes

1 I acknowledge with gratitude the editorial and research support of Nataya Friedan and Terry McGovern in preparing this written reflection.
2 Intergovernmental Panel on Climate Change, "Summary for Policymakers," in *Climate Change 2014: Impacts, Adaptation, and Vulnerability. Part A: Global and Sectoral Aspects. Contribution of Working Group II to the Fifth Assessment Report of the Intergovernmental Panel on Climate Change,* ed. Christopher B. Field, Vicente R. Barros, D.J. Dokken, Katherine J. Mach, Michael D. Mastrandrea, T.E. Bilir, Monalisa Chatterjee, K.L. Ebi, Y.O. Estrada, R.C. Genova, B. Girma, E.S. Kissel, A.N. Levy, S. MacCracken, P.R. Mastrandrea, and L.L. White (Cambridge and New York: Cambridge University Press, 2014), 1–32.
3 Koko Warner, Kees van der Geest, Sonke Kreft, Saleemul Huq, Sven Harmeling, Koen Kusters, and Alex de Sherbinin, *Evidence from the Front Lines of Climate Change: Loss and Damage to Communities Despite Coping and Adaption,* Loss and Damage in Vulnerable Communities Initiative Report No. 9, United Nations University Institute for Environment and Human Security, 2012, http://i.unu.edu/media/unu.edu/publication/31467/6815.pdf.
4 International Program on the State of the Ocean and International Union for the Conservation of Nature, *The State of the Ocean 2013; Perils, Prognoses and Proposals,* 13 October 2013, www.stateoftheocean.org/pdfs/IPSO-Summary-Oct13-FINAL.pdf.
5 Intergovernmental Panel on Climate Change, *Climate Change 2007: Impacts, Adaption and Vulnerability. Contribution of the Working Group II to the Fourth Assessment Report of the Intergovernmental Panel on Climate Change,* ed. M.L. Parry, O.F. Canziani, J.P. Paluikof, P.J. van der Linden, and C.E. Hanson (Cambridge: Cambridge University Press, 2007).
6 Intergovernmental Panel on Climate Change, "Summary for Policymakers," in: *Climate Change 2014: Impacts, Adaptation, and Vulnerability. Part A: Global and Sectoral Aspects. Contribution of Working Group II to the Fifth Assessment Report of the Intergovernmental Panel on Climate Change,* ed. Christopher B. Field, Vicente R. Barros, D.J. Dokken, Katherine J. Mach, Michael D. Mastrandrea, T.E. Bilir, Monalisa Chatterjee, K.L. Ebi, Y.O. Estrada, R.C. Genova, B. Girma, E.S. Kissel, A.N. Levy, S. MacCracken, P.R. Mastrandrea, and L.L. White (Cambridge and New York: Cambridge University Press, 2014), 6–7.
7 Intergovernmental Panel on Climate Change, "Summary for Policymakers," in: *Climate Change 2014: Impacts, Adaptation, and Vulnerability. Part A: Global and Sectoral Aspects. Contribution of Working Group II to*

the *Fifth Assessment Report of the Intergovernmental Panel on Climate Change*, ed. Christopher B. Field, Vicente R. Barros, D.J. Dokken, Katherine J. Mach, Michael D. Mastrandrea, T.E. Bilir, Monalisa Chatterjee, K.L. Ebi, Y.O. Estrada, R.C. Genova, B. Girma, E.S. Kissel, A.N. Levy, S. MacCracken, P.R. Mastrandrea, and L.L. White (Cambridge and New York: Cambridge University Press, 2014), 7.

8 World Health Organization, *Climate Change and Health: Key facts*, www. who.int/mediacentre/factsheets/fs266/en/.

9 Shakoor Hajat, Sotiris Vardoulakis, Clare Heaviside, and Bernd Eggen, "Climate Change Effects on Human Health: Projections of Temperature-related Mortality for the UK during the 2020s, 2050s and 2080s," *Journal of Epidemiology and Community Health* (2014).

10 World Health Organization, *Climate Change and Hhealth: Key facts*, www. who.int/mediacentre/factsheets/fs266/en/.

11 Noelene Nabulivou, "Extractive Feminists and Women's Movements: Proposals Toward Post-extractivist, Ecologically Sustainable and Just Futures," in *Gender Equality, Women's Rights and Women's Priorities – Recommendations for the Proposed SDGs and the Post 2015 Development Agenda*, ed. Women's Major Group (2013), 114–116.

12 Women's Major Group, "We will not be mainstreamed into a polluted stream: feminist visions of structural transformations for achieving women's human rights and gender equality in the 2015 development agenda." Statement read at *Advancing the Post-2015 Sustainable Development Agenda: Reconfirming Rights – Recognising Limits – Redefining Goals*, Bonn, Germany, 20–22 March 2013.

13 "Governments Gamble with Our Future. South Feminists Demand Responsible Action Now," Joint Statement by Women Activists from the Economic South Rio+20, Rio de Janeiro, Brazil, 22 June 2012, www.da wnnet.org/advocacy-cso.php?id=248.

14 "Governments Gamble with Our Future. South Feminists Demand Responsible Action Now," Joint Statement by Women Activists from the Economic South Rio+20, Rio de Janiero, Brazil, 22 June 2012, http://www. dawnnet.org/advocacy-cso.php?id=248.

15 Geraldine Terry, "No climate justice without gender justice: an overview of the issues," *Gender & Development* 17, no. 1 (2009): 5–18.

16 Olubayo Oluduro and Ebenezer Durojaye, "The Implications of Oil Pollution for the Enjoyment of Sexual and Reproductive Rights of Women in Niger Delta Area of Nigeria," *The International Journal of Human Rights* 17, nos 7–8 (2013): 772–795.

17 Olubayo Oluduro and Ebenezer Durojaye, "The Implications of Oil Pollution for the Enjoyment of Sexual and Reproductive Rights of Women in Niger Delta Area of Nigeria," *The International Journal of Human Rights* 17, nos 7–8 (2013): 772–795.

18 GRAVIS, *Women Miners in Rajasthan, India: A Reflection on their Life, Challenges and Future*, 2010, www.indianet.nl/pdf/WomenMinersInRaja sthan.pdf.

19 Olubayo Oluduro and Ebenezer Durojaye, "The Implications of Oil Pollution for the Enjoyment of Sexual and Reproductive Rights of Women in Niger Delta Area of Nigeria," *The International Journal of Human Rights* 17, nos 7–8 (2013): 772–795.

20 Olubayo Oluduro and Ebenezer Durojaye, "The Implications of Oil Pollution for the Enjoyment of Sexual and Reproductive Rights of Women in Niger Delta Area of Nigeria," *The International Journal of Human Rights* 17, nos 7–8 (2013): 772–795.

21 Michael Warren and Natacha Pisarenko, "Argentines Link Health Problems to Agrochemicals," *The Associated Press*, 20 October 2013, http://bigstory.ap.org/article/argentines-link-health-problems-agrochemicals-2.

22 The Women's Major Group was created at the Earth Summit in Rio de Janeiro, Brazil in 1992, where governments recognized women as one of the nine key societal constituencies for sustained input to achieve sustainable development. Others include indigenous people, children and youth, farmers, trade unions, etc.

23 See the full statement *Mobilize and organize to Stop and Prevent Planet Fever*, at http://climatespace2013.wordpress.com/2014/09/16/mobilize-and-organize-to-stop-and-prevent-planet-fever/.

24 *Key Messages for the COP 20 and Ministers Meeting at the 2014 PreCOP, Island of Margarita*, 6 November 2013, www.precopsocial.org/sites/default/files/key_messages_for_ministers_social_precop_2014.pdf.

25 Diverse Voices and Action of Equality (DIVA), "Statement at the Conclusion of UNFCCC, COP20," Lima, Peru, 14 December 2014. Pacific Partnerships to Strengthen Gender, Climate Change Response and Sustainable Development, "Outcome Statement by Government and Civil Society Participants: Equitable, Effective and Meaningful Partnerships to Address Gender Equality and Climate Change in Pursuit of Sustainable Development," Nadi, Fiji, 9–10 June 2014, www.divafiji.com/gender-cc-sustainable-dev.

26 Human Rights Council of the General Assembly, "Elaboration of an International Legally Binding Instrument on Transnational Corporations and Other Business Enterprises with Respect to Human Rights," 2014, 26th session (A/HRC/26/L.22).

27 Women's Major Group, *Women's "8 Red Flags" Following the Conclusion of the Open Working Group on Sustainable Development Goals (SDGs)*, www.womenmajorgroup.org/wp-content/uploads/2014/07/Womens-Major-Group_OWG_FINALSTATEMENT_21July.pdf.

28 Women's Major Group, *Women's "8 Red Flags" Following the Conclusion of the Open Working Group on Sustainable Development Goals (SDGs)*, www.womenmajorgroup.org/wp-content/uploads/2014/07/Womens-Major-Group_OWG_FINALSTATEMENT_21July.pdf.

29 Radhika Balakrishnan and Ignacio Saiz, "Transforming the Development Agenda Requires More, not Less, Attention to Human Rights," *Open Democracy*, 15 September 2014, www.opendemocracy.net/openglobalrights-blog/radhika-balakrishnan-and-ignacio-saiz/transforming-development-agenda-requires.

30 Women's role in energy access solutions to climate change

A reflection

Wanjira Mathai

The Seventh Assessment of the Intergovernmental Panel on Climate Change acknowledges that Africa is one of the most vulnerable continents to climate change and climate variability. The continent will see increased drought, erratic rainfall, floods, crop failures, and a consequent migration of large numbers of people, which will exacerbate already existing tensions. In 2007, my late mother, the Nobel Prize-winning Professor Wangari Mutta Maathai, observed that while climate change will negatively affect the economies of wealthy countries, in Africa, where people's daily lives are closely linked to their environment, the consequences will be a matter of life and death.

This is why it is essential that African leaders and civil society be involved in global decision-making on how to address the climate crisis in ways both effective and equitable. In turn, as major polluters, the industrialized countries have a responsibility to assist Africa and other developing regions by sharing technologies and identifying funding to reduce the vulnerability of the prime victims of the climate crisis who are likely to be poor, very young, and, more often than not, female.

This chapter reflects on and advocates for the continued expansion of one such effort: the promotion of clean energy entrepreneurship by women. Women's leadership in clean energy technologies such as solar lamps and clean cookstoves provides one of our best opportunities to address both energy access and climate change. Since 2010, the Global Alliance for Clean Cookstoves (GACC) has led the way in highlighting this little known issue, and in collaboration with local partners has reached an estimated 20 million households with cleaner and more efficient cookstoves and fuels.[1] In 2013, the US Department of State, in association with the Wangari Maathai Institute for Peace & Environmental Studies in Kenya, among others, launched our own collaboration to these ends—the Partnership on Women's Entrepreneurship in

Renewables, simply called the wPOWER Hub. Our goal is to empower more than 8,000 women across East Africa, Nigeria, and India who will, in turn, reach an estimated 3.5 million people over the next three years. The program builds on the work of the GACC and incorporates strategies developed by Kenya's own Green Belt Movement founded by my mother nearly 40 years ago.

The dimensions of the challenge

Globally, more than 1.3 billion people lack access to electricity, and some 2.7 billion people lack access to clean cooking technologies and fuels and instead cook on open fires or inefficient cooking technologies mainly fueled by solid biomass such as wood or charcoal. Although not the primary source of climate pollution, inefficient lighting and cooking contribute to climate change and the degradation of natural resources by increasing emissions into the atmosphere from the incomplete combustion of traditional, inefficient cooking technologies, which release pollutants at 100 times the recommended levels. Burning solid biomass is inefficient at converting energy to heat and releases a toxic mix of health-damaging pollutants, such as black carbon, which contributes about a quarter of all carbon dioxide-induced warming globally, and methane, the second-largest cause of climate change after carbon dioxide.

Increased demand for biomass fuel—mainly charcoal and firewood— also promotes illegal logging, and ultimately affects the livelihood of millions of families who live near forests and rely on them for subsistence. One vital component of a sustainable future must be standing forests. They contain the biodiversity that makes life possible for numerous animal species, including humans. Thick, healthy stands of indigenous trees also absorb huge amounts of carbon dioxide and hold vast reserves of carbon in their soils. As trees are felled for timber, charcoal, agriculture, human settlements, or commercial development, the world loses a vital component needed to slow, and ultimately reverse, global warming. Depletion of wood-based biomass is estimated to be responsible for 18 percent of all greenhouse gas emissions.

The Swedish Environmental Institute also reports that in Sub Saharan Africa the impact of inefficient biomass energy use is felt across multiple sectors.[2] Indoor air pollution adversely affects health, leading to an estimated 1.5 million deaths, disproportionately of women and children who spend more time at home. It impacts agriculture as communities cut down timber for fuel and tillable land. It limits opportunities for education because fuel wood collection can take close to five hours and require travel of up to 15 kilometers per day, leaving less time, especially for girls, to attend school. It reduces capacity for growth in formal economic activity and trade, as the informal charcoal sector in Sub Saharan Africa is estimated to be worth over eight billion US dollars and to employ over seven million people. In Kenya alone, over 65 percent of the population relies on firewood and charcoal for cooking and heating. Firewood is the fuel of choice for 85 percent of the country's rural population—charcoal, for 80 percent of the urban population. These statistics seen together tell a compelling story.

Investing in alternative approaches with women at the center

What is needed is a more integrated approach to biodiversity conversation and biomass energy—one that integrates women directly into the energy access value chain. This at once makes them beneficiaries of improved energy technologies and also managers and entrepreneurs with the power to purchase the energy alternatives their families need and also to make environmentally sound decisions. Clean energy technologies are being adopted in greater numbers as women entrepreneurs market, sell, and use them themselves. The natural environment and human health are also protected as women increase the efficiency of energy used for cooking and lighting.

According to the GACC "Women can play a unique role within the cookstove and fuel value chains, as they often excel in entrepreneurial activities and can leverage their existing networks for distribution, marketing, and sales." The GACC has included the empowerment of women as an explicit goal in its mission statement, recognizing that clean cookstoves and fuel solutions cannot be successfully designed or promoted without their full participation and input.[3]

Forging the wPOWER Hub partnership

To these ends, the US Department of State and USAID have recently teamed up with the GACC, the MacArthur Foundation, CARE International, Solar Sister, Swayam Shikshan Prayog of India, and the Wangari Maathai Institute for Peace & Environmental Studies in Kenya. The wPOWER Hub aims to empower women entrepreneurs by training them in best practices for sustainable clean energy entrepreneurship, creating platforms for experience-based learning, and building a body of sound program evaluation and research. In just a short time we have supported the training of 27 sustainable clean energy leaders from India, Nigeria, and East Africa to, in turn, train grassroots entrepreneurs. In 2015, we plan to reach an additional 360.

The Hub is working to accomplish these goals by engaging women as leaders of their communities and as agents to promote sound environmental stewardship by distributing clean cooking and lighting solutions. We are playing a critical role by sponsoring our Train the Trainer (TOT) workshops, by facilitating African and Indian women leadership exchanges, and by building broader public awareness of the critical role of women entrepreneurs in the clean energy value chain.

With the input of leading experts and practitioners, GACC has identified market-based approaches as the most sustainable way to achieve universal adoption of clean cooking solutions. Without the ability to sell tens of millions of new appliances a year, it will not be possible to meet the cooking needs of the more than 600 million households around the world still using solid fuels in inefficient cookstoves and open fires.[4] Despite decades of prior effort, programs that were targeted geographically and heavily subsidized to simply give away new appliances, without developing competitive models for consumers, and without educating or incentivizing them to have a stake in those new appliances and maintain them, have generally not been successful.

It has now been widely demonstrated that a more comprehensive undertaking combining community education and social marketing with financing for consumers to select from a range of competitive products and with easily available repair services after sales—in essence a market-based approach—is more effective. This approach is described in *Igniting Change: A Strategy for Universal Adoption of Clean Cookstoves and Fuels* published by GACC.[5] Currently the market for clean cookstoves is highly fragmented and underdeveloped. What is necessary to catalyze a thriving market is donor support and subsidies for new product development and marketing, for the training of women entrepreneurs as a sales force, and for the provision of credit to consumers at point of purchase.

Building on the insights of the Green Belt Movement

The establishment of the wPOWER Hub at the Wangari Maathai Institute recognizes my late mother's success in building Africa's Green Belt Movement (GBM), which for nearly 40 years has worked to empower grassroots women by engaging them in environmental, social, and civic activities. Founded in 1977, GBM has long responded to the concerns of rural Kenyan women who saw their streams drying up and their food and fuel supplies depleting. GBM builds confidence and skills with a combination of personal counseling and technical assistance to grow seedlings and plant new trees that bind the soil, store rainwater, and provide food and fuel.

Early on my mother recognized that the everyday hardships these women and their communities face poverty, unemployment, environmental degradation, water scarcity, deforestation, and food insecurity are symptoms of deeper issues of poor governance, inequalities, and, especially for the women, a sense of disempowerment and disenfranchisement. She understood that to resolve larger economic hardships, one first must address these deeper psychosocial challenges. To that end, she developed what remains a cornerstone of GBM's programming, its Community Education and Empowerment Seminars facilitated discussions that inspire communities, largely of women, to reject an often deeply entrenched sense of fatalism, awaken their own agency, and take action. These involve exercises in what we call *kwimenya* or self-knowledge on issues of democratic governance, such as the need to vote, to manage resources wisely, to respect the rights of others, and to maintain a peaceful order.[6] And we have seen that over time this empowerment process can transform entire communities by promoting the authority and confidence of women to engage as volunteers, or in formal leadership roles and income-generating activities. The Wangari Maathai Institute's curriculum on "Sustainable Clean Energy Entrepreneurship" incorporates GBM's module on transformative leadership.[7] Research abounds to support the role of women entrepreneurs in the energy sector.[8]

Conclusion

Wangari Maathai spent half her life trying to tackle what she considered to be one of Africa's greatest predicaments. In *The Challenge for Africa* she describes the dilemma of a woman farmer in Cameroon through whom she illustrates our collective challenge and opportunity.[9]

My mother had been appointed by the leaders of ten African governments to serve as a goodwill ambassador for the Congo Basin Forest Ecosystem. As she stood outside her hotel in the town of Yaoundé, waiting to be driven to her meetings, she looked up at farmers working a nearby hillside. On keener observation she noticed one in particular—a woman tilling the land, along the gradient of the hill, in a manner sure to result in severe soil erosion when the rains fell.[10] The hardworking woman did not have the benefit of scientific training in soil conservation to sustain crops and protect her family's livelihood.

My mother believed passionately that unless we reach this ordinary woman with information, appropriate technologies and a sense of her own capacity for action, all of our efforts elsewhere are futile. As she wrote, "unless that farmer—and millions of others like her—acquires what she needs to develop her skills, and educates herself and her children, and is encouraged to make decisions that take her on a different path, the future generations will look back fifty or a hundred years from now and shake their heads."[11] The GACC and the wPOWER Project present two new reasons for hope in a better future achieved through improved technologies and the training of women leaders and entrepreneurs to promote sustainable clean energy and address climate change.

Notes

1 Global Alliance for Clean Cookstoves (GACC), *Igniting Change: A Strategy for Universal Adoption of Clean Cookstoves & Fuels*, November 2011.

2 Stockholm Environmental A # 20, 2014; Stockholm Environmental Institute, *From Cleaner Cookstoves to Clean Cooking. Thinking Beyond Technology to a Systems Approach*, Technical Brief, May 2014; Stockholm Environmental Institute, *Achieving Sustainable Charcoal in Kenya, Harnessing the Opportunities for Cross-Sectoral Integration*, Technical Brief, May 2014.

3 GACC, *Igniting Change: A Strategy for Universal Adoption of Clean Cookstoves & Fuels*, November 2011.

4 GACC, *Factsheet: General Cookstoves*, 2014; GACC, *Factsheet: Cookstoves & Climate Change*, 2014; and GACC, *Factsheet: Women & Livelihoods & Clean Cookstoves Can Save Lives & Improve Livelihoods*

5 GACC, *Igniting Change: A Strategy for Universal Adoption of Clean Cookstoves and Fuels*, November 2011.

6 Wangari Maathai, *Unbowed: A Memoir* (New York: Alfred A. Knopf, 2006), 170.

7 Wangari Maathai Institute, *Wangari Maathai Institute for Peace and Environmental Studies. Strategic Plan 2010–2020* (Nairobi, Kenya: Wangari Maathai Institute, 2010).

8 Frances M. Amatucci and Daria C. Crawley, "Financial Self-Efficacy among Women Entrepreneurs," *International Journal of Gender and Entrepreneurship* 3, no. 1 (2010): 23–37; Candida G. Brush, Patricia G. Greene, Donna J. Kelley, and Yana Litovsky, *Global Entrepreneurship Monitor 2010 Women's Report: Women Entrepreneurship Worldwide,* Babson College, 2011; Leslie Corders, Gail Karlsson, and Richenda Van Leeuwen, *Leveraging New Technology for Women's Empowerment: Setting the Context: Challenges and Opportunities* (Audio), Council on Foreign Relations, 2010; Corporate Citizenship, *Women Mean Business: Empowerment in Developing Markets*, Corporate Citizenship, 2012; Ernst & Young, *Scaling up: Why Women-owned Businesses Can Recharge Global Economy* (London: Ernst & Young, 2012); Srilatha Batliwala and Amulya K.N Reddy, "Energy for

Women and Women for Energy: A Proposal for Women's Energy Entrepreneurship," *ENERGIA News* 1 (December 1996): 11–13; Srilatha Batliwala and Amulya K.N Reddy, "Energy for Women and Women for Energy: Engendering Energy and Empowering Women," *Energy for Sustainable Development* 3, no. 3 (2003); Elizabeth Cecelski, *The Role of Women in Sustainable Energy Development*, National Renewable Energy Laboratory, Subcontractor Report, June 2000; Joy Clancy, Tanja Winther, Magi Matinga, and Sheila Oparaocha, *Gender Equity in Access to and Benefits from Modern Energy and Improved Energy Technologies: World Development Report Background Paper*, ETC and ENERGIA, September 2011; Joy S. Clancy and Margaret Skutsch, *The Gender-energy Poverty Nexus: Finding the Energy to Address Gender Concerns in Developing Countries*, UK Department for International Development, 2002; UNDP, *Generating Opportunities: Case Studies on Energy and Women*, ed. Gail V. Karlsson and Salome Misana (New York: UNDP, 2001).

9   Wangari Maathai, *The Challenge for Africa* (New York: Pantheon Books, 2009).
10 Wangari Maathai, *The Challenge for Africa*.
11 Wangari Maathai, *The Challenge for Africa*, 17.

Afterword

The Honorable Hillary Rodham Clinton

IN CONVERSATION WITH LISSA MUSCATINE

In 1995, Hillary Rodham Clinton traveled to the United Nations Fourth World Conference on Women in Beijing and delivered a speech that has since been widely acclaimed as among the most important of her tenure as First Lady.

She argued that criminal behaviors against women must no longer be hidden behind the protective shroud of religion and culture. She demanded universal legal remedies to harmful discriminatory practices long condoned under claims of respect for pluralism. She framed the issue of women's rights as a moral imperative first and foremost, but also as a necessary condition for success in US diplomacy, development, and defense policies—if America's aim is to meet the world's most critical challenges. Adapting a central tenet of the global women's movement, she said most memorably that women's rights are human rights, and human rights are women's rights, once and for all—a paradigm that has since become a global mantra.

Many at home, especially conservatives, but also a number of skeptics on her husband's national security team, opposed the trip. And the Chinese government banned coverage of her speech by local media. Yet through her efforts then and since, large numbers of people around the world who simply never thought this way before have come to understand that investing in women and girls is a good in its own right and a critical tool to help secure nations by stimulating economic growth, reducing poverty, improving public health, and helping to sustain the natural environment.

As US Secretary of State in the first term of the Obama administration, Mrs. Clinton translated these principles into enduring US policies and programs. Through her recent work at the Clinton Foundation, she led an effort to measure and assess the practical impact of new gender norms as a necessary foundation for future investment and progress.

Secretary Clinton spoke to the Roosevelt Institute's Women and Girls Rising conference on September 12, 2014 in conversation with Lissa Muscatine, currently the proprietor of Washington's renowned Politics and Prose bookstore, but for many years, a senior aide to Mrs. Clinton at the State Department and in the White House, who traveled with her to Beijing. The interview appears here, adapted from a transcript and edited for context.

HRC: Oh my goodness! This is like a reunion, looking out at the audience here!

LM: I wonder if you can take yourself back, a little more than 19 years ago today, when you landed in Beijing. Let's be honest, the months leading up to that moment were a diplomatic and political minefield. Many people here at home, especially conservatives, did not want you to go. There were tensions with China over Taiwan and nuclear proliferation. Even many officials in your husband's own State Department were a little uneasy. And then, of course there was the arrest of Harry Wu.[1] For six or seven weeks, it appeared you would not make the trip. And by the way, I could tell some very funny stories about how determined you were to do so. Many of us thought you would get a boat and row yourself across the Pacific, if necessary. But finally, Harry Wu was released, and you were able to go. Why did the conference matter so much to you?

HRC: Well first, my thanks to all of you in this audience, many of whom have been the stalwart leaders of the women's movement here in the United States and around the world over the last 30, 40 years. Part of the reason I was so determined to go to Beijing is that I had not gone to the UN women's meetings in Mexico City, Copenhagen, or Nairobi, which a number of you were instrumental in shaping. I thought that those conferences had begun to raise important issues about women and girls, but that we still had not coalesced around a practical program for action.

We needed a program for action that could be used from the capital cities of the most highly developed, industrialized countries to remote rural villages in the developing world. Having myself worked over many years on behalf of women's rights, I was excited by the prospect of seeing the many strands—the broad spectrum—of the global women's movement coalesce, not only at the official conference of UN parliamentarians, but also at the NGO conference in Hairou.

As Lissa said, my getting there was not an easy task. We did have a formal delegation, made up of a lot of wonderful people and had long been counting on having a very strong US presence. But for both personal and political reasons I wanted to be there too. We had to jump a lot of hurdles to get that to happen.

There was a good deal of indifference and some very active opposition. On the indifference side, there were a lot of people in our government at that time and in Congress who really didn't believe that issues affecting women should be a high priority. "If you want to go to the UN Conference in Beijing, go ahead," they kept saying, "but don't make a big deal out of it because who knows what might happen?"

And then there was the active opposition primarily around Harry Wu. Even some of our best friends in the Congress were dead set against my going because of his arrest. They saw my going at this time as a concession to China. I saw a UN conference that happened to be in Beijing and thought it would be a serious mistake if we did not participate. But thankfully the stars did align. Harry Wu was released, the congressional opposition receded, and the internal governmental indifference was overcome.

As the honorary chair of the US delegation, I was then asked to speak. This gave us a platform to make a very strong case on behalf of human rights as women's rights and women's rights as human rights. Lissa was my partner in drafting that speech and spent many, many hours gathering good input from many people, including our friend Madeleine Albright, who was then serving as US Ambassador to the UN. We had a great group in our official delegation and an even bigger and more wonderful collection of participants at the NGO Forum in Hairou.

LM: Speaking of the convening power of this conference, let's talk for a moment about Hairou, which became such a symbol of determination and resilience for many women who were essentially exiled to this very undersized venue in monsoon-like weather. It was pretty dramatic.

HRC: Many of you know Donna Shalala, who was Secretary of Health and Human Services in those years and my wonderful friend—a great, great person in every way. She co-chaired the delegation, and there was so much pushing and shoving through the storm, and a lot of security officials trying to keep people out of the venue where I was speaking. Donna, who is not the tallest person in the room, was being knocked around, and honest-to-goodness I think she just crawled under their legs. She was indefatigable, and determined to get there. I have a mental image of my asking "Where's Donna," and suddenly I heard her say: "I'm coming, I'm coming!"

LM: A human chain of Secret Service agents roping us all in, but I was thinking about this in the context of an unrelated famous photo taken a while later of you and Madeleine Albright darting into a women's room to exchange a confidential word. So many such serendipitous things happened in Beijing, with official delegates and NGO representatives meeting not just in formal conference rooms, but in corridors and hotel rooms. I'm wondering if Beijing was in a way that photo of you and Madeleine, writ large—a moment that gave women space and propelled the global women's movement to another level.

HRC: Well, historians will have to decide, but I recall that the Platform for Action, though hotly and heavily negotiated and attacked from many different perspectives, was a giant step forward. Bella Abzug was especially fabulous, as always, in standing her ground on behalf of a number of the difficult issues addressed. But the United States wasn't alone. We worked with many partners. The Platform for Action set forth a template for moving toward achieving the full participation of girls and women in a broad range of political, social, economic, and security arenas. Historically, it's a very important document, along with the Declaration of Sentiments from Seneca Falls and other milestones along the way. It was important for two overriding reasons. It represented a hard won consensus. UN meetings require unanimity, and we achieved it. That gives us a point of departure with every country in the world that signed on and pledged to continue to move toward full participation of women.

The second reason is that it really did tackle the issues most pressing at that time. As some of you who are working with us know, Melinda Gates and her foundation staff are partnering with the Clinton Foundation on a project to take stock of how much progress the world has made in achieving those 12 full participation goals from Beijing. (I think they are watching the videostream of this conference now). Five years after Beijing, we also got the UN Millennium Development Goals, with gender equity central to many of them, so now, for the first time, we really can chart progress and hold nations accountable.

We call this "No Ceilings: the Full Participation Project" to try to pull together all the data to really understand the gaps. This is work I started as Secretary of State, working with the UN Foundation, whose president, Kathy Calvin, is also in the audience. We know there are big gaps in data. We're still not collecting enough data that are usable about girls and women in many places in the world. We are aiming toward the 20th anniversary of Beijing, which happens to coincide with the next round of UN development goals, to build on top of the Millennium Development Goals and address some of these gaps. So much of what we are doing arises out of the agreed-upon Platform for Action from Beijing. So I think in the future it is really going to be seen as an extraordinarily historic achievement for women and girls, and especially for young people everywhere.

LM: This goes part and parcel with the whole notion of needing to get women's issues off the margins onto the front-and-center stage of foreign policy and domestic policy. This is something I have heard you say as long as I've known you, and I'm sure you were saying it before that. These are not tangential issues. They're not soft issues. They must be dealt with holistically. Where are we on that? Some of this is evolutionary, some of it is revolutionary, some of it is visible, some invisible, but how far along have we gotten in making sure this is happening? I also want to say that in addition to work you did in Arkansas and as First Lady, you started Vital Voices with Madeleine Albright at the State Department, and you did even more in the Senate to give voice to women. Bringing women from Afghanistan who had lived under the Taliban to testify in Congress, and your choices of whom to meet or what countries to visit, were often making a statement. Then, of course, as Secretary you are able to institutionalize gender equity as part of the foreign policy agenda. These are really important steps, they came in fits and starts, but overall where do things stand?

HRC: Well, as Secretary of State, building on these experiences, I strongly believed we needed to make the rights of girls and women a central focus of American foreign policy. Now when I raised this, there was a standard reaction from many people in our own government and elsewhere: "Well that's nice, every secretary has his or her pet project. This is yours, really very understandable, so go off and do whatever it is you're going to do."

I quickly realized that for me, as I know for many of you, recognizing women's rights as human rights is a fundamental moral issue. It is integral and essential to everything I believe about human dignity, about freedom, about agency, and I have made that argument and continue to do so.

But I also realized, as I know a number of you have, that making the moral argument—the human rights argument—however critical and essential, may not change people's minds. As First Lady, as a Senator, and then as Secretary of State—especially in the beginning of my tenure, I literally would watch eyes roll when I started to talk about how women and girls deserve to be at the center of American foreign policy. "It's reflective of our values. It's part of who we are. It's the unfinished business of the twenty-first century," I would say. "We defeated slavery in the nineteenth century. We defeated Fascism and Communism in the twentieth century. Now we need to unleash respect for women and girls and further defend their rights." But more than in the past, I realized as Secretary that I also had to figure out ways to break through that sense of "been-there-done-that, let's talk about the real issues."

So we began in the State Department to institutionalize the importance of the rights of women and girls—their full participation in our foreign policy—by several steps. One, we created the first ever position of Ambassador for Global Women's Issues, and I really appreciate the fact that President Obama was right there with me on this. We appointed Melanne Verveer. Before that there had been pockets within the State Department—a woman's office, here, a woman's issue there—but we wanted these issues elevated to the same importance as anything else we were dealing with. Literally the last day of my tenure, the President signed an executive order making that ambassadorship permanent. So we have a focal point, we have an office, and we have a visible woman to carry this on with Melanne's successor, Cathy Rogers.

Number two, when we did the first ever review of the State Department and USAID we integrated women's issues across the exercise. We thought it important that they not be an afterthought—not be marginalized. So we began to integrate women's issues in the State Department across all of the bureaus.

Then I sent out the first all-person cable. Secretaries of State do this on urgent matters. I sent a cable to everybody working for the State Department around the world, saying that gender equity is a key goal. We then worked on the first ever US National Plan on Women, Peace and Security, worked closely with the Defense Department. (And now, under Melanne's leadership Georgetown University has the first academic program anywhere in the world on women, peace, and security.) We also changed the curriculum of the Foreign Service Institute, which is where Foreign Service officers get trained and re-trained for their postings. So, there is a long list of what we tried to do to institutionalize gender equity.

In addition, we began to comb through the data looking for better ways to make the argument about women's rights as a moral imperative more understandable to people who give you lip service but don't change their behaviors. That's when we began working on the data conference we held in Washington hosted by the Gallup Organization, which has polled for 50 years around the world. Gallup has a lot of good information about what people are thinking and how you position arguments to change people's minds, and we began looking for where we had accomplishments and where we were falling short.

The easiest way of describing this is that we've made progress on girls' education, and we've made progress on health, particularly maternal mortality and access to health care. But we have not made much progress on economic participation, on political and civil rights and on peace and security. And even where we have made progress, it is often limited.

I'll give you an example; we've made enormous progress in enabling girls to achieve primary education, but then they drop out. There are many reasons, often deeply cultural or religious, or just the result of simple concerns about security. I've visited a number of villages in South Asia and Africa, for example, where girls go to the primary school because it's nearby, but the high school, as you might expect, is a mile or two away, and parents are afraid to let their daughters travel that far alone. So how do you tackle that specific issue—is it transportation, or boarding during the week, or organized groups to accompany the girls?

Now on economics, during the nineties as First Lady I was in Africa meeting with a group of economists, anthropologists, and others. Everywhere I'd ever been during my trip, I'd seen women working; in the fields, in markets, carrying firewood, carrying water, caring for children, tilling the fields. So I asked: "How do you account for the contributions that women's labor makes?" And again I got one of those looks, "Well that's not part of the economy," the experts responded. "Really," I said. "Well if all the women in Africa, Asia, Latin America, and the United States stop working, our economies will be in bad shape."

But the informal economy was still not considered part of the economy. Therefore, the many contributions of women to gross domestic product went uncounted. We were not able to make the argument, until finally, the World Bank, the IMF, and other respected groups began making the case that leaving women out of the formal economy, or putting obstacles in their way, along with not counting their contributions in the informal economy, means that countries are overlooking potential economic growth.

So I gave a speech before something called the Asia-Pacific Economic Community, which the United States hosted in 2011 in

Hawaii, reviewing all the data and making the argument that every country in the world has barriers to women's full economic participation. If countries started to tear those barriers down, their gross domestic product will rise.

The world leader who paid the most attention was Prime Minister Abe of Japan, and he's actually in Tokyo right now holding a big conference about how to get more Japanese women into the formal economy. He's now convinced that doing so will raise the Japanese GDP by an estimated 9 percent. In a country like Egypt, it would be more like 34 percent.

So let's see what we've accomplished. Let's be grateful, even proud in some cases, but by no means have we accomplished enough. Let's try to address what is not happening, and let's try to marshal data and arguments to get more people to look at the areas where we're the furthest behind.

LM: What you're doing at No Ceilings creates a fresh paradigm. Everyone in this room knows the Chinese saying that women hold up half the sky. Well, actually, it's more than half the sky. If we do this data collection, we can actually prove that.

As we all know from reading the newspaper or watching the news, unfathomable challenges for women and girls remain in this country and beyond our borders, from gender-based violence to pay equity—still only 77 cents on the dollar on average in the United States. I want to circle back to Beijing. Something happened on the plane flying into Beijing that I will never forget as long as I live, and I just want to tell this story quickly. We had the final draft of the speech pretty much in shape, and I made it up to your cabin to get one last read through, and forgive me for sounding extremely corny, but I handed you the speech, and you paused and said, "I just want to push the envelope on women's rights as far as I can."

It was one of those moments when I felt so proud to be an American—so proud that you were our First Lady, and despite the political and diplomatic minefield this trip presented, that you were willing to push the envelope. So, last question: what does it mean to push the envelope in today's world?

HRC: Right. I think a lot about that because my daughter Chelsea is co-chairing No Ceilings with me at the foundation. First of all, we need to know the facts—we can't push the envelope if we don't know where the envelope is. We have to do a better job sorting out what has happened, and then coming forth with an agenda for the next 20 years.

I invite everyone here to participate in this exercise, to give us your thoughts, your ideas. We'll have several more convenings as we go forward over the next year to talk through what the data tell us, because I really think data is our friend. We have to be smart about it and utilize it effectively.

But I've also found that young women, especially the so-called Millennials, but some who are older as well, have a different view on what the struggle is for women going forward in our country and around the world. I was not as aware of that fact as I needed to be when we began our foundation project. Chelsea is the one who first said: "I bet that there are lots and lots of women, my age and younger, who have no idea Beijing ever happened—no idea of all the conferences, all the efforts, on behalf of women and girls over the years."

They bring no historical context to what we're talking about. In the United States especially, we have a public communications challenge, and this may be true for other advanced economies and societies. Here and elsewhere around the world, we also have to fight to prevent the clock from being turned back even on the limited progress that's been made. So my hope is that we can put forward an agenda that is understood and accepted as a follow-up to Beijing and to the MDGs, which moving forward will be known as the UN's Sustainable Development Goals or SDGs.

Talking about this challenge, even the meaning of reproductive freedom differs depending on the age, location, and experience of the audience. It takes some careful thought. A perfect example is the subject of female genital mutilation, historically and still today a sensitive cultural issue. How do we try to persuade governments, communities, and families, of the adverse health consequences for their daughters? It's different depending on where you are. There's a lot to be done here in understanding what the facts are and the best way of communicating the agenda we all need to rally around. We're also working closely with UN Women, which is particularly focused on engaging men and boys to realize that these issues affect them, not just their mothers, sisters, and daughters. So there's a lot of work to be done.

LM: We have time for a couple of audience questions. First question: "Your remarks on LGBT rights at the UN Human Rights Council played a major role in advancing US leadership internationally on that issue. How can the United States play a similar role in reinvigorating international attention to discrimination and violence against women?"

HRC: Thanks for what you said about the speech I gave in Geneva, because I tried to frame the rights of LGBT communities around the world in a sensitive way that would begin the same kind of conversation. This is a difficult issue in many places. Similarly, the issue of violence against women remains difficult, although we have made progress.

Despite the headlines, laws have been passed and better enforcement mechanisms created, including unusual ones, such as training of police officers and judges, and the creation of women-led police stations or teams as an institutional response, including here in the United States.

Still, there are three kinds of violence to address: domestic violence involving a member of the family or a close acquaintance, which is the most common; harassment and violence from strangers; and victimization of women and girls as a strategy of conflict and war, as we've seen so horrifically with young girls kidnapped by Boko Haram in Nigeria, by ISIL (Islamic State of Iraq and the Levant), by the Lord's Resistance Army in northern Uganda, which also kidnapped girls to serve as sex slaves—"wives," as they called them, along with boys to be soldiers—by raiding villages and convent schools.[2]

First, we have consistently said since 1995 that domestic violence is not cultural, it is criminal. And we have to keep pushing for more effective criminal justice responses, a well-trained police force, etc., to be able to respond. Second, we have to do much more to raise the visibility of attacks on women and girls by strangers and the accountability of local governments primarily to deal with them. Regarding war and conflict, we need to do much more on peace and security by including women at the peace table and as law enforcement officials and soldiers. There's still a huge agenda awaiting us and a long way to go, but we have some solutions.

LM: Second question: "How likely is US ratification of CEDAW (The UN Convention on all Forms of Discrimination against Women)?"

HRC: Well, you would think the answer is likely. But having tried as a senator and as a Secretary of State, first we have to change the Senate! We first submitted the Disabilities Treaty, which you would think would be easy to pass. It is modeled on the Americans with Disabilities Act, but even Bob Dole in a wheelchair on the floor of the Senate couldn't secure the necessary votes. On CEDAW, we are still struggling to get a favorable committee to send it to the floor for a vote. Congresswoman Carolyn Maloney of New York, who is in the audience, has also introduced a House resolution calling for another bill on the ERA—an equal rights amendment to the US constitution.

REPRESENTATIVE CAROLYN MALONEY: (from the audience): I also introduced a bill similar to what the State Department has been doing with great impact by rating countries on sexual trafficking. We ought to rate countries on how they treat women across a spectrum of policies to empower and educate them. And we should name the bill after you!

HRC: CEDAW does exactly that, so we should ratify it! But I love Carolyn, who is so creative. So in the absence of getting CEDAW ratified by the Senate, let's support what she is trying to do in the House! Still, the short answer is we just have to keep working. It is embarrassing, I mean really embarrassing.

LM: Last question. A couple of people in their questions mention Nigeria. You already spoke of Boko Haram. This is a somber note to end on, but what do you think about the new threats women are facing from terrorism?

HRC: It's really serious—part of the backlash we are seeing in many parts of the world. I became involved with this issue back in the nineties and as Secretary of State pushed hard for the US to train Ugandan troops to track down Joseph Kony, the leader of the Lord's Resistance Army, and end his reign of terror.[3] Unfortunately, these tactics have now been adopted by other terrorist groups.

In some countries the kidnapping is simply not taken seriously. You don't see sufficient government outrage and commitment to action, especially when the violence is to vulnerable children in isolated regions, as happened with the Yazidis in Iraq, when hundreds of girls and women were kidnapped and forced to become so-called wives of the ISIL terrorists.[4] This is a very ancient tactic, but we had reason to believe it would not persist in the twenty-first century. We need a much more vigorous response through the UN, which has already passed a number of resolutions. I chaired a UN Security Council meeting to try to focus attention on the use of terrorist tactics, including gender-based violence against women and girls in conflict.

It is a somber question to end on, but I'm afraid that unfortunately we see a trend for terrorist groups to prey on women, especially if they're recruiting foreign fighters from elsewhere. It's an ancient, horrible tale of snatching women to be part of their entourage. It's a very unfortunate fact that the girls kidnapped by Boko Haram have never been heard from again. Nobody claims to know where they are, and there has not been any adequate rescue mission, so the kidnappings continue. This demonstrates what we're up against.

With the metastasizing of terrorist groups across Africa, North Africa particularly, into the Middle East—with the continued presence of the Taliban and other groups in Afghanistan and Pakistan—it's going to be a hard struggle to figure out how best to deal with their threats in general and give special attention to their turning the clock back for women and girls. This will be a big issue for the next couple of years at least. We need the UN to come up with a unified strategy out of the Security Council and to deploy technical and human resources immediately to try to track down those who have been kidnapped and prevent reoccurrence. I can't give you an easy, quick answer about what we can do, except that I think that we need a process put in place very quickly, which we can rely on as we go forward.

LM: And maybe keep giving voice to the "Malalas" of the world and all those who are resisting.

HRC: The Pakistanis claim they arrested 10 militants today for the shooting of Malala. We'll see how that unfolds.

LM: And that is a good thing to end on. Thank you so much. Thank you all so much.

Notes

1 Harry Wu was born to an affluent family in Shanghai in 1937. Arrested at the age of 23 when he protested policies of the regime of Mao Zedong, he spent 19 years in Chinese labor camps before his life sentence was commuted. He left China in 1985 for an academic position in the United States, where he became a prominent China critic and human rights activist. Arrested on entering China in 1995 carrying a valid US passport, he was held for 66 days and sentenced to 15 years in prison but then immediately deported.

2 Boko Haram, which translates literally as "Western education is forbidden," is a militant Islamist movement in northeast Nigeria, whose membership has been estimated between a mere few hundred and a few thousand. Designated by the United States as a terrorist organization in 2013, it has killed more than 5,000 civilians since 2009 but came to international attention with the recent kidnapping of young school girls.

3 Kony was indicted for war crimes and crimes against humanity by the International Criminal Court in 2005 but has evaded capture.

4 The Yazidis are a Kurdish ethno-religious community.

Index

Routledge Global Institutions Series

2 The UN Secretary-General and Secretariat (2005)
by Leon Gordenker (Princeton University)

1 The United Nations and Human Rights (2005)
A guide for a new era
by Julie A. Mertus (American University)

Books currently under contract include:

The Regional Development Banks
Lending with a regional flavor
by Jonathan R. Strand (University of Nevada)

Millennium Development Goals (MDGs)
For a people-centered development agenda?
by Sakiko Fukada-Parr (The New School)

The Bank for International Settlements
The politics of global financial supervision in the age of high finance
by Kevin Ozgercin (SUNY College at Old Westbury)

International Migration
by Khalid Koser (Geneva Centre for Security Policy)

Human Development
by Richard Ponzio

The International Monetary Fund (2nd edition)
Politics of conditional lending
by James Raymond Vreeland (Georgetown University)

The UN Global Compact
by Catia Gregoratti (Lund University)

Institutions for Women's Rights
by Charlotte Patton (York College, CUNY) and
Carolyn Stephenson (University of Hawaii)

International Aid
by Paul Mosley (University of Sheffield)

Global Consumer Policy
by Karsten Ronit (University of Copenhagen)

The Changing Political Map of Global Governance
*by Anthony Payne (University of Sheffield) and
Stephen Robert Buzdugan (Manchester Metropolitan University)*

Coping with Nuclear Weapons
by W. Pal Sidhu

Global Governance and China
The dragon's learning curve
edited by Scott Kennedy (Indiana University)

The Politics of Global Economic Surveillance
by Martin S. Edwards (Seton Hall University)

Mercy and Mercenaries
Humanitarian agencies and private security companies
by Peter Hoffman

Regional Organizations in the Middle East
by James Worrall (University of Leeds)

Reforming the UN Development System
The Politics of Incrementalism
by Silke Weinlich (Duisburg-Essen University)

The United Nations as a Knowledge Organization
by Nanette Svenson (Tulane University)

The International Criminal Court
The Politics and practice of prosecuting atrocity crimes
by Martin Mennecke (University of Copenhagen)

BRICS
*by João Pontes Nogueira (Catholic University, Rio de Janeiro) and
Monica Herz (Catholic University, Rio de Janeiro)*

Expert Knowledge in Global Trade
edited by Erin Hannah (University of Western Ontario),
James Scott (University of Manchester), and
Silke Trommer (Murdoch University)

The European Union (2nd edition)
by Clive Archer (Manchester Metropolitan University)

Governing Climate Change (2nd edition)
by Peter Newell (University of East Anglia) and
Harriet A. Bulkeley (Durham University)

Protecting the Internally Displaced
Rhetoric and reality
by Phil Orchard (University of Queensland)

The Arctic Council
Within the far north
by Douglas C. Nord (Umea University)

For further information regarding the series, please contact:

Nicola Parkin, Editor, Politics & International Studies
Taylor & Francis
2 Park Square, Milton Park, Abingdon
Oxford OX14 4RN, UK
Nicola.parkin@tandf.co.uk
www.routledge.com

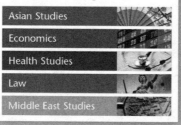